THE FOREIGN AFFAIRS READER

PUBLICATIONS OF THE

COUNCIL ON FOREIGN RELATIONS

FOREIGN AFFAIRS (quarterly), edited by Hamilton Fish Armstrong.

THE UNITED STATES IN WORLD AFFAIRS (annual). Volumes for 1931, 1932 and 1933 by Walter Lippmann and William O. Scroggs; for 1934-1935, 1936, 1937, 1938, 1939 and 1940 by Whitney H. Shepardson and William O. Scroggs; for 1945-1947 by John C. Campbell.

POLITICAL HANDBOOK OF THE WORLD (annual), edited by Walter H. Mallory.

SURVEY OF AMERICAN FOREIGN RELATIONS (in four volumes, 1928-1931), prepared under the direction of Charles P. Howland.

THE FOREIGN AFFAIRS READER, edited by Hamilton Fish Armstrong.

THE STUDY OF INTERNATIONAL RELATIONS IN AMERICAN COLLEGES AND UNIVERSITIES, by Grayson Kirk.

FOREIGN AFFAIRS BIBLIOGRAPHY, 1932-1942, by Robert Gale Woolbert.

THE STRUGGLE FOR AIRWAYS IN LATIN AMERICA, by William A. M. Burden.

WORLD ECONOMY IN TRANSITION, by Eugene Staley.

MOBILIZING CIVILIAN AMERICA, by Harold J. Tobin and Percy W. Bidwell.

THE FAR EASTERN CRISIS, by Henry L. Stimson.

THE INVISIBLE TARIFF, by Percy W. Bidwell.

RAW MATERIALS IN PEACE AND WAR, by Eugene Staley.

OUR TRADE WITH BRITAIN, by Percy W. Bidwell.

PEACEFUL CHANGE, by Frederick Sherwood Dunn.

CAN WE BE NEUTRAL?, by Allen W. Dulles and Hamilton Fish Armstrong.

ORES AND INDUSTRY IN THE FAR EAST, by H. Foster Bain.

LIMITS OF LAND SETTLEMENT, prepared under the direction of Isaiah Bowman.

INTERNATIONAL SECURITY, by Philip C. Jessup.

AMERICAN AGENCIES INTERESTED IN INTERNATIONAL AFFAIRS, compiled by Ruth Savord.

DOLLARS IN LATIN AMERICA, by Willy Feuerlein and Elizabeth Hannan.

NEW DIRECTIONS IN OUR TRADE POLICY, by William Diebold, Jr.

INTERNATIONAL AIR TRANSPORT AND NATIONAL POLICY, by Oliver J. Lissitzyn.

THE UNITED STATES IN A MULTI-NATIONAL ECONOMY, by Jacob Viner and Others.

THE PROBLEM OF GERMANY, by Hoyt Price and Carl E. Schorske.

THE FOREIGN AFFAIRS READER

EDITED BY

Hamilton Fish Armstrong

Published for the

COUNCIL ON FOREIGN RELATIONS

by

HARPER & BROTHERS

New York and London

1947

Printed in the United States of America

SECOND EDITION

American Book–Stratford Press, Inc., New York

FOREWORD

WELL over a thousand articles have appeared in FOREIGN AFFAIRS since the first issue in the autumn of 1922. The ones chosen for this anniversary volume do not pretend to be the "best" of the thousand. Some of the others may have been better as literature, or may have exercised a deeper influence on a particular aspect of current public thinking or government action. These articles have been selected because what their authors had to say seems a permanent part of the record of this past quarter century. Many have intrinsic intellectual or moral significance; others remind us that a situation or mode of thought which troubles us today had its parallel in the past. As often noted, historic parallels can be misleading; but they can also be of deadly accuracy.

In 1923, the year following the appearance of the first issue of FOREIGN AFFAIRS, Colonel George Harvey made a memorable statement on relinquishing his post as American Ambassador at the Court of St. James'. "The national American foreign policy," he said, "is to have no foreign policy." The unfolding scroll of history—carrying chapters headed "Pearl Harbor," "D-Day," "Okinawa" and "United Nations"—was in due course to give that ineffably complacent remark its full measure of futility and likewise its full weight of warning. No topic of discourse can so readily secure an audience today as animadversions on our foreign policy—surely a great gain in principle, if not always in substance. If sometimes we still fall short of practising the precepts for "learning the business" which a great American diplomat, Elihu Root, sets forth in the article he wrote for the first issue of FOREIGN AFFAIRS (reprinted as the leading essay in the present volume), we at least are aware of the importance of the subject. How far we have come from the easy provincialism of the Harding era; how far we have still to go in developing a foreign policy which will be foresighted in the protection of our rights and prompt in the execution of our duties; and how challenging to the best resources of mind and imagination a study of foreign relations can be, the following pages will, I hope, help to reveal.

In the task of selection, and in preparing the historical notes that knit the contributions together, the knowledge and judgment of my colleague Byron Dexter have played a great part. The thanks of FOREIGN AFFAIRS go to him, and also to Mary H. Stevens and Ann W. Viner who have helped make the manuscript ready for the press.

H. F. A.

CONTENTS

THE FOREIGN AFFAIRS READER

❖ ❖ ❖

THE article which Elihu Root wrote for the first issue of FOREIGN AFFAIRS in the autumn of 1922 has become something of a classic. The thesis was a simple one. Since the people in a democracy are responsible for the control and conduct of foreign policy they should learn the business.

Elihu Root was, in 1922, our most eminent elder statesman. He had been Secretary of War under McKinley, Secretary of State under Theodore Roosevelt, United States Senator from 1909 to 1915, and Ambassador Extraordinary to Russia in 1917. Now 77, he wrote out of deep concern for the safety of his country, launched on waters which his experience told him were more perilous than most of his fellow citizens perceived or, at any rate, were willing to admit. Two years earlier, the United States had rejected the Treaty of Versailles, the Covenant of the League of Nations and the military guarantee to France; only the previous year it had concluded a separate peace with Germany. Domestic affairs engrossed the American mind.

In so far as problems of foreign relations impinged at all on the public consciousness, it was in the form of questions left over from the recent time of troubles. On most of them the American public had opinions, but, as events were to show, not much knowledge. Should the United States join the World Court? Leaders of both parties advocated it; a majority of Republicans vetoed it; and public opinion soon forgot it. How rapidly could the moral satisfactions and dollar savings of disarmament be achieved? A rapprochement with Japan in this connection was applauded; but a reduction in the strength of the British fleet relative to our own was vaguely thought to be an even more important American objective. And the war debts? That they should be paid was obviously a matter of simple right and wrong. Calvin Coolidge was to state this with the force of moral virtue unhampered by knowledge: "They hired the money, didn't they?" And *how* were they to be paid? If Presidents Harding, Coolidge or Hoover understood the exchange problem involved in asking for payment in dollars and refusing to admit the imports which alone could produce them, they did not by word or act reveal it. And if this was the attitude of our leaders, how was the public to know better?

One way for the public to "know better" on these and other similar problems was to approach them in the attitude recommended by Elihu Root in such simple and reasonable language. After a quarter century his advice is still good.

❖ ❖ ❖

A REQUISITE FOR THE SUCCESS OF POPULAR DIPLOMACY

By Elihu Root

THE control of foreign relations by modern democracies creates a new and pressing demand for popular education in international affairs. When the difficult art of regulating the conduct of nations toward each other, in such a way as to preserve rights and avoid offense and promote peaceful intercourse, was left to the foreign offices of the world the public in each country could judge policies by results, and, in the various ways by which public opinion expresses itself, could reward or punish the success or failure of government. To perform that particular function it was not very important that the public should be familiar with the affairs out of which success or failure came. That condition, however, is passing away. In the democratic countries generally, the great body of citizens are refusing to wait until negotiations are over or policies are acted upon or even determined. They demand to know what is going on and to have an opportunity to express their opinions at all stages of diplomatic proceedings. This tendency is due partly to a desire to escape from certain well recognized evils in diplomacy as it has been practised. It is due in part doubtless to the natural disposition of democracies to revert to the conditions which existed before the invention of representative government and thus to avoid the temporary inequalities involved in delegations of power to official representatives however selected.

The new condition has undoubtedly been accelerated by the great war and its lessons. We have learned that war is essentially a popular business. All the people in the countries

concerned are enlisted in carrying it on. It cannot be carried on without their general participation. And whoever wins the war all the people of all the countries involved suffer grievous consequences. There is a general conviction that there has been something wrong about the conduct of diplomacy under which peoples have so often found themselves embarked in war without intending it and without wishing for it and there is a strong desire to stop that sort of thing. Democracies determined to control their own destinies object to being led, without their knowledge, into situations where they have no choice.

The demand for open diplomacy and contemporaneous public information, although in its application there is frequently an element of mere curiosity or news gathering business, nevertheless rests upon the substantial basis of democratic instinct for unhampered self-government. It is incident to the awakening sense of opportunity which, among the unskilled majority, has followed the exercise of universal suffrage, the spread of elementary education, and the revelation of the power of organization. The change is therefore not to be considered as temporary but as a step in the direct line of development of democratic government, which, according to the nature of democracies, will not be retraced. The new conditions and such developments as may grow from them are the conditions under which diplomacy will be carried on hereafter. Of course, as in all practical human affairs, limitations and safeguards will be found necessary, but the substance will continue, and public opinion will be increasingly not merely the ultimate judge but an immediate and active force in negotiation.

The usefulness of this new departure is subject to one inevitable condition. That is, that the democracy which is undertaking to direct the business of diplomacy shall learn the business. The controlling democracy must acquire a knowledge of the fundamental and essential facts and principles upon which the relations of nations depend. Without such a knowledge there can be no intelligent discussion and consideration of foreign policy and diplomatic conduct. Misrepresentation will have a clear field and ignorance and

error will make wild work with foreign relations. This is a point to which the sincere people who are holding meetings and issuing publications in opposition to war in general may well direct their attention if they wish to treat the cause of disease rather than the effects. Given the nature of man, war results from the spiritual condition that follows real or fancied injury or insult. It is a familiar observation that in most wars each side believes itself to be right and both pray with equal sincerity for the blessing of heaven upon their arms. Back of this there must lie a mistake. However much ambition, trade competition, or sinister personal motives of whatever kind, may have led towards the warlike situation, two great bodies of human beings, without whose consent war cannot be carried on, can never have come to two diametrically opposed genuine beliefs as to the justice of the quarrel without one side or the other, and probably both, being mistaken about their country's rights and their country's duties. Here is the real advantage of the change from the old diplomacy to the new. Irresponsible governments may fight without being in the least mistaken about their rights and duties. They may be quite willing to make cannon fodder of their own people in order to get more territory or more power; but two democracies will not fight unless they believe themselves to be right. They may have been brought to their belief by misrepresentation as to facts, by a misunderstanding of rules of right conduct, or through having the blank of ignorance filled by racial or national prejudice and passion to the exclusion of inquiry and thought; but they will fight not because they mean to do wrong but because they think they are doing right. When foreign affairs were ruled by autocracies or oligarchies the danger of war was in sinister purpose. When foreign affairs are ruled by democracies the danger of war will be in mistaken beliefs. The world will be the gainer by the change, for, while there is no human way to prevent a king from having a bad heart, there is a human way to prevent a people from having an erroneous opinion. That way is to furnish the whole people, as a part of their ordinary education, with correct information about their relations to other peoples, about the limitations upon their own rights, about their duties to respect the rights of others, about what has happened and is happening in international affairs, and about the effects upon national life of the things that are done or refused as between nations; so that the people themselves will have the means to test misinformation and appeals to prejudice and passion based upon error.

This is a laborious and difficult undertaking. It must be begun early and continued long, with patience and persistence, but it is the very same process as that by which all the people of the great democracies have learned within their own countries to respect law and to follow wise and salutary customs in their communities, and to consider the rights of others while they assert their own rights, and to maintain orderly self-government.

It so happens that our own people in the United States have been peculiarly without that kind of education in foreign affairs. Not only have we been very busy over the development of our own country and our own institutions, but our comparatively isolated position has prevented the foreign relations of the old world from becoming matters of immediate vital interest to the American people, and they have not been interested in the subject. Naturally enough a great part of our public men have neglected to study the subject. The great body of Americans in office would study questions of transportation and tariff and internal improvements and currency because their constituents were interested in these subjects; but there was no incentive for them to study foreign affairs because their constituents were indifferent to them. The conditions are now widely different. Our people have been taught by events to realize that with the increased intercommunication and interdependence of civilized states all our production is a part of the world's production, and all our trade is a part of the world's trade, and a large part of the influences which make for prosperity or disaster within our own country consists of forces and movements which may arise anywhere in the world beyond our direct and immediate control. I suppose that the people of the United States have learned more about international relations within the past eight years than they had learned in the preceding eighty years. They are, however, only at the beginning of the task.

The subject is extensive and difficult and a fair working knowledge of it, even of the most general kind, requires long and attentive study. Underlying it are the great differences in the modes of thought and feeling of different races of men. Thousands of years of differing usages under different conditions forming different customs and special traditions have given to each separate race its own body of preconceived ideas, its own ways of looking at life and human conduct, its own views of what is natural and proper and desirable. These prepossessions play the chief part in determining thought and action in life. Given two groups of men, each having a different inheritance of custom and tradition, each will have a different understanding of written and spoken words, of the reasons for conduct and the meaning of conduct, and each will to a very considerable degree fail to understand the other. Neither can judge the other by itself. If the instinctive occidental reformer and the instinctive oriental fatalist are to work together they must make biological studies of each other. Add to these differences the selfish passions which have not yet been bred out of mankind and there inevitably follow in the contacts of international intercourse a multitude of situations which cannot be solved by the men of any one nation assuming that the rest of the world is going to think and feel as they themselves do and to act accordingly.

The organization of independent nations which has followed the disappearance of the Holy Roman Empire is in the main the outgrowth of that progress in civilization which leads peoples to seek the liberty of local self-government according to their own ideas. Whatever may be the form of local governments there can be no tyranny so galling as the intimate control of the local affairs of life by foreign rulers who are entirely indifferent to the local conceptions of how life ought to be conducted. National independence is an organized defense against that kind of tyranny. Probably the organization of nations is but a stage of development, but it is the nearest that mankind has yet come towards securing for itself a reasonable degree of liberty with a reasonable degree of order.

It is manifest that the differences of thought and feeling and selfish desire which separate nations in general, have to be dealt with in particular in the multitude of controversies which are sure to arise between them and between their respective citizens in a world of universal trade and travel and inter-communication. The process of such adjustment without war is the proper subject of diplomacy. During some centuries of that process many usages have grown up which have been found necessary or convenient for carrying on friendly intercourse, and many of these have hardened into generally accepted customs in manners or in morals which no longer require to be discussed but which every nation has a right to assume that other nations will observe. Many rules of right conduct have been accepted and universally agreed upon as law to govern the conduct of nations. In England and America these rules of international law are authoritatively declared to be a part of the municipal law of the country enforceable by the courts. In this way the nations founded upon differences have been gradually rescuing from the field of difference and controversy, and transferring to the field of common understanding and agreement, one subject after another of practical importance in the affairs of the world. The process is in the direction of that unity of thought and feeling, the absence of which hitherto has caused the failure of all schemes and efforts for the unity of mankind. The study of international relations means not only study of some particular controversy but study of this long history of the process of adjustment between differing ideas and of the prejudices and passions and hitherto irreconcilable differences which have baffled adjustment and which affect the relations and probable conduct of the nations concerned. All these are in the background of every international question and are often of vital importance to its right understanding.

The process I have described has created a community of nations. That community has grown just as communities of natural persons grow. Men cannot live in neighborhood with each other without having reciprocal rights and obligations towards each other arising from their being neighbors. The practical recognition of these rights and obligations creates the community. It is not a matter of contract. It is a matter of usage arising from the necessities of self-protection. It is not a voluntary matter. It is compelled by the situation. The neighbors generally must govern their conduct by the accepted standards or the community will break up. It is the same with nations. No nation whose citizens trade and travel—that is to say, no nation which lives in neighborhood with other nations—need consider whether or not it will be a member of the community of nations. It cannot help itself. It may be a good member or a bad member, but it is a member by reason of the simple fact of neighborhood life and intercourse. The Bolshevik rulers of Russia are illustrating this. They have been trying to repudiate all the obligations resulting from their country's membership in the community of nations, and one result is that intercourse is impossible.

This great fact of the community of nations is not involved at all in any question about the League of Nations or any other association of nations founded upon contract. The League of Nations is merely a contract between the signers of the instrument by which they agree to super-add to the existing usages, customs, laws, rights and obligations of the existing community of nations certain other rights and obligations which shall bind the signers as matter of contract. Whether a country enters into that contract or not, its membership in the community of nations continues with all the rights and obligations incident to that membership.

A self-respecting democracy which undertakes to control the action of its government as a member of this community of nations, and wishes to respond fairly and fully, not only to the demands of its own interests, but to the moral obligations of a member of the community, is bound to try to understand this great and complicated subject so that it may act not upon prejudice and error but upon knowledge and understanding.

There is one specially important result which should follow from such a popular understanding of foreign affairs. That is, a sense of public responsibility in speech and writing, or perhaps it would be better stated as a public sense of private responsibility for words used in discussing international affairs. More fights between natural persons come from insult than from injury. Under our common law, libel was treated as a crime, not because of the injury which it did to the person libeled, but because it tended to provoke a breach of the peace. Nations are even more sensitive to insult than individuals. One of the most useful and imperative lessons learned by all civilized governments in the practice of international intercourse has been the necessity of politeness and restraint in expression. Without these, the peaceful settlement of controversy is impossible. This lesson should be learned by every free democracy which seeks to control foreign relations.

It cannot, however, be expected that every individual in a great democracy will naturally practise restraint. Political demagogues will seek popularity by public speeches full of insult to foreign countries, and yellow journals will seek to increase their circulation by appeals to prejudice against foreigners. Hitherto these have been passed over because the speakers and writers were regarded as irresponsible, but if the democracy of which the speakers and publishers are a part is to control international intercourse that irresponsibility ends, and it is the business of the democracy to see to it that practices by its members which lead directly towards war are discouraged and condemned. Offenses of this character are frequently committed in this country by political speakers and sensational newspapers and because we are a great nation the expressions used become known in the other countries concerned and cause resentment and bitter feeling. What especially concerns us is that these are very injurious offenses against our own country. Such public expressions by our own citizens bring discredit upon our country and injure its business and imperil its peace. They answer to the description of crime in the old indictments as an act "against the peace and dignity" of the state. They will practically cease whenever the American public really condemns and resents them so that neither public office nor newspaper advertising or circulation can be obtained by them. That will come when the American public more fully understands the business of international intercourse and feels a sense of the obligations which it incurs by asserting the right to control the conduct of foreign relations.

❖ ❖ ❖

In 1925, when President Thomas Garrigue Masaryk, of Czechoslovakia, published his article "Reflections on the Question of War Guilt," the German effort to shift the responsibility for the war to the shoulders of the Allies was in full cry.

Masaryk, born the son of a coachman in Moravia in 1850, knew Pan-Germanism well. Long before 1914 he had perceived that Austria-Hungary was fated to be the tool of German expansion, and it was precisely in the name of necessary opposition to Pan-Germanism that he had declared for the breaking up of that corrupt and decrepit Empire. His belief that a free Czechoslovak state was an essential factor in creating a free and liberal Europe, and his insight into the nervous irritation and suicidal mania which underlay German militarism, were to be given deadly corroboration, for a second time, 15 years after he composed the article which follows.

To many students of history, Masaryk, the professor of philosophy at Prague who, with his young assistant Dr. Beneš and with the extraordinarily close and confident coöperation of the Czech and Slovak people, created the Czechoslovak state, is one of the truly great men of his time and one of the wisest of statesmen in history. This brief essay suggests the quality of his mind. Thought and action in Masaryk seemed exactly in balance. Though his judgments and aims were clear, he never pretended that the conditions which gave rise to great political developments were simple. "Policy, *i.e.,* the principle of the politics of states, is complicated," he wrote. He knew that the outburst of German militarism which the world had just fought off was only a particularly deadly manifestation of the cultural crisis which existed everywhere in modern civilization. His remedy, however, was not that modern men should turn their backs on freedom and civilization. He had only condemnation for absolutisms of any kind. He proposed "a calm, direct analysis and criticism of our culture and its elements . . . by thinking people." Not the least remarkable aspect of Masaryk's achievements was that he accomplished his prodigies of practical politics by emphasizing his ideals, not by sacrificing them.

REFLECTIONS ON THE QUESTION OF WAR GUILT

By Thomas G. Masaryk

WHAT is the significance of the World War? What is the meaning of this enormous common manifestation in the history of Europe and of humanity?

The Marxian interpretation of war will not hold. Not that a specifically capitalistic interpretation of economic history is entirely wrong; but it is one-sided, incomplete and uncertain. The conception of capitalism itself is vague; there were certainly wars before capitalism—and nobody has demonstrated the extent to which capitalism is responsible for the genesis and development of this latest war. Are we to understand by "capitalism" a whole and complete economic system or, specifically, finance? Or great industrial development? And in what countries? Capitalism is to be found in all countries, and capitalism has always opposed capitalism. Which capitalism is the deciding factor? We always return to one main question: Which of the combatant parties was conducting an offensive war, and which a defensive?—for this distinction is of great importance in estimating the character of the war.

Nobody doubts that economic interests have always been an important reason for making wars. But there are, in addition, other deciding factors. Historians are always teaching (as are also the historical Marxists) that in modern times wars are made in order that states, their rulers and their statesmen may increase their power and prestige, that they may extend their sway over portions of neighboring countries, and that they may get colonies. They talk much about imperialism, especially in the case of large states. The proponents of this point of view stress ambition, the desire to dominate, greed, and racial and national hatred as the motives for a military offensive.

An interpretation of the World War in the light of nationalism is likewise one-sided and vague. Nationalism differs in various countries, and again the question is raised as to what sort of nationalism was responsible. Who began the offensive, and who was on the defensive? What is implied by this "nationalism"? Certainly, nationalist quarrels and disputes were one of the causes of the war. But the war cannot be regarded as exclusively a war of nationalities. Nations are not yet quite synonymous with states; the states were at war, the nations so only indirectly, or as far as they were organized by their states and were represented in them. Moreover, the policy of the states was not merely national. Policy, *i.e.,* the principle of the politics of states, is complicated. It is affected by dynasties, governments, influential statesmen and politicians, journalists, parliaments, parties, and by intellectual and moral movements. To define scientifically exactly who conducted, and was responsible for, the policy of a given state—who, in a given instance, made the decision and why—who had greater and who less influence upon it—this is a task for genuine history and the philosophy of history. It is impossible to say that wars are nationalist, that is, nationalist only. England and America certainly did not take part in the war for reasons of nationalism, at any rate nationalism of the type common on the Continent, although they recognized the principle of nationality and especially the rights of small nations in Europe to be free and independent. It cannot, therefore, be said that the war was a contest between the Germans and Slavs, or between the Germans and the Romance peoples. It was a World War. The genesis and development of the war clearly demonstrate that nationality—at times national chauvinism—was only one factor among others.

The war has sometimes been regarded as an ecclesiastical and religious quarrel between the Orthodoxy of Russians and Serbs and the Catholicism of Austria, the Protestantism of the Germans and the Catholicism of the French. These religious influences were also factors, but again only factors among others.

The character of this war can to a certain extent be realized by a comparison of the military aims of the contestants and their programs; that of the west, leading the enormous majority of mankind, and that of Germany, leading a minority composed of the Central Powers. This division had more than a temporary military significance; it expressed the whole situation. Ideas faced each other in a life and death struggle.

In modern times, the independence of states and peoples has been substituted for the mediaeval theocracy which centered in the spiritual leadership of the Papacy as an international authority. The Reformation, humanism, science, art and philosophy laid down new spiritual and moral ideals as the foundation for the organization of a new society. A great revolution was prepared in England, France and America. In this revolution the enormous gain was that the State and the Church (or rather the churches) became independent of one another. With the passage of time, State and Church have become more and more separated in the west, that is, in Europe and America, not to the detriment of religion but on the contrary to its gain, as also to the gain of political life. And as the state gradually became emancipated from ecclesiastical influence all institutions and strata of society—science, together with philosophy, education and morality—became emancipated also.

In the state which after the Reformation took over the leadership of society and, following the example of the church, became absolutist, the French Revolution proclaimed the great watchword "Liberty, Equality, Fraternity." The rights of man and of citizens were enunciated and codified, France and America became republics, England, and for a time France also, constitutional monarchies. Against the old aristocratic system—for monarchy is but a form of aristocracy—democracy developed in different forms and degrees. The revolutionary process was not exhausted by the French Revolution. A succession of revolutions followed, and we are still in the midst of them. It may even be that in the World War we not only overthrew the old régime but also the earlier stages of revolution.

The ideal of the whole revolution was humanity. Morally, this signified mutual sympathy and respect between individuals, and the recognition of the principle that one man must not be used by another as a tool. Politically and socially, it meant the equality of all citizens in the state, the alliance of nations and states, and through them the coming together of the whole of humanity. This idea of natural right was an old one which we had inherited from the Greeks and Romans, and in some respects it had been consecrated by the church and by the churches, though the social and political content of this natural right was only gradually formulated. Closely allied to this ideal of humanity was the conception of enlightenment, expressed in a striving for knowledge and education. From this grew, in the last century, the universal recognition of science and the attempts to develop a new philosophy with a scientific basis, as also the continual efforts to organize general education, to make attendance at schools obligatory, to popularize science, and to develop journalism, publicity and the press generally.

The revolution, and the great changes which it wrought in the outlook on life, fixed the idea and the ideal of progress in all branches of human effort, and spread the faith that nations as well as humanity in general would gradually, through their own efforts, reach a higher and higher degree of achievement and satisfaction.

These, it seems to me, are the dominating ideas of western Europe. I say western Europe, although I am chiefly thinking of France, since the west (France and the adjoining nations, England and America, and Italy and the other Romance nations) forms a cultural whole, as is clearly demonstrated by the history of the reciprocal influences exerted by the various nations mentioned.

During the Middle Ages, Germany also belonged to the cultural body of Europe. But in modern times she has steadily separated herself, more and more, in her culture. Prussia, an aggressive state from the very beginning, strengthened by the Reformation, came to dominate Germany. A noticeable *étatisme* also prevailed in the west, but there the state grew to be the organ of Parliament and of public opinion, while in Germany a monarchistic state was deified and its absolutism generally recognized. Not till the end of the World War did the Prussian King, as German Emperor, decide for the parliamentarization of the government. Prussia and Germany were really an organized Caesarism; certainly Frederick the Great, Bismarck and the Wilhelms in contrast to Napoleon were Caesars and Tsars. The soldier, the Prussian officer, was for the Germans the standard of social organization, in fact of the organization of the world. The soldier and war became institutions. In Germany the Reformation, humanism, science, art and philosophy did not expel theocracy as thoroughly as they did in the west; the German people accepted the Reformation only in part, and in its German form (Lutheranism) adapted it to Catholicism. A kind of Caesaro-Papism arose, although different from the Russian Caesaro-Papism. The humanitarian ideals of Lessing, Herder, Goethe, Kant and Schiller, derived from observing and from collaborating in the development of the west and of the world in general, came to be replaced by a Pan-Germanic imperialism. The Berlin-Baghdad scheme was characteristic of the effort to dominate Europe and Asia and Africa—an effort in which is to be seen the ideal of the ancient world! Germany maintains and develops the ideal of the Roman *imperium*.

In contrast with this, the ideal of the west is the organization of the whole of humanity—the alliance (before everything) of Europe with America, and by this means the alliance of the other parts of the world. The World War furthered this unification.

Pan-Germanism did not recognize the rights of peoples to independence. It wished to be the sole leader and ruler of all. In its arrogance it announced that the ideal was a multi-national state. It rejected natural right and substituted for it historical right. Kant is certainly recognized as a leading philosopher; but his inclination towards natural right and Rousseau was rejected by Germany, as were humanitarian ideals in general. Historical right was strengthened with the aid of Darwinism, through the theory of mechanical evolution, guaranteeing success to the strongest. War and the making of war became divine institutions. Prussian militarism utilized the theory of the English naturalist to strengthen its military aristocracy, which proclaimed as its chief dogma the so-called *Realpolitik,* the notion that all right is born of might. Power and force were identified.[1] The German nation was described as a nation of born rulers.

The results of Prussianism can be seen not only in politics, but also in German philosophy, science, art and, of course, in theology. When in a nation the leading men and classes begin to rely upon power and force, eschewing sympathy, people cease to have any interest in finding out about the feelings and thoughts of those who are near to them, and finally of foreigners; for all contact with them is made through the state mechanism. They cease to think freely, and knowledge becomes devoid of living ideas.

This is an interpretation of the great errors of German history and of German thought before and after the war. Bismarck, with his use of force in his relations with the people near to him, is the type of the domineering Prussian spirit. I should describe the development schematically as follows: Goethe, Kant, Frederick the Great, Hegel, Lagarde, Marx, Moltke, Bismarck, William II.

In Hegel we see the synthesis of both tendencies of German culture; he accepted the Prussian idea of the state, namely that it is the chief expression of nationality and the leader of all society. By his pantheism and his imaginative philosophy he constitutes a transition from Goethe, and in the practical domain a transition to Prussianism and its mechanism, materialism and force. Not for nothing was Hegel originally a theologian—even in this connection he formulated the principles of the Prussian theocracy. Bismarck and Wilhelm were always calling on God, of course the Prussian God; Hegel, with his "absolute idealism,"

[1] The proof of this Pan-German identification of right and might is given by Professor Schafer in "Staat und Gesellschaft," 1922 (*i.e.,* after the war). He shows that right is only an expression of conditions of power, particularly external right; but under his hands power becomes force. "The thing cannot be otherwise, force and power can create right." (p. 264)

served the "authoritism" of the Prussian state, abandoned humanity and the universal outlook of Goethe and Kant, and laid a foundation for the theoretical and practical employment of force. Bismarck and Bismarckism absorbed Goethe—the Prussian state became the infallible leader of the nation and the arbiter of its spiritual and cultural efforts.

Marx, having passed through the philosophy of Feuerbach (" a man is what he eats"), turned Hegel's pantheism and absolute idealism into materialism and accepted the mechanism of Prussian organization and *étatisme* (all-powerful centralization), although he made the state subject to economic laws. The fact that during the war the German Marxians, in spite of their Socialism and revolutionary tendencies, accepted without criticism the Prussian policy and remained so long in alliance with the Pan-Germans, is due to their relationship with them in method and tactics. The undemocratic conception regarding the necessity of large economic units corresponds to the Prussian theory of super-humanity. Marx himself had the same view of the Slav peoples as Treitschke and Lagarde.

German thought, beginning with Kant, took a wrong road. Kant set opposite the one-sided English empiricism, and especially the skepticism of Hume, the one-sided intellectualism of so-called pure creative reason. He constructed a whole system of *a priori* eternal truths and thus began the reign of German subjectivism, leading inevitably to solipsistic isolation and egoism, to an aristocratic individualism and a super-humanity based on force. This metaphysical titanism necessarily led the German subjectivists to moral isolation. The phantasy of Fichte and Schelling gave birth to the nihilism and pessimism of Schopenhauer. The titans became wrathful, ironical—and anger and irony and titanism are a *contradictio in adjecto*—and finally desperate. Hegel and Feuerbach sought a refuge in the police state and in materialism, through which they avoided metaphysical imagination; they submitted to the régime of Prussian "corporalism," for which Kant had given strong justification by his categorical imperative. The German universities became the spiritual barracks of this philosophical absolutism, which reached its consummation in the idea of the Prussian state and kingdom, deified by Hegel. Hegel created absolutism for the state, and justified right by strength and force. Nietzsche, like Schopenhauer, rejects this development, but only in words; in reality Nietzsche became a philosophical prophet of the Hohenzollern parvenus and of Pan-German absolutism. Nietzsche is the type of the modern hair-splitting scholastic, intoxicating and satisfying himself with big words.

Hegel proclaimed not only the infallibility of the state, but the "self-saving" quality of war and militarism; Lagarde and his followers then conceived a philosophy and policy of pan-Germanism. This it was which was defeated in France. With the Prussian regiments there fell the philosophy which stood for the doctrines "exterminate the Poles" (von Hartmann); "break the thick skulls of the Czechs" (Mommsen); "destroy the decadent French and the haughty English." Prussian Pan-Germanism was overthrown by the war.

In rejecting the one-sidedness of German thought which was initiated by Kant, I do not say that German philosophy is entirely faulty, nor do I say that it is superficial or uninteresting. On the contrary, German philosophy is interesting and profound, but profound for the reason that it is not, and cannot be, free. It is a scholasticism of the mediaeval type, ready-made, a predetermined official creed. Like the Prussian state and Prussianism generally, German philosophy, and also German idealism, is absolutist, violent, unjust to the greatness of free united humanity.

In my first work, "Suicide as a Collective Social Phenomenon in Modern Civilization" (1881), I attempted to interpret the surprising and terrible fact that in modern times, from the end of the eighteenth century, the number of suicides has increased everywhere in Europe and in America, and particularly amongst the most enlightened peoples, and this to such an extent that it is necessary to speak of suicide as a pathological condition of modern society. This tendency to suicide in the modern individual is allied to his increasing psychism. Through a detailed analysis of the causes and motives of isolated suicides I was forced to the recognition of the fact that the instigating, and often the deciding, factor in suicide is a weakening of character through the loss of religion. Seen in historical perspective, modern suicide and psychism appear as the result of the precocity or crudity of the new conception of the world and the inadequate organization of the society inhabiting it.

Mediaeval Catholic theocracy consolidated throughout Christendom a unified conception of the world and, corresponding to it, a moral and political régime; but the power of the Catholic theocracy in modern times (and this is what makes them modern!) decreased, and is still decreasing. Revolution—scientific, philosophical, artistic, religious, political and social—characterized the transition from the Middle Ages. Hume and Kant, skepticism and the attempt to overcome skepticism, are both characteristic of modern times. Against infallibility, absolutism and inquisition, mankind protested and revolted; there developed a revolutionary and excessive individualism and subjectivism, leading to spiritual and moral isolation, to general anarchy instead of the previous catholicity. Skepticism, criticism, irony and negation have forced faith into the background; man has become uneasy, inconstant, restless, nervous; through his very energy, often artificially increased, he has fallen into Utopianism; through his continual searching and enterprise he has been deceived again and again; the idealist has plunged himself into gluttony, but has not found satisfaction; pessimism, not only theoretical, but also practical, has become widespread—as also joylessness and anxiety, hate and despair, and from these exhaustion, nervousness, psychism and suicide. Modern society is pathologically irritated, torn, disintegrated—always in one transition after another. In the number of suicides we find a direct arithmetical measure of this psychic sickness, at once moral and psychological.

The psychological opposite of suicide and the suicidal mania is murder. Suicide is violence done by the soul to itself and is intrinsically egocentric and subjective; murder is violence to the soul, turned outwards—it is abnormal objectivization. Subjectivistic individualism, reaching a higher stage in solipsism and titanic equality with God, is unendurable to man—finally he uses force, either on himself or on somebody near him: suicide and murder are degrees of the same violence.

Modern militarism, especially Prussian militarism, is a violent flight from morbid subjectivity and the suicidal mania. I repeat, modern militarism; for, psychologically and morally, the bellicosity of the savage, the barbarian, and even of the medieval knight and mercenary, is different from the scientifically calculated military system of the modern absolutist states. The savage and the barbarian fight from original savagery; but in the World War, there were to be found in the trenches disciples of Rousseau and Kant, Goethe and Herder, Byron and Musset! If Sombart praises German militarism in the spirit of Hegel, and is proud of the fact that Fausts and Zarathustras are fighting in the trenches, he does not realize that he is thus condemning the bloodthirstiness of German civilization and European civilization.

The warfare of these modern civilized peoples is in actuality a violent flight from the narrow conditions imposed by the conception of the superhuman "I." For this reason the intelligentsia, as far as bellicosity went, were not eclipsed by countrymen and laborers, but on the contrary took a leading part in the war. In modern war the opponents do not stand opposite to one another, eye to eye; it is not a battle, as it used to be; they destroy one another at a distance, abstractly, one man not seeing the other, killing one another through ideas and in ideas—German idealism turned into "Kruppism." The *natural* man knows nothing of suicide from modern reasons of exhaustion, nervousness and boredom; only in isolated instances does he commit suicide from anger at the lack of recognition or from general failure of his energy. The *modern* man, through exhaustion and narrow conditions due to spiritual and moral isolation, from a fruitless desire for greatness, and from "superhumanism," suffers from a morbid desire for suicide. Militarism is the attempt of this superman to flee from his malady, but it only constitutes an aggravation of it. It is a nation of thinkers and philosophers which has had the greatest number of suicides, which has produced the most perfected militarism, and which was responsible for the World War.

I am of the opinion that this connection between the modern suicidal mania and Prussian militarism is very real. The World War was a war of peoples. Not the old, permanent armies were opposed to one another, but new armies created through a universal obligation to military service, armies consisting chiefly of reserves. Not many of the soldiers engaged on opposing sides were soldiers by profession, though, of course, the Kaiser and the military leaders, as well as a portion of the *personnel,* were soldiers of the old type. The fact, however, that the World War was conducted on a huge scale gave it a peculiar stamp—the characteristics of the combatant peoples themselves were made manifest. The character of the war depends on the character of the soldiers. If the war, as the pacifists assure us, let loose all the evil forces such as hate, ill-will and bellicosity, then these qualities did not arise only in the war, but were characteristic of the people before the war; the devils of the year 1914 were not the angels of 1913. The World War had, as has been said, an abstract, scientific quality. It was the preëminence of scientific military industry and the mathematical employment of great masses which finally brought victory.

I am of the opinion that the moral significance of the World War as an attempt at objectivization after excessive subjectivism is plain enough; the war and the method of making war arose from this moral and spiritual condition of the modern man and of his whole culture, as I have briefly set it forth. The modern contest between objectivization and subjectivization, expressed in literature and philosophy, and therefore in life, is a protracted historical process and expressed itself in the war also and particularly in its long duration. The war demonstrated what the modern man is capable of and what he would be capable of if he were to rid himself of his desire for domination and did not suppress in himself that love for his neighbor which is innate in every man.

The German historian, Lamprecht, in endeavoring so

enthusiastically and energetically to justify the Germans in the war, supports my analysis in spite of himself. In his history of modern Germany, written before the war,[2] he rightly characterizes the time as an epoch of nervous irritation (he coined the word *Reizsamkeit*), and quotes not only Wilhelm but also Bismarck as types of this neurosis. In fact, the German superman, the titan, is nervous and seeks either for death or war as an acute excitement in the place of chronic excitement.

This applies to all nations, but before everything to the German nation. In their spiritual isolation the German philosophers and scientists, historians and politicians, declared German civilization and culture to constitute the zenith of human development, and in the name of this self-appointed eminence Prussian Pan-Germanism announced the right of conquest and the right generally to subdue by power and force. The Prussian state, its army and militarism, became a corrective to morbid subjectivism; Prussian Pan-Germanism is responsible for the World War, is the moral cause of it.

The crisis of the modern man is a general one; it is a crisis of the whole man in his whole spiritual existence. Modern life, our institutions, our views on the world, must be revised. The internal disintegration and disharmony of the modern man and his life, the disintegration and disharmony of society and the general spiritual anarchy, the contest between the present and the past, between fathers and children, the war between the churches and science, philosophy, art and the state, these penetrate the whole of modern culture. We are seeking for the peace of our own souls—how and where shall we find it? In our effort to attain spiritual freedom we fell into an excessive individualism and subjectivity, which were the source of this general spiritual and moral anarchy. Many of us gave ourselves up to materialism and mechanics. We have cultivated intellectualism one-sidedly and have forgotten the harmonious cultivation of all our spiritual and physical powers and qualities. In opposing the churches and religion, we have

[2] "Zur jungsten deutschen Vergangenheit," 1904.

contented ourselves with doubt and denial, we have snatched at revolutionary politicism, although we have convinced ourselves that at least in the primary conceptions of life and of the world a permanent social organization is impossible without harmony. We have revolted against the discipline of the church, but we have become slaves to programs and to the principles of parties and factions. To talk about and to demand morality and moral discipline is considered to be an exhibition of old-world moralizing. Restlessness, anxiety, skepticism, exhaustion, pessimism, hate, despair, suicide, militarism, going to war—that is the end of the modern man, the modern superman.

The postwar situation led many to the conviction that Europe and the civilization of peoples were declining, declining definitely. Before the war, the Pan-Germans often announced the decline of the Romance peoples, especially of the French; now the German philosophers of history (Spengler) talk about the decline of the Germans and of the whole of the west. Some, on the other hand, hope for salvation from Russia or even from further east, although Russia fell in the war just as did Germany and Austria.

I do not believe in a general and definite degeneration and decadence. As a consequence of the war we are living through an acute and chronic crisis. Not we alone are responsible for this crisis, but our forefathers also. We could not refrain from altering what they left us; but the alterations we made were erroneous, and we continue to err. However, an honest recognition of a mistake is the beginning of improvement. The war and its horrors upset all of us—we stand helpless before a tremendous historical mystery, faced with an occurrence of a type which has never been known before in the history of humanity. But perturbation is not a program. We need a calm, direct analysis and criticism of our culture and its elements, and we must decide upon a concrete improvement in every sphere of thought and action. In all the enlightened nations there are enough thinking people to carry out this reform in concert.

❖ ❖ ❖

GIOVANNI GENTILE, Italian philosopher and Senator, was the Minister of Public Instruction in the first Cabinet of Benito Mussolini. His article, "The Philosophic Basis of Fascism," written for the January 1928 issue of FOREIGN AFFAIRS, did not make pleasant reading then, nor does it now; but it is, perhaps, the most authoritative summary of the body of ideas which Mussolini chose to parade as the Fascist philosophy.

The First World War left Italy a dissatisfied and restless nation. She received only part of the territories which had been promised her, in reward for her participation, before the United States entered the war and Wilson introduced self-determination as a condition of the peace. The catch-all program of Fascism attracted romantic youths, nationalists stirred to frantic excitement by d'Annunzio's extravagances of word and action, demobilized and disillusioned soldiers and officers, intellectuals without any sure orientation, and such divergent elements as syndicalist disciples of Sorel and monarchists who followed the ultramontane teaching of De Maistre. The binding ideal of all these groups was a glorification of force; and the material sinews for putting their will to force into operation was provided by the landed and industrial bourgeoisie, who backed the movement in the belief it was a safeguard against Bolshevism.

Huey Long, author of the famous aphorism that if Fascism ever comes to the United States it will do so in the guise of anti-Fascism, almost surely never read Professor Gentile's rhetoric. But one finds here interesting confirmation of what Huey Long meant. Fascism, as Gentile explained it, was idealism and anti-materialism and the Fascist state was a spiritual and democratic creation—a collection of phrases which nevertheless led to a simple conclusion: "The authority of the State is absolute." Mussolini, who did not take himself quite seriously, enjoyed this sort of mystification. Hitler, who took himself very seriously, borrowed large amounts of it to make a philosophy for Germans, and they efficiently organized its inherent viciousness.

Professor Gentile was reported shot by anti-Fascists in Florence on April 17, 1944.

❖ ❖ ❖

THE PHILOSOPHIC BASIS OF FASCISM

By Giovanni Gentile

FOR the Italian nation the World War was the solution of a deep spiritual crisis. They willed and fought it long before they felt and evaluated it. But they willed, fought, felt and evaluated it in a certain spirit which Italy's generals and statesmen exploited, but which also worked on them, conditioning their policies and their action. The spirit in question was not altogether clear and self-consistent. That it lacked unanimity was particularly apparent just before and again just after the war when feelings were not subject to war discipline. It was as though the Italian character were crossed by two different currents which divided it into two irreconcilable sections. One need think only of the days of Italian neutrality and of the debates that raged between interventionists and neutralists. The ease with which the most inconsistent ideas were pressed into service by both parties showed that the issue was not between two opposing political opinions, two conflicting concepts of history, but actually between two different temperaments, two different souls.

For one kind of person the important point was to fight the war, either on the side of Germany or against Germany: but in either event to fight the war, without regard to specific advantages—to fight the war in order that at last the Italian nation, created rather by favoring conditions than by the will of its people to be a nation, might receive its test in blood, such a test as only war can bring by uniting all citizens in a single thought, a single passion, a single hope, emphasizing to each individual that all have something in common, something transcending private interests.

This was the very thing that frightened the other kind of person, the prudent man, the realist, who had a clear view of the mortal risks a young, inexperienced, badly prepared nation would be running in such a war, and who also saw—a most significant point—that, all things considered, a bargaining neutrality would surely win the country tangible rewards, as great as victorious participation itself.

The point at issue was just that: the Italian neutralists stood for material advantages, advantages tangible, ponderable, palpable; the interventionists stood for moral advantages, intangible, impalpable, imponderable—imponderable at least on the scales used by their antagonists. On the eve of the war these two Italian characters stood facing each other, scowling and irreconcilable—the one on the aggressive, asserting itself ever more forcefully through the various organs of public opinion; the other on the defensive, offering resistance through the parliament which in those days still seemed to be the basic repository of state sovereignty. Civil conflict seemed inevitable in Italy, and civil war was in fact averted only because the King took advantage of one of his prerogatives and declared war against the Central Powers.

This act of the King was the first decisive step toward the solution of the crisis.

II

The crisis had ancient origins. Its roots sank deep into the inner spirit of the Italian people.

What were the creative forces of the *Risorgimento?* The "Italian people," to whom some historians are now tending to attribute an important if not a decisive rôle in our struggle for national unity and independence, was hardly on the scene at all. The active agency was always an idea become a person—it was one or several determined wills which were fixed on determined goals. There can be no question that the birth of modern Italy was the work of the few. And it could not be otherwise. It is always the few who represent the self-consciousness and the will of an epoch and determine what its history shall be; for it is they who see the forces at their disposal and through those forces actuate the one truly active and productive force—their own will.

That will we find in the song of the poets and the ideas of the political writers, who know how to use a language harmonious with a universal sentiment or with a sentiment capable of becoming universal. In the case of Italy, in all our bards, philosophers and leaders, from Alfieri to Foscolo, from Leopardi to Manzoni, from Mazzini to Gioberti, we are able to pick up the threads of a new fabric, which is a new kind of thought, a new kind of soul, a new kind of Italy. This new Italy differed from the old Italy in something that was very simple but yet was of the greatest importance: this new Italy took life seriously, while the old one did not. People in every age had dreamed of an Italy and talked of an Italy. The notion of Italy had been sung in all kinds of music, propounded in all kinds of philosophy. But it was always an Italy that existed in the brain of some scholar whose learning was more or less divorced from reality. Now reality demands that convictions be taken seriously, that ideas become actions. Accordingly it was necessary that this Italy, which was an affair of brains only, become also an affair of hearts, become, that is, something serious, something alive. This, and no other, was the meaning of Mazzini's great slogan: "Thought and Action." It was the essence of the great revolution which he preached and which he accomplished by instilling his doctrine into the hearts of others. Not many others—a small minority! But they were numerous enough and powerful enough to raise the question where it could be answered—in Italian public opinion (taken in conjunction with the political situation prevailing in the rest of Europe). They were able to establish the doctrine that life is not a game, but a mission; that, therefore, the individual has a law and a purpose in obedience to which and in fulfillment of which he alone attains his true value; that, accordingly, he must make sacrifices, now of personal comfort, now of private interest, now of life itself.

No revolution ever possessed more markedly than did the Italian *Risorgimento* this characteristic of ideality, of thought preceding action. Our revolt was not concerned with the material needs of life, nor did it spring from elementary and widely diffused sentiments breaking out in popular uprisings and mass disturbances. The movements of 1847 and 1848 were demonstrations, as we would say today, of "intellectuals;" they were efforts toward a goal on the part of a minority of patriots who were standard bearers of an ideal and were driving governments and peoples toward its attainment. Idealism—understood as faith in the advent of an ideal reality, as a manner of conceiving life not as fixed within the limits of existing fact, but as incessant progress and transformation toward the level of a higher law which controls men with the very force of the idea—was the sum and substance of Mazzini's teaching; and it supplied the most conspicuous characteristic of our great Italian revolution. In this sense all the patriots who worked for the foundation of the new kingdom were Mazzinians—Gioberti, Cavour, Victor Emmanuel, Garibaldi. To be sure, our writers of the first rank, such as Manzoni and Rosmini, had no historical connection with Mazzini; but they had the same general tendency as Mazzini. Working along diverging lines, they all came together on the essential point: that true life is not the life which is, but also the life which ought to be. It was a conviction essentially religious in character, essentially anti-materialistic.

III

This religious and idealistic manner of looking at life, so characteristic of the *Risorgimento,* prevails even beyond the heroic age of the revolution and the establishment of the Kingdom. It survives down through Ricasoli, Lanza, Sella and Minghetti, down, that is, to the occupation of Rome and the systemization of our national finances. The parliamentary overturn of 1876, indeed, marks not the end, but rather an interruption, on the road that Italy had been following since the beginning of the century. The outlook then changed, and not by the capriciousness or weakness of men, but by a necessity of history which it would be idiotic in our day to deplore. At that time the fall of the Right, which had ruled continuously between 1861 and 1876, seemed to most people the real conquest of freedom.

To be sure the Right cannot be accused of too great scruple in respecting the liberties guaranteed by our Constitution; but the real truth was that the Right conceived liberty in a sense directly opposite to the notions of the Left. The Left moved from the individual to the State: the Right moved from the State to the individual. The men of the Left thought of "the people" as merely the agglomerate of the citizens composing it. They therefore made the individual the center and the point of departure of all the rights and prerogatives which a régime of freedom was bound to respect.

The men of the Right, on the contrary, were firmly set in the notion that no freedom can be conceived except within the State, that freedom can have no important content apart from a solid régime of law indisputably sovereign over the activities and the interests of individuals. For the Right there could be no individual freedom not reconcilable with the authority of the State. In their eyes the general interest was always paramount over private interests. The law, therefore, should have absolute efficacy and embrace the whole life of the people.

This conception of the Right was evidently sound; but it involved great dangers when applied without regard to the motives which provoked it. Unless we are careful, too much law leads to stasis and therefore to the annihilation of the life which it is the State's function to regulate but which the State cannot suppress. The State may easily become a form indifferent to its content—something extraneous to the substance it would regulate. If the law comes upon the individual from without, if the individual is not absorbed in the life of the State, the individual feels the law and the State as limitations on his activity, as chains which will eventually strangle him unless he can break them down.

This was just the feeling of the men of '76. The country

needed a breath of air. Its moral, economic and social forces demanded the right to develop without interference from a law which took no account of them. This was the historical reason for the overturn of that year; and with the transference of power from Right to Left begins the period of growth and development in our nation: economic growth in industry, commerce, railroads, agriculture; intellectual growth in science, education. The nation had received its form from above. It had now to struggle to its new level, giving to a state which already had its constitution, its administrative and political organization, its army and its finance, a living content of forces springing from individual initiative prompted by interests which the *Risorgimento,* absorbed in its great ideals, had either neglected or altogether disregarded.

The accomplishment of this constitutes the credit side of the balance sheet of King Humbert I. It was the error of King Humbert's greatest minister, Francesco Crispi, not to have understood his age. Crispi strove vigorously to restore the authority and the prestige of the state as against an individualism gone rampant, to reassert religious ideals as against triumphant materialism. He fell, therefore, before the assaults of so-called democracy.

Crispi was wrong. That was not the moment for re-hoisting the time-honored banner of idealism. At that time there could be no talk of wars, of national dignity, of competition with the Great Powers; no talk of setting limits to personal liberties in the interests of the abstract entity called "state." The word "God," which Crispi sometimes used, was singularly out of place. It was a question rather of bringing the popular classes to prosperity, self-consciousness, participation in political life. Campaigns against illiteracy, all kinds of social legislation, the elimination of the clergy from the public schools, which must be secular and anticlerical. During this period Freemasonry became solidly established in the bureaucracy, the army, the judiciary. The central power of the state was weakened and made subservient to the fleeting variations of popular will as reflected in a suffrage absolved from all control from above. The growth of big industry favored the rise of a Socialism of Marxian stamp as a new kind of moral and political education for our proletariat. The conception of humanity was not indeed lost from view: but such moral restraints as were placed on the free individual were all based on the feeling that each man must instinctively seek his own well-being and defend it. This was the very conception which Mazzini had fought in Socialism, though he rightly saw that it was not peculiar to Socialism alone, but belonged to any political theory, whether liberal, democratic, or anti-Socialistic, which urges men toward the exaction of rights rather than to the fulfillment of duties.

From 1876 till the Great War, accordingly, we had an Italy that was materialistic and anti-Mazzinian, though an Italy far superior to the Italy of and before Mazzini's time. All our culture, whether in the natural or the moral sciences, in letters or in the arts, was dominated by a crude positivism, which conceived of the reality in which we live as something given, something ready-made, and which therefore limits and conditions human activity quite apart from so-called arbitrary and illusory demands of morality. Everybody wanted "facts," "positive facts." Everybody laughed at "metaphysical dreams," at impalpable realities. The truth was there before the eyes of men. They had only to open their eyes to see it. The Beautiful itself could only be the mirror of the Truth present before us in Nature. Patriotism, like all the other virtues based on a religious attitude of mind, and which can be mentioned only when people have the courage to talk in earnest, became a rhetorical theme on which it was rather bad taste to touch.

This period, which anyone born during the last half of the past century can well remember, might be called the demo-Socialistic phase of the modern Italian state. It was the period which elaborated the characteristically democratic attitude of mind on a basis of personal freedom, and which resulted in the establishment of Socialism as the primary and controlling force in the state. It was a period of growth and of prosperity during which the moral forces developed during the *Risorgimento* were crowded into the background or off the stage.

IV

But toward the end of the nineteenth century and in the first years of the twentieth a vigorous spirit of reaction began to manifest itself in the young men of Italy against the preceding generation's ideas in politics, literature, science and philosophy. It was as though they were weary of the prosaic bourgeois life which they had inherited from their fathers and were eager to return to the lofty moral enthusiasms of their grandfathers. Rosmini and Gioberti had been long forgotten. They were now exhumed, read, discussed. As for Mazzini, an edition of his writings was financed by the state itself. Vico, the great Vico, a formidable preacher of idealistic philosophy and a great anti-Cartesian and anti-rationalist, became the object of a new cult.

Positivism began forthwith to be attacked by neo-idealism. Materialistic approaches to the study of literature and art were refuted and discredited. Within the Church itself modernism came to rouse the Italian clergy to the need of a deeper and more modern culture. Even Socialism was brought under the philosophical probe and criticized like other doctrines for its weaknesses and errors; and when, in France, George Sorel went beyond the fallacies of the materialistic theories of the Marxist social-democracy to his theory of syndicalism, our young Italian Socialists turned to him. In Sorel's ideas they saw two things: first, the end of a hypocritical "collaborationism" which betrayed both proletariat and nation; and second, faith in a moral and ideal reality for which it was the individual's duty to sacrifice himself, and to defend which even violence was justified. The anti-parliamentarian spirit and the moral spirit of syndicalism brought Italian Socialists within the Mazzinian orbit.

Of great importance, too, was nationalism, a new movement then just coming to the fore. Our Italian nationalism was less literary and more political in character than the similar movement in France, because with us it was attached to the old historic Right which had a long political tradition. The new nationalism differed from the old Right in the stress it laid on the idea of "nation;" but it was at one with the Right in regarding the state as the necessary premise to the individual rights and values. It was the special achievement of nationalism to rekindle faith in the nation in Italian hearts, to arouse the country against parliamentary Socialism, and to lead an open attack on Freemasonry, before which the Italian bourgeoisie was terrifiedly prostrating itself. Syndicalists, nationalists, idealists succeeded, between them, in bringing the great majority of Italian youth back to the spirit of Mazzini.

Official, legal, parliamentary Italy, the Italy that was anti-Mazzinian and anti-idealistic, stood against all this, finding its leader in a man of unfailing political intuition, and master as well of the political mechanism of the country, a man skeptical of all high-sounding words, impatient of complicated concepts, ironical, cold, hard-headed, practical—what Mazzini would have called a "shrewd materialist." In the persons, indeed, of Mazzini and Giolitti, we may find a picture of the two aspects of prewar Italy, of that irreconcilable duality which paralyzed the vitality of the country and which the Great War was to solve.

V

The effect of the war seemed at first to be quite in an opposite sense—to mark the beginning of a general débâcle of the Italian state and of the moral forces that must underlie any state. If entrance into the war had been a triumph of ideal Italy over materialistic Italy, the advent of peace seemed to give ample justification to the neutralists who had represented the latter. After the Armistice our Allies turned their backs upon us. Our victory assumed all the aspects of a defeat. A defeatist psychology, as they say, took possession of the Italian people and expressed itself in hatred of the war, of those responsible for the war, even of our Army which had won our war. An anarchical spirit of dissolution rose against all authority. The ganglia of our economic life seemed struck with mortal disease. Labor ran riot in strike after strike. The very bureaucracy seemed to align itself against the state. The measure of our spiritual dispersion was the return to power of Giolitti—the execrated neutralist—who for five years had been held up as the exponent of an Italy which had died with the war.

But, curiously enough, it was under Giolitti that things suddenly changed in aspect, that against the Giolittian state a new state arose. Our soldiers, our genuine soldiers, men who had willed our war and fought it in full consciousness of what they were doing, had the good fortune to find as their leader a man who could express in words things that were in all their hearts and who could make those words audible above the tumult.

Mussolini had left Italian Socialism in 1915 in order to be a more faithful interpreter of "the Italian People" (the name he chose for his new paper.) He was one of those who saw the necessity of our war, one of those mainly responsible for our entering the war. Already as a Socialist he had fought Freemasonry; and, drawing his inspiration from Sorel's syndicalism, he had assailed the parliamentary corruption of reformist Socialism with the idealistic postulates of revolution and violence. Then, later, on leaving the party and in defending the cause of intervention, he had come to oppose the illusory fancies of proletarian internationalism with an assertion of the infrangible integrity, not only moral but economic as well, of the national organism, affirming therefore the sanctity of country for the working classes as for other classes. Mussolini was a Mazzinian of that pure-blooded breed which Mazzini seemed somehow always to find in the province of Romagna. First by instinct, later by reflection, Mussolini had come to despise the futility of the Socialists who kept preaching a revolution which they had neither the power nor the will to bring to pass even under the most favorable circumstances. More keenly than anyone else he had come to feel the necessity of a state which would be a state, of a law which would be respected as law, of an authority capable of exacting obedience but at the same time able to give indisputable evidence of its worthiness so to act. It seemed incredible to Mussolini that a country capable of fighting and winning such a war as Italy had fought and won should be thrown into disorder and held at the mercy of a handful of faithless politicians.

When Mussolini founded his Fasci in Milan in March 1919, the movement toward dissolution and negation that featured the postwar period in Italy had virtually ceased. The Fasci made their appeal to Italians who, in spite of the disappointments of the peace, continued to believe in the war, and who, in order to validate the victory which was the proof of the war's value, were bent on recovering for Italy that control over her own destinies which could come only through a restoration of discipline and a reorganization of social and political forces. From the first, the Fascist Party was not one of believers but of action. What it needed was not a platform of principles, but an idea which would indicate a goal and a road by which the goal could be reached.

The four years between 1919 and 1923 inclusive were characterized by the development of the Fascist revolution through the action of "the squads." The Fascist "squads" were really the force of a state not yet born but on the way to being. In its first period, Fascist "squadrism" transgressed the law of the old régime because it was determined to suppress that régime as incompatible with the national state to which Fascism was aspiring. The March on Rome was not the beginning, it was the end of that phase of the revolution; because, with Mussolini's advent to power, Fascism entered the sphere of legality. After October 28, 1922, Fascism was no longer at war with the state; it *was* the state, looking about for the organization which would realize Fascism as a concept of state. Fascism already had control of all the instruments necessary for the upbuilding of a new state. The Italy of Giolitti had been superseded, at least so far as militant politics were concerned. Between Giolitti's Italy and the new Italy there flowed, as an imaginative orator once said in the Chamber, "a torrent of blood" that would prevent any return to the past. The century-old crisis had been solved. The war at last had begun to bear fruit for Italy.

VI

Now to understand the distinctive essence of Fascism, nothing is more instructive than a comparison of it with the point of view of Mazzini to which I have so often referred.

Mazzini did have a political conception, but his politic was a sort of integral politic, which cannot be so sharply distinguished from morals, religion, and ideas of life as a whole, as to be considered apart from these other fundamental interests of the human spirit. If one tries to separate what is purely political from his religious beliefs, his ethical consciousness and his metaphysical concepts, it becomes impossible to understand the vast influence which his credo and his propaganda exerted. Unless we assume the unity of the whole man, we arrive not at the clarification but at the destruction of those ideas of his which proved so powerful.

In the definition of Fascism, the first point to grasp is the comprehensive, or, as Fascists say, the "totalitarian" scope of its doctrine, which concerns itself not only with political organization and political tendency, but with the whole will and thought and feeling of the nation.

There is a second and equally important point. Fascism is not a philosophy. Much less is it a religion. It is not even a political theory which may be stated in a series of formulas. The significance of Fascism is not to be grasped in the special theses which it from time to time assumes. When on occasion it has announced a program, a goal, a concept to be realized in action, Fascism has not hesitated to abandon them when in practice these were found to be inadequate or inconsistent with the principle of Fascism. Fascism has never been willing to compromise its future. Mussolini has boasted that he is a *tempista,* that his real pride is in "good timing." He makes decisions and acts on them at the precise moment when all the conditions and considerations which make them feasible and opportune are properly matured. This is a way of saying that Fascism returns to the most rigorous meaning of Mazzini's "Thought and Action," whereby the two terms are so perfectly coincident that no thought has value which is not already expressed in action. The real "views" of the Duce are those which he formulates and executes at one and the same time.

Is Fascism therefore "anti-intellectual," as has been so often charged? It is eminently anti-intellectual, eminently Mazzinian, that is, if by intellectualism we mean the divorce of thought from action, of knowledge from life, of brain from heart, of theory from practice. Fascism is hostile to all Utopian systems which are destined never to face the test of reality. It is hostile to all science and all philosophy which remain matters of mere fancy or intelligence. It is not that Fascism denies value to culture, to the higher intellectual pursuits by which thought is invigorated as a source of action. Fascist anti-intellectualism holds in scorn a product peculiarly typical of the educated classes in Italy: the *letterato* —the man who plays with knowledge and with thought without any sense of responsibility for the practical world. It is hostile not so much to culture as to bad culture, the culture which does not educate, which does not make men, but rather creates pedants and aesthetes, egotists in a word, men morally and politically indifferent. It has no use, for instance, for the man who is "above the conflict" when his country or its important interests are at stake.

By virtue of its repugnance for "intellectualism," Fascism prefers not to waste time constructing abstract theories about itself. But when we say that it is not a system or a doctrine we must not conclude that it is a blind praxis or a purely instinctive method. If by system or philosophy we mean a living thought, a principle of universal character daily revealing its inner fertility and significance, then Fascism is a perfect system, with a solidly established foundation and with a rigorous logic in its development; and all who feel the truth and the vitality of the principle work day by day for its development, now doing, now undoing, now going forward, now retracing their steps, according as the things they do prove to be in harmony with the principle or to deviate from it.

And we come finally to a third point.

The Fascist system is not a political system, but it has its center of gravity in politics. Fascism came into being to meet serious problems of politics in postwar Italy. And it presents itself as a political method. But in confronting and solving political problems it is carried by its very nature, that is to say by its method, to consider moral, religious and philosophical questions and to unfold and demonstrate the comprehensive totalitarian character peculiar to it. It is only after we have grasped the political character of the Fascist principle that we are able adequately to appreciate the deeper concept of life which underlies that principle and from which the principle springs. The political doctrine of Fascism is not the whole of Fascism. It is rather its more prominent aspect and in general its most interesting one.

VII

The politic of Fascism revolves wholly about the concept of the national state; and accordingly it has points of contact with nationalist doctrines, along with distinctions from the latter which it is important to bear in mind.

Both Fascism and nationalism regard the state as the foundation of all rights and the source of all values in the individuals composing it. For the one as for the other the state is not a consequence—it is a principle. But in the case of nationalism, the relation which individualistic liberalism, and for that matter Socialism also, assumed between individual and state is inverted. Since the state is a principle, the individual becomes a consequence—he is something which finds an antecedent in the state: the state limits him and determines his manner of existence, restricting his freedom, binding him to a piece of ground whereon he was born, whereon he must live and will die. In the case of Fascism, state and individual are one and the same thing, or rather, they are inseparable terms of a necessary synthesis.

Nationalism, in fact, founds the state on the concept of nation, the nation being an entity which transcends the will and the life of the individual because it is conceived as objectively existing apart from the consciousness of individuals, existing even if the individual does nothing to bring it into being. For the nationalist, the nation exists not by virtue of the citizen's will, but as datum, a fact, of nature.

For Fascism, on the contrary, the state is a wholly spiritual creation. It is a national state, because, from the Fascist point of view, the nation itself is a creation of the mind and is not a material presupposition, is not a datum of nature. The nation, says the Fascist, is never really made; neither, therefore, can the state attain an absolute form, since it is merely the nation in the latter's concrete, political manifestation. For the Fascist, the state is always *in fieri*. It is in our hands, wholly; whence our very serious responsibility towards it.

But this state of the Fascists which is created by the consciousness and the will of the citizen, and is not a force descending on the citizen from above or from without, cannot have toward the mass of the population the relationship which was presumed by nationalism.

Nationalism identified state with nation, and made of the nation an entity preëxisting, which needed not to be created but merely to be recognized or known. The nationalists, therefore, required a ruling class of an intellectual character, which was conscious of the nation and could understand, appreciate and exalt it. The authority of the state, furthermore, was not a product but a presupposition. It could not depend on the people—rather the people depended on the state and on the state's authority as the source of the life which they lived and apart from which they could not live. The nationalistic state was, therefore, an aristocratic state, enforcing itself upon the masses through the power conferred upon it by its origins.

The Fascist state, on the contrary, is a people's state, and, as such, the democratic state *par excellence*. The relationship between state and citizen (not this or that citizen, but all citizens) is accordingly so intimate that the state exists only as, and in so far as, the citizen causes it to exist. Its formation therefore is the formation of a consciousness of it in individuals, in the masses. Hence the need of the Party, and of all the instruments of propaganda and education which Fascism uses to make the thought and will of the Duce the thought and will of the masses. Hence the enormous task which Fascism sets itself in trying to bring the whole mass of the people, beginning with the little children, inside the fold of the Party.

On the popular character of the Fascist state likewise depends its greatest social and constitutional reform—the foundation of the Corporations of Syndicates. In this reform Fascism took over from syndicalism the notion of the moral and educational function of the syndicate. But the Corporations of Syndicates were necessary in order to reduce the syndicates to state discipline and make them an expression of the state's organism from within. The Corporations of Syndicates are a device through which the Fascist state goes looking for the individual in order to create itself through the individual's will. But the individual it seeks is not the abstract political individual whom the old liberalism took for granted. He is the only individual who can ever be found, the individual who exists as a specialized productive force, and who, by the fact of his specialization, is brought to unite with other individuals of his same category and comes to belong with them to the one great economic unit which is none other than the nation.

This great reform is already well under way. Toward it nationalism, syndicalism, and even liberalism itself, were already tending in the past. For even liberalism was beginning to criticize the older forms of political representation, seeking some system of organic representation which would correspond to the structural reality of the state.

The Fascist conception of liberty merits passing notice. The Duce of Fascism once chose to discuss the theme of "Force or Consent"; and he concluded that the two terms are inseparable, that the one implies the other and cannot exist apart from the other; that, in other words, the authority of the state and the freedom of the citizen constitute a continuous circle wherein authority presupposes liberty and liberty authority. For freedom can exist only within the state, and the state means authority. But the state is not an entity hovering in the air over the heads of its citizens. It is one with the personality of the citizen. Fascism, indeed, envisages the contrast not as between liberty and authority, but as between a true, a concrete liberty which exists, and an abstract, illusory liberty which cannot exist.

Liberalism broke the circle above referred to, setting the individual against the state and liberty against authority. What the liberal desired was liberty as against the state, a liberty which was a limitation of the state; though the liberal had to resign himself, as the lesser of the evils, to a state which was a limitation on liberty. The absurdities inherent in the liberal concept of freedom were apparent to liberals themselves early in the nineteenth century. It is no merit of Fascism to have again indicated them. Fascism has its own solution of the paradox of liberty and authority. The authority of the state is absolute. It does not compromise, it does not bargain, it does not surrender any portion of its field to other moral or religious principles which may interfere with the individual conscience. But on the other hand, the state becomes a reality only in the consciousness of its individuals. And the Fascist corporative state supplies a representative system more sincere and more in touch with realities than any other previously devised and is therefore freer than the old liberal state.

❖ ❖ ❖

Less than a year after Mussolini took power in Italy, Harold Laski, a young professor in the London School of Economics, contributed to Foreign Affairs a piece of political analysis which sounded with remarkable prescience the theme which was to be the central one in world history for the next 25 years, and perhaps much longer—the similarities and disparities of Communism and Fascism.

The interaction of the two ideologies has been a process of hands around. Communism first offered itself as the implacable enemy of constituted society, and Fascism replied by presenting itself as its savior. Before long, however, German National Socialism fully revealed the profound hostility of the Fascist ideal to western civilization. But it attacked not only the nations which were the citadel of that civilization, but the Bolshevik state also. As a result, the tolerance or in some cases even evidence of support which some leaders of the capitalist Powers had been foolish enough to show toward Fascism was now reversed; and the Bolshevist state found itself for a time the beneficiary of capitalist indulgence.

There now has come another break in the music, and the performance seems to have come again to the point at which Professor Laski viewed it so shrewdly in September 1923—save, of course, that Mussolini has been hung by his heels, Hitler has immolated himself in order to avoid a like fate, and the Fascist spirit possesses no formal chieftain.

For 25 years, in short, our western society was acted upon alternately by one group of desperate revolutionaries and by another. Perhaps the history of the next 25 years will depend upon the ability of our society to grasp the significance of Professor Laski's analysis of the challenge of the Red and the Black, and to move from a passive to an active rôle.

In the later 1920's, and the 1930's, Harold Laski replaced the viewpoint of the English tradition of Bentham and Mill, who laid their emphasis on free enquiry, reason and persuasion, with a Marxist analysis which, he believed, gave him a better insight into the processes of history. What thesis he will develop in the 1940's and 1950's to elucidate the meaning of the incipient conflict between Marxism and democracy remains to be revealed.

❖ ❖ ❖

LENIN AND MUSSOLINI

By Harold J. Laski

THE progress of science in the past century has reduced the world to the unity of interdependence. A civil war in America brings starvation to the cotton towns of Lancashire. An injury to the credit-structure of Germany may involve a panic on the Paris Bourse. Not less notable than this web of complex interweaving is the pace at which change proceeds. Feudal Japan can become, as it were overnight, the modern state. Men are still living to whom the railway was an incredible innovation; and their children will doubtless watch aerial traffic blot out the distance between London and New York.

We pay, of course, the price for scientific development. The complexity that ensues involves a necessary fragility in the machine. The working of our social institution depends, as never before, upon the maintenance of peace. The mechanisms of civilization are so delicate that they respond like the needle of the compass to every gust of wind; and without their continuous functioning we are, to continue the metaphor, like sailors upon an uncharted sea. We cannot maintain the vast system of interrelationships we have built unless men are prepared to follow consistently the path of reason in their affairs. We need a minimum of social unity that will at least persuade mankind that the path of social change is a matter for deliberation and argument, not for violence and physical conflict.

Yet our interdependence has not procured a unified outlook. Racial hatred, national suspicion, the war of class and class, all these remain to emphasize to us the error of optimism. Confidence, in fact, is the more dangerous because the weapons that science has placed at the service of destruction are now so powerful that their utilization is incompatible with civilized life. We have learned in the last decade that the impulses of savagery that are loosed by war are utterly destructive of the foundations of a decent existence. If men cease to trust the good will of institutions, if, that is, they sacrifice the winning of conviction to the attainment of their desires, civilization could quite easily be reduced to the condition where, as in Mr. Wells' imaginary picture, some aged survivor may tell of an organized and coherent world as a legend which his grandchildren cannot hope to understand. The plain lesson of scientific knowledge is the making of social change in terms of peace. We must utilize our institutions. To destroy them is to destroy ourselves.

Such, at least, seems the plain lesson of recent experience. It implies, of course, the general realization that great events suggest the importance of continuous social reform. The mass of men has now been entrusted with political power; and the governments of the modern state must discover ways and means of translating the will of an electorate which has hardly known the amenities life can offer into terms of statutes. It is possible that so long as the process of legislation can offer proof to the democracy of a good will that results in solid benefit the transition to a new social order will be accomplished in peace. But the good will must be demonstrated; and the benefits must affect those who feel that they have now too small a stake in the present order to make its preservation a matter of urgency to themselves.

Such an attitude is the more important because the desirability of social peace has recently been attacked from what, at first sight, might seem two opposite directions. In Russia, a revolution made in the name of the workers has enthroned in authority men whose boast it is that they hold power without regard to the will of their subjects. In Italy, there developed alongside the constitutional government an extra-legal organization to which, at the first definite challenge, the former was compelled to yield. In Russia, the Bolsheviks have won and maintained power only at the cost of immense bloodshed, in large part, doubtless, the result of foreign intervention. In Italy, the Fascisti met with relatively little opposition at home, and with no external challenge. It is common to both movements that their power is built upon the force they can command. It is common to them, also, that they have rigorously suppressed all opposition to themselves and dismissed as unimportant the forms of constitutionalism. Each has exalted the end it has in view as superior to all problems implied in the means that have been used. Each has declared its own will so clearly identical with the good of the community as to make invalid, on *a priori* grounds, the notion of its critical analysis. Each, that is to say, has abandoned the path of reason and declared, in substance, that a great end transcends the doubts to which its methods have given rise. It is worth while to examine in some detail the principles and possibilities which lie behind this attitude.

II

A revolution in Russia was doubtless implied in the logic of events. No government which is vicious in principle and corrupt in practice can hope, particularly in the atmosphere of military defeat, to retain the allegiance of those who do not share in the benefits of its dishonesty. But the Russian Revolution differs from all its predecessors in that it came in the name of a consistent system of doctrine; and it was largely made by men to whom that system contained the quintessence of social truth. No one can fail to be impressed by the contrast between France in 1789 and the Bolshevik Revolution of November 1917. At no stage in the drama of Versailles was a body of coherent principles given validity in the event. 1789 was a revolution of occasion; November 1917 was a revolution of theory. Lenin and his disciples came to do battle in the name of a social philosophy each item of which was built upon historic interpretation. Accident might have defeated their effort; Kerensky might have been a strong man; the Allies might have had a definite policy; the nation might not have been welded into unity by external invasion. But granted that the opportunity was given, Lenin was the first author of an attempt to translate the Marxian creed into the institutions of a state. His was a root-and-branch challenge to western civilization. It was not merely a rejection of social reform; it was not merely an insistence on the overwhelming superiority of Communism. It was preëmiently the argument that Communism is so obviously desirable that the cost of its establishment must not be counted; and the methods to that end were drawn from the system inherited by Lenin from Marx.

The theses upon which Lenin has proceeded have at any rate the merit of comparative simplicity. The political institutions of society, he argues, are merely a façade to conceal the real nature of the state's organization. The state is in fact a method of protecting the owners of property; and the true division of men is into those who own and those who do not own possessions other than their power to labor. The life of the state is an eternal struggle between them. They have no interests in common. The class which owns property moulds the civilization of society in the service of its own interests. It controls the government, it makes the laws, it builds the institutions of the commonwealth in accordance with its own desires. It divides the society into free men and slaves; and with the advent of capitalism the last stage of that historic antithesis is reached. Just as the social order of the past has secreted within its womb the germ of its successor, as, for example, feudalism produced capitalism, so does the latter contain within itself the germ of its Communist successor. Capitalism, as Marx said, produces its own grave-digger. The conflict between owner and proletariat is an inevitable one, and it is bound to result in the victory of the proletariat. The process is predetermined; and there is nothing in Lenin's writings to suggest that a doubt of ultimate success has ever crossed his mind.

The method he advocates is, of course, the method of Marx. The workers are to assume the reins of power by a revolutionary act; and a dictatorship of iron rigor is to consolidate the new system until the period of transition has been effectively bridged. Lenin has never blinded himself to what this implies. The history of capitalism seems to him the history of a relentless defense of every phase of the rights of property. These were maintained at every point by methods unconnected with morality. If the conflict was extreme, as in the days of June 1848, or as with the Commune of Paris, the last ounce of misery was wrung from its opponents that capitalism might be secure. A period of comparative quiescence may produce the concession of social reform, but this is merely deception. Once a really vital point is touched by the workers' demands, they are met by armed resistance. This means that only a conscious and violent intervention can realize Communism. The proletariat must seize a propitious moment for the revolution; and until the revolution comes it must do all in its power to disturb the existing régime. For Communists have only two functions, to prepare for the revolution and to consolidate it successfully when it has been prepared.

The period of consolidation has always seemed to Lenin a period of iron dictatorship. He has had no illusions about the possibility, in such an hour, of democratic governance. Ideals of freedom and equality are bourgeois myths which cannot be admitted until the ground won has been secured. Revolution provokes counterrevolution; and a victorious proletariat must be on its guard against reaction. Revolution, in fact, demands of the revolutionary class that it secure its purpose by every method at its disposal. For compassion or remorse it has neither time nor opportunity. It must disarm antagonism by execution, imprisonment, forced labor, control of the press. For as it cannot allow any effort at the violent overthrow of what it has established, so must it stamp out such criticism as might engender further attack. Revolution is war, and war is founded upon terror. The Communist must use, in fact, the methods of capitalism to extinguish capitalism. For as capitalism has made of life itself the cheapest of commodities, there need be no repining at its sacrifice, and the result, in the end, is worth the cost, since it destroys the possibility of future sale. It would be, as Marx said of the Paris Commune, a wanton betrayal of trust to observe the traditional forms of liberalism. The end involved is too great to be nice about the means used.

Nor, Lenin argues, can revolutionary Communism halt at its own frontiers. The best defensive is the offensive method; it must attack other states lest they become centers of attack against itself. Of this attitude the Moscow International has been a not ineffective expression. It has allied itself to every center of proletarian discontent. It has sought everywhere to create revolutionary working-class organizations hostile to the constitutional weapons of the middle-class state. Communists all over the world have been invited to arm the class-conscious proletariat. They have been invited to do all they could to cut down the army of the state as the chief weapon of defense possessed by the bourgeoisie. They have been urged to form their independent, if hidden, military force and acquire arms by every method. They have been asked to discredit influential democrats to whose word the working class seemed to respond. For everywhere, Lenin has insisted, a violent struggle is inevitable. In England, for example, the workers might capture Parliament at the polls, but political power is in any case a shadow, and were it used for an attack on property it would inevitably provoke an armed resistance. Lenin, indeed, has gone further, and is openly contemptuous of democracy. It is for him a bourgeois institution intended only to deceive the people. The proletariat will always be deceived; and there can be no reliance save upon the class-conscious minority which accepts his views. For in his eyes there is no place in history for the majority-principle. The record of states is of a clash between determined minorities contending for the seat of power. To introduce considerations of consent, to wait on in the belief that the obvious rightness of Communist doctrine will ultimately persuade them to its acceptance, is entirely to ignore reality.

A generation which, like our own, has seen these dogmas applied by armed battalions is unlikely to underestimate their importance. Nor are they less significant because Lenin has retreated from the full substance of his original position. Compromise may have been made with the peasants; internal difficulties may have called a halt to international propaganda; the pressure of circumstance may have admitted a small measure of private trading. What is here in dispute is not the end the Russian Revolution seeks to serve. The idea of emancipating a people from economic servitude is unquestionably a noble one; and there is a fundamental sense in which the atmosphere of that effort marks a great epoch in the history of mankind. Lenin is quite obviously informed by high sincerity. No work has been too difficult or too dangerous for either himself or his disciples to undertake. They have shrunk from no labor, however hard; and they have pursued throughout impersonal ends.

The question involved is a different one. Capitalism may be all that Lenin believes; and, indeed, the indictment against it is, on any impartial view, a formidable one. The question is whether the overthrow of institutions by violent means is ever likely to serve its intended purpose. It entails, and has entailed in Russia, the suppression of tolerance and kindliness. It has sown cruelty and hatred, anger and suspicion, into the soil of human relations. It has impaired at every point the intellectual heritage of the Russian people. It has been impatient of reason and fanatically hostile to critical inquiry. Its method, in fact, has been that by which every militant religion in past history has propagated its creed. The religion may have been true; but a religion which has sought to enforce its truth by the sword has always been in ultimate conflict with what is most precious in the nature of men.

III

The Italian movement is different in origin, but its ultimate spirit is in nowise dissimilar. Leninism has been the dictatorship of a party, Fascism is the dictatorship of a man. Its rise is in part due to the endeavor to escape from the disillusion which seized Italy after the Treaty of Versailles, and in part to the ill-considered effort of the left-wing Italian Socialists not merely to link themselves to the Third International but also to seize control of industry in some of the great towns. Violence assumed the character of a habit in postwar Italy. D'Annunzio's defiance of the Allies at Fiume awoke everywhere a vivid enthusiasm; and the ultimate expulsion of his troops by the government was a profound blow to the new pride of irredentist victory. Hardly less dissatisfaction was caused by the supineness of the government before the progress of Socialism. Its refusal to expel the workers from the occupied factories was taken, not as a wise effort to avoid unnecessary bloodshed—since their surrender was inevitable—but as a failure to accept the challenge of Bolshevism. The older politicians were thoroughly discredited. Giolitti had been opposed to Italy's entrance into the war; Orlando had surrendered to the prestige of President Wilson; Nitti's conversion to the outlook of a "good European" did not square with the inflamed ambitions of victory. There had, moreover, been for many years a profound unreality about the alignment of Italian parties. They were in the control of machines bankrupt of ideas and—the clericals apart—little different from each other. A revivification of political life was essential if Italy was to realize the new possibilities opened by her part in the victory.

It was as the symbol of that revivification that Mussolini came to do battle with the old order. In part he represented the passionate optimism of youth, eager to control what seemed a great destiny, and in part the desire of the small property-owner for security against the advance of Socialism. Fascist ideas found a ready acceptance wherever men were ambitious of power or apprehensive of novelty. As a soldier in the late war, Mussolini could claim a part in the victory. As a former member of the Socialist Party, he had the credit which always attaches to those who abandon unpopular views. The small bands of his supporters grew rapidly until they were the one organized and disciplined party in the state. They were able by direct action to drive out the Socialists from their municipal strongholds. They met criticism and dissent not by words but by deeds. They destroyed the printing-presses of their opponents. They broke up public meetings. They beat strikers into submission. Where they encountered resistance, they did not hesitate even at assassination to enforce their will. The district authorities were cowed into submission to their local leaders. They infected the army and navy with their spirit; and the government did not dare to challenge their power. Mussolini, as chairman of the central council, exacted and received an iron obedience from his followers. They were organized like an army; they wore a uniform. By the summer of 1922 Mussolini had half a million soldiers under his command. The time had come to move from the atmosphere of influence to the realm of government. He marched to Rome. The cabinet resigned its authority into the King's hands; and the latter had no alternative save to make Mussolini Prime Minister.

He was not even within sight of a parliamentary majority; but the Chambers abdicated before his avowed contempt for them. Either, he asserted, they must accept his will, or he would act without regard to their constitutional power. The ethos of Italy was incarnate in himself; and to oppose him was to invite disaster. The result was a remarkable triumph of dominant personality. The deputies did not hesitate to surrender their authority; if they criticized, they were beaten in the street or subjected to humiliating personal attack. Foreign policy and domestic policy alike were simply the will of Mussolini. His followers became the national militia. It is now a legal offense to publish material which serves to bring either the government or its policies into contempt. Freedom of speech has so far ceased to exist that older statesmen like Giolitti and Orlando have hastened to salute the new star. The Chamber of Deputies has passed a bill by which any party which receives one-quarter of the votes at a general election will secure automatically two-thirds of the seats in the Chamber; and since every Italian Government controls the elections Mussolini has granted himself at least four years of power.

He has openly thrown overboard all pretense of majority rule. He will obtain power not because the mass of the electorate supports his views, but because his followers will not allow opposition to make itself heard. Government, for him, exists to fulfil needs, not to give effect to wills; and its first requirement is an overwhelming strength incompatible with liberty. For liberty, indeed, Mussolini professes no affection. He has called it a nineteenth-century concept which has exhausted its utility. Liberty, for him, is the parent of anarchy if it implies hostility from opponents, and the proof of disloyalty, involving expulsion from the party, if it comes from his declared supporters. He is hostile, also, to notions of equality. Though Fascism was, in its first phases, republican, since its accession to power it has found reasons to believe in monarchical government. It is avowedly favorable to a régime of classes; and it regards the hierarchical structure of society as the natural reward of ability in an order where the weaker must go to the wall. It is opposed to public enterprise at a period when the increasing control of basic monopolies is more and more regarded as a vital part of social policy. It is imperialistic in foreign affairs. It regards the League of Nations as the ill-begotten child of Anglo-Saxon plutocracy. It is determined to expel England and France from the domination of the Mediterranean. It regards Jugoslavia with suspicion. Wherever Italians dwell in foreign lands, it proposes to create enclaves of Fascismo that they may "be brought to live the Italian life more intimately" and be protected "legally and extralegally" where they are dependent upon foreign employers. It seeks the domination, in particular, of the Adriatic, which involves the economic penetration of Albania. It demands a sympathetic policy towards Turkey in its new form.

The student of Fascismo who desires to glean from its literature any definite system of ideas will be astonished at its incoherent naïveté. The Italian mind has always been prolific of eloquence; but Cavour and Mazzini, whatever their limitations, had always in view a tangible ideal. Mussolini has offered no such hostages to fortune. His writings and speeches have been sedulously kept within the realm of the impalpable. He emphasizes the importance of patriotism and the duty of upholding the national interest, as at Fiume, at all costs. He denies the validity of class warfare. Capital must be protected; but labor must be given a due coöperation in its management. He believes, particularly, in the promotion of peasant proprietorship. It is at once a safeguard against Bolshevism and a means of giving individualism the opportunity of active expression. He believes in law, but, so to say, in a lawless sense. When government is weak it must be made strong; and direct action is the path to strength. For the subversive tyranny of Lenin there is substituted the creative tyranny of Mussolini. He has a ruthless will to power; and the extreme situation in which he found himself seemed to demand heroic remedies. The will to power justifies the assumption of power. Its victory means the close of the period of internal trouble and foreign disappointment. Production is to be intensified; all political and economic deficiencies are to be repaired. When life "has resumed its peaceful rhythm" violence may be discarded; but it is an essential method until the national reconstruction is complete.

No one who has seen a political party constructing its electoral program can fail to recognize phrases of this kind. The promise of a new heaven and a new earth are part of the common stock-in-trade of those who traffic in the art of government. Where, perhaps, Mussolini differs from his predecessors is in the passionate conviction by which his activity is inspired. He literally regards opposition to his views as a crime. He literally insists that all Italian history since the time of Virgil finds its consummation in the movement he leads. Any party, of course, which regards its dogmas as a religion is bound to derive strength from its fanaticism. It is too early yet to pronounce a judgment upon the meaning of this victory. Declarations of truth are inevitably easier than their realization in the event. Insistence that violence must give place to order is more easily announced than applied. Expectations that one's opponents will start from the acceptance of the condition one has established are often doomed to disappointment. Mussolini has used all the weapons at the disposal of force to hew his way to power. He has trampled down all opposition. He has cowed his critics into silence. He may have yielded a little here, as in his support of England's policy to Germany, or his conciliatory attitude to the Vatican; in general, he holds office without conditions or limitations of any kind. He has made a revolution as vital as any in the history of the last decade by methods which Machiavelli would have understood and admired. If he establishes at length the rule of reason, it will be in terms of the rejection of its essential instruments. For there is no connection between conviction that is won by persuasion, and acceptance that is extorted by force. The victories of the former are enduring; but the conquests of violence produce a reaction conceived in the tragic terms of the model they create.

IV

The historian of the next generation cannot fail to be impressed by the different reception accorded to the changes of which Lenin and Mussolini have been the chief authors. Where Lenin's system has won for itself international ostracism and armed intervention, that of Mussolini has been the subject of widespread enthusiasm. He himself has been decorated by the governments of foreign powers; ambassadors have exhausted the language of eulogy at official banquets; and great men of business have not hesitated to say that only the emulation of his methods can reduce the working classes to a proper state of mind. Yet, save in intensity, there has been no difference in the method pursued by the two men; and it is difficult to avoid the conclusion that the different reception of their effort is the outcome of their antithetic attitudes to property.

Yet the danger implicit in each philosophy is a similar one. We have spent so many years in war that we have grown accustomed to a code of conduct peculiar to times of disorder, and we have even erected laws of behavior which are special to periods of rebellion. In Greece, in Turkey, in Bulgaria, the writ of violence alone receives allegiance; and the news of murder and pillage is accepted without a sense of outrage. We are training to the thought of seizing power numbers of desperate men who are careless of the historic tradition and contemptuous of the morality upon which our civilization has been built. The same temper may be found in America and Ireland; and evidence of its existence in England and France can be found on every hand. Mussolini and Lenin are merely the last term in a series which pervades the circumference of western civilization.

The attitude they represent is the simple one that they serve a great end, and that barriers in the way of their goal must be removed at any cost. Yet it is obvious that if any group of men may, because of ardent belief, ignore the tested constitution of society, there is no prospect of peaceful development. For it is the plain lesson of experience that the only permanent basis of power is action built upon the wills and desires of the mass of men; and those who govern must be humble enough to be so skeptical of their conclusions as to be willing continuously to submit them to the judgment of their fellows.

Since, at least, the Renaissance, what improvement we have made in matters of social organization has been built upon the maintenance of this temper. The willingness to abide by free inquiry is the one certain avenue of progress. We may dislike the result; and we may seek to persuade men by further investigation to reject decisions that have been made. What is above all important is the notion that toleration is the persistent atmosphere of experiment. Once we are willing to be aggressively dogmatic about what are, after all, the most difficult of all questions, we invite the abandonment of reason. For every system of government which fails to rely upon persuasion and argument will always attract to itself men who are capable of neither. They may begin by asserting that they have seized power for a great end; they are bound to continue by holding power for its own sake. And they are certain to hold power by penalizing dissent from their views.

Such systems have been tried before in history, most notably in the case of religion. They have always failed for the final reason that the bonds which unite the social fabric are too fragile to survive a constant assault. Medieval dogmatism did not produce conviction; it involved the wars of religion. The price we pay for militant certitude in social affairs is always the establishment of a despotism. From despotism to conflict the step is near and logical.

Lenin and Mussolini alike have established a government not of laws but of men. They have degraded public morality by refusing to admit the terms upon which civilized intercourse alone becomes possible. By treating their opponents as criminals, they have made thought itself a disastrous adventure; and that at a time when what is needed, above all, is inventiveness in social affairs. They have penalized sincerity in politics. They have given rein to passions which are incompatible with the security of life. They have insisted on the indispensability of themselves and their dogmas even though we cannot afford to pay the price incurred in the enforcement of that notion. If, as with both men, the problem of social change is to be restricted to a struggle between property and poverty, we shall end either by the establishment of an iron industrial feudalism or an anarchy in which our intellectual heritage will perish.

It may well be that the time has come for a revolution in the temper of human affairs; certainly no modern state can at once widely distribute political power and seek to maintain great disparities of fortune. But the only revolution that can hope for permanence is that which wins by slow persuasion the organized conviction of men. To endanger that process by exalting violence will not merely destroy a law here and a government there. It will, in the end, disrupt the foundations of the social fabric. Great events are not produced by the mechanism of law or the efforts of single men. They depend, in the last analysis, upon the spirit which surrounds the circumstances of government. If that spirit is habituated to methods of violence, we cannot maintain the traditions of civilization.

❖ ❖ ❖

THE story described here in 1922 by Philip Kerr (later Lord Lothian, British Ambassador to the United States at his death in 1940), which constituted one of the few truly heartening major political developments of the period between the wars, failed almost completely to find lodging in the American mind. It was one of the conventions of the time that politics, by definition, was a subject fit only for debunking; and the idea that from the old roots of British imperialism had sprung a system of free yet firmly united nations was dismissed as a chimera. Either the Commonwealth was described as a device to enable Britain to cast six votes in the League of Nations, or, if there was reality in the independence of the Dominions, then the British Empire was considered to have at last fallen apart, in the pattern of 1776 but without the fighting.

Even those who studied the new arrangement with sympathy often failed to grasp its import, for the British Commonwealth was an original political institution. It is only in the light of the world's experience in the full 25-year span since Kerr wrote that the central significance of this political development is apparent. What we have seen is a demonstration that independent nations can be grouped in a workable political system other than by the method of federalism. The question of the nature of the cohesive force in this union remains unanswered and extremely interesting. Balfour, in a memorandum, ascribed it to: "Patriotism. Loyalty. Custom. Religion. Race. Pride in various manifestations. Habit. Language." Yet since Balfour jotted down that comment, we have the almost incredible spectacle of the closing out of British rule in India in the spirit of mutual good will, and with the apparent possibility that the structure of the British Commonwealth will be flexible enough to attract and contain great Hindu and Moslem states. The story of the Commonwealth seems still in its early chapters, but a world awake to the importance of the problem of uniting sovereign states in a firm political system no longer disregards its lesson and its challenge.

❖ ❖ ❖

FROM EMPIRE TO COMMONWEALTH

By Philip Kerr

DURING the past twenty years a very marked change has taken place in the character and constitutional system of what is known as the British Empire. The old view was described in 1911 in *The Round Table*, a quarterly devoted to discussion of the political problems of the Empire, as follows:

Forty years ago the British Empire was regarded as a failure. Contemporary judgment, conscious of the difficulties and burdens of the day and of the doleful lessons of the past, could see no future before it . . . As Seeley said, 'We had not learnt from experience wisdom, but only despair.' History, indeed, seemed to prove that human beings failed of the capacity to rise above a certain territorial nationalism. In Turgot's phrase, colonies had always been 'like ripe fruits which cling till they ripen.' Was it not the manifest destiny of the British colonies also to declare their independence so soon as they could stand alone? Gladstone, indeed, went so far as to suggest that we should anticipate the inevitable end and settle the difficulties between England and America over the Civil War by an immediate transfer to America of British territory in Canada.

There was much the same feeling about the dependencies. India and the West Indies were England's chief possessions—an empire she had gained by no deliberate policy, but which had been forced upon her in her struggles with France and Spain, and by the restless enterprise of traders and adventurers. Her own political traditions—especially as embodied in the phrase 'no taxation without representation'—compelled her to abandon the methods of earlier empires and refrain from levying tribute from subject peoples. There was, therefore, no great enthusiasm for the dependencies. The trade with them was considerable, but it affected only a small portion of the British population, while the burdens for their defence all had to bear. . . . In fact, to use a phrase of Mr. Asquith's, the Empire 'was regarded as a regrettable necessity, to be apologized for as half blunder, half crime.'

In the colonies themselves there was a complete indifference to the subject. People were absorbed in the task of settling and developing a virgin country, and in casting off the thraldom of a somewhat ignorant, narrow, and unsympathetic office in Downing Street, Whitehall. They had little knowledge of world problems beyond their borders, they had but little consciousness of their own, and were content to let events shape their destiny.

Finally, there was no imperial constitutional machinery of any kind. The government of the Empire was conducted from Downing Street, at the unfettered discretion of the British Government save in the then unfederated provinces or states of Canada, Australia and South Africa, which governed themselves.

Nobody would say that this was a true picture of the British Empire today. It has been so transformed that even its name has been changed. In the Anglo-Irish treaty of 1921 it is officially described as "the British Commonwealth of Nations." It is the purpose of this article to describe the nature of this transformation, and the forces which have brought it about.

I. THE DOMINIONS

In the middle of the last century the territories now known as the Dominions, namely Canada, Australia, South Africa and New Zealand, consisted of a number of provinces, mostly governing themselves, but with no machinery for conducting their common affairs save the ordinances of the British Governor-General and the colonial office, and no means at all for participating in the management of the Empire of which they formed part. As population flowed in, however, the necessity for dealing with the problems of the colonies on a national basis became apparent, and the movement for federation everywhere began to grow. It was successful first in Canada, in 1867. Australia followed suit in 1900; South Africa in 1909, after the Boer War had removed the obstacle of the two flags.

The achievement of federation, in every case the work of

purely local movements, produced two effects. It involved the final elimination of the power of the British Government in the internal affairs of the colonies. The Dominions, as they later came to be termed, became, so far as their internal politics were concerned, practically independent self-governing nations, united to the rest of the Empire by sentiment and by certain legal ties symbolized by allegiance to a common crown, but not linked to it by any governmental control.

The second effect was a rapid growth of national feeling, which manifested itself in protective tariffs designed to develop local industries, and a determined resistance to anything like interference or dictation from England.

In proportion, however, as the independence of the Dominions grew and the authority of Great Britain diminished, the feeling of loyalty to the Empire as a composite of free nations—independent of one another, but united in patriotism, pride in their institutions, and for common defense—steadily strengthened. The first outward manifestation of this new spirit appeared in 1887 on the occasion of Queen Victoria's jubilee. Then the first Colonial Conference was called, because, as the British Government declared, of their "conviction that there is on all sides a growing desire to draw closer in every practicable way the bonds which unite the various portions of the Empire."

In summoning the conference the British Government expressly disclaimed the desire to discuss "what was known as Political Federation." They said that their chief desire, in view of the new era of international expansion symbolized by the march of Russia across Asia, the union of Germany, and the general grab for African territory, was to examine the problem of improving the common organization for defense. The colonies, however, were not impressed at that time with the necessity of contributing to the common defense. The policy of the colonial representatives was rather to promote imperial unity by introducing a system of tariff preferences for Empire goods.

This first Colonial Conference accomplished little. Its main importance is that its deliberations show the sentiment which then existed about the Empire. It was clear that there was no dissatisfaction with the organization of the Empire, as it then was. It was England's business to run the Empire as a whole, to conduct its foreign relations, to defend it from attack, to govern the dependencies. Colonial legislatures, on the other hand, were recognized as being solely responsible for the government of their own territories, but they assumed no responsibility for defending themselves from invasion across the seas or for assisting in the defense of the Empire as a whole.

In the ensuing 25 years, five further conferences were held—in 1897, in 1902, in 1907, in 1909, and in 1911. The tendency throughout all these meetings is quite uniform. There is a steady refusal on the part of the Dominions to consider any form of federal or constitutional union, and an ever increasing insistence on their status as independent nations within the Empire. On the other hand, there is a steady increase in the insistence by the British Government on the importance of the problem of defense, and in the sentiment on the part of the colonies in favor of inter-imperial commercial preferences.

In 1907, 20 years after the first Colonial Conference, the position was crystallized in a constitutional resolution. There were in future to be regular meetings, every four years and oftener if need be, of what was to be called the Imperial Conference. The Imperial Conference, however, was to have no legislative or executive authority. It was to be a conference between governments, represented normally by prime ministers, for the discussion of "questions of common interest." The decisions of the Imperial Conference were to be effective only if endorsed by the respective Dominion parliaments.

This was the first step taken by the peoples of the Empire in evolving a rudimentary organization and in the transition from Empire to Commonwealth. Apart from this resolution, however, the Imperial Conference of 1907 did not accomplish much. The question of defense was not seriously discussed because the British Government at the time was trying to make an agreement for the limitation of armaments with Germany, and because, having just been returned to power on a free trade policy, it could not fall into line with the Dominion policy of Empire preference.

Two years later, however, when the announcement of the new German naval program, which provided for the creation of a navy greater than any then in existence, showed that the peace movement had failed, a special imperial defense conference was summoned to consider the situation. The British Government had in the past been inclined to ask the Dominions to contribute in cash towards the cost of the British navy and in men towards the imperial army. But the larger Dominions, Canada and Australia, had made it clear that while they were perfectly willing to share in the burden their assistance must be in the form of Dominion navies and national armies, and not of contributions in money or men to an imperial army. At the defense conference of 1909 the British Government accepted this view, and Australia agreed to maintain, in Australian waters and under her own control, an Australian fleet unit consisting of one dreadnought, three armored cruisers, destroyers, etc.; Canada undertook to keep up two smaller units, one on the Atlantic, the other on the Pacific; while New Zealand and South Africa, which could not afford separate units of their own, contributed in ships or money directly to the British navy. Each, too, undertook to take steps to increase their national forces and to train them on uniform lines, so that coöperation should be easy in case war broke out.

It was immediately recognized, however, that if the Dominions were thus to share in the burden of defense it was essential that they should be consulted about the foreign policy which might lead to war. Accordingly, at the Imperial Conference of 1911, two years later, foreign policy for the first time figured upon the agenda.

The Great War did not change in the least the general line of constitutional development in the Empire. It only hastened and intensified it. To the amazement of the world the Dominions threw themselves from the outset wholeheartedly into the struggle against Prussianism. Out of a scattered population of about 15,000,000 they sent no less than 700,000 men to Europe. But even so the character of the coöperation of the Dominions grew steadily more national. At first the Dominion units were brigaded with the more experienced and trained British troops, but by the end of the war the Canadian and the Australian troops had become self-contained national armies, organized and commanded exclusively by Dominion officers, though under the orders of the British Commander-in-Chief for the purposes of the war.

The same process is to be seen in the direction of the war itself. In 1917, to quote the War Cabinet report, the Prime Ministers of the Dominions together with representatives of India "were invited to London to attend a series of special meetings of the War Cabinet in order to discuss the problems of the war and the possible conditions of peace.... The sessions of the Cabinet thus enlarged came to be known as the Imperial War Cabinet." In 1918, the Imperial War Cabinet again convened, remained in session as the supreme directing body until the armistice and then went to Paris in 1919 as the British Empire delegation to the Peace Conference. Throughout this period the main questions of British policy were settled at meetings in which Dominion ministers took part on equal terms and with equal responsibility with British ministers.

The process of development from a colonial to an equal status reached its climax in Paris. While Great Britain and the Dominion delegates sat together as the British Empire delegation, the Dominions insisted upon being separately represented in the Peace Conference itself. They claimed that they had done a great deal more to win the war than many of the nations participating, and they would not tolerate being excluded in their individual national capacity.

The extent to which the new concept of the Empire as a commonwealth of free and equal nations has grown is shown by the fact that on one occasion the Prime Minister of Canada took a line in a public session at variance with the rest, and that the British ratification of the treaty of peace could be deposited only after it had been separately approved by all the Dominion Parliaments. Finally, when the

Covenant of the League of Nations came to be considered, the Dominions insisted upon independent representation within it, for the same reasons that they had insisted upon separate representation in the Peace Conference. This fact was afterward used in the campaign against the League of Nations in the United States in the form of the six votes to one slogan, to the general surprise of people in England, who thought that the United States had far more real control over the votes of Cuba and Panama or some of the Central American republics than Great Britain was ever likely to have over the votes of the Dominion nations.

Since the war, the Dominions have sent delegations to the League of Nations which have acted and voted more or less independently. On the other hand, at the Washington Conference the British Empire delegation, consisting of representatives of all its parts, acted more or less as a whole.

In 1921 the Prime Ministers reassembled in London to consider the postwar situation and the policy to be pursued at the Washington Conference. The anomalies of the present constitutional position are well illustrated by the difficulty which arose over the title to be given the gathering. The official title of the conference was "The Conference of Prime Ministers and Representatives of the United Kingdom, the Dominions and India." And this is the only name by which the body which in fact determines the policy of a commonwealth containing more than a quarter of mankind is officially known!

A second question which arose centered on whether Canada should send a minister of its own to Washington. Great Britain had already agreed to this being done. But the other Dominions objected on the ground that if Canada did this they would have to follow suit, and that they did not wish to have to incur the expense of sending ministers all over the world. So far no minister has been appointed.

But the chief problem before the conference centered about the control of foreign policy. Each self-governing part of the Commonwealth is independent so far as concerns its defensive preparations and the action it should take to deal with imperial or international crises as they arise. But who is to control foreign policy? That is the important thing, for it is foreign policy which leads nations into war and international complications or keeps them out of them. Yet foreign policy is not a matter which can wait for endless deliberation and consultation. Its essence is prompt decision and prompt action. How, therefore, is the foreign policy of a commonwealth of nations scattered all over the face of the globe to be conducted and controlled?

The conclusion arrived at by the Prime Ministers in 1921 was summarized in *The Round Table* in the following terms:

> Now, the "Conference of Prime Ministers and Representatives" is recognized as the body which formulates the policy of the Empire, especially in foreign matters; while the British Government becomes charged with the duty of carrying out that policy in the intervals between the assembling of the Conference, subject to such consultation as is possible through resident or visiting ministers or the cables and the mails. From now onwards policy is a matter for the people of the Empire, and the British Government will occupy a position somewhat similar to that of the President of the United States, whose foreign policy, to be effective, requires the consent and coöperation of the Senate—in our case, the Dominions.

Since then the only change, and it is a very great one, has been the establishment of Ireland as a Dominion with the same status in the British Commonwealth of Nations as Canada. The self-governing portion of the Commonwealth now consists of six independent nations united under a single crown, linked in a common loyalty to one another, but possessing no common governmental organ save the occasional conference already described. Whether the Commonwealth is likely to develop a more effective organism of its own, or whether it will tend to develop along the League of Nations lines, I will briefly consider in the last section of this article.

II. THE NON-SELF-GOVERNING EMPIRE

The total population of the British Empire is given in the "Statesman's Year Book for 1922" as being 440,923,000, or more than a quarter of the whole population of the world. Not more than 65,000,000 of them are Europeans in origin, and 47,000,000 of them live in the British Isles. What of the balance?

The overwhelming majority, no less than 319,000,000, live in India, leaving about 65,000,000 people in about 50 other areas scattered all over the world, from territories like Nigeria through mandated territories like Palestine, down to miscellaneous islands like St. Helena or Fiji.

To the average American mind this whole Empire stands for "imperialism." To some extent this is true. The British Empire has grown partly because the dominant classes in Great Britain in the past valued the prestige and power and the commercial gains that Empire seemed to bring. But there were two other causes at work which, if one studies the history and the feats of the past, will be found to have been far more decisive. One has been rivalry and struggle with other Powers. The other has been the problem of what to do with backward territories after civilization has begun to affect them.

The expansion of Great Britain in India, America, Africa and the isles of the sea has been fundamentally caused by exactly the same forces that led to the elimination of France and Spain from the hinterland of the 13 original colonies, and to the incorporation of Texas, the purchase of Alaska, the annexation of Hawaii, the inclusion of the Philippines, and the exercise of tutelage over Cuba and the Central American republics, by the United States. Probably nobody deliberately planned to annex these territories. But if it came to a question of whether Japan or the United States was going to have Hawaii, or whether Russia was going to spread over to North America, or whether some European Power or the United States was going to end disorder in Central America, America had no two opinions. This same factor has been the biggest single element in the growth of the British Empire proper. It was the reluctance to allow the new world to fall under the control of Bourbon and Napoleonic France, and later of Bismarckian Germany, which was the primary cause of the expansion of the British Empire during the last 200 years.

And this same factor will continue to operate until the whole world is brought under some system of law which will define the rights of nations, give security to all, promote self-government in the backward parts and so end the rivalry and suspicion which necessarily dominate the policy and action of all powers, so long as they remain in a "state of nature" towards one another.

The second cause is hardly less potent. Few people realize the effect of the impact of civilization upon a primitive community. It usually disorganizes it altogether. The only African or Asiatic state which has been able to absorb the methods of the west without disintegrating has been Japan. At the other extreme take the following case. Forty years ago Swaziland was an ordinary Kaffir community, ruled by a paramount chief and his advisers, and living extremely primitively but in comparative happiness, though subject to tribal wars with its neighbors. The first person who came along was the trader. He sold beads and blankets and later bicycles and gramophones in return for gold or ivory or anything else of value. Then he brought in liquor, then firearms. The old chief developed a taste for liquor, other natives for other things. They had no experience of how to deal in western ideas. They soon had nothing to give in exchange for what they wanted save land and mining concessions. The last stage of the story of Swaziland was that the paramount chief, having signed away every concession he could, his own and his people's, signed a concession on his deathbed for "all those concessions I have not already given," in return for a final consignment of gin. By 1902 the country was in chaos.

There is only one way of dealing with people as primitive as these, and that is for a civilized government to step in and control the foreign trader and concession seeker, whether he wants to do legitimate or illegitimate business, in the interests of the backward people. Some people say: "Leave them alone." It cannot be done. Every community can run its own affairs if left entirely to itself. But primitive communities do not know how to resist the deleterious aspects of modern civilization. It is obviously impossible to erect a ring fence round Africa and allow nobody to go in or out. In the case of Swaziland, George Grey, the brother of Sir Edward Grey, was sent in. He cancelled all concessions which interfered with the legitimate life of the people, redistributed the rest on fair terms, and set up a British resident with power to see that such things did not happen again.

If we study the history of the expansion of European states or of the United States we shall find this process operating everywhere. The primary cause of the entry of the British into Egypt was the disorder which followed the misgovernment and oppression of the Khedive when he tried to get taxes to pay for loans he had borrowed abroad. The greatest menace to China's future is the money which its military leaders and ministers can borrow in return for concessions and which they spend in fighting wars of their own. The United States had to stay in the Philippines because it could not leave the Filipinos without any government after the Spaniards had withdrawn. And Great Britain had to stay in Mesopotamia and other German colonies for exactly the same reason.

This does not mean that foreign intervention has not often been brutally oppressive and exploiting. Some of the worst scandals of history have occurred under this plea. Nor does it mean, as I shall show, that Great Britain has always been wise in the way she has governed the politically backward peoples. But it does mean that the problem is quite different from being a mere question of "imperialism." The problem of adjusting the relations between advanced and relatively backward communities is one of the most urgent in the world. It cannot be ignored or solved by phrasemaking. It has to be dealt with somehow or other.

A study, indeed, of the history of Great Britain will show that at almost every stage her governments have been reluctant to increase the burden of her overseas responsibilities, but have felt forced to do so by one of the two fundamental considerations I have named, the general international situation, or the necessity of doing something to protect peoples ruined by the deleterious effects of western civilization or by the consequences of war. Further, since the great trial of Warren Hastings towards the end of the eighteenth century awakened the public conscience, the British government of its dependencies has been benevolent. The testimony of impartial foreign witnesses is practically uniform that wherever Great Britain has gone she has introduced law and order, honest justice, good government and sound finance, and that railways and telegraphs, irrigation works, sanitary services, forestry work have sprung into being and that famines and private oppression have lessened. The evidence, indeed, is overwhelming that she has governed the peoples primarily for their own interest, that she has derived no tribute from them, and that prosperity has followed her footsteps everywhere. There is practically no doubt that in all these countries the people have never before in recorded history enjoyed such uninterrupted good government, peace, and order.

That does not mean that she has not benefited also. Though she has always maintained the open door to the trade and commerce of all nations, the fact that the territory is under British rule is undoubtedly an advantage to British traders, and the task of government affords employment to a certain number of soldiers and administrators. Great Britain undoubtedly derives great advantages from her Empire, though it also imposes upon her shoulders a burden of responsibility and taxation. Nonetheless, if Britain gains the peoples she has governed have gained also. As in every sound commercial arrangement, both parties have profited.

It is interesting to contrast the ordinary British criticism of America's attitude with the current American criticism of Britain on this subject. To the American, Britain is an international profiteer, who gets something out of every war, and he is inclined to regard his own attitude of renunciation as evidence of virtue. To the Englishman, the American renunciation is simply that of a man finding an excuse for refusing to take a hand in a difficult world job. The advice of the American, "Why don't you leave all these peoples to run their own affairs?" strikes him as having about as much to do with the problem as the action of the United States in sending a warship full of toys for the suffering children of Europe in 1914 had to do with the problem of saving democracy and freedom. Unless the civilized peoples take steps to maintain some supervision and control, many of the backward peoples have no chance of progress at all, for either predatory and reactionary powers or deleterious elements of civilization will lay them in ruins. Every informed Britisher knows this, but few Americans have yet realized that it is true. Moreover, the Englishman feels the less inclined to admit the superiority of the American attitude when he remembers that whereas Great Britain has always maintained the policy of the Open Door in the territory she is responsible for, on the ground that she was a trustee and not entitled to profiteer, the United States has rejected the Open Door and keeps the trade in her dependencies for herself, practically excluding the foreigner altogether.

III. INDIA AND SELF-GOVERNMENT

Is there nothing, then, to be said against the British Empire? I think there is, and it is a serious criticism. It is that the British have paid undue attention to administration and material progress and not enough to education and self-government. The basis of this criticism is embodied in the aphorism: Good government is no substitute for self-government. In making this criticism, however, it must be remembered that modern democracy is comparatively a recent thing. The United States did not begin upon the basis of universal suffrage. At first barely one in three of its population had the vote. Democracy did not find a firm footing among the Great Powers of Europe until 1870, when France finally established the republic. Democracy was unknown to Asia until 1911, when China became a republic, and even in China democracy in any true sense of the word has not yet been successfully worked.

Nonetheless, though Great Britain had established law

and order in India and had planted the seeds of western ideas of self-government and liberalism, she did little or nothing to prepare to train the people in the exercise of political responsibility.

The Ripon reforms of 1880 were a step in this direction, but came to nought, partly because the British officials were prepared to take all the responsibility and the Indian representatives were content to leave it to them.

Up till the beginning of the present century, however, there was no real demand for self-government. But the leaven of western civilization and contact with Britain was steadily working, and after the success of Japan against Russia the nationalist movement rapidly grew. For a time it was regarded as seditious. In 1908, however, a long step forward was made in the Morley-Minto reforms, which constituted elected assemblies in all the chief provinces and for India itself. But these assemblies were really consultative. The Government kept an official majority, and while they improved government they did not place any real responsibility for it upon Indians themselves.

The war, however, brought about a great change. India, like the rest of the world, was profoundly moved by the cause for which the Allied Powers were fighting and by the utterances in which that cause was expressed. It threw itself generously into the struggle and nearly 1,000,000 men were enlisted for service in some capacity or other. Inevitably, however, the demand grew loud and insistent that further and immediate steps should be taken to make India self-governing. The British Government admitted fully the justice of the claims and in August 1920 the famous pronouncement was made that the policy of the Government was that "of increasing the association of Indians in every branch of the administration and the gradual development of self-governing institutions with a view to the progressive realization of responsible government in India as an integral part of the British Empire."

The decision, however, to introduce responsible government into India was simple as compared with the problem of finding ways and means.

In order to understand that problem it is necessary to realize what India is. India is not a territory containing ten or 20 million people, homogeneous in race, language or culture. It is tantamount to a continent. It contains almost as many people as Europe, and as many races, languages and religions. The 1921 census showed a total population of 319,156,396 people, of whom 71,000,000 lived in native states, mostly governed by hereditary autocratic princes. There were 11 main languages, with more than 10,000,000 speaking each, 12 languages spoken by between 1,000,000 and 10,000,000 people and ten lesser dialects. There are two main religions, the Hindu religion with 217,580,000 adherents and the Mohammedan with 66,640,000, while there are also 10,721,000 Buddhists, 3,870,000 Christians, 3,010,000 Sikhs, 1,248,000 Jains, and 10,000,000 animists, or primitives. There was the all-pervading factor of caste, which is far more rigid even than the social hierarchies of Europe.

Democracy, beyond the limits of the village, has never existed in historic India. It has always been autocratically governed. There was no class with political training, no electorates, and even the vernacular press had only just sprung into being. How was self-government to be introduced into this vast area? Many people are now wondering whether it will be possible for the United States to work efficiently a federal system swelled to include much more than 110,000,000 people. How, then, was democracy to be introduced in a territory containing three times as many people, none of whom had any traditions or any experience of self-government, with no common language and with threatening military neighbors?

The solution which was adopted, and which was afterwards embodied in the Montagu-Chelmsford reforms, was known as dyarchy. It was recognized that the transference of responsibility for government in India must be gradual. If chaos was to be avoided a class of Indians must grow up with practical experience of government and of the working of democratic institutions. It was necessary, too, for electorates to develop of sufficient size and education and responsibility to control intelligently their representatives. Nothing but responsibility for the effects of their own actions would convert either electorates or representatives from mere critics into constructively minded administrators. Yet, obviously, untrammeled responsibility for so great an organism could not be suddenly transferred to inexperienced hands.

Under the plan of dyarchy, the functions of government are divided into two categories, one of which is entrusted to the control of India Ministers, responsible to elected legislatures. Over this branch of administration Indian control and responsibility is complete. The control over the other category is retained in the hands of the Governor-General or Governor, as the case might be, subject only to the criticism of the legislatures.

Under the Montagu-Chelmsford reforms two all-India bodies are created—the India Council of State containing 60 members, 20 of whom are official, and the Indian Legislative assembly containing 144 members, of whom 26 are official. Finally, as an essential part of the scheme it is provided that a Royal Commission should go to India every ten years to examine into the working of the Act and advise, on the basis of the practical success or failure of the Indian legislatures in working the powers entrusted to them, whether those powers should be increased or not.

That is the system which has been working for the last two years in that part of India governed by the British. It has been attacked from two sides. It has been attacked by reactionaries on the ground that it is bound to lead to chaos, that all the foundational work accomplished in the last century will be thrown away, because there is no sufficient number of Indians competent to work the system. It has been attacked from the other side by Mahatma Gandhi and the non-coöperationists, either on the ground that India is quite capable of taking over the whole work of government immediately, or on the ground that they want to break down the whole influence of western civilization and that they object to the reformed system nearly as much as to the old system because it involves westernization.

Whether India should follow in the path of western civilization or strike out a line of her own is for the Indian people to decide. But they can do this only when they have learnt how to govern themselves. India will not gain peace or the ideal age by destroying government, but by creating for herself a better government. Fortunately, perhaps, for mankind, the blind worship of the word democracy and its mechanism is passing away. People everywhere are coming to see that the mere existence of the vote and the mere erection of democratic institutions is not self-government. The mere machinery of democracy, indeed, may lead to a more subtle and paralyzing form of autocracy and corruption than absolutism itself. True democracy exists only where there is a sufficient degree of self-control and a sufficiently high moral standard among the people to enable it to choose capable leaders and wise policies. India under the new system has the opportunity to prove and make good her capacity to govern herself.

IV. THE FUTURE

The foregoing pages will have made clear the immense transformation which has come over the British Empire in recent years. On the one hand the self-governing Dominions are now separate nations, completely independent within the Commonwealth and participating on equal terms in the direction of British policy so far as geography and circumstances permit. On the other hand Great Britain is now committed to the development of self-government in all other parts of the Empire, as rapidly as the inhabitants can take over responsible control. The process which has been begun in India is being extended in various ways to Egypt, Palestine and Malta, and its gradual development everywhere is inevitable.

They will have shown, also, that with all its defects and mistakes the modern British Commonwealth does serve a great purpose in the world. It maintains some kind of constitution and law among a quarter of the population of the earth, comprising within itself peoples of every race and color and degree of civilization, and it keeps the peace between them while promoting the growth of self-government everywhere.

What of the future? In my judgment the problems of the British Commonwealth are becoming merged in the world problem. It is no longer a question of maintaining law and order and promoting orderly self-government over sections of the earth's surface, but over the earth as a whole. Obviously there is going to be no peace or prosperity for mankind so long as it remains divided into 50 or 60 independent states, brought hourly into closer contact with one another, yet with no real machinery for adjusting their relations save diplomacy and war. Equally obviously there is going to be no steady progress in civilization or self-government among the more backward peoples until some kind of international system is created which will put an end to the diplomatic struggles incident to the attempt of every nation to make itself secure, and which will hold in check, under a mandatory or other régime, those deleterious forces of civilization already described.

The real problem today is that of world government. Every month that passes will bring home to people more and more clearly that all political problems—whether of preventing war, of establishing stable conditions for trade and commerce, of ending unemployment and bettering social and economic conditions, of improving constitutional organization—all ultimately come back to the problem of ending international lawlessness upon the earth and establishing some method by which world problems can be discussed and settled by constitutional means rather than by force or the threat to use force.

There is no doubt that the combination known as the British Commonwealth is doing much to maintain peace, develop freedom and promote prosperity in the world. Its directing nations manifestly cannot carry a greater burden than they do today. If peace and freedom and prosperity are to be made universal over the earth, the United States and other Powers must take their share of the burden and coöperate in some such scheme as the League of Nations.

The alternatives before us, indeed, are obvious—on the one side chaos ending in another world war, on the other side the work and self-sacrifice necessary to substitute law for force throughout the world. What part is the United States going to play? Is she going to take a hand in the greatest enterprise for human betterment that has ever been presented to a people, or is she going to shatter that hope and reap the rewards that inevitably befall those who think only of themselves?

❖ ❖ ❖

CONTEMPORANEOUS with the story of the evolution of the British Empire during the inter-war years, and woven into it, is the demand of the colored races for political and economic justice at the hands of the white race. W. E. B. DuBois, whose "Worlds of Color" appeared in the April 1925 FOREIGN AFFAIRS, has been one of the great leaders of the movement. Born in Massachusetts in 1868, he took degrees at Fisk and Harvard Universities and at the University of Berlin, taught history and economics at Atlanta and Wilberforce Universities, organized the Niagara Movement which produced the National Association for the Advancement of Colored People, and was the prime mover in the calling of the first Pan-African Congress which met in Paris in 1919. As Editor of the *Crisis* and author of many books, his voice has been among the most powerful and effective in arousing the members of the Negro race to their opportunities and their responsibilities, and in educating members of the white race to their obligations and to the danger of complacent acceptance of caste privileges. Possibly more than any other man, he helped change the attitude of American Negroes from one of acquiescence in a dependent status to a militant demand for the rights (as he himself has phrased it) belonging to members of the civilization of which they are a part.

In his latter days, DuBois has championed the belief that only through Socialism can Negroes achieve these rights. As is natural enough for one whose task is to arouse and awaken, he uses the methods of combat—broad, hard strokes, not fine distinctions. In the perspective of a quarter-century more, the British Empire is less the villain of the drama than it could once be represented to be; indeed, it seems possible that the Commonwealth institutions are the ones which will provide great areas inhabited by colored peoples with the best opportunities for self-government. (The interested reader may be referred to "African Facts and American Criticisms" by Margery Perham, in the April 1944 FOREIGN AFFAIRS, for a further account of the situation discussed in the following pages.) It may nonetheless be noted that the lessening of complacence has been hastened by tragedies more terrible and defeats more humiliating than any forecast in 1922—and that the final results of neither complacency, injustice, nor Socialism have yet been registered.

❖ ❖ ❖

WORLDS OF COLOR

By W. E. B. DuBois

ONCE upon a time in my younger years and in the dawn of this century I wrote: "The problem of the twentieth century is the problem of the color line." It was a pert phrase which I then liked and which since I have often rehearsed to myself, asking how far was it prophecy and how far speculation? Today, in the last year of the century's first quarter, I propose to examine this matter again, and more especially in the memory of the great event of these great years, the World War. How deep were the roots of this catastrophe entwined about the color line? And of the legacy left, what of the darker race problems will the world inherit?

THE LABOR PROBLEM

Most men would agree that our present problem of problems is what we call labor: the problem of allocating work and income in the tremendous and increasingly intricate world-embracing industrial machine which we have built. But, despite our study and good will, is it not possible that our research is not directed to the right geographical spots and our good will too often confined to that labor which we see and feel and exercise right around us rather than to the periphery of the vast circle and to the unseen and inarticulate workers within the world shadow? And may not the continual baffling of our effort and failure of our formula be due to just such mistakes? At least it will be of interest to step within these shadows and, looking backward, view the European and white American labor problem from this external vantage ground—or, better, ground of disadvantage.

With nearly every great European empire today walks its dark colonial shadow, while over all Europe there stretches the yellow shadow of Asia that lies across the world. One might indeed rede the riddle of Europe by making its present plight a matter of colonial shadows and speculate wisely on what might not happen if Europe became suddenly shadowless—if Asia and Africa and the islands were cut permanently away. At any rate here is a field of inquiry, of likening and contrasting each land and its far-off shadow.

THE SHADOW OF PORTUGAL

I was attending the Third Pan-African Congress and I walked to the Palacio dos Cortes with Magellan. It was in December 1923, and in Lisbon. I was rather proud. You see Magalhaes (to give him the Portuguese spelling) is a mulatto—small, light-brown and his hands quick with gestures. Dr. José de Magalhaes is a busy man: a practising specialist; professor in the School of Tropical Medicine whose new buildings are rising; and, above all, deputy in the Portuguese Parliament from São Thomé, Africa. Thus this Angolese African, educated in Lisbon and Paris, is one of the nine colored members of European parliaments. Portugal has had colored ministers and now has three colored deputies and a senator. I saw two Portuguese in succession kissing one colored member on the floor of the house. Or was he but a dark native? There is so much ancient black blood in this peninsula.

Between the Portuguese and the African and near African there is naturally no "racial" antipathy—no accumulated historical hatreds, dislikes, despisings. Not that you would likely find a black man married to a Portuguese of family and wealth, but on the other hand it seemed quite natural for Portugal to make all the blacks of her African empire citizens of Portugal with the rights of the European born.

Magalhaes and another represent São Thomé. They are elected by black folk independent of party. Again and again I meet black folk from São Thomé—young students, well-dressed, well-bred, evidently sons of well-to-do if not wealthy parents, studying in Portugal, which harbors annually a hundred such black students.

São Thomé illustrates some phases of European imperialism in Africa. This industrial rule involves cheap land and labor in Africa and large manufacturing capital in Europe, with a resultant opportunity for the exercise of pressure from home investors and the press. Once in a while—not often—a feud between the capitalists and the manufacturers at home throws sudden light on Africa. For instance, in the Boer War the "cocoa press" backed by the anti-war Liberals attacked the Unionists and exposed labor conditions in South Africa. In retaliation, after the war and when the Liberals were in power, the Unionists attacked labor conditions in the Portuguese cocoa colonies.

For a long time the cocoa industry flourished on the islands of São Thomé and Principe, on large plantations run by Portuguese and backed by English capital. Here under a system of labor recruiting and indentures which amounted to slavery these little islands led the world in cocoa production and here was the basis of the great English and American cocoa industry. When this system was attacked there immediately arose the situation which is characteristic of modern industrial imperialism and differentiates it from past imperialism. Modern expansion has to use democracy at home as its central authority. This democracy is strangely curbed by industrial organization but it does help select officials, and public opinion, once aroused, rules. Thus with a democratic face at home modern imperialism turns a visage of stern and unyielding autocracy toward its darker colonies. This double-faced attitude is difficult to maintain and puts hard strain on the national soul that tries it.

In England the attack of the Unionists on the Liberals and the "cocoa press," proving slavery on the São Thomé plantations, led to a demand for drastic labor reform in Portuguese Africa. Now the profits of the great Portuguese plantation owners could not afford this nor could they understand this sudden virtue on the part of capitalists who had known all along how labor was "recruited." They charged "hypocrisy," not understanding that English capitalists had an inconvenient democracy at home that often cracked its whip over them. The cocoa industry was forced by public opinion to boycott Portuguese cocoa; the great Portuguese proprietors were forced to give place to smaller Negro and mulatto cultivators who could afford smaller profits. At the same time the center of cocoa raising crossed the straits and seated itself in the English colonies of the Gold Coast and Nigeria, formerly the ancient kingdoms of Ashanti, Yoruba, Haussaland and others. Thus in this part of Portuguese Africa the worst aspects of slavery melted away and colonial proprietors with smaller holdings could afford to compete with the great planters; wherefore democracy, both industrially and politically, took new life in black Portugal. Intelligent black deputies appeared in the Portuguese parliaments, a hundred black students studied in the Portuguese universities and a new colonial code made black men citizens of Portugal with full rights.

But in Portugal, alas! no adequate democratic control has been established, nor can it be established with an illiteracy of 75 percent; so that while the colonial code is liberally worded and economic power has brought some freedom in São Thomé, unrestrained Portuguese and English capital rules in parts of Angola and in Portuguese East Africa, where no resisting public opinion in England has yet been aroused.

The African shadows of Spain and Italy are but drafts on some imperial future not yet realized, and touch home industry and democracy only through the war budget. As Spain is pouring treasure into a future Spanish Morocco, so Italy has already poured out fabulous sums in the attempt to annex north and northeast Africa, especially Abyssinia. The prince who yesterday visited Europe is the first adult successor of that black Menelik who humbled Italy to the dust at Adowa in 1896.

Insurgent Morocco and dependent Egypt, independent Abyssinia and Liberia are, as it were, shadows of Europe on Africa, unattached, and as such they curiously threaten the whole imperial program. On the one hand they arouse democratic sympathy in homelands which makes it difficult to submerge them; and again they are temptations to agitation for freedom and autonomy on the part of other black and subject populations.

THE SHADOW OF BELGIUM

There is a little black man in Belgium whose name is Mfumu Paul Panda. He is filled with a certain resentment against me and American Negroes. He writes me now and then but fairly spits his letters at me, and they are always filled with some defense of Belgium in Africa, or rather with some accusation against England, France and Portugal there. I do not blame Panda although I do not agree with his reasoning. Unwittingly, the summer before last, I tore his soul in two. His reason knows that I am right but his heart denies his reason. He is nephew and therefore by African custom heir of a great chief who for thirty years, back to the time of Stanley, has coöperated with white Belgium. As a child of five young Panda was brought home from the Belgian Congo by a Belgian official and given to that official's maiden sister. This sister reared the little black boy as her own, nursed him, dressed him, schooled him, and defended against the criticism of her friends his right to university training. She was his mother, his friend. He loved her and revered her. She guided and loved him. When the second Pan-African Congress came to Brussels it found Panda leader of the small black colony there and spokesman for black Belgium. He had revisited the Congo and was full of plans for reform. And he thought of the uplift of his black compatriots in terms of reform. All this the Pan-African Congress changed. First it brought on his head a storm of unmerited abuse from the industrial press: we were enemies of Belgium; we were pensioners of the Bolsheviks; we were partisans of England. Panda hotly defended us until he heard our speeches and read our resolutions.

The Pan-African Congress revealed itself to him with a

new and inexplicable program. It talked of Africans as intelligent, thinking, self-directing and voting men. It envisaged an Africa for the Africans and governed by and for Africans and it arraigned white Europe, including Belgium, for nameless and deliberate wrong in Africa. Panda was perplexed and astonished; and then his white friends and white mother rushed to the defense of Belgium and blamed him for consorting with persons with ideas so dangerous and unfair to Belgium. He turned upon us black folk in complaining wrath. He felt in a sense deceived and betrayed. He considered us foolishly radical. Belgium was not perfect but was far less blood guilty than other European Powers. Panda continues to send me clippings and facts to prove this.

In this last matter he is in a sense right. England and France and Germany deliberately laid their shadow across Africa. Belgium had Africa thrust upon her. Bismarck intended the Congo Free State for Germany and he cynically made vain and foolish Leopold temporary custodian; and even after Bismarck's fall Germany dreamed of an African empire which should include the Congo, half the Portuguese territory and all the French, making Germany the dominant African Power. For this she fought the Great War.

Meantime, and slowly, Belgium became dazzled by the dream of empire. Africa is but a small part of Britain; Africa is but a half of larger France. But the Congo is eighty-two times the size of little Belgium, and at Tervurien wily Leopold laid a magic mirror—an intriguing flash of light, set like a museum in rare beauty and approached by magnificent vistas—a flash of revealing knowledge such as no other modern land possesses of its colonial possessions. The rank and file of the Belgians were impressed. They dreamed of wealth and glory. They received the Congo from Leopold as a royal gift—shyly, but with secret pride. What nation of the world had so wonderful a colony! And Belgium started to plan its development.

Meantime the same power that exploited the Congo and made red rubber under Leopold—these same great merchants and bankers—still ruled and guided the vast territory. Moreover, Belgium, impoverished by war and conquest, needed revenue as never before. The only difference, then, between the new Congo and the old was that a Belgian liberal public opinion had a right to ask questions and must be informed. Propaganda intimating that this criticism of Belgium was mainly international jealousy and that the exploitation of black Belgium would eventually lower taxes for the whites was nearly enough to leave the old taskmasters and methods in control in spite of wide plans for eventual education and reform.

I remember my interview with the Socialist Minister for Colonies. He hesitated to talk with me. He knew what Socialism had promised the worker and what it was unable to do for the African worker, but he told me his plans for education and uplift. They were fine plans, but they remain plans even today and the Belgian Congo is still a land of silence and ignorance, with few schools, with forced industry, with all the land and natural resources taken from the people and handed over to the state, and the state, so far as the Congo is concerned, ruled well-nigh absolutely by profitable industry. Thus the African shadow of Belgium gravely and dangerously overshadows that little land.

THE SHADOW OF FRANCE

I know two black men in France. One is Candace, black West Indian deputy, an out-and-out defender of the nation and more French than the French. The other is René Maran, black Goncourt prize-man and author of "Batouala." Maran's attack on France and on the black French deputy from Senegal has gone into the courts and marks an era. Never before have Negroes criticized the work of the French in Africa.

France's attitude toward black and colored folk is peculiar. England knows Negroes chiefly as colonial "natives" or as occasional curiosities on London streets. America knows Negroes mainly as freedmen and servants. But for nearly two centuries France has known educated and well-bred persons of Negro descent; they filtered in from the French

West Indies, sons and relatives of French families and recognized as such under the Code Napoleon, while under English law similar folk were but nameless bastards. All the great French schools have had black students here and there; the professions have known many and the fine arts a few scattered over decades; but all this was enough to make it impossible to say in France as elsewhere that Negroes cannot be educated. That is an absurd statement to a Frenchman. It was not that the French loved or hated Negroes as such; they simply grew to regard them as men with the possibilities and shortcomings of men, added to an unusual natural personal appearance.

Then came the war and France needed black men. She recruited them by every method, by appeal, by deceit, by half-concealed force. She threw them ruthlessly into horrible slaughter. She made them "shock" troops. They walked from the tall palms of Guinea and looked into the mouths of Krupp guns without hesitation, with scarcely a tremor. France watched them offer the blood sacrifice for their adopted motherland with splendid *sang-froid,* often with utter abandon.

But for Black Africa Germany would have overwhelmed France before American help was in sight. A tremendous wave of sentiment toward black folk welled up in the French heart. And back of this sentiment came fear for the future, not simply fear of Germany reborn but fear of changing English interests, fear of unstable America. What Africa did for France in military protection she could easily repeat on a vaster scale; wherefore France proposes to protect herself in future from military aggression by using half a million or more of trained troops from yellow, brown and black Africa. France has 40,000,000 Frenchmen and 60,000,000 Colonials. Of these Colonials, 845,000 served in France during the war, of whom 535,000 were soldiers and 310,000 in labor contingents. Of the soldiers, 440,000 came from north and west Africa. The peace footing of the French army is now 660,000, to whom must be added 189,000 Colonial troops. With three years' service and seven years' reserve, France hopes in ten years' time to have 400,-

000 trained Colonial troops and 450,000 more ready to be trained. These Colonial troops will serve part of their time in France.

This program brings France face to face with the problem of democratic rule in her colonies. French industry has had wide experience in the manipulation of democracy at home but her colonial experience is negligible. Legally, of course, the colonies are part of France. Theoretically Colonials are French citizens and already the blacks of the French West Indies and the yellows and browns of north Africa are so recognized and represented in parliament. Four towns of Senegal have similar representation; but beyond this matters hesitate.

All this, however, brings both political and economic difficulties. Diagne, black deputy from Senegal, was expelled from the Socialist Party because he had made no attempt to organize a branch of the party in his district. And the whole colonial bloc stands outside the interests of home political parties, while these parties know little of the particular demands of local colonies. As this situation develops there will come the question of the practicability of ruling a world nation with one law-making body. And if devolution of power takes place what will be the relation of self-governing colonies to the mother country?

But beyond this more or less nebulous theory looms the immediately practical problem of French industry. The French nation and French private industry have invested huge sums in African colonies, considering black Africa alone. Dakar is a modern city superimposed on a native market place. Its public buildings, its vast harbor, its traffic are imposing. Conakry has miles of warehouses beneath its beautiful palms. No European country is so rapidly extending its African railways—one may ride from St. Louis more than halfway to Timbuktu and from Dakar 1,500 miles to the Gulf of Guinea.

The question is, then, is France able to make her colonies paying industrial investments and at the same time centers for such a new birth of Negro civilization and freedom as will attach to France the mass of black folk in unswerving loyalty and will to sacrifice. Such a double possibility is today by no means clear. French industry is fighting today a terrific battle in Europe for the hegemony of reborn Central Europe. The present probabilities are that the future spread of the industrial imperialism of the west will be largely under French leadership. French and Latin imperialism in industry will depend on alliance with western Asia and northern and central Africa, with the Congo rather than the Mediterranean as the southern boundary. Suppose that this new Latin imperialism emerging from the Great War developed a new antithesis to English imperialism where blacks and browns and yellows, subdued, cajoled and governed by white men, form a laboring proletariat subject to a European white democracy which industry controls; suppose that, contrary to this, Latin Europe should evolve political control with black men and the Asiatics having a real voice in colonial government, while both at home and in the colonies democracy in industry continued to progress; what would this cost? It would mean, of course, nothing less than the giving up of the idea of an exclusive white man's world. It would be a revolt and a tremendous revolt against the solidarity of the west in opposition to the south and east. France moving along this line would perforce carry Italy, Portugal and Spain with it, and it is the fear of such a possible idea that explains the deep-seated resentment against France on the part of England and America. It is not so much the attitude of France toward Germany that frightens white Europe, as her apparent flaunting of the white fetish. The plans of those who would build a world of white men have always assumed the ultimate acquiescence of the colored world in the face of their military power and industrial efficiency, because of the darker world's lack of unity and babel of tongues and wide cleft of religious difference. If now one part of the white world bids for dark support by gifts of at least partial manhood rights, the remainder of the white world scents treason and remains grim and unyielding in its heart. But is it certain that France is going to follow this program?

I walked through the native market at St. Louis in French

Senegal—a busy, colorful scene. There was wonderful work in gold filigree and in leather, all kinds of beads and bracelets and fish and foods. Mohammedans salaamed at sunset, black-veiled Moorish women glided like somber ghosts with living eyes; mighty black men in pale burnooses strode by—it was all curious, exotic, alluring. And yet I could not see quite the new thing that I was looking for. There was no color line particularly visible and yet there was all the raw material for it. Most of the white people were in command holding government office and getting large incomes. Most of the colored and black folk were laborers with small incomes. In the fashionable cafés you seldom saw colored folk, but you did see them now and then and no one seemed to object. There were schools, good schools, but they fell short of anything like universal education for the natives. White and colored school children ran and played together, but the great mass of children were not in school.

As I looked more narrowly, what seemed to be happening was this: the white Frenchmen were exploiting black Africans in practically the same way as white Englishmen, but they had not yet erected or tried to erect caste lines. Consequently, into the ranks of the exploiters there arose continually black men and mulattoes, but these dark men were also exploiters. They had the psychology of the exploiters. They looked upon the mass of people as means of wealth. The mass therefore had no leadership. There was no one in the colony except the unrisen and undeveloped blacks who thought of the colony as developing and being developed for its own sake and for the sake of the mass of the people there. Everyone of intelligence thought that Senegal was being developed for the sake of France and inevitably they tended to measure its development by the amount of profit.

If this sort of thing goes on will not France find herself in the same profit-taking colonial industry as England? Indeed, unless she follows English methods in African colonies can she compete with England in the amount of profit made, and if she does not make profit out of her colonies how long will her industrial masters submit without tremendous industrial returns? Or, if these industrial returns come, what will be the plight of black French Africa? "Batouala" voices it. In the depths of the French Congo one finds the same exploitation of black folk as in the Belgian Congo or British West Africa. The only mitigation is that here and there in the Civil Service are black Frenchmen like René Maran who can speak out; but they seldom do.

For the most part, as I have said, in French Africa educated Africans are Europeans. But if education goes far and develops in Africa a change in this respect must come. For this France has a complete theoretical system of education beginning with the African village and going up to the colleges and technical schools at Goree. But at present it is, of course, only a plan and the merest skeleton of accomplishment. On the picturesque island of Goree whose ancient ramparts face modern and commercial Dakar I saw two or three hundred fine black boys of high school rank gathered in from all Senegal by competitive tests and taught thoroughly by excellent French teachers in accordance with a curriculum which, as far as it went, was equal to that of any European school; and graduates could enter the higher schools of France. A few hundred students out of a black population of 19,000,000 is certainly but a start. This development will call for money and trained guidance and will interfere with industry. It is not likely that the path will be followed and followed fast unless black French leaders encourage and push France, unless they see the pitfalls of American and English race leadership and bring the black apostle to devote himself to race uplift not by the compulsion of outer hate but by the lure of inner vision.

As yet I see few signs of this. I have walked in Paris with Diagne who represents Senegal—all Senegal, white and black—in the French parliament. But Diagne is a Frenchman who is accidentally black. I suspect Diagne rather despises his own black Wolofs. I have talked with Candace, black deputy of Guadaloupe. Candace is virulently French. He has no conception of Negro uplift, as apart from French development. One black deputy alone, Boisneuf of Martinique, has the vision. His voice rings in parliament. He made the American soldiers keep their hands off the

Senegalese. He made the Governor of Congo apologize and explain; he made Poincaré issue that extraordinary warning against American prejudice. Is Boisneuf an exception or a prophecy?

One looks on present France and her African shadow, then, as standing at the parting of tremendous ways; one way leads toward democracy for black as well as white—a thorny way made more difficult by the organized greed of the imperial profit-takers within and without the nation; the other road is the way of the white world, and of its contradictions and dangers English colonies may tell.

THE SHADOW OF ENGLAND

I landed in Sierra Leone last January. The great Mountain of the Lion crouched above us, its green sides trimmed with the pretty white villas of the whites, while black town sweltered below. Despite my diplomatic status I was haled before the police and in the same room where criminals were examined I was put through the sharpest grilling I ever met in a presumably civilized land. Why? I was a black American and the English fear black folk who have even tasted freedom. Everything that America has done crudely and shamelessly to suppress the Negro, England in Sierra Leone has done legally and suavely so that the Negroes themselves sometimes doubt the evidence of their own senses: segregation, disfranchisement, trial without jury, over-taxation, "Jim Crow" cars, neglect of education, economic serfdom. Yet all this can be and is technically denied. Segregation? "Oh no," says the colonial official, "anyone can live where he will—only that beautiful and cool side of the mountain with fine roads, golf and tennis and bungalows is assigned to government officials." Are there black officials? "Oh yes, and they can be assigned residences there, too." But they never have been. The Negroes vote and hold office in Freetown—I met the comely black and cultured mayor—but Freetown has almost no revenues and its powers have been gradually absorbed by the autocratic white colonial government which has five million dollars a year to spend. Any government prosecutor can abolish trial by jury in any case with the consent of the judge and all judges are white. White officials ride in special railway carriages and I am morally certain—I cannot prove it—that more is spent by the government on tennis and golf in the colony than on popular education.

These things, and powerful efforts of English industry to reap every penny of profit for England in colonial trade, leaving the black inhabitants in helpless serfdom, has aroused West Africa, and aroused it at this time because of two things—the war, and cocoa in Nigeria. The burden of war fell hard on black and British West Africa. Their troops conquered German Africa for England and France at bitter cost and helped hold back the Turk. Yet there was not a single black officer in the British army or a single real reward save citations and new and drastic taxation even on exports.

But British West Africa had certain advantages. After the decline of the slave trade and before the discovery that slavery and serfdom in Africa could be made to pay more than the removal of the laboring forces to other parts of the world, there was a disposition to give over to the natives the black colonies on the fever coast and the British Government announced the intention of gradually preparing West Africans for self-government. Missionary education and the sending of black students to England raised a small Negro intelligentsia which long struggled to place itself at the head of affairs. It had some success but lacked an economic foundation. When the new industrial imperialism swept Africa, with England in the lead, the presence of these educated black leaders was a thorn in the flesh of the new English industrialists. Their method was to crowd these leaders aside into narrower and narrower confines as we have seen in Sierra Leone. But the Negroes in the older colonies retained possession of their land and, suddenly, when the cocoa industry was transferred from Portuguese Africa, they gained in one or two colonies a new and undreamed of economic foundation. Instead of following the large plantation industry, cocoa became the product of the small individual native farm. In 1891 a native sold 80 pounds of the first cocoa raised on the Gold Coast. By 1911 this had increased to 45,000 tons and in 1916 to 72,000 tons. In Nigeria there has also been a large increase, making these colonies today the greatest cocoa producing countries in the world.

Moreover, this progress showed again the new democratic problems of colonization, since it began and was fostered by a certain type of white colonial official who was interested in the black man and wanted him to develop. But this official was interested in the primitive black and not in the educated black. He feared and despised the educated West African and did not believe him capable of leading his primitive brother. He sowed seeds of dissension between the two. On the other hand, the educated West African hated the white colonial leader as a supplanter and deceiver whose ultimate aims must be selfish and wrong; and as ever, between these two, the English exploiting company worked gradually its perfect will.

Determined effort was thus made by the English, both merchants and philanthropists, to cut the natives off from any union of forces or of interests with the educated West Africans. "Protectorates" under autocratic white rule were attached to the colonies and the natives in the protectorates were threatened with loss of land, given almost no education and left to the mercy of a white colonial staff whose chief duty gradually came to be the encouragement of profitable industry for the great companies. These companies were represented in the governing councils, they influenced appointments at home and especially they spread in England a carefully prepared propaganda which represented the educated "nigger" as a bumptious, unreasoning fool in a silk hat, while the untutored and unspoiled native under white control was nature's original nobleman. Also they suggested that this "white" control must not admit too many visionaries and idealists.

This policy has not been altogether successful, for the educated Negro is appealing to English democracy and the native is beginning to seek educated black leadership. After many vicissitudes, in 1920 a Congress of West Africa was assembled on the Gold Coast, and from this a delegation was sent to London "to lay before His Majesty the King in Council through the Colonial Ministry certain grievances." This was an epoch-making effort and, as was natural, the Colonial Office, where imperial industry is entrenched, refused to recognize the delegation, claiming that they did not really represent black West Africa. Nevertheless, through the League of Nations Union and the public press this delegation succeeded in putting its case before the world. They described themselves as "of that particular class of peaceful citizens who, apprehensive of the culminating danger resulting from the present political unrest in West Africa—an unrest which is silently moving throughout the length and breadth of that continent—and also appreciating the fact that the present system of administration will inevitably lead to a serious deadlock between the 'Government and the Governed,' decided to set themselves to the task of ameliorating this pending disaster by putting forward constitutionally a programme, the carrying of which into operation will alleviate all pains and misgivings."

The final resolutions of the Congress said, "that in the opinion of this Conference the time has arrived for a change in the Constitution of several British West African colonies, so as to give the people an effective voice in their affairs both in the Legislative and Municipal Governments, and that the Conference pledges itself to submit proposals for such reforms."

The reasons for this demand are thus described:

"In the demand for the franchise by the people of British West Africa, it is not to be supposed that they are asking to be allowed to copy a foreign institution. On the contrary, it is important to notice that the principle of electing representatives to local councils and bodies is inherent in all the systems of British West Africa. . . . From the foregoing it is obvious that a system by which the Governor of a Crown Colony nominates whom he thinks proper to represent the people is considered by them as a great anomaly and constitutes a grievance and a disability which they now request should be remedied."

Since the war not only has West Africa thus spoken but the colored West Indies have complained. They want home rule and they are demanding it. They asked after the war: Why was it that no black man sat in the Imperial Conference? Why is it that one of the oldest parts of the empire lingers in political serfdom to England and industrial bondage to America? Why is there not a great British West Indian Federation, stretching from Bermuda to Honduras and Guiana, and ranking with the free dominions? The answer was clear and concise—color.

In 1916 a new agitation for representative government began in Grenada. The fire spread to all the West Indies and in 1921 a delegation was received by the Colonial Office in London at the same time that the Second Pan-African Congress was in session.

Here were unusual appeals to English democracy—appeals that not even commercial propaganda could wholly hush. But there was a force that curiously counteracted them. Liberal England, wanting world peace and fearing French militarism, backed by the English thrift that is interested in the restored economic equilibrium, found as one of its most prominent spokesmen Jan Smuts of South Africa, and unfortunately Jan Smuts stands for the suppression of the blacks.

Jan Smuts is today, in his world aspects, the greatest protagonist of the white race. He is fighting to take control of Laurenço Marques from a nation that recognizes, even though it does not realize, the equality of black folk; he is fighting to keep India from political and social equality in the empire; he is fighting to insure the continued and eternal subordination of black to white in Africa; and he is fighting for peace and good will in a white Europe which can by union present a united front to the yellow, brown and black worlds. In all this he expresses bluntly, and yet not without finesse, what a powerful host of white folk believe but do not plainly say in Melbourne, New Orleans, San Francisco, Hong Kong, Berlin and London.

The words of Smuts in the recent Imperial Conference were transcribed as follows: "The tendencies in South Africa, just as elsewhere, were all democratic. If there was to be equal manhood suffrage over the Union, the whites would be swamped by the blacks. A distinction could not be made between Indians and Africans. They would be impelled by the inevitable force of logic to go the whole hog, and the result would be that not only would the whites be swamped in Natal by the Indians but the whites would be swamped all over South Africa by the blacks and the whole position for which the whites had striven for two hundred years or more now would be given up. So far as South Africa was concerned, therefore, it was a question of impossibility. For white South Africa it was not a question of dignity but a question of existence."

This almost naïve setting of the darker races beyond the pale of democracy and of modern humanity was listened to with sympathetic attention in England. It is without doubt today the dominant policy of the British Empire. Can this policy be carried out? It involves two things—acquiescence of the darker peoples and agreement between capital and labor in white democracies to hold colored labor in perpetual subordination.

This agreement between capital and labor in regard to colored folk cannot be depended on. First of all, no sooner is colored labor duly subordinate, voiceless in government, efficient for the purpose and cheap, than the division of the resultant profit is a matter of dispute. This is the case in South Africa and it came as a singular answer to Smuts. In South Africa white labor is highly paid, can vote, and by a system of black helpers occupies an easy and powerful position. It can retain this position only by vigorously excluding blacks from certain occupations and by beating their wages down to the lowest point even when as helpers they are really doing the prohibited work. It is to the manifest interest of capitalists and investors to breach if not overthrow this caste wall and thus secure higher profits by cheaper and more pliable labor. Already South African courts are slowly moving toward mitigating the law of labor caste and in retaliation the white labor unions have joined Smuts' political enemies, the English-hating Boer party of independence, and have overthrown the great Premier.

But how curious are these bedfellows—English capital and African black labor against Dutch home-rulers and the trades unions. The combinations are as illogical as they are thought-producing, for after all if South Africa is really bent on independence she must make economic and political peace with the blacks; and if she hates Negroes more than she hates low wages she must submit even more than now to English rule.

Now what is English rule over colored folk destined to be? Here comes the second puzzling result of the Smuts philosophy. I was in London on the night of the Guild Hall banquet when the Prime Minister spoke on "Empire Policy and World Peace" and gave a sort of summing up of the work of the Imperial Conference. It was significant that in the forefront of his words, cheek by jowl with Imperial "foreign policy," stood the "intensity of feeling in India on the question of the status of British Indians in the Empire." What indeed could be more fundamental than this in the building of world peace? Are the brown Indians to share equally in the ruling of the British Empire or are they an inferior race? And curiously enough, the battle on this point is impending not simply in the unchecked movement toward "swaraj" in India but in Africa—in the Union of South Africa and in Kenya.

In South Africa, despite all Imperial explanations and attempts to smooth things out, Smuts and the Boers have taken firm ground: Indians are to be classed with Negroes in their social and political exclusion. South Africa is to be ruled by its minority of whites. But if this is blunt and unswerving, how much more startling is Kenya. Kenya is the British East Africa of prewar days and extends from the Indian Ocean to the Victoria Nyanza and from German East Africa to Ethiopia. It is that great roof of the African world where, beneath the silver heads of the Mountains of the Moon, came down in ancient days those waters and races which founded Egypt. The descendant races still live there with fine physique and noble heads—the Masai warriors whom Schweinfurth heralded, the Dinka, the Galla, and Nile Negroes—the herdsmen and primitive artisans of the beautiful highlands. Here was a land largely untainted by the fevers of the tropics and here England proposed to send her sick and impoverished soldiers of the war. Following the lead of South Africa, she took over five million acres of the best lands from the 3,000,000 natives, herded them gradually toward the swamps and gave them, even there, no sure title; then by taxation she forced 60 percent of the black adults into working for the ten thousand white owners for the lowest wage. Here was opportunity not simply for the great landholder and slave-driver but also for the small trader, and 24,000 Indians came. These Indians claimed the rights of free subjects of the Empire—a right to buy land, a right to exploit labor, a right to a voice in the government now confined to the handful of whites.

Suddenly a great race conflict swept East Africa—Orient and Occident, white, brown and black, landlord, trader and landless serf. When the Indians asked rights the whites replied that this would injure the rights of the natives. Immediately the natives began to awake. Few of them were educated but they began to form societies and formulate grievances. A black political consciousness arose for the first time in Kenya. Immediately the Indians made a bid for the support of this new force and asked rights and privileges for all British subjects—white, brown and black. As the Indian pressed his case, white South Africa rose in alarm. If the Indian became a recognized man, landholder and voter in Kenya, what of Natal?

The British Government speculated and procrastinated and then announced its decision: East Africa was primarily a "trusteeship" for the Africans and not for the Indians. The Indians, then, must be satisfied with limited industrial and political rights, while for the black native—the white Englishman spoke! A conservative Indian leader speaking in England after this decision said that if the Indian problem in South Africa were allowed to fester much longer it would pass beyond the bounds of domestic issue and would become a question of foreign policy upon which the unity of the Empire might founder irretrievably. The Empire could never keep its colored races within it by force, he said, but only by preserving and safeguarding their sentiments.

Perhaps this shrewd Kenya decision was too shrewd. It preserved white control of Kenya but it said in effect: "Africa for the Africans!" What then about Uganda and the Sudan, where a black leadership exists under ancient forms; and, above all, what about the educated black leadership in the West Indies and West Africa? Why should black West Africa with its industrial triumphs like Nigeria be content forever with a Crown Government, if Africa is for the Africans?

The result has been a yielding by England to the darker world—not a yielding of much, but yielding. India is to have a revision of the impossible "dyarchy;" all West Africa is to have a small elective element in its governing councils; and even the far West Indies have been visited by a colonial under-secretary and parliamentary committee, the first of its kind in the long history of the islands. Their report is worth quoting in part: "Several reasons combine to make it likely that the common demand for a measure of representative government will in the long run prove irresistible. The wave of democratic sentiment has been powerfully stimulated by the war. Education is rapidly spreading and tending to produce a colored and black intelligentsia of which the members are quick to absorb elements of knowledge requisite for entry into learned professions and return from travel abroad with minds emancipated and enlarged, ready to devote time and energy to propaganda among their own people."

Egypt is Africa and the Bilad-es-Sudan, Land of the Blacks, has in its eastern reaches belonged to Egypt ever since Egypt belonged to the Sudan—ever since the Pharaohs bowed to the Lords of Meroe. Fifty times England has promised freedom and independence to Egypt and today she keeps her word by seizing the Sudan with 1,000,000 square miles, 6,000,000 black folk and $20,000,000 of annual revenue. But Egypt without the Sudan can never be free and independent and this England well knows, but she will hold the Sudan against Egypt as "trustee" for the blacks. That was a fateful step that the new Conservatives took after the Sirdar was murdered by hot revolutionists. Its echo will long haunt the world.

If now England is literally forced to yield some measure of self-government to her darker colonies; if France remains steadfast in the way in which her feet seem to be tending; if Asia arises from the dead and can no longer be rendered impotent by the opium of international finance, what will happen to imperialistic world industry as exemplified in the great expansion of the nineteenth and early twentieth centuries?

LABOR IN THE SHADOWS

This is the question that faces the new labor parties of the world—the new political organizations which are determined to force a larger measure of democracy in industry than now obtains. The trade-union labor movement dominant in Australia, South Africa and the United States has been hitherto autocratic and at heart capitalistic, believing in profit-making industry and wishing only to secure a larger share of profits for particular guilds. But the larger labor movement following the war envisages through democratic political action real democratic power of the mass of workers in industry and commerce. Two questions here arise: Will the new labor parties welcome the darker race to this industrial democracy? And, if they do, how will this affect industry?

The attitude of the white laborer toward colored folk is largely a matter of long continued propaganda and gossip. The white laborers can read and write, but beyond this their education and experience are limited and they live in a world of color prejudice. The curious, most childish propaganda dominates us, by which good, earnest, even intelligent men have come by millions to believe almost religiously that white folk are a peculiar and chosen people whose one great accomplishment is civilization and that civilization must be protected from the rest of the world by cheating, stealing, lying and murder. The propaganda, the terrible, ceaseless propaganda that buttresses this belief day by day—the propaganda of poet and novelist, the uncanny welter of romance, the half knowledge of scientists, the pseudo-science of statesmen—all this, united in the myth of mass inferiority of most men, has built a wall which many centuries will not break down. Born into such a spiritual world, the average white worker is absolutely at the mercy of its beliefs and prejudices. Color hate easily assumes the form of a religion and the laborer becomes the blind executive of the decrees of the masters of the white world; he votes armies and navies for "punitive" expeditions; he sends his sons as soldiers and sailors; he composes the Negro-hating mob, demands Japanese exclusion and lynches untried prisoners. What hope is there that such a mass of dimly thinking and misled men will ever demand universal democracy for all men?

The chief hope lies in the gradual but inevitable spread of the knowledge that the denial of democracy in Asia and Africa hinders its complete realization in Europe. It is this that makes the color problem and the labor problem to so great an extent two sides of the same human tangle. How far does white labor see this? Not far, as yet. Its attitude toward colored labor varies from the Russian extreme to the extreme in South Africa and Australia. Russia has been seeking a *rapprochement* with colored labor. She is making her peace with China and Japan. Her leaders have come in close touch with the leaders of India. Claude McKay, an American Negro poet traveling in Russia, declares: "Lenin himself grappled with the question of the American Negroes and spoke on the subject before the Second Congress of the Third International. He consulted with John Reed, the American journalist, and dwelt on the urgent necessity of propaganda and organization work among the Negroes of the South."

Between these extremes waver the white workers of the rest of the world. On the whole they still lean rather toward the attitude of South Africa than that of Russia. They exclude colored labor from empty Australia. They sit in armed truce against them in America where the Negroes are forcing their way into ranks of union labor by breaking strikes and underbidding them in wage.

It is precisely by these tactics, however, and by hindering the natural flow of labor toward the highest wage and the best conditions in the world that white labor is segregating colored labor in just those parts of the world where it can be most easily exploited by white capital and thus giving white capital the power to rule all labor, white and black, in the rest of the world. White labor is beginning dimly to see this. Colored labor knows it, and as colored labor becomes more organized and more intelligent it is going to spread this grievance through the white world.

THE SHADOW OF SHADOWS

How much intelligent organization is there for this purpose on the part of the colored world? So far there is very little. For while the colored people of today are common victims of white culture, there is a vast gulf between the red-black south and the yellow-brown east. In the east long since, centuries ago, there were mastered a technique and philosophy which still stand among the greatest the world has known; and the black and African south, beginning in the dim dawn of time when beginnings were everything, has evolved a physique and an art, a will to be and to enjoy, which the world has never done without and never can. But these cultures have little in common, either today or yesterday, and are being pounded together artificially and not attracting each other naturally. And yet quickened India, the South and West African Congresses, the Pan-African movement, the National Association for the Advancement of Colored People in America, together with rising China and risen Japan—all these at no distant day may come to common consciousness of aim and be able to give to the labor parties of the world a message that they will understand.

THE COLOR LINE

My ship seeks Africa. Ten days we crept across the Atlantic; five days we sailed to the Canaries. And then, turning, we sought the curve of that mighty and fateful shoulder of gigantic Africa. Slowly, slowly we creep down the coast in a little German cargo boat. Yonder behind the horizon is Cape Bojador, whence in 1441 came the brown Moors and black Moors who, through the slave trade, built America and modern commerce and let loose the furies on the world. Another day afar we glide past Dakar, city and center of French Senegal. Thereupon we fall down, down to the burning equator, past Guinea and Gambia, to where the Lion Mountain glares, toward the vast gulf whose sides are lined with silver and gold and ivory. And now we stand before Liberia—Liberia that is a little thing set upon a hill—thirty or forty thousand square miles and 2,000,000 folk. But it represents to me the world. Here political power has tried to resist the concentration in the power of modern capital. It has not yet succeeded, but its partial failure is not because the republic is black but because the world has failed in this same battle; because the oligarchy that owns organized industry owns and rules England, France, Germany, America and Heaven. And it fastens this ownership by the Color Line. Can Liberia escape the power that rules the world? I do not know. But I do know that unless the world escapes, world democracy as well as Liberia will die: and if Liberia lives it will be because the world is reborn as in that vision splendid that came in the higher dreams of the World War.

And thus again in 1925, as in 1899, I seem to see the problem of the twentieth century as the problem of the color line.

❖ ❖ ❖

THE brothers Jules and Paul Cambon have become a legendary pair in the annals of diplomacy; only the existence of one, it was said, made it incorrect to call the other the greatest diplomat in the service of the French Republic. Jules Cambon, author of this essay on "The Permanent Bases of French Foreign Policy," had been French Ambassador at Washington and at Madrid before he was named to Berlin in 1907. Throughout the ensuing crucial years before the First World War he represented his country in Germany while his brother was Ambassador to Great Britain. These two men played major rôles in the construction of the Triple Entente and are to be thanked for the fact that when the German assault broke upon France in 1914 she did not have to stand up to it alone.

Some of the characteristics of the old diplomacy at its best are to be seen in this article—one of the classic statements of French policy—published in FOREIGN AFFAIRS in January 1930. Jules Cambon was a man of learning and culture, with a wide knowledge of the ingredients of his trade—perhaps they could be called history and men. He was exact, unfailingly courteous, and inclined to be skeptical: neither human nature nor the governments which are its instruments of policy change much, he thought. He could understand a view different from his own, as was, indeed, one of the plain obligations of his profession. The League of Nations, he saw, was a step beyond precise "qualitative analysis of opposing forces"—that is to say, a step in advance, peculiarly American (though America had withdrawn from it). As such he respected it and hoped for the best from it. At the same time, he felt that prudence recommended the maintenance of "a certain balance between the Powers." French foreign policy was as clear as the facts which conditioned it, namely that the French northeast frontier was open to easy invasion and on the other side waited the Germans. The policy which best met this specific danger was the creation of specific alliances to maintain a preponderance of power against Germany. Perhaps the American mind had difficulty in understanding the policy because, paradoxically, it seemed too simple. Unfortunately, it proved to be correct. At the time Cambon wrote, the Weimar Republic was steadily rearming; the Allied occupation of the Rhineland was to end in a few months; three years later Hitler was to seize power; and under his blows the system set up at Versailles to restrain Germany was to collapse.

❖ ❖ ❖

THE PERMANENT BASES OF FRENCH FOREIGN POLICY

By Jules Cambon

AIMLESS and contradictory as appear the happenings in the history of each nation, one nevertheless is able to discern, when one surveys them as a whole and in their proper sequence, that they are not disobedient to certain laws. Revolutions do not work any definite change; the institutions which a people set up are only the expression of its ideas at a certain moment, and they do not modify its position with regard to other nations. The relations of a government with foreign governments may be affected, but not the necessities imposed upon it by its geographical position, its history, its need to live. That is what we call its traditions. At the present moment, we have a striking example of this fact. The policy of the Soviet Government in the Far East may differ in method from that which the Tsarist Government followed; but it does not differ from it in spirit or in objective.

The geographical position of a nation, indeed, is the principal factor conditioning its foreign policy—the principal reason why it must have a foreign policy at all.

This is a truism of which the whole history of England is a demonstration. English history is determined and limited by the fact that Great Britain is an island. She is a European Power, but as she is separated from the Continent by the sea she has not experienced the constant tribulations of the Continental states. Twice, in the times of Philip II and of Napoleon I, she has feared attacks on her own territory; but the history of those events showed how impossible it was for her adversaries to penetrate her natural defenses. Hence her disdain for the military establishments of the Continent, and her inbred dislike of the system of conscription. Oftentimes she has mixed in European quarrels, but only to play the rôle of an umpire who is unwilling for the victor to be too victorious. And when the time came to make peace it has not been hard to sense that she did not consider her own security as being in the least at stake. Elizabeth and Cromwell, Pitt and Palmerston, had the same views, which one may characterize as "insular" in the real sense of the word. On the other hand, the naval policy of England has had quite a different character, because it was essential that she should never encounter any superior sea power. All the other nations have had to struggle against her for the freedom of the seas. Her maritime imperialism grew out of her need of assuring her security and her sources of supply.

And cannot what I have said of England also be said of the United States of America? Separated from the Old Worlds by two oceans, her only neighbors too weak to dare to contradict her, free from any fears regarding security, possessing in her immense territory all the riches of the earth, all the forces and products of industry, she has almost limitless liberty of action. That is why expressions of the noble idealism which is the real honor of the American spirit sometimes sound strange in the ears of the European nations, brought up as they have been in other circumstances and preoccupied with hopes and fears in which the United States has no share. The geographical isolation of the American people has given it its force, has allowed it to become great and powerful. The Monroe Doctrine is nothing but the expression of its determination to let nothing impair that isolation. This celebrated doctrine has been the cornerstone of the American Government's policy for a century, and today it explains why the United States has not wished to participate in the League of Nations.

France, like England, has sought through the centuries to realize her destiny; but, like England, which by reason of her special situation has put her trust in a preponderant naval power, France, whose frontiers to the north and to the east were open to invasion, has put her trust in military power. And so these two Powers, whose behavior at first glance, seems to have been so different, in reality obey the same instinct: both look for security, but each looks for it in the manner dictated by its particular geographical position.

It is true that sometimes accidental happenings have misled or bewildered foreign opinion as to the real objectives of England and France. But we do not understand history if we do not give the right value to accidents, as well as to the personal schemes of those who play great historical rôles at particular moments. I should like to cite two examples from the history of France.

France is often accused of imperialism because throughout her history she has wished to make the Rhine her frontier. The origin of this tendency, which goes far back, must be made clear. Caesar in his "Commentaries," Tacitus in his "Customs of the Germans," Strabo himself, fixed the Rhine as the boundary of Gaul; the jurists who played so important a part in the policy of the ancient kings and who loved to rely on old texts to justify their territorial claims, never failed to cite these hoary traditions, which gradually became part of the national soul. When, during the wars of the French Revolution, the armies of the Republic entered into the Rhenish provinces, they certainly believed that they were taking possession again of what had always belonged to them. And our long occupation of those lands left a deep imprint on the Rhenish people themselves. The Foreign Minister of the German Empire, Kiderlen-Waechter, one day admitted to me that up to 1866 France would have been able to reëstablish the Rhine frontier without encountering any opposition from the local population. It was the foundation of the new Germany, he said, which had changed this state of mind.

Napoleon and his prodigious conquests intoxicated France. In spite of that, and glorious as his achievement was, it is not paradoxical to say that this epoch in our history was an "accident." At St. Helena he avowed that he had wanted to set up a great Germany and a great Italy, to join in a single mass all the peoples of the same race. He foresaw the future.

But the very grandiosity of his views proved how foreign his genius was to the traditional policy of France, who always regarded herself as the guardian of weak princes. Napoleon's imperial spirit, founded on the memories of the grandeur that was Rome, was not hampered by a consideration of French interests *per se*. His gaze went beyond our frontiers. But the tradition of our policy was something altogether different; it cared only for France; it was essentially conservative, circumspect, deliberate. That is what Rivarol indicated very well when in 1783, in his celebrated essay on the universality of the French language, he wrote: "France acts against her best interests and misunderstands her rôle when she lends herself to the spirit of conquest." And Vergennes, the great Minister of Louis XVI, said in 1777, in his report to the King: "France must fear expansion much more than desire it." These principles were merely the practical application of the ideas of Montesquieu, who in his "Spirit of Laws" invited sovereigns always to have a wary eye open to the inconveniences, not to say the dangers, of grandeur.

In the eighteenth century, then, the policy of France, as defined by her philosophers and her statesmen, was far from being imperialistic. It based itself rather upon the idea of the balance of power. It seemed as though the peace of Europe and the security of each of its component parts would necessarily result from an equilibrium. Here is the explanation of the sudden transformation of French policy in the eighteenth century, sometimes called the overthrow of the alliances. France had supported Prussia in her early stages and had aided her to become strong. When Frederick II openly menaced the established order in Germany, the government at Versailles ranged itself on the side of Austria and Maria Theresa. French opinion received this abandonment of the Prussian alliance with every sign of mistrust; but the shift of position undoubtedly was in conformity with the policy of the balance of power followed by M. de Choiseul.

For the rest, we must admit that at the start this policy of equilibrium was of a purely empirical character and grew out of events. Later on, naturally enough, theorists were found to give it its name and to make of it the fundamental law on which rested peace between the European Powers.

Today, after the war of 1914, people jeer at the guarantee of peace afforded by the old system of the balance of power. It is described as an illusion. That is going too far, but we must recognize that democracy does not rest content with quantitative analyses of opposing forces, carried on quietly in diplomatic offices. It demands new methods which will permit weak nations, like the strong, to play a rôle in the settlement of matters of general concern. This is a step forward; the League of Nations is constantly taking on more importance and authority, and assuredly is destined to develop further still. But all that does not make it any less prudent always to maintain a certain balance between the Powers. What is happening today in the case of naval disarmament is evidence of what I say. The United States and Great Britain seek to adjust their naval armaments, but the condition which they set to any action is that it shall not impair naval parity between them. To each the idea that it might wake up one day to find itself in the presence of a superior naval force is intolerable.

It is useful, then, to search the past and learn why and how the system of the balance of power came into being, and to follow through successive centuries the application which has been made of it. Perhaps I shall be pardoned a historical digression. It will allow us—in spite of momentary accidents which now and then break the sequence—to recognize the unity of purpose which has characterized French policy in dealing with the difficulties which have always faced it. So we shall be led to understand what are its permanent characteristics.

We must go back to the end of the Middle Ages to find the origins of French foreign policy in modern times. The Hundred Years' War between France and England, which marked the end of this formative period, at first had the characteristics of a feudal war, but even in the midst of their miseries the French people developed a common consciousness. Jeanne d'Arc personified the dawn of national feeling, and that is why she appears to us the greatest figure in our history. It was not long afterwards, at the time of the Renaissance, that the French people, having at last constituted themselves into a nation, found that they were encircled on all sides—south, east and north—by a single sovereign power. The House of Austria ruled Germany, the Low Countries, Spain. The Emperor Charles V was the most powerful potentate that the world has known since Charlemagne, and the common saying was that the sun never set on his dominions. He had genius, ambition and prodigious activity, and immense forces under his control. Inevitably he wished to stifle the independence of France, which, placed in the center of his possessions, prevented him from unifying them. Nature itself had made Francis I, who reigned at Paris, his rival and his enemy. Poets and writers of romance have been pleased to paint Francis I merely as a lover of the arts and of pleasure. They have not seen in him the politician that he was. He was unlucky in war, but he was the initiator of a policy which his successors had to follow, a policy which triumphed in the eighteenth century and which since then has been followed through many changing circumstances—I dare to say it—down to the present day. It should be noted that from the very beginning this policy, which was to unite all the French, was disturbed and endangered by the passions which divided Frenchmen amongst themselves. Religious wars rent the country for nearly a century and brought the Spaniards to Paris itself. Two tendencies have always existed in France and have thrown her statesmen into two camps. Those who in the sixteenth century had a liberal and aristocratic spirit and tended toward reform were partisans of union with England. Admiral Coligny, who represented this party, maintained relations with Queen Elizabeth. On the contrary, those who belonged to the Catholic party, the Guises and the chiefs of the League, wished to rely on Spain and Germany. Between the two, the King and his policies manœuvred as best they could. It sometimes seems as though even in our day these two tendencies still exist and continue to set Frenchmen against each other.

Be that as it may, the nature of things led the Monarchy to seek allies against the might of the German Emperor. In this way she became the supporter of the weak German princes who were trying to escape the talons of the imperial eagle, and who for the most part became partisans of the Reformation. Hence the rôle of France in the Thirty Years' War. And hence the policy of France always to be the ally of the little Powers of Europe. It was this same search for an equilibrium which led Francis I to court the friendship of the Grand Turk (to the great scandal of Christendom), which had for its consequence the opening up of the east to Christian traders of all nationalities.

Our great Henry IV was one of the first to inaugurate the policy of coöperating with the weak and of showing moderation in spite of strength. His favorite minister, Sully, defined it when he wrote in one of his reports: "The Kings of France should aim to acquire friends, allies and confederates, bound by the sure ties of commerce and common interests, rather than to nourish ambitious projects and thus draw irreconcilable hatreds down upon their heads."

Princes of the Church though they were, both Richelieu and Mazarin backed the Protestant princes of Germany against the Emperor. Mazarin even went so far as to form an alliance with Cromwell. The steady pursuit of this policy resulted in the Treaty of Westphalia which, through the Rhine League, secured the independence of the Protestant princes and gave Germany a constitution that lasted two centuries. This policy of alliances and compromises constituted what has been known as the classic system of French diplomacy. It corresponded to the national temperament, which mistrusts imagination in matters of state. The men responsible for this policy were not theorists who stuck to their preconceptions regardless of hard facts; Jean Jacques Rousseau and his disciples had not yet been born; and, as our eminent historian, Albert Sorel, observes, "these great men had method without having any spirit of system."

Europe relied upon the balance of power, but when Louis XIV, abandoning the policy of moderation which France had followed until his time, appeared on the point of shattering it, he found aligned against him a coalition which included even our old allies. He has been reproached by many historians for accepting the inheritance of Charles II and thus entering upon the disastrous war of the Spanish Succession. However, he had serious reasons for acting as he did. If his grandson, the Duke of Anjou, had not ascended the throne of Spain, it would have passed into the hands of an Austrian Archduke, and once again France would have been faced with a united Spain and Austria, a combination which she had fought against for centuries. The war ended in a compromise. France no longer threatened Europe. By renouncing for himself and his descendants the right to reign in Paris, a Bourbon was permitted to reign in Madrid.

In my opinion, the worst result of Louis XIV's abandonment of our traditional policy was the distrust which it aroused towards us abroad. Perhaps we suffer from it even today.

Throughout the eighteenth century the policy of every European government was one of intrigue and ambition: the period is well represented by the skeptical and realistic Frederick II, who knew how to exploit the jealousies of the various courts. In France, statecraft completely lacked continuity. Louis XV, intelligent and weak, was typical of his epoch. He followed a policy separate and distinct from that of his ministers—what was called "le secret du Roi"—with results easy to imagine. By the time the Seven Years' War was over, France had lost all influence and authority. This became obvious when Prussia, Austria and Russia started to dismember Poland, and France found herself in no position to oppose them. The eclipse of French prestige was a tragedy for the little nations.

France learned her lesson. Vergennes, to whom Louis XVI intrusted the portfolio of foreign affairs, was imbued with the traditional ideals of the old régime, the ideals in particular of Henry IV and of Richelieu. His policy was one of moderation, of collaboration with the lesser Powers and support of the weak. Public opinion, piqued by the decline of national prestige under his predecessors, backed him up when he offered French military, financial and moral support to the United States, who wished to become an independent nation. In this he was but repeating the assistance given by France early in the seventeenth century to Portugal and the Low Countries.

Meanwhile the German Emperor, Joseph II, an ambitious and restless sovereign, wished to follow in the footsteps of Frederick II. Thinking to profit by his sister Marie Antoinette's influence at Versailles, he dreamed great dreams; he dreamed of annexing Bavaria to Austria, of creating a kingdom for the Elector of Bavaria in the Netherlands, and of buying French complicity by ceding part of Belgium to her. He even went so far as to offer us Luxembourg. Vergennes spurned these proposals; in fact he urged the German princes (who were of course much disturbed) to unite against the Emperor, and in a memorandum on this subject for the King he wrote: "If one stops to consider the crying injustice which would be entailed by the acceptance of the idea of partitioning the Netherlands, no honest man can contemplate it seriously." And the Ambassador, Baron de Breuteuil, said: "The King should look upon himself as guardian of the lesser princes. This policy has for centuries constituted the glory and security of the Crown." These statesmen, in other words, based the country's security upon the principle of respecting the rights of others and they did not separate the peace of France from that of Europe.

Such were the ideas, also, of two men destined one day to play an important rôle at the start of the Revolution, Mirabeau and Talleyrand. Both were partisans of the English alliance and hated the spirit of conquest. Territorial bargainings between states, wrote Mirabeau in his book on the Prussian Monarchy, are iniquitous, and added: "It is arbitrary and tyrannous to make such exchanges without consulting the inhabitants."

"Consulting the inhabitants"—these are new words and new ideas in international relations. Despite the storm of revolution, despite the Napoleonic wars, despite the reaction of the Holy Alliance, they persisted and little by little made their way. They reappeared in the nineteenth century, and they furnish the main clue to an understanding of its events.

But the Revolution, which at first had made much of its renunciation of the spirit of war and conquest, was to be swept along by its enemies into a war lasting for almost twenty-five years. The European courts were on the whole quite indifferent to the fate of the unfortunate Louis XVI; indeed, they congratulated one another upon the weakened and distracted state of France, and, profiting by a situation which left them with free hands, made haste to finish off what remained of Poland amongst themselves. Nevertheless, a certain sense of the community of royal interests held them from going too far and led them to combat the Revolution as such. Brunswick made his pronouncement. But he had not counted upon what the enthusiasm of a people can do. Twenty-three years later the war ended at Waterloo with the defeat of Napoleon, but the ideas which his army had sowed across Europe were to germinate during the course of the nineteenth century. The Emperor had indeed been vanquished, but the Revolution triumphed.

I have already noted how the imagination of Napoleon, who when a young man in Egypt had dreamed like Alexander of eastern conquests, broke through all the traditional limits of French policy. According to Montesquieu, France is in the happy position of having a territory proportionate to her strength and abilities. This was also the opinion of Frenchmen of the eighteenth century, and particularly of Mirabeau's old friend Talleyrand, who used to say that real richness is to be won not by invading the territory of others, but by exploiting one's own to the utmost. He felt Europe's growing fear of the Emperor's insatiable ambition and he dreaded the future consequences of this ambition for France. He realized the dangerous fragility of the imperial edifice, and detached himself from the Napoleonic cause. His conceptions were those of the old school of French diplomacy; they could not be harnessed up with the grandiose schemes of the hero whose servant he had been. And when Napoleon had fallen, and Louis XVIII sent Talleyrand in 1814 to the Congress of Vienna, he drafted his own instructions so that they should carefully point out the need for France to inspire those around her with her spirit of moderation and her desire to be of service by aiding the cause of justice.

At Vienna, Talleyrand faced Europe's natural reaction against all the works of the Empire. Greedy ambitions demanded satisfaction on all sides. Prussia in particular gave herself over to the same spirit of conquest which had caused her so much suffering; in Germany, she hoped to aggrandize herself at the expense of the King of Saxony, who had long been the ally of Napoleon, and in France to seize our eastern provinces, which had formed part of the territory of the old Monarchy. Basing his claim on the principle of legitimacy, Talleyrand set himself to obtain the reëstablishment of the pre-Revolutionary territorial status, including of course the maintenance of our old frontiers. He returned to the old doctrines of our diplomacy, and undertook the defense of the lesser states against Prussia. He managed to secure the support of England, and even of Austria, whom the Russian specter was beginning to alarm. He triumphed, and with him triumphed the essential factor in French diplomacy which I have several times described. These negotiations at Vienna may be considered Talleyrand's diplomatic *chef-d'oeuvre*. It was based on a principle which is of course open to discussion, that of legitimacy, and it thus introduced into the settlement of diplomatic problems the consideration of abstract ideas in a disinterested way and above the passions of the moment.

Fifteen years later, in 1830, the Belgian people rose against Holland, to whom they had been arbitrarily united in 1815. France was faithful to her past; she intervened to assist them to gain their independence, and her army took Antwerp. But though she thus was responsible for the triumph of liberty, she proved that she wished to draw no special profits from it, for when the Belgians offered the crown of Belgium to the Duke de Nemours, son of Louis Philippe, the King refused it. In consequence of this refusal Prince Leopold of Coburg became King of the Belgians.

This policy of restraint was so thoroughly a national policy, without distinction of party, that when on February 24, 1848, France proclaimed herself a Republic and Europe was being rocked to its foundations by the storm of revolution, the head of the provisional government, M. de Lamartine, sent our agents abroad a celebrated circular in which he reaffirmed the conservative intentions of the Paris cabinet. This declaration meant much, because since the fall of Napoleon the slogan of the advanced parties of Europe had been the destruction of the European order as constituted by the Congress of Vienna.

When the republican régime was overthrown in its turn, the Emperor Napoleon III, fired by his uncle's example, dreamed of remaking Europe. Nevertheless, when he joined England in defense of Turkey against the Emperor Nicholas of Russia, his action was in accord with the precepts of the old Monarchy. In the same spirit at the Congress of Paris he undertook to establish the independence of Rumania, up to that time a mere Turkish province. The wave of democracy then sweeping Europe found in him a convinced supporter. He upheld Piedmont against Austria, and one may say without exaggeration that his benevolent attitude toward the states of the peninsula made him the chief author of Italian unity. But many who had applauded him for assisting the weak against the strong began to be troubled when it appeared that he was dominated by the Napoleonic rather than the old French tradition, and that national security was no longer his principal aim. The war of 1866 between Austria and Prussia justified these anxieties; the Europe of the Treaties of Westphalia and Vienna vanished. Public opinion in France was bewildered. The war of 1870 put the finishing touch to what had been begun in 1866. It marked the end of that balance of power which, under the leadership of France, had guaranteed some sort of order in Europe during two centuries.

In France, however, the Republic had succeeded the Empire. For forty-four years it acted wisely and prudently. France came to enjoy the esteem and friendship of all the Powers which were harassed by the presumptuous policies of Berlin.

Never before had the supreme objectives of a long line of our greatest statesmen imposed themselves so insistently upon France. We sought—we sought *only*—security. I remember how once, while I was Ambassador at Berlin, a high German official suggested to me in the course of a private conversation that Germany, France and England might agree among themselves to divide up the Belgian Congo. I promptly repelled the suggestion, basing my position on our policy of always upholding the smaller states. In this I simply conformed with the *dicta* of Vergennes, Mirabeau and Talleyrand; and the ideas which led my German colleague to speak as he did were those of Frederick II, Hardenberg and Bismarck.

After the World War, at the Peace Conference of 1919, France naturally became the protagonist of all the nationalities which had been suppressed in centuries past; they wished to live again, and they invoked the principles of justice and liberty which had been avowed by the Allies throughout the long struggle. Poland came to life. The Czechs of Bohemia, who since the time of John Hus had often revolted against the Austrian domination, formed a young republic. Rumania won back her kinsmen in Transylvania. The Slavs of Croatia and of Illyria united with the Serbs of old Serbia to form Jugoslavia. And the French Republic gave these young nationalities the support which the old Monarchy, from Henry IV to Louis XVI, had given all nationalities who wished to live an independent life.

Democracy, dominant in the world at last, was unwilling to limit itself to the ordinary methods of the old diplomacy. And when President Wilson took the initiative in proposing that a League of Nations be set up he was merely responding to the obvious need for the creation of some new international instrument. Despite scoffs and misgivings the League of Nations was established; its authority has grown; and it has become the most efficient instrument yet found for preventing international disputes from degenerating into armed conflicts. France's rôle at Geneva has been in keeping with her tradition. She is happy to see the lesser states granted a hearing on world problems on an equality with the Great Powers, for in this she sees the endorsement of her age-long policy towards them.

M. Briand, who has been active at Geneva and who put

forward the anti-war proposal which has since become the Briand-Kellogg Pact, has found his inspiration in the same order of ideas that governed apostles of the balance of power. Political methods change, but the objectives remain the same. In essence, the traditional aims of France, the aims which she has today, center about the quest for security. And what is that but the maintenance of peace?

To sum up. If in the past France has sometimes given herself over to the spirit of conquest, either she was led to do so in the enthusiasm of victory after attacks had been launched against her, or because she felt that she was carrying the torch of liberty to the peoples of other nations. Even then, in the hours of their greatest triumphs, our statesmen (knowing how quickly the French spirit can change) thought like Talleyrand that the surest foundation of peace lay in the reëstablishment of the balance of power. This view we still hold.

Of course the situation is not precisely the same today as formerly. At Geneva discussions are carried on in public, and for that reason a preoccupation with the principle of the balance of power seems out of date. But it would be a mistake to take this view. There are groups, cabals and oppositions inside the League of Nations, and though political action may take new forms, at heart it is the same. National aspirations are the expression of national interests, and these, as I have said, persist through the ages because human nature does not change. They condition the relations of peoples, and according to circumstances bring them together or set them one against the other. So it was with France and England; they had long been enemies, but they united at last in the face of a common danger. It is true that by the Briand-Kellogg Pact most of the nations have solemnly renounced war, but in 1914 how little the most solemn engagements were worth when the German Chancellor, Bethmann-Hollweg, declared that necessity knows no law! We therefore are under compulsion to neglect nothing which can guarantee us against the danger of war.

When I have said that security has always been the cardinal aim of France, that term must be understood in its fullest sense. There is a France outside our own frontiers. Just as England cannot permit her communications with India to be menaced in Egypt, and just as the United States considers that one of her elementary interests is to safeguard the Panama Canal, just so France must guard her communications with her possessions in North Africa and preserve her freedom of action in the Mediterranean. Here we touch the problem of the relations of states at its most delicate point. For it is when states come into direct contact that practical accommodations become imperative.

Security! The term signifies more indeed than the maintenance of a people's homeland, or even of their territories beyond the seas. It also means the maintenance of the world's respect for them, the maintenance of their economic interests, everything, in a word, which goes to make up the grandeur, the life itself, of the nation. But all peoples have not the same ideal; each follows what it considers to be its national interests in accordance with its own traditions. If the nations are to live in peace, those who direct the foreign affairs of each state must try diligently and long to understand and respect the aspirations of others. For by a statesman's comprehension of the forces which direct the destiny of nations one measures the breadth and depth of his genius.

❖ ❖ ❖

THE American demand that neutral commerce should have the unhampered use of the oceans of the world in time of war—the question which engaged Lord Grey in his analysis entitled "Freedom of the Seas" in April 1930—seems about as close to present realities as the problem of controlling the speed of trotting horses on public highways. During most of the 1920's and 1930's, however, United States foreign policy revolved around an effort to strengthen the laws of neutrality. Most Americans believed that this was the realistic way to safeguard their country from the menacing effects of conflicting European interests and passions.

But Lord Grey's pages deserve study not merely because they deal with a major phase of the history of the inter-war years. The English approach to foreign relations is as distinctive as the French one; and for the exemplification of it one may look to Grey, as one looks to Jules Cambon to learn the French approach. The word "reason" is applicable to both attitudes. But for Jules Cambon, reason in foreign policy was the expression of a clear thesis; for Grey, reason was reasonableness. Incidentally, the two "reasons" can supplement one another magnificently, as Paul Cambon and Grey showed in London, when they made the arrangements which saved Europe in 1914. In the light of later efforts to cope with the German question, their achievement seems more remarkable than once supposed.

As we read this quiet analysis we cannot but wonder whether the ocean bulwarks that compartmented America from the world were really as stout in Grey's eyes as he was ready to grant. After all, the airplane, the submarine, the wireless, were potent actualities in 1930; but Grey (in the courteous tradition of the old diplomacy) was expressly dealing with the American interests as Americans declared them to be, not as they might be argued to be from some other view. The emphasis on the interchangeability of rôles in the matter of neutrality and freedom of the seas, and the patience and skill with which Grey pressed the case for the British interest, are also worth studying in the light of current intimations that the rôles of 1940 may not necessarily be the ones to which these two particular countries will under all circumstances incline. If Americans found it necessary to reverse the arguments presented here, again in the interest of the two peoples, one ventures to believe that Grey would say that that, too, was reasonable.

❖ ❖ ❖

FREEDOM OF THE SEAS

By Viscount Grey of Fallodon

THE Freedom of the Seas, like the Monroe Doctrine, is understood to be a phrase representing an aspect of the policy of the United States. Every nation has the right to define its own policy, and a British Secretary of State once provoked indignation by sending a dispatch to Washington in which it was argued that the Monroe Doctrine was not what the President of the United States described it to be. It is for the United States alone to define the Monroe Doctrine as being part of her own policy. But as other nations also have the right to define their own policies, it is for them to say how far the declared policy of another nation is compatible or conflicts with their own policies.

As far as the Monroe Doctrine is concerned, no friction except on the one occasion referred to above has arisen or is likely to arise between America and Britain. I am not aware that the United States has ever given any definition or declaration of the Monroe Doctrine which conflicts with British policy or aims. It is therefore unnecessary that there should be any discussion of the subject or exchange of views upon it. The United States has declared her policy to the world at large, and there is no likelihood of British policy running counter to it.

It is different with the Freedom of the Seas. The policy thus named applies not to one geographical area, as the Monroe Doctrine does, but to the whole world. Differences of opinion about right of capture at sea still exist. Even in peacetime the sense of this difference causes a feeling of uneasiness between Britain and the United States; in the event of future war this might be not only serious but dangerous. It is therefore very desirable that the two nations should discuss the subject freely, when this can be done calmly and at leisure.

It is necessary, however, that we should know what is meant by Freedom of the Seas. The phrase has become so familiar that it is used as if the meaning was as familiar as the sound of the words; whereas in point of fact I doubt whether we are quite sure what it really does mean. Let us try to arrive at this by eliminating certain things which it presumably does not mean.

The full, literal, unqualified sense of the words would abolish national right to control territorial waters. This presumably is not meant. Whatever is contended about Freedom of the Seas, it will be agreed that there are to be such things as territorial waters and that freedom to use such waters will remain qualified and conditioned by national rights within these limits.

The "seas," therefore, for the purpose of this discussion, are to be regarded as the high seas outside territorial waters. For this purpose it may be desirable to have a clear understanding as to what are territorial waters. Even so, Freedom of the Seas must be still further qualified so as not to give immunity to battleships and other armed vessels of a belligerent nation. Each belligerent must retain the right to sink, capture or pursue the armed vessels of an opponent on the high seas.

If this be agreed, as I assume it is, then Freedom of the Seas applies only to merchant vessels. Here we come on to debatable ground, and it becomes necessary to ask questions as to what is meant. In the first place, is it the American view that the merchant vessels of a belligerent should be absolutely free from interference or capture on the high seas by the armed vessels of another belligerent? I have no right to assume the answer that the United States will give to this question, but let it be supposed for the purpose of further discussion that the answer will be in the negative—that is to say, that Freedom of the Seas will not be construed so as to deprive a belligerent of all right to interfere with merchant vessels flying an enemy flag.

The next question will be whether a belligerent nation is

to have no right to interfere with the merchant vessel of any neutral nation, no matter what the nature of the cargo or the destination of the vessel may be. In other words, is the whole doctrine of contraband of war to be swept away? This would be a great change, and here again, though I have no right to assume what is now meant by Freedom of the Seas, I will suppose that some right of capture or search on the high seas will still be left to a belligerent. The discussion will then be not whether there should be any belligerent rights as regards neutral merchant ships on the high seas at all, but what is to be the extent and the limits of such rights. This has hitherto been the ground of controversy on several occasions between Britain and the United States, and for the purpose of this paper I will assume that it will be the basis of discussion now.

It seems to be commonly supposed that there has been an American view of belligerent rights on the high seas and a British view, and that each view has been consistently opposed to the other. This is not accurate: it is indeed a misleading statement. American views and practice on this subject have not been consistent: nor have British views and practice. Let the British record be considered first.

British practice and arguments have varied. When Britain has been neutral, its public opinion has resented interference by belligerents with neutral ships and cargoes. I write from memory only, but I am confident that this can be proved by reference to the correspondence that passed between the British and French Governments when France was at war with China in the latter part of the last century. The French then declared rice to be contraband and argued for an extended view of belligerent rights. Britain disputed the French contention and argued for the limitation of belligerent rights. On the other hand, when Britain has been a belligerent, public opinion has insisted upon the utmost use of the navy to prevent supplies from reaching an enemy. The correspondence between the British and United States Governments in the first two years of the Great War is sufficient proof of this.

The United States record is similar. When neutral, she

has contended for the rights of neutrals as against belligerent rights of interference with commerce; but when in the Great War she became a belligerent, she stood for the most extended rights of belligerents to control or supervise neutral commerce.

It is difficult to find in the practice of either nation anything that has not its parallel in the practice of the other. Each has had not one view, but varying views. Difficulties have arisen between Britain and the United States not because each has differed in principle from the other, but because they have not always held the same view at the same time. The record of practice shows that, had they always been neutrals together or belligerents together, they would never have differed about belligerent rights.

It is as if each had used a telescope. Each when neutral looked at belligerent rights through the end of the telescope that makes all objects seem very small. Each when belligerent has looked at these rights through the end of the telescope that makes objects seem very large.

Thus in the first part of the Great War Britain surveyed belligerent rights through the magnifying end of the telescope, the United States through the small end: the difference between their two points of view was naturally enormous. But when the United States entered the war she reversed her telescope, and all difference of view or practice disappeared. Indeed, it was as if the magnifying powers of the American telescope and of that of Britain were combined: for belligerent rights to interfere with neutral commerce were carried by the two nations together to an extreme that had never before been practised, claimed or contemplated. America and the Allies ceased to bother about technical questions such as continuous voyage or the ultimate destination of particular cargoes. They discarded all argument and by *force majeure* put neutral neighbors of Germany on rations as regards everything that might help Germany to carry on the war.

Now the war is over and America and Britain are occupying different points of view as to what belligerent rights should be in future. American opinion recalls the intolerable nuisance of interference with American commerce by belligerents in a war in which America at first seemed to have no concern. American opinion seems to assume that in the next war the United States will be neutral and has therefore reverted to the neutral point of view: and this finds expression in the doctrine of the Freedom of the Seas.

British opinion, on the other hand, feels that its country has passed through a terrible crisis in which its liberty and its very status as an independent nation were at stake, and in which the issue was for a long time in doubt. Many people in Britain believe that had it not been for the sustained pressure of the British naval blockade of Germany the issue might have gone against the Allies and all that was at stake might have been lost: and that but for the pressure of the blockade even American help might not have been in time or have availed to save the Allies.

It is this very right of blockade that would be taken away by the Freedom of the Seas. Under modern conditions blockade could not be effective, it would indeed be a mere farce, if the limiting view of belligerent rights at sea which is now being put forward were adopted. The result would be that so long as an enemy fleet did not put to sea, the British Navy would be reduced to inactivity. Britain would in fact become a Power that could not hurt an aggressor; for the British Army, like that of the United States, is not maintained on a scale that can be regarded as a striking force. To this consideration must be added another disadvantage. London, the British capital and most vital spot, is more accessible to an air attack from a possible Continental enemy than are corresponding vital spots on the Continent to air attack from Britain. The conclusion is that with a navy reduced to a mere watching rôle in war, we should, if attacked by a Continental Power, be *ab initio* at a disadvantage. We should have more to fear than anyone else would have reason to fear from us.

The doctrine of the Freedom of the Seas has an altruistic or humanitarian as well as a commercial side. This higher aspect of it is illustrated by President Hoover's suggestion that in time of war food ships at any rate should be free.

It may well be, therefore, that there are some people in America who feel impatient at British hesitation or reluctance to discuss the Freedom of the Seas—an impatience that may feel conscious of a moral as well as a material justification.

If such impatience there be, I would ask those who feel it to imagine for a moment the mind of those who live in Britain. It may not be easy for an American to enter into this mind. For never since the independence of the United States was established in the eighteenth cntury have her people been in such peril from a foreign enemy as we were in the Great War; and never, as far as human foresight can see—having regard to the geographical position of the United States, to her vast self-contained resources, and to the numbers and power of the people—can she be made by any foreign foe to face an ordeal so terrible or an anxiety so intense as that from which we have but recently emerged. The margin by which we did emerge safely was narrow enough: the weapon of blockade was a great—perhaps a really essential—factor in winning our safety. Is it any wonder, when we are asked to discuss something which involves a pledge never to use this weapon again, that we should approach the discussion with misgiving and much caution? Some people in Britain probably feel the considerations here set forth to be conclusive against entering into the discussion at all. I do not agree with such a conclusion and will state the reasons for my opinion.

In the latter half of the Great War our most serious anxiety was lest German submarines preying upon merchant vessels should starve us into defeat. We could still prevent our enemies from getting oversea supplies, but under modern conditions it was more difficult than ever before to keep the sea open for our own supplies. Long range guns that could command the Channel, mines in the sea, aircraft, submarines, the recent inventions of science, have impaired our island security, for we must ever be dependent on imported food supplies. There are people who hold that the counter-inventions of science will master those that are unfavorable to us. Who can be sure of this? Would it not be well to accept President Hoover's suggestion that food ships in time of war should be free? We might by accepting it be impairing or retarding our chance of victory in a future war, but we should be greatly increasing our own security.

There are, however, one or two questions to be asked. The matter is not altogether simple.

The League of Nations and the Pact for the Renunciation of War have made it difficult for war to come in future between great nations without one of them having broken its obligations under one or both of these peace treaties. A nation which has set these obligations at naught will have no scruple about breaking other promises. If we are at war with such a nation, and it sinks or captures food ships destined for our ports, are we still to be bound by our pledge to respect food ships? The pledge will have been one given to all nations and the action of our enemy in breaking it can release us from it only in so far as it may justify us in retaliating upon ships or cargoes that actually belong to the enemy. The Covenant of the League of Nations and the Pact for the Renunciation of War have greatly diminished the prospect of future war. But these two treaties have also made us feel that if a nation does break these great and solemn obligations, no rules of war will be kept. We hope by these two treaties to be saved from war, but if in spite of them war does come, we must be prepared for a breach of every rule that has previously been accepted.

A further point remains. There is the need to secure that if food is to be free from capture in time of war the ships that carry food will carry nothing else. This difficulty might be overcome by strict supervision of the loading in neutral ports, but the supervision would have to be very strict and the food supplies confined to ships specially chartered for the purpose and loaded under this supervision.

Let us pass to consideration of supplies other than food, which, though not actual munitions, are yet essential to carry on war: copper and rubber may be taken as examples. If we have observed every treaty obligation for the security of peace, and another nation has broken these and attacked us, are we to let all these supplies go through? Is the British fleet to remain inactive, to look on in acquiescence, while ships pass by conveying these supplies in unlimited quantity to a neutral port neighboring to the enemy, whence they can pour in an uninterrupted stream into the enemy country?

I have assumed that actual munitions, shells, rifles, guns will be regarded as contraband of war and legitimate capture. But is everything else, and not only food alone, to be guaranteed free passage?

Let it be supposed that a guarantee of free food supplies in time of war would have a balance of advantage in Britain's favor, and that in return for this it would be worth our while to concede some points about Freedom of the Seas that would have a balance of disadvantage to us. The question still remains: What is to be the position if an enemy breaks a rule that is to our advantage, and how can we be sure that this will not happen?

It will be observed that I have written thus far on two assumptions. One is that if we are at war it will be because some other nation has broken one or both of the great treaties to secure world peace. I have ignored the possibility of a British Government being thus to blame, because if it were thus in fault I should urge no plea that its interests should be considered. Nor has the contingency of a war in which neither belligerents could be charged with a breach of treaty been contemplated. Such an event is not inconceivable, at any rate technically, but to multiply in advance conceivable contingencies is an intolerable complication. Discussion should begin by contemplating one broad, clear and simple issue. This is the way to promote discussion of such a question as Freedom of the Seas; to overload the discussion at the outset by multiplying hypotheses is to choke it.

The other assumption on which this has been written is that the United States will not enter into any treaty or agreement about Freedom of the Seas that involves any obligation to take action or apply sanctions if the rules are broken. I have assumed that any such proposal must be excluded from the discussion. This assumption we are not only entitled but bound to make after the statements made by President Hoover, and by others made in connection with the Pact for the Renunciation of War. The first reason, then, why Britain should be willing to enter into discussion is as follows: It is a mistake to suppose that Britain has everything to lose and nothing to gain by Freedom of the Seas. We are more dependent upon overseas supplies, particularly of food, than any Continental country. As long as we could deny Freedom of the Seas to enemy supplies and maintain it for ourselves in time of war the position was naturally very satisfactory to us; but the inventions of science have already put the matter in doubt, and should they progress to a point at which even a superior navy cannot keep the sea open in time of war for its national supplies, then Britain has at least as much as any other nation to gain by an assured Freedom of the Seas.

Some will not be convinced by the above consideration and will ask: "Why should we not leave the question alone? Why should we not keep our hands free, and in the event of future war do as we did in the last war?" The answer is this:

In the last war, before the United States entered it, we pressed the right of blockade as far as we could without a breach with America. We knew this matter to be delicate; it was even more dangerous than we knew. Such books as the life of Walter Hines Page and the papers of Colonel House show that in the first part of the war we came nearer to a breach with the United States than even the most cautious of us realized at the time. It may seem illogical that we should have been brought near to a breach with the United States by doing less than the United States was ready to participate in herself directly she entered the war, but logic and consistency have not hitherto governed the views that nations have held about belligerent rights at sea. Or the same thing may be put positively by saying that every nation has been consistent in taking the view that suited its own interest at the time. The risk of a breach with America was not the only unpleasantness for the British Government in the first years of the war. We were exposed to reproach and obloquy from our own people: the demand was insistent that we should press belligerent rights at sea to the point of defying the United States, that is to a point that would have been fatal to the cause of our Allies and to our own.

As it was in the last war so would it be in another war. Britain in 1914 to 1917 did indeed come through without disaster, but as we look back with all the knowledge that we have since gained of the feeling at Washington it is surprising that we did come through; and it is to be hoped that no British Government ever will again have to engage in negotiations so critical and delicate with so powerful a neutral and at the same time be exposed to the pressure and reproaches of a public opinion at home for refusing to do what must certainly bring that neutral into the war against us. But should there be a future war in which Britain is again a belligerent and the United States is neutral the same dangerous situation will assuredly recur if we have meanwhile refused even to discuss the Freedom of the Seas.

Thus far the subject has been considered from the point of view of British national interest; and it is natural and reasonable that this should be our first consideration. We have but recently escaped great national peril, and experience has shown us that under modern conditions our island security is not, and probably can never again be, what it has been in history. But it is not on this basis, however, that coöperation and friendship with the United States can be sought. Friendship based on vital national interests takes the form of alliance or political entente. These can be based only on a conviction that the security of each nation depends on friendship with the other. There can be no such reciprocal conviction between the United States and any other nation. The intrinsic strength and geographical position of the United States make it independent of the support of any other nation. This it is, I imagine, which makes the historic American warning against foreign alliances or entanglements as potent in America today as it was when it was first enunciated. And so no doubt it will remain; for every nation would gladly avoid foreign entanglements as long as it felt that it could safely do so. Nor can friendship with the United States be based on the fact of common language or racial kinship. The latter as between the United States and Britain is only partial. These two factors, language and race, may and do make intercourse between individuals easy and pleasant, but neither one nor the other nor both together qualify or affect the fact that the national feeling of the United States is purely American and distinct from the national feeling of Britain, which is British; and that in any clash of policies or aims between the two countries their respective national feelings will draw apart as separate entities. In fact, in so far as American national sentiment can be said to have manifested any predilection at all, it has, owing to historical associations, been for France.

Friendship between the United States and any other nation cannot therefore be based on mutual national interest. It can come only by coöperation in something that is not exclusive: that is, in something that transcends any individual national interest, something in which the national interest of every nation may have a share and in which every nation may join.

Such an opportunity occurred when President Wilson proposed and pursued the policy of founding the League of Nations; then came the decision of the United States not to become a member of the League and the opportunity seemed to disappear. But the forces that make for world peace were still active. The League of Nations began to function and the United States showed that, though her decision not to join the League was unaltered, the motive and the ideal that had prompted its formation were still active in America. The attitude of the United States to the League was not unfriendly; on the contrary, it was one of good will, as was shown by the sending of friendly American observers to conferences and committees initiated or organized by the League. There followed an American initiative in movements for the reduction of armaments and finally in proposing the Pact for the Renunciation of War.

Thus the opportunity for coöperation with the United States for world peace has grown, has been fruitful, and continues. To refuse discussion of the Freedom of the Seas, if the United States proposes it, would be a distinct check to this coöperation. For the question has in the past been a cause of serious international controversy and is therefore very relevant to the security of future peace, which is concerned with the removal of potential causes of conflict as well as with the settlement of disputes after they have arisen.

Such is my final plea for agreeing to discuss the Freedom of the Seas. This does not imply that whatever the United States proposes must at once be accepted. Nor, I am sure, would the United States expect this. If she did so it would be quite contrary to the spirit in which all her peace initiatives have been taken. Difficulties will be met with—some of them have been indicated here—and these should not be left to arise as unforeseen obstacles in a formal conference. There should be, as in the case of the Five Power Naval Conference, preliminary, frank and informal discussion between the Governments. Especially should they consider what bearing the existence of the Pact for the Renunciation of War and the Covenant of the League of Nations has upon the question of the Freedom of the Seas. If either of these instruments is broken, the situation will not be the same as in previous wars. The Freedom of the Seas must be considered in the light not only of previous controversies, but also of these new future contingencies.

❖ ❖ ❖

THE fundamental assumption of the American people and of American foreign policy which Grey and Cambon had been so careful not to question at the end of the 1920's—that in and of itself the strength of the United States was impregnable—had by the early 1930's suddenly and surprisingly vanished, not under the impact of weapons of war but by the working of the impalpable acid of economic decay. The corrosive filled the world. But where it came from, what produced it, and what, indeed, it was, Americans did not understand. In bewilderment, anger and bitterly divided counsels, but also in renewed vigor and determination, there began the reëxamination of the basic premise of self-sufficiency—"the great debate"—which set the tone of American life for the next ten years and resulted in the sweeping political and economic reorientation of American foreign policy which is still in progress.

The first response of Americans to the dissolution of the barriers which had been counted on to fence out the problems of a less fortunate world was, not unnaturally, a blind effort to build them stronger. Politically, this took the form of the drive for neutrality. Economically, its expression was the Smoot-Hawley tariff. In 1931 came a corresponding endeavor by nations everywhere around the globe to seal off their preserves against the universal malady—culminating in the abandonment by Great Britain of its traditional free-trade policy. Every man for himself.

Even at the height of the panic of economic nationalism voices of reason were heard. One which was influential in the United States was that of Edwin F. Gay, Professor of Economic History at Harvard and the first Dean of the Harvard Graduate School of Business Administration, whose article entitled "The Great Depression" appeared in FOREIGN AFFAIRS in July 1932. The article is especially noteworthy, since Gay himself wrote little—yet, as has been said, "through teaching and guidance of research he dominated economic history as very few American scholars have ever dominated any major academic field." It is interesting to note that Gay also played an important, if unpublicized, part in practical affairs. He was called one of the "miracle men" of 1917, for his part in finding shipping to transport American troops to France: as head of the Import Bureau of the War Trade Board, he made a million tons of additional shipping available by rearranging imports.

❖ ❖ ❖

THE GREAT DEPRESSION

By Edwin F. Gay

A RECENT statement by Mr. Justice Brandeis has been widely quoted. "The people of the United States," he said, "are now confronted with an emergency more serious than war. Misery is widespread, in a time, not of scarcity, but of overabundance. The long-continued depression has brought unprecedented unemployment, a catastrophic fall in commodity prices and a volume of economic losses which threatens our financial institutions."

The economic losses both of the World War and the present depression, in their full volume and extent, are incalculable, but it is not only of such losses that Mr. Justice Brandeis was speaking. The gravity of the present situation lies not merely in the widespread suffering, vast as that is, but in the questions it excites concerning the fundamental strength and character of our economic structure and in the series of decisions which must be made, indeed are now in process of making. These decisions are much more difficult than those of war. In war the chief problem is clearly set and calls for immediate action, unifying in its effect. In such a depression as this the problem is infinitely complex, decisions are beset by doubt, action seems always too late or has effects contrary to what were expected, and disunion and disruption have spread as each centrifugal force, seeking to strengthen itself, weakens the whole. War stimulates the full expansion of productive energy, but the deep depression cripples every economic process and discourages even the most sanguine business leaders. There are many confusing prescriptions offered from all sides. But no one, however skilled, really knows the character of or the specific cure for what some practitioners diagnose as a wasting disease.

Whether or not a phenomenon regularly recurring, though at unequal intervals and with varying intensity, may properly be called a disease is questionable. A continuous succession of wave-like fluctuations, each with its phases of rising business activity, boom, recession and depression, may more properly be regarded as the result of the normal functioning of a competitive economy. Multitudes of business men, each making his individual calculation of gain in a future market, but each affected by the contagious movement of contemporary business hopes or fears, unconsciously coöperate in creating the fluctuations known as business cycles. In this ebb and flow, however, there is more than the repeated concurrence of a mass of individual plans and expectations. Physical determinants are clearly present in other types of contemporary fluctuations, such as those affecting agriculture and the short seasonal swings. Monetary and other technological factors enter largely into the long secular trends. All the different types of fluctuations interact. It is possible, in the present instance, that a business cycle has been intensified by an agricultural cycle and by greater seasonal fluctuations, and then prolonged by the impact of a longer downward-moving secular trend in prices. There are also to be considered the stresses and strains which may result when the normally uneven operation of the economic forces in the business cycle, never fully balanced, develops from time to time a state of acute disequilibrium. And, in addition to these and many other disturbing factors, come the irregular influences named by the economists, rather inadequately, as "random perturbations," such as cyclones, earthquakes, widespread visitations of disease, and wars. The economists find the analysis of business cycles no simple thing, and the present deep depression, transcending in depth and extent the usual amplitudes and intensities of business cycles, is still more difficult to explain.

It is generally recognized, however, that the World War has had serious effects upon the economic conditions of the postwar period, such as the depletion of manpower, the stimulus to over-capacity of some essential industrial, including American agriculture, the forcing process in the industrial development of regions cut off from their former sources of supply and of the newly-created states, the widespread monetary disorders, and the staggering burden of internal debts and foreign obligations. The World War left deep wounds, but they could be healed. As Sir Arthur Salter has just pointed out in his admirable book, "Recovery, the Second Effort," the war—except in Russia—meant not the destruction but the dislocation of the economic structure. This seemed to be demonstrated by the remarkable economic recovery in the decade after the war, and especially after 1924, even in ravaged Europe. But now we are wondering whether this recovery was not simply a respite rather than a cure.

The range of the great depression is unprecedentedly wide. Past crises have affected many countries simultaneously; but, despite the growing economic international interdependence, even in previous major crises some important countries have been little affected. The timing of the business cycles as between countries has not been parallel, nor their incidence equal. At the close of 1929, when the crash came in the United States, about half the countries for which statistical evidence is available were already suffering a decline in prosperity. But thereafter the process continued, with brief deceptive pauses, until after the middle of 1931 the disastrous, deepening depression had become world-wide. The depression is also unprecedentedly deep. Experience as measured in statistics of prices, production, foreign and domestic trade, and unemployment, shows nothing comparable in intensity. The United States has suffered bitterly during former depressions, notably in the years following 1837, and 1873, and 1893, but it then had free land to absorb its unemployed and an expanding European market for its increased agricultural production. During those former crises banks failed and specie payments ceased to an extent which the present experience has not equalled, but this was the habitual behavior of a young and rapidly growing country. Finally, after the crisis of 1907, when the banks had again been prostrated, the Federal Reserve System was created to put an end to an intolerable weakness. Now, despite strong banks in the leading countries, despite a productive equipment in materials and men unmatched in the world's history, deep business depression is universal.

That the World War and the World Depression are intimately linked, as fundamental cause and ultimate effect, is beginning to be realized. There are other coöperating causes of our present distress, some antedating the war and some coming in its wake; but the war accentuated the prior trends of change and was largely responsible for the later dislocations. The economists in 1930 at first looked for the familiar signs of a business cycle. There seemed in 1929 to be no such accumulation of inventory in the hands of producers as in 1920, but in the form of goods bought on credit, installment purchases, housing and the like, a great inventory was being carried by consumers. In many lines of productive activity, both industrial and agricultural, it appeared that an excess capacity was facing a saturated market. "Cumulative disequilibria" of various sorts were seen to have strained the economic system: the increase in the consumer's spending power had not kept pace with the increase in productive power, the wage-earner's income had not grown as rapidly as that of the entrepreneur, and the flow of savings toward investment in capital goods and in durable consumption goods was exceptionally great. The technological advance had been more rapid than the growth of the market demand for new or cheaper products, so that, despite the great mobility of the working population, there was a steady increase of unemployment. These and similar unbalancing elements, it was thought, went far to explain the break in the economic mechanism with its slackening business activity and increasing unemployment. But as the depression was prolonged and intensified through the first half of 1931 it became clear that changes of greater range and longer duration were operating than those ordinarily engendered afield. They noted the shift in monetary gold supply and the demonstrable alterations in the money markets of the world; the declining birth rate; the rise in the standard of living and the changes in habits of consumption tending to make the market more sensitive to fluctuations;

the increasing mechanization which was revolutionizing agriculture and affecting many other industries; the development of large-scale organizations in industry, banking and labor; and the spread of price agreements and market controls which tended to introduce dangerous rigidities into the flexible system of free competition.

Then came the collapse of the Austrian Kredit Anstalt in May 1931, the breakdown of the German financial system in June, England's abandonment of the gold standard in September, followed promptly by many other countries, the cessation of international lending, and the further and alarming deepening of depression everywhere. The factors producing business cycles and the changes in long-time trends have exerted their influence upon the depression, but the specialists in the study of business fluctuations, after arraying the factors and weighing those which are measurable, acknowledge that their accustomed methods of analysis are inadequate. A more incalculable force seems to be at work. The situation suggests that the credit economy, not alone of nations as separate units but of all, is involved; and that recovery demands both separate and common efforts.

"We have still inadequately realized," writes Sir Arthur Salter, "how deeply the foundations of the system of credit have been undermined." The World Depression reveals many related causes at work, but it now is evident that the break in the stream of credit should be especially emphasized and carefully studied. The sapping process, undermining credit, goes back to the war, to the huge unproductive debts which it created and which, by the financial illusions engendered, have been continually extended. The war was fought with determination through four interminable years; and the confidence of all its participants was buoyed up, and in turn supported an enormous inflation of credit. The exaltation of war made possible the incredible toll it exacted. Unmindful of postwar consequences, the contestants piled mountainously high their demands upon the future and thus mobilized for war's exigent present the productive resources of the world. To the people of the United States especially the war revealed possibilities of credit expansion which seemed boundless; the whole world shared in the illusion, but not so riotously in the exploitation of it. The military contribution of the United States in the war's concluding year was of decisive character, but the country's primary function was the furnishing of supplies, in the first two years paid for largely by shipments of gold from Europe and the repatriation of American securities, and in the last two supported by great domestic credits, which financed the production of war materials both for the American armies and for their associates.

The war fervor, aided and inflamed by energetic organization, placed government bonds in the hands of millions of people who never before had possessed such instruments of credit. They were not thereby educated in the use of credit; they simply received a new vision of its possibilities. The basis was thus laid for the vast and credulous postwar market for credit which culminated in the portentous speculation of 1928 and 1929. Great enterprises learned that they could distribute their shares and bonds by direct sale to the public, and smaller enterprises were recapitalized by busy investment houses to float new securities in a national market canvassed by high-pressure bond salesmen. Despite the heavy inflow of gold to the United States, particularly during the first half of the decade, despite the easy money policy of the Federal Reserve Board, especially in 1927, and despite the large repayments by the United States Treasury of the principal of the domestic debt, prices of commodities did not rise. Instead, after 1924, they showed a slight tendency downward, in consonance probably with the more pronounced price-fall outside the United States. It was perhaps because the pressure for a rise was checked in this section of the elastic tissue of the price system that it burst forth with such redoubled vigor in the stock market. Here was presented the greatest scene in the history of speculation. Stock values were pyramided again and again as they soared to heights out of all rational relationship to earnings present or prospective. The mania spread in unexampled breadth; where millions had bought Liberty Bonds, tens of millions now were buying shares or speculating on margin at the new brokerage offices springing up everywhere.

Below these paper values, the easy credit was stimulating actual production. American economic progress during the postwar period was rapid but uneven. Certain regions, whose old staple industries or agricultural products were in competition with the new mechanization or with virgin land, lagged in the race; but the pace was set by relatively new industries like the electrical or chemical industries, with the giant automobile industry far in the lead both in methods of mass production and in volume of mass sales. The construction industry in all its branches, and the machine-tool industry, especially in its export trade, grew amazingly. Spending (though toward the close it showed signs of "sales resistance," even though reinforced by abundant consumers' credit) seemed on the whole to be holding its place with production. Public spending by governmental agencies—federal, state and municipal—likewise mightily increased. The fructifying stream, attracted by high interest rates, overflowed in foreign loans, which in turn financed the growth in exports. Foreign states, towns and business concerns, especially those of Germany and Latin American, sought, or were sought by, the American investment houses and banks, until the total volume of private postwar loans surpassed, or on a net reckoning fully equalled, the public war loans.

All this was the work of credit, of which the war had taught the lesson of apparently unlimited expansion. Credit on the great scale is a modern invention, an instrument of immense power, comparable with the prime-movers in the physical field for whose introduction through the industrial revolution it had prepared the way. Together these new powers are transforming the world. But the engineers of credit know far less about the limitations and control of their new organ than the engineers of steam and electricity do about theirs. Credit is a social force, operating upon masses of people through its own specialized institutions. It has become robust and resilient and yet sensitively flexible, adjusting itself to daily repeated shocks. Its outer limits of expansion and contraction are not ordinarily reached and tested, and hence in part the reason for our lack of scientific knowledge. Nevertheless, as historical experience if not yet economic theory has demonstrated, it has limits in both directions. Its essential form is that of a continuous stream of debts, constantly renewed, flowing where profitable enterprise beckons. Since these debts or advances rest upon a conglomerate of human estimates of future gains, some near and more certain, others distant and more speculative, wastage is inevitable, and so long as it is not excessive this does not check the stream. It flows confidently on and draws new volume from its watershed of supply.

The continuous and excessive waste of credit by unproductive use was initiated by the war, and has been continued under the habit inherited from the war of drawing freely upon the future for the immediate enhancement of productive power and of living standards. Credit has been used in unprecedented volume, but it has also been abused, in a manner not indeed different in kind but enormously increased in degree as compared with earlier experiences. When finally (as in the time of John Law's great speculative venture, a period of inflated credit in many respects like our own) the *realisateurs* commenced to cash in on their paper gains, the swollen stream contracted and for the first time the great body of investors became aware that it was fed by inadequate earnings. Then panics began. The domestic and foreign capital which had been drawn into the maelstrom by the lure of high call-rates was hastily withdrawn. The stream of American credit which had been diverted to the speculative market suddenly left the foreign debtors stranded, and their distress today adds to the depression. Abroad some of the unproductive debts cannot pay their interest; at home extravagantly invested funds, supplied by credit, fail to pay dividends or rent. Investors widely come to feel that the public trust which credit implies has been betrayed and their confidence abused. People complain of the paradox that poverty appears in the midst of abundance. It is no paradox; abundance is freighted on credit and credit stretched beyond its limits of safety must withdraw.

While America has been experiencing the elation and suffering of excessive overconfidence, bred from the war's extravagance and its aftereffects, Europe has not been immune. She was left shattered by the war. The monetary systems of combatants and neutrals were tottering. Some of these systems succumbed utterly, in the case of others the fall was checked. But by the middle of the postwar decade order had been restored, the bulk of the work of reconstruction seemed to have been accomplished, and Europe was turning hopefully to the modernization of her industries and to the redemption of her pledges, expressed or tacit, to make her lands fit for heroes to live in. The strong desire for social betterment, running from peasant land allotments to recreation facilities, was matched, on the part of peoples who had during the war seen money poured out like water, by a belief that a material improvement in the conditions of life was attainable. The same miraculous rock could be tapped again; and in fact the stream of credit did again flow. Furthermore, since the menace of social upheaval is a reality in Europe (where an example lies close on her eastern border), her rulers feel that measures of social amelioration are more than desirable: they are necessary. The debts for reconstruction added to the war debts were crushing, but in many countries they have been greatly alleviated by the valuations of currency, shifting part of the loss to the *rentier* class and the recipients of fixed incomes. When the currencies had been re-stabilized new hope made possible new credits.

But it now becomes apparent that the war left a legacy of fundamental insecurity to the continent of Europe. To the manifestly continuing political insecurity has been added a persistent undercurrent of economic insecurity, which has made itself felt in repeated emergencies and in various ways. The nervousness of European investors, great and small, has been shown in the more conspicuous episodes of the successive "flights" from the mark, the franc or other currencies; it has been allayed for periods, but still has been instant to take alarm. Largely for this reason the flow of capital from country to country has tended to be spasmodic and unpredictable; investors have sought security by shifting funds from one financial center to another without primary regard to differences in interest rates. They have thus contributed to impede the quasi-automatic operation of the mechanism of foreign exchange which before the war, when security was taken for granted, affected national price levels and regulated the international movements of goods and gold.

In the quest for security, especially during the respite afforded by the relative improvement in economic conditions for a few years after 1925, many countries, anxious to stabilize their disordered currencies, adopted an equivalent for the gold standard. Their equivalent was the gold exchange standard which permitted them to place bills of exchange in their portfolios instead of gold bullion in their vaults. This gave them rights to call on gold held in the great Central Banks, but the innovation not only laid an increased load of responsibility on the Central Banks, especially during periods of sudden emergency, but it acted as another impediment to the normal regulating flow of foreign exchange. Meanwhile the Central Banks were sweeping up gold from private holdings, and much of this, together with the newly-mined monetary gold (because of the abnormally functioning forces of the period) flowed into two great reservoirs—before 1925 mainly to the Federal Reserve System of the United States, and since that date the larger portion to the Bank of France. By the end of 1931 a substantial part (probably a fifth) of the banking reserves of the world was in the exposed form of foreign exchange, the "cushion" of domestic circulating gold had everywhere disappeared, and about three-quarters of the world's monetary stock of gold had been so withdrawn as to intensify the downward movement of world commodity prices. Monetary security was sought, but on an unstable basis; and since England, the first establisher and maintainer of the gold standard, has departed from it, monetary insecurity and difficult experimentation with "managed" currencies have again returned.

The effort to maintain stability in the agitated postwar world has been the underlying motive for the renewal of the great movement not merely toward large-scale business organizations but toward combinations, cartels and similar agreements for the maintenance of prices or the division and control of markets. The combination movement has been long-continued, for in industry it commenced its first great operations in the eighties and nineties of the last century, after the railroads had shown the way; it is world-wide; it is paralleled by an analogous growth of social organizations in many other fields, such as labor and agricultural and consumers' coöperatives; it shows variety, adaptiveness and increasing strength; in short, it is an organic development of revolutionary importance. For it has begun to modify profoundly the system of free competition and the social attitudes which accompanied that blindly "automatic" system. A free system which in a community of small competitive producers worked satisfactorily for the mass of consumers, since it furnished its products at the lowest price compatible with adequate remuneration to the more efficient producers and ruthlessly discarded the less efficient, was bound ultimately to force the strongest or most adaptable producers to increase their scale of operations. And the larger and better organized these operations become, the more inevitable it is that the small group of great producers, accustomed to order and discipline in their factories, should combine to regulate the disorderly, crisis-ridden market. It seems apparent that this tendency toward a planned economy, already initiated each in its own sphere by a growing number of the great industries, sponsored governmentally by the necessities of the Great War, and now filling men's minds, should proceed further. It obviously faces great difficulties both in organization and in public control; and stability, if it is gradually attained, is likely to entail a slowing up of technical progress and a degree of social regimentation for which perhaps the public's mind is already being prepared. The process of readaptation of the economic system is likely to be long and full of unexpected disappointments, but the successes and failures of the various nations already experimenting with economic planning will be instructive.

Meantime, the postwar developments of industrial planning have served to add to our present difficulties rather than to aid in solving them. They have taken mainly the form of stabilizing, by price or market agreements, a number of the great raw material producers, some of them with governmental aid and supervision, like the Brazilian valorization schemes or the Stevenson plan for rubber, others, like the international organization of copper producers, by private agreements. Some of them failed or were in process of failure before the depression, some have succumbed or seem about to succumb under the pressure of the disastrous fall in prices. Only two great raw material industries, both practically monopolies, nickel and sulphur, have thus far maintained prices in the face of serious decreases in production. There is evident danger of intensifying the stresses and strains in the system of prices if the fixity of great sections increases the fluctuations of the unorganized remainder, but the danger would be much less if the attempt were made to obtain stability by intelligent and timely price adjustments instead of to obtain rigidity by price maintenance. The great difficulty of a price maintenance policy, supposing all the producers, national and international, to be combined, is not only its possible repercussions on the price system and therefore the economic system in general, but its almost certain inability to restrain producers from overproductions and to check the entrance of new competitors into the profitable field, not to speak of the competition of substitute commodities. By mistaking rigidity for stability most of the postwar so-called stabilization plans have thus far failed to give the security so ardently desired.

If in this outline of some of the economic consequences of the World War in their bearing on the World Depression only cursory mention has been made of reparations and war debts, it is because they have become matters even more for political than for economic discussion. The two payments, while theoretically distinct, are in European opinion and practice so closely connected as to form practically one problem in two phases—receiving from Germany in order to pay to the United States. Since the cessation of American lending to Germany and since the rise of nationalist propaganda, Germany has come passionately to believe, and her political leaders declare, that an end must be made of reparation payments. Indeed, it seems highly probable that no government could stand which proposed to continue these payments. In the interest not merely of European but of world appeasement and of the economic recovery which depends thereupon, some settlement must promptly be arrived at. An extended moratorium, which in any case must be granted, seems likely only to prolong the disquiet, not to allay it. France, pressed by her own economic insecurity, may prefer to take the best obtainable terms which Germany can now offer rather than run the risk of another Ruhr occupation and the even graver risk of thereby unsettling further an economic world already in peril. The United States, then, must come to grips with the related problem of the war debts. Will it prefer a radical revision of the debts to meet the radically changed position of the debtors, or will it prefer a futile and embittered altercation, charged with national animosities? A reasonable end to the debt problem would not, indeed, at once stop the World Depression, but it would be a great step toward the appeasement which is necessary for recovery. The steady exacerbation of international feelings resulting from a settlement of reparations and debts which was not a settlement reveals in a clearer light the fundamental error of continuing the economic war after peace had been signed. It has only added continuously to postwar insecurity.

What has especially aggravated the European feeling about the war debts has been the American tariff. This has been held responsible for the relative decline in the imports from the European debtors to the United States. Supplementary causes may be found for the general decline in imports of European commodities into the United States, from the 48 percent of total imports in 1913 to the 30 percent of recent years. And there has been an offset, which should be taken into account, in the increase of expenditures by American tourists abroad. But the fact remains that the narrowly nationalistic policy of the United States, as exemplified again in the tariff of 1930—inexcusable from an economic point of view and definitely harmful from a broader national standpoint—has been one of the great complicating and accelerating factors in the cumulation of abnormal unbalances and rigidities which brought the world to the Great Depression.

A time must come when the United States as a powerful world state and a great creditor nation, hence vitally interested in world trade and world prosperity, will face the realities of its new position. It will realize that a policy of self-sufficiency is not only impossible, but that a policy which presupposes it to be possible is stultifying and impoverishing. To say, as one frequently hears it said, that because the value of American exports is less than 10 percent of the total American production, we may therefore go our own way regardless of foreign trade or international responsibilities is to misinterpret the plain facts. The whole network of domestic prices and domestic credit in the United States is bound indissolubly with the system of world prices and with the stream of world credit. A dislocation anywhere in the fabric is now felt everywhere. The World War affirmed the international political responsibilities of the United States; the World Depression demonstrates the economic interdependence of the United States with other states. It cannot be a hermit nation.

❖ ❖ ❖

ONE who wanted to estimate the speed and volume of the water that has flowed under the bridge in American foreign relations since October 1933, when Newton D. Baker wrote his article "The 'New Spirit' and Its Critics," might take as a point of reference the extent of patient exposition which he felt compelled to summon to his aid in the effort to persuade Americans that it really was neither moral nor practical to look for national safety in a program which authorized the impartial sale of weapons to both the highwayman and the occupants of the stagecoach. It was still the period when references to "liberty" or "democracy" were held to be in bad taste. But Newton D. Baker, Mayor of Cleveland from 1912 to 1916, and Secretary of War from 1916 to 1921, was not at all of that school of thought. He had respect enough for his fellow-citizens to appeal to them by reason, and faith enough in their common sense to believe that they would respond to it. He also had such a strong belief in democracy that he was willing to ask Americans to fight for it if necessary, and such a belief in their ideals that he was confident they would. It was this characteristic belief in the virtue of reason and the triumph of courage for the right that brought him the steadily growing esteem of his countrymen, from the day he entered Woodrow Wilson's Cabinet, unknown to most of them, to the hour of his death on Christmas Day, 1937.

The "new spirit" for which Newton D. Baker wrote this fighting credo had (like all ideas in which Baker believed) a definite objective, and as always he had a clear program by which it was to be achieved. The objective was to settle controversies between nations in their early stages by pacific means. To accomplish this, he recommended that the United States join the League of Nations and the World Court, participate in international conferences (then thought by some Americans a dangerous exposure to foreign contamination), and make plain its readiness to support with armed force the new standard of judgment expressed in the Pact of Paris, which outlawed aggressive war.

Here are themes which have recurred ever since. The reader will also note the presence of another major theme—the interplay of the "new spirit" and the old diplomacy as represented by the alliances and the balance-of-power policies which Baker did not recommend. The reconciliation of these two major lines of international efforts for peace, each of which has its great spokesmen, is a particular problem of the present era.

❖ ❖ ❖

THE "NEW SPIRIT" AND ITS CRITICS

By Newton D. Baker

IN 1754 the long-heralded philosophical works of Lord Bolingbroke were published. To Edmund Burke they constituted an effort to exclude God from his universe as a wholly unnecessary phenomenon, and he composed "A Vindication of Natural Society" as an indignant protest. The form of this protest was a seriously argued examination of all merely human institutions, with a view to demonstrating "that every endeavor which the art and policy of mankind has used from the beginning of the world until this day, in order to relieve or cure natural ills, has only served to introduce new mischiefs or to aggravate or inflame the old." This thesis, set forth with stately logic and illustrated by critical examinations in all the fields of political activity, leads the reader, with solemn power, to the conviction that all human efforts to improve the world in which we live are necessarily fruitless and that the only true state of happiness for mankind is that Edenic condition in which our first parents were before wisdom, in the form of a serpent, had beguiled them into a reliance upon mere human powers for improvement.

But, of course, Burke was playful and was imposing upon us with sham artillery. By using Bolingbroke's method, he destroys his conclusion and then proves that man, too, is worse than useless in the universe in which Bolingbroke had sought to place him as the dominant and supreme if not solitary figure. Burke knew, as we know when we read his paper, that he was exemplifying one of those common states of mind which make progress difficult. The fact is that all efforts to solve human problems are beset by unidentic twin evils. On the one hand, we have the enthusiast who declines to see difficulties, is indifferent to the lessons of history, takes no account of the deep ruts worn by mental habit and, by expecting too much, either in speed or achievement, takes a flight from reality and accomplishes less than the possible. On the other, we have the pessimist, his ranks all too often recruited by disillusioned enthusiasts. Starting with an assumption of human incorrigibility, he soon despairs of any progress in a tough and obdurate world and looks with sour disfavor upon those who would disturb any arrangement which has been found to ease the galling of a burden which it is the inescapable lot of mankind to carry. This acceptance of failure as a guide for future conduct is easily fortified by a selective reading of history, and Burke's "Vindication of Natural Society," if read without the humor which underlies it, is a classical illustration of how fiercely learned and at the same time unwise this temper can be.

Somewhere between these temperamental extremes lies the great mass of mankind; neither credulous nor incredulous, neither foolishly hopeful nor foolishly hopeless, aware of the fact that progress is not a steadily ascending spiral but a jagged thing on a chart, with peaks and valleys and yet constantly rising, as is shown by the median line in the diagram which marks increasing comfort, security, beauty and nobility in the life of man. This great mass of people, unnumbed by learning, are yet aware that old abuses have been swept away, tyrannies over the body and spirit of man abolished, superstitions and fears dissipated, and that all this has come about by experimental processes, many of which were failures, all of which were assailed, and only some of which fruited in lasting good. It may well be, therefore, that the "new spirit" had been greeted with too much enthusiasm by some of its proponents; but it is certainly true that the emanations of that new spirit, in practical efforts to establish a better order in international relations, have been too quickly distrusted and condemned by those who stand at the other extreme in philosophical outlook.

In the course of his "Vindication of Natural Society,"

Burke examines war as one of the results of man's effort at political organization. He says: "The first accounts we have of mankind are but so many accounts of their butcheries. All empires have been cemented in blood, and in these early periods when the races of mankind first began to form themselves into parties and combinations, the first effect of the combination and, indeed, the thing for which it seems purposely formed and best calculated, was their mutual destruction." Following this, he makes what he calls "a small calculation" of the number of people done to death by war as a political institution, from the earliest times to the middle of the eighteenth century, and comes to the serious conclusion that the number is not less than 35 billion human beings. To this number no doubt would have to be added indirect losses from epidemics and famines resulting from wars. These ragings of the heathen and more refined slaughterings among the civilized had taken place with undiminished ferocity, in spite of diplomacy, resident ambassadorial representation, and all manner of other efforts, by way of offensive and defensive alliances and bargains, which from time to time constituted the mechanism of international relations. Since Burke made this estimate the world has gone steadily on, increasing the possibility of large-scale mobilization and wholesale destruction, until in our own day we have had actual world war with losses counted in tens of millions and dislocations of normal life world-wide in extent and covering decades—how many we do not know—in their duration.

Thus war has presented historically, and still presents, the major catastrophe in human relations. In its modern forms it challenges the very continuance of organized society. It is no longer fought by selected champions but engages the energies of whole peoples. Its stage is no longer some remote and confined battlefield but the whole area of the combatant nations. It is fought in three dimensions and with weapons which, like Satan's dart, seize us with "strange terrors, pangs unfelt before." The consequences of modern wars, we have now learned, threaten an integrated world with the complete dissolution of the foundations upon which organized and expanding life must rest. Whether history is encouraging or discouraging, we cannot contemplate the World War, and the world which has resulted from it, without realizing that no spirit can be too bold which refuses to accept war as a constantly recurring menace and that no experiment can be too rash, however much the books on international law and history may creak on their shelves, if its intention is to rescue the race from this threat of destruction. The time has come for somebody to be "a fool in Christ" if necessary.

Clearly, if there is any substitute for war it must lie in the pacific settlement of controversies out of which wars grow. Throughout the long period of recorded history, efforts of one sort or another to establish the means of such pacific settlements have been made. They have, however, been sporadic rather than consecutive, and for the most part were responses to war weariness, religious enthusiasm, the brief ascendancy of a philosophical spirit, or a change in political policy in a dominant state. Writers on international law have, since Vattel, given the subject some attention. But until recent years the discussion of pacific settlements usually revolved around the possibility of a substitution of arbitration or adjudication for an appeal to arms; and, of course, both of these agencies take hold of a full-grown conflict, and the likelihood of their being used is diminished by the fact that passion has already been engendered before they can be appealed to. They are envisaged, frankly, as alternatives to war rather than as anticipatory adjusters of incipient controversies in which the seeds of conflict have only begun to germinate. For the most part, statesmen have preferred to try one or the other of two policies to preserve the peace of the world: either a Roman Peace, dictated by a single authoritative state, strong enough to impose its will upon the rest of the world, or a balance of power, which seeks to divide the world into an equipoise by systems of alliances and understandings. Both of these types of effort, repeated under every variation of time and circumstance, have failed. The spirit of nationality has always been too strong to endure an imposed peace. Balances of power, being organized with war in mind, become unstable as one side or the other feels that it has acquired a momentary supremacy or has detached from the other side and annexed to itself an ally, thus putting itself in a position to overpower its adversaries and accomplish certain long-cherished political objectives of its own group.

As against these policies, based frankly upon power, the intermittent suggestion of securing pacific settlement by using among nations the agencies worked out in the domestic policy of civilized states secured a hearing with difficulty. One obvious reason for this lies in the fact that the people who made wars and resorted to them to accomplish their political objectives were not the people who suffered in wars, while the people who did suffer and pay the price had no voice in the councils where the extent of their sacrifices might be weighed against the advantage of a political policy which the governing class sought to pursue. King William of Prussia had a violent quarrel with Bismarck, after the humiliation of Austria, because of Bismarck's unwillingness to annex Austrian territory from the defeated enemy. The King said to him that it had been the policy of his House to enlarge Prussia and that each of his ancestors had annexed territory as the result of his conquests. The whole diplomatic history of the world has revolved around the dreams of empire builders; and the historic policies of states, lying buried in the archives of their foreign offices, have contemplated conquest and acquisitions based on opportunities, as they might arise, for advantageous wars. Sometimes these policies have been purely defensive, as for instance the interest of England in Persia and Afghanistan to protect the Indian frontier. Sometimes they are aggressive, like the policy which has for centuries dictated to the Russian mind the dominance of Asia and an outlet through the Bosporus to the Mediterranean. Under the old order, each new foreign minister came to his task with orders to follow the chart. Necessity might require gestures, opportunity might have to be waited for; but all concessions and all combinations looked to the ultimate accomplishment of objectives which, though often undeclared and unexposed, were the final and supreme concern of the state. As these policies were hopelessly irreconcilable, the relations of the nations which entertained them were necessarily transitory and unstable. That this picture is not fanciful is illustrated by any realistic view of the relations of modern Europe. Bismarck's Reinsurance Treaty, Caprivi's failure to renew it, the hesitance of Germany as between friendship with England and friendship with Russia, the effort to build a European anti-English alliance, these and a hundred other episodes in modern European diplomatic history evidence the uneasy tension of nationalistic policies against the restraints of world order and world peace. Even the United States was captured by "manifest destiny" and made overnight into an Asiatic power by exactly the sort of impulse which has led Russia and Japan through a long period of years to look with acquiring eyes on Manchuria and Chosen.

The existence of these forces, controlled only by considerations of national advantage, has always been perfectly well known, but the cost of leaving them so controlled has only gradually come to be realized. The scientific spirit, which has given us in the realm of material things the courage to look unpleasant facts in the face and to follow truth wherever it may lead, has, in recent years, begun increasingly to make itself felt in considerations of the social and political relations of men, and this has given both new dignity to the speculations of philosophers and new hopefulness to the efforts of statesmen in the international field. If wider knowledge and franker thinking have bred a new spirit which by searching has found common interests in the preservation of peace that are of higher value than the ruthless pursuit of national objectives, we may be permitted to hope that the moral equivalent of war, if not at hand, is at least not so remote as it was when these matters of life and death were held to be games for princes to play at and, like the wills of princes, not subject to moral restraint. Surely, too, the triumphs of science in the material world encourage us to do some laboratory work with the human spirit. A peaceful world would have been less amazing to George Washington than wireless telegraphy. We must not think too well of atoms at the expense of thinking too ill of men.

From its beginnings the United States has had an attitude favoring the pacific settlement of international controversies. This has been manifested particularly in our attitude toward arbitration. But we early began to advocate the addition of adjudication to the means of settlement. Long before the World War, American public opinion had reached the settled conviction that coöperative international action was necessary for the preservation of peace, and but for the controversy of prestige between the Senate and the President it seems likely that an enlightened sentiment against war would have made the United States a partner, if not the leader, in widespread arrangements—perhaps compulsory in character—for pacific settlements.

Theodore Roosevelt was certainly one of the most combative and valiant of modern Americans. Yet, in accepting the Nobel Peace Prize, he said in 1910:

> Finally, it would be a master stroke if those Great Powers honestly bent on peace would form a league of peace, not only to keep the peace among themselves, but to prevent, by force if necessary, its being broken by others. The supreme difficulty in connection with developing the peace work of The Hague arises from the lack of any executive power, of any police power to enforce the decrees of the court. In any community of any size the authority of the courts rests upon actual or potential force; on the existence of a police, or on the knowledge that the able-bodied men of the country are both ready and willing to see that the decrees of judicial and legislative bodies are put into effect. In new and wild communities where there is violence, an honest man must protect himself; and until other means of securing his safety are devised, it is both foolish and wicked to persuade him to surrender his arms while the men who are dangerous to the community retain theirs. He should not renounce the right to protect himself by his own efforts until the community is so organized that it can effectively relieve the individual of the duty of putting down violence. So it is with nations. Each nation must keep well prepared to defend itself until the establishment of some form of international police power, competent and willing to prevent violence as between nations. As things are now, such power to command peace throughout the world could best be assured by some combination between those great nations which sincerely desire peace and have no thought themselves

of committing aggressions. The combination might at first be only to secure peace within certain definite limits and certain definite conditions; but the ruler or statesman who should bring about such a combination would have earned his place in history for all time and his title to the gratitude of all mankind.

That this was not a mere rhetorical flourish by a retired President was shortly made manifest, for about a month later, by joint resolution, the Congress of the United States authorized the President to appoint a commission in relation to universal peace, its duty being to consider the expediency of utilizing existing international agencies for the purpose of limiting the armaments of the nations of the world by international agreement; and it was especially charged to consider and report upon any other means "to lessen the probabilities of war."

After the Great War had broken upon the world, the League to Enforce Peace enlisted in support of its program the highest types of Americans, men trained in the practical administration of affairs, and the idea of the League was universally acclaimed as perhaps the greatest gift of the American spirit to a world forced to admit the complete breakdown of its system of international relations. It was not a plan to deal with the existing war, but to deal with the future after that war.

Later, of course, we ourselves became involved in the conflict. But America's attitude toward war remained unchanged and is best illustrated by the fact that the two slogans which most profoundly affected the American mind in all those years were first, "He kept us out of war;" and second, "This is a war to end war." It has become the fashion nowadays to be cynical about the latter of these slogans and to say that America's participation was in fact no crusade in behalf of peace, but rather the pursuit of any one of a half-dozen sordid objectives which have come as afterthoughts of partisan rancor; but no one who lived through the days of America's participation can fail still to feel the thrill and exaltation which we had then from the belief that we were unselfish and fought both for a just and a permanent peace. And the soldiers of a country which had not denied knowledge to its citizens died on French battlefields believing that they were contributing their lives to the cause of peace. Since the end of the war, the world has been seeking with quickened zeal the means of pacific settlement. If some of these means in the future turn out to be frail reliances, America's background requires that we should exercise toward them, in their hour of trial, a great charity of judgment and that we should extend to the effort to improve them and use them a spirit of patient and sympathetic coöperation.

What, then, is the new spirit, what is its approach to the problem of pacific settlement, and what agencies has it established, experimental or otherwise, to accomplish its purpose? Perhaps it is enough to say that the new spirit is an awakened conscience, chastened by experience, informed by research, and driven by the necessity of finding a solution for the problem presented by man's most destructive enemy. The principles underlying the agencies so far established or suggested are principally four—adjudication, arbitration, conciliation, and conference.

The World Court is the embodiment of the first of these. As we have already seen, it is equipped to deal only with matured controversies, and of these, only those which lie within the field of legal rights. It can interpret and apply treaties which define, by contract, the obligations which the high contracting parties are willing to assume toward each other. To a more limited extent it can determine rights upon generally accepted principles of law, and it may be expected that, as time goes on, larger areas of jurisdiction will be conceded to it as confidence in its wisdom and disinterestedness grows. It has not been and ought not now to be given any jurisdiction over political questions. Whether it should ever be given such jurisdiction is a profitless speculation. Our own Supreme Court at the beginning moved with hesitant steps and slow, and in an early case its judgment was flouted by a State in the Union, so that its contemporary critics foresaw its early dissolution. It was in that spirit that the judgment of the World Court in the Anschluss case was assailed until John W. Davis, in a dispassionate and irresistible paper, demonstrated that the Court had acted judicially upon questions of intricacy and difficulty, and had reached a judgment about which conflict of opinion was possible but with the weight of argument strongly with the judgment of the Court. But with the years our Supreme Court has been tried in the fire of fierce contests and has acquired finality for its judgments based upon unshakable confidence in its wisdom and integrity. The controversies which our Supreme Court now decides are such as in Europe cause general mobilizations and marching armies. In the so-called Chicago Drainage Canal case, the plaintiff State, Wisconsin, and the States associated with it in interest aggregated a population of 39,000,000, while on the other side were arrayed Illinois and the States of the Mississippi Valley with an aggregate population of about 22,000,000. The issue was believed on both sides to have vital economic implications. Yet it was argued, determined, and the judgment accepted, without any emotional outburst due to wounded pride or loss of prestige. In like manner the judgments of the World Court will come to have authority in great matters. This precedent of our own Supreme Court in adjudicating controversies among 48 sovereign States makes the idea of a world court peculiarly congenial to our mode of thought, as is evidenced by the practically unanimous judgment of the American people outside of the Senate in favor of adhesion to its protocol. Even in the Senate, where the appetite for reservations and interpretations is as yet unsatisfied, the sentiment is practically unanimous for a court, even on the part of those who are critical of the one which exists.

It would be idle to set out again the extent to which the World Court as now constituted is an American institution, but it is difficult for an American lawyer to check an expression of his pride that at The Hague conference and elsewhere this great idea was exploited as an expression of American confidence in the supremacy of law and the efficacy of justice, and even more difficult for him to restrain an exclamation of grateful admiration for his countryman, Elihu Root, whose services in connection with the Court dignify the profession of which he is the leader as they nobly express the political philosophy of the people for whom he spoke.

But useful as is the function of the Court, its limitations are obvious. It must sit at the door of its tent until the controversy is brought to it. It may not anticipate controversies, and especially it may not deal with political and economic questions. And it is out of these latter that wars are likely to arise. As a part of the modern peace machinery the World Court is indispensable, but it is probable that the very nature of adjudication has retarded the acceptance of the other agencies which have been suggested for use in the field which the Court cannot cover. Conciliation and conference are more remote and less tangible in their operation.

When they succeed, they are not known to have averted tragedies, and, like the undisclosed charities of the really benevolent, they are recorded in no books except those of the Guardian Angel. Everything about our modern life makes us thirst for the dramatic. Conciliation and conference administer no knockout blows, and yet, if we are to find modes of pacific settlement, they will have to be based upon long-range wisdom which must see the cloud of controversy while it is still no larger than a man's hand. The process must afford no opportunity for diplomatic triumphs and either the gaining or losing of face.

These considerations have perhaps tended to make very practical people impatient and cause them to point out that the world always has enough real and threatening troubles to make it unnecessary to go poking about to see if there are any merely possible future troubles to be borrowed. To this is to be added a difficulty which arises from the fact that international conferences in the past have rather served the purpose of dramatically registering conclusions arrived at before the conference was held than actually reaching and adopting conclusions as the result of the conference itself. But when all of these difficulties are recognized, it must still be admitted that conference belongs in the scheme of pacific settlement. Great international conferences, with agenda prepared long in advance, serve a useful purpose even when they collapse without apparent result. The mere fact that nations are willing to meet and discuss their problems in public is a gain. They will continue to afford opportunities for the making of nationalistic speeches for home consumption and the adoption of intransigent attitudes upon questions which engage popular passion; but, even in such an atmosphere, agreements are often reached upon questions of real significance while the conferees maintain unyielding attitudes on others, and the ground is laid for future consideration, in a cleared atmosphere, of contentious and for the moment intractable differences. Nor is it to be forgotten that with each such conference the technique improves. A more patient and scholarly research, a more sympathetic comprehension of the facts in issue, a longer view of the history of the questions in controversy, and a more sobered realization of the value of agreement can be expected as the novelty of international conference wears off and the value of frank discussion becomes more apparent. We have a long way to go before we can feel that we have given conference a fair trial. It is to be hoped that we will more and more move away from the selection of personages as delegates and to an increasing degree give scholarship and character first consideration in the selection of conferees. If we can acquire the habit of appointing, not politicians with an eye on retaining or obtaining an office, but men who are willing to play for the long verdict of history, and surround them with knowledge dispassionately collected by men who work in the scientific spirit, the possibilities of conference are unlimited. If such improvements in the make-up and technique of conferences be regarded as fanciful, I can only reply that I write this paper in the deep conviction that the natural tendency of man is upward, that what is good will ultimately come to pass, and without the least impatience at not being able instantly to accomplish the best if I can but be sure that our aim is constantly toward the good.

The League of Nations is, of course, the visible and ultimate embodiment of all these principles of pacific settlement. Established in the peace treaty which ended the World War, it has always been beset by difficulties growing out of territorial and political arrangements made by other parts of the treaty in which the Covenant is contained, which it has no power *suo motu* to revise. Nations prostrated by their losses, paupered by their expenditures, and eager both for revenge for the past and security for the future wrote their triumphant passions in the treaty and then said their prayers in the Covenant. The League of Nations is neither so authoritative nor so dentate as the Roosevelt-Taft-Lodge proposal for a League to Enforce Peace. Both its nature and its machinery rely on research, consultation and conciliation; and the restraint of its deliberations and actions from the day of its organization has been in accordance with this theory of its functions. America's relationship to the League was at the outset confused by a wholly shabby, domestic, partisan controversy. As the years have gone by, however, a graver question has arisen, and while the United States no longer denies the existence of the League and does increasingly coöperate with it, we are far from having settled upon any practical basis by which a democracy like ours can so combine and delegate its power in foreign affairs, which is distributed by the Constitution between the Executive and the Senate, as to make full participation on our part helpful. Indeed, as the world comes to be more and more governed by democracies, in the sense of being ultimately controlled by popular opinion, the whole problem of foreign affairs becomes infinitely more complicated, for democracies will brook no check upon their emotions and yet, in the very nature of the case, must operate under inescapable limitations upon their information, thus making the agitation of demagogues and the appeal of super-nationalists peculiarly effective. The absence of the United States from the League has caused difficulties too well known to need recital. Without, for the moment, considering the possible use of force or even sanctions, the moral authority of the League is diminished by the absence from its composite voice of the disinterested and detached note which, in many controversies, the United States alone can strike. The League has, therefore, like the children in Maeterlinck's "Blue Bird," had certain infirmities handed to it before its birth, and to these have been added the grave misfortune of abstention by the United States, together with a third difficulty, arising out of exaggerated expectations on the one side and exaggerated fears on the other, according to the temperament of the particular critics who have watched its proceedings.

To me it has always seemed irrational to expect instant *ad hoc* solutions of age-old difficulties and to criticize the League because there is still abroad in some parts of the world the spirit of Jenghiz Khan. It has seemed to me equally irrational to criticize the League as envisioning war as the ultimate recourse. It may be possible to dispute whether the good offices of the League, to date, have prevented this or that threatened outbreak of hostility; the "ifs" and "ands" of an event which has not happened are always numerous. But it is certainly impossible to assert that any action of the League has in the slightest degree tended to cause or increase the likelihood of hostility. To a dispassionate view, the offices of the League seem to have been wholly conciliatory in the postwar agitations, and the labors of the devoted scholars and statesmen who have worked in and for the League have developed a new and sounder technique of international inquiry and promoted a broad basis of understanding and sympathy among the nations whose delegates, sitting in the Council and Assembly, have discussed international problems and policies with thoughts of understanding and peace always uppermost in their minds. Of the League as an institution we may say that Paul has planted, Apollos has watered, and all sincere lovers of their kind pray that God will give the increase.

The things which have grown out of the League, the fruit of its spirit as well as the developments of its experience, form the great body of mechanisms which now constitute the agencies for pacific settlement. The League has developed the principles underlying the Bryan Treaties of Arbitration: it promoted the Locarno Treaty and its congeners. In 1925 it created a preparatory commission to study the possibilities of world disarmament. On the basis of its work the present Disarmament Conference is still laboring, and whatever formal treaties it may or may not achieve, an immense gain has already been had from its frank discussions and disclosures. In 1928 the Assembly prepared and promulgated a series of model conventions, many of which have been adopted as bilateral arrangements, for pacific settlements by definite provision for arbitration and conciliation. Ultimately there came out of the troubled waters the healing influence of the Pact of Paris, which was opened to general accession in 1928 and has since been adhered to by practically all the nations of the world, including, *mirabile dictu,* the United States.

I suppose when Moses brought down the Tables of the Law from Mount Sinai there was an immediate division of opinion about them. The sage but weary fathers in Israel doubtless asked on the one side, "Where are the sanctions?" and on the other, "Why all these innovations? Is not the old law, which was good enough for our fathers, good enough for us?" But truth has its own sanctions and so the Pact of Paris, enunciating a great moral datum, will continue to stand, as the Tables of the Law have stood, violated by casual lawbreakers but avenged in the consequences as the moral sense of mankind unites to rebuke the transgressor. In a world which has throughout its history treated war as an instrument of policy, a moral revolution is manifest when the nations of that world unite in a declaration condemning recourse to war for the solution of international controversies, and renouncing it as an instrument of national policy in their relations with one another. A new standard of judgment is set up. This is a thing around which world opinion can gather; and in the future of the world, so far as we can foresee it, the controlling force is going to be the slow-moving but irresistible tide of public opinion.

Whether, and by what means, and how fast the Pact of Paris should be implemented, the evolutions of time alone can determine. To criticize the Pact because the right of self-defense is reserved, or because nations retained freedom of action in special areas, or because certain Senators of the United States made slighting remarks about it when they voted for it, is all beside the point. For thousands of years the right to make war has been regarded as an attribute of sovereignty and it was inconceivable that anybody should question the discretion of a sovereign in resorting to it. Under that theory, war always lay in the field of normal expectation. Under this new theory, the normal expectation is pacific settlement. The burden of proof has shifted. The irrebuttable presumption of the right of the sovereign to go to war for political objectives has been abolished and the war-maker is put upon the defensive. How important this is any soldier will testify. Big guns are important, but a defensible cause is indispensable to ultimate success in war. Some of the criticism of the Briand-Kellogg Pact, and indeed of all this pacific settlement machinery, proceeds on the theory that when the world goes mad it pays no attention to previously enacted self-denying ordinances; and it must be conceded that the world has gone mad occasionally and ruthlessly disregarded prudential checks set upon its own behavior. But I fancy the best we can do is to legislate for a sane world and, so far as we can, set up standards of conduct so that departures from the normal will be recognized and all possible restraints exerted. The whole of mankind's conventional morality has grown by that process and there would seem to be no reason why the growth of an international morality might not be similarly fostered.

Particularly since the adoption of the Briand-Kellogg Pact, there has grown up the practice of multilateral treaties dealing with special circumstances and regional situations. These treaties include provisions for consultation upon the occasion of alleged violation by one of the high contracting parties, and among the critics of modern peace machinery this provision causes special concern. The fear, apparently, is that if ten nations make a treaty and one of them appears to have violated it, if the other nine get together and consult about what ought to be done, their propensity will be to declare war at once or at least to make among themselves such commitments as may ultimately carry them into a war which they might otherwise avoid. This entirely overlooks the fact that both the purpose and spirit of such proposed consultation is to find a peaceful solution. So far as the United States is concerned, it would seem adequate to reply that the power to declare war rests with Congress and any consultation in which the United States was a party would necessarily be subject to that final safeguard. But the only alternative to consultations is not to consult, and the consequences of not consulting are either that the treaty will be violated with impunity, in which case it might as well not have been made, or the alleged violation will go unanalyzed and unredressed, breeding ill will and suspicion and war if the point of the violation is of sufficient interest to justify war by any one or more of the contracting parties which feel themselves sufficiently powerful to enforce the treaty. After all, it ought to be easy to prevent consultations from automatically becoming conspiracies, and if such consultations are conducted in the spirit of the modern devices for pacific settlement the danger from improper commitments would seem to be far less than that from a failure to consult. But consultation is not a novelty. Under the old procedure, consultation *ad hoc* was common. When war threatened, hurriedly gathered groups of ambassadors or foreign ministers got together to consult with a view to averting the outbreak. There are not wanting those who feel that if there had been some standing machinery for consultation in Europe in August 1914 the World War could have been averted. Sir Edward Grey's noble but pathetic effort to secure consultation is an excellent illustration of the point under consideration. If Russia, Austria, Germany, France and England had been under a treaty arrangement which required consultation, his fatal race against the limitations of time might not have been in vain.

But the chief flutter in the dovecote of all this criticism of arrangements for pacific settlement seems to grow out of the possible effect it may have upon the doctrine of neutrality.

When the World War broke out, President Wilson, issuing a proclamation of neutrality, called upon the American people not merely to be neutral within the restraints of legal definitions of that status, but to be neutral "in thought as well as action." This was in August 1914. In April 1917 President Wilson declared "neutrality is no longer feasible or desirable where the peace of the world is involved and the freedom of its peoples." And it must be admitted that Article 16 of the Covenant of the League of Nations, in effect, recognizes that resort to war by a member of the League in disregard of the restraints of the Covenant is an act of war against all other members of the League, to the extent at least of justifying immediate severance of all trade or financial relations between them and the aggressor and ultimate coöperative action, by force if necessary. It ought to be admitted that while the machinery for pacific settlement counts heavily—or perhaps it ought to be said, hopes fervently—for success through peaceful agencies, it does not and cannot close its eyes to the possibility of failure and the ultimate necessity of resort to force. But surely advocates of the doctrine of neutrality offer no more attractive prospect; for the rights of neutrals are, and always have been, no stronger than the power of the neutral to enforce them against the interest of a belligerent to break them. I am not here speaking of the status of perpetual neutrality accorded to certain areas of the world by the concerted action of surrounding states, like that of Switzerland, although in this connection it is wise to remember that Belgium had such a status and that Germany was a co-guarantor.

Temporary neutrality has had a long and varied history. Its periods of success have been largely those in which there were many strong nations neutral as to a particular conflict. Its periods of failure have been those when the dominant nations of the world were at war and their interest led them to disregard so-called neutral rights. Grotius considered the subject in the third book of his treatise "On the Law of War and Peace" and suggested that neutrals should form an opinion upon the justice or injustice of the hostility and then do nothing which would further the cause of the one in the wrong or hamper the movements of the one in the right. Vattel dissented from this view, holding that the neutral should not constitute himself a judge but that his greater safety lay in equal treatment of the belligerents. Modern statesmen and international lawyers have sought to build around the idea of neutrality a system of principles, with a view of restricting the extent of the conflict by defining the limits of conduct permissible to a neutral state and its nationals.

In its essence neutrality is a sort of indifferentism based on the theory that one is not obliged to imperil one's interests by espousing the cause of another, however innocent the victim or vicious his assailant. It has always been conceded that the doctrine of neutrality does not prevent a state from going to war when it has a sufficient interest to justify its intervention. It would seem, therefore, that the doctrine is really a system of rules of conduct for a state which has no interest justifying intervention and hopes to have, either alone or in concert with other states like-minded, the power to stay out of the conflict. Undoubtedly the doctrine has been highly useful to small states with warlike neighbors, but its dignity as a principle has often been marred by the fact that it has been used as a counter in bargains made in anticipation of aggression. A single example will suffice. Germany's neutrality in the Russo-Japanese War was the equivalent of an alliance. It protected Russia on her western frontier and at Constantinople and thus freed her to exert her entire power in Manchuria. A somewhat different case was presented when Germany in 1875 and 1887 contemplated fresh aggressions upon France to retard her recovery from the Franco-Prussian War. Bismarck inquired whether England would be neutral, and being unable to secure a promise of neutrality refrained from a fresh war upon France. In this aspect, neutrality is in effect intervention. The assumption of British neutrality in 1914 was Bethmann-Hollweg's fatal mistake. On the basis of its history, therefore, the doctrine of neutrality can hardly claim to be an adequate safeguard, or indeed to be a basis which, however extended and developed, will sustain peace even to the peaceful.

The World War experience with the doctrine of neutrality was disastrous. Not only were solemn obligations to respect neutrality disregarded, but a world situation was created in which neutrality was impossible. How can an integrated world, in which finance and commerce are thoroughly internationalized, be neutral when the high seas are marked out into lanes of permitted but limited travel and the list of contraband is extended beyond all the categories of arms and munitions so as to include, not the subsistence of armies alone, but the raw materials and manufactured products which sustain civilian life? If the doctrine of neutrality ever had a friend, it was President Wilson. He hoped with passionate fervor that the United States might remain neutral. He prayed that the United States might "speak the counsels of peace and accommodation not as a partisan but as a friend," and he struggled with all the belligerent governments to protect some vestige of America's right as a neutral, to remain at peace and store up a great reservoir of good will with which to bind up the wounds of the belligerents and make possible the restoration of peace and ultimate understanding among them. There were times when it was thought that we might be forced into the war to defend the definition of neutral goods. By 1917 he had come to realize that under the conditions of modern war neutrality had become impossible and, in the presence of so devastating a spectacle, that it was undesirable. After all, there is no reflection upon the soldier who lives up to the exact letter of the bond of his military obligation; but Congressional Medals of Honor are awarded for heroism above and beyond the call of duty. The law of neutrality and the rights of neutrals are brands plucked from the burning. They ought to be preserved, made more definite and certain, and every effort made to secure for them wider usefulness and more general acceptance. But there are situations, and the world has just faced one of them, where neutrality is not enough and where the thing needed is the sword of righteousness and not the mere security of a bomb-proof while our common civilization is being destroyed.

This was, to be sure, a special case, and no general way

of defining aggression or determining the aggressor can be easily formulated. Even if we had a formula, the facts can rarely be gathered, in the midst of conflict, with final completeness. Don Quixote's procedures are not to be recommended for international action. But can we abandon the problem because it is difficult? There are both moral responsibilities and practical difficulties about being indifferent to the distinction between right and wrong. To insist on the right to sell pistols both to the highwaymen and to the occupants of the stagecoach is bad morals and, when we have occasion to use the stagecoach, may prove inconvenient if not fatal. But if this be a dilemma it is a very old one, and one which, for all practical purposes, has long been solved in all domestic matters. We let the community decide. We have determined that the chances of a wrong decision are immeasurably less serious than either not having it decided at all or letting each man decide for himself. The analogy is persuasive. The nations of the world are coming more and more to be a family or a community of nations, and the new mechanisms seek its judgments. The neutrality which merely refuses to decide has a hard case to make against an international consciousness which coöperates to decide and so to prevent the conflict. Even if a war, prevented by joint international action, would have been "a good war" the loss is not irreparable. The result may still be worked out by some other means, or the war started later, with a better chance for the side now known to be in the right.

Within its limited sphere neutrality is a useful doctrine, but its defense does not require an attack upon measures conceived in a bolder spirit and designed to avert catastrophes of a kind where neutrality is, as we have seen, impossible or undesirable. Indeed, we should remember that neutrality does not even aim to prevent war. Its more modest and local object is to restrain its extension.

The world is cursed by its common fears. It is made better by its great faiths. The new spirit is the evidence of such a fighting faith. The agencies it has so far devised have in them the seeds of growth. Lawyers with their doubts and statesmen with their policies may encumber this spirit and delay its achievements. Its progress by trial and error may be slow and its course may sometimes seem to be inviting new perils. Some of the steps it eagerly takes may have to be retraced and fresh starts made, but if this is ever to be a world in which nations, like civilized men, are governed by moral restraints, and from which licensed war for the private objectives of ambitious states will disappear, it must be fought for in this spirit. Those who share this faith and work in this hope have no apology to make to their own or future generations.

❖ ❖ ❖

WITH this article by Karl Radek, "The Bases of Soviet Foreign Policy," and the companion piece by Nicolai Bukharin which follows it, the reader is plunged into the nightmare world of the immeasurable self-dedication, infinite capacity for double-dealing, grandiose visions of the betterment of mankind and total contempt for human life which make up the Soviet Russian version of the ancient resolve of exceptional men to impose their particular creed upon their fellows, by force.

It is a world in which purposes are sometimes ruthlessly disclosed, yet in which little can be taken to be what it seems. Radek, who here set forth so confidently the main outlines of Soviet foreign policy, was one of the original group of Bolsheviks who created the Soviet state under Lenin's leadership. After Lenin's death, he fell under suspicion as a member of the Trotskyist opposition, and Stalin deposed him as Editor of *Pravda.* At the time he wrote this article (January 1934) he had apparently weathered that crisis. He was then Editor of *Izvestia.* But three years later, he was broken again, and sentenced to ten years' imprisonment in the purge of that year. His present whereabouts, if indeed he is alive, are unknown.

This second liquidation of oppositionists also embraced those who stood for a slower pace of industrialization and collectivization. Estimates of executions and deportations of peasants in the collectivization campaign vary from one to several million. How many of the 3,000,000 to 7,000,000 deaths from starvation in the early thirties resulted from the program of collectivization no one can say. The extent of the purge can likewise be expressed only in general terms: thousands were executed and hundreds of thousands were exiled. The dominant clique considered these as essential measures in preparation for the inevitable war with capitalist imperialism—of which the Nazi or Japanese dictatorships or the western democracies were, with little Marxist differentiation, the representatives.

Lenin had written that to have dealings with one of these enemies, if that would help in settling with another, was not to be condemned as "dishonest, shameful, unclean." The phrasing of the statement, and Radek's gloss upon it, epitomize the history of the inter-war years. When one imperialist enemy was repulsed, the Communist state would turn to confront the next. No wonder these men of powerful imagination cry "peace," when by their doctrine there can be no peace.

❖ ❖ ❖

THE BASES OF SOVIET FOREIGN POLICY

By Karl Radek

I AM fully aware of the difficulties of the task which I undertake in attempting to give the readers of FOREIGN AFFAIRS an account of the main lines of Soviet foreign policy and the fundamental considerations which govern it. The first difficulty arises from the fact that the foreign policy of the Soviet Government differs as much from the foreign policy of the other Great Powers as the domestic policy of this first Socialist state differs from the domestic policy of the states belonging to the capitalist system. Men and women who accept the capitalist point of view find it just as hard to understand the Socialist state's foreign policy as its domestic policy. Moreover, this primary difficulty is increased by several propositions generally accepted in the capitalist world, although even there they are of questionable validity. I mean the theory of the priority of foreign over domestic policy and the theory of the continuity of foreign policy. In order to clear the way for an understanding of the foreign policy of the Soviet Union the reader must attempt to grasp our attitude toward these two propositions. We consider them erroneous because they are in contradiction with generally-known historical facts.

Foreign policy is a function of domestic policy. It solves problems which result from the development of a given society, a given state, under definite historical conditions.

The wars of the era when modern capitalism was born, the wars of Cromwell and Louis XIV, were the product of the struggle for the emancipation of the youthful capitalism, which gained strength under the mercantilist system, from the oppression of the domestic market, largely based on a peasant economy which met the requirements of the peasant and of his feudal exploiter. There was a need for colonies as sources of raw materials and as markets for the produce of young industries, and also for the plundering which provided the stimulus for the growth of manufactures, which became in turn the basis for the eventual development of machine industry. Industrial capitalism relegates the struggle for colonies to the background because industrial capitalism itself creates an immense domestic market as well as immense means of accumulation and has in cheap mass production a magnificent weapon for mobilizing raw materials from the colonies.

The wars of the industrial era served either as a means for breaking through the Chinese wall which separates the backward nations from the capitalist world (the Anglo-Chinese war, the Anglo-American threats to Japan), or as a way for achieving national unity, which means creating a large domestic market for infant industries (the unification of Germany, Italy, the United States).

Under monopolistic capitalism the mad struggle for colonies was again accentuated. In the war of 1914–1918 the attempt was made to re-distribute the world's surface in accordance with the strength of the imperialistic Powers which took part in the struggle. The difference between the aims and methods of the imperialistic policy of the twentieth century and those of the foreign policy of the mercantilist era is made clear, despite their superficial similarity, by the consequences of that imperialistic policy. Whereas during the period of manufactures England did everything in her power to prevent the development of industry in the colonies, the policy of modern imperialism is a policy of exporting capital, that is, a policy of exporting the means of production. This policy, regardless of the intentions of its originators, leads to a certain degree of industrialization in the colonies—although the survivals of feudalism and the exploitation of the colonial countries hinder the process of industrialization and prevent emancipation. The revolutionary movement in the colonies, centering as it does around the young proletariat, shows how different are the policies of mercantilism and imperialism. The fate of India, the fate of China, furnish the proofs.

Where, in this process, is the priority of foreign policy and where is its continuity? Its aims are seen to be shaped by the economic and political structure of changing forms of society. Therefore they are not permanent but on the contrary variable.

The attempt to represent the foreign policy of the Soviet Union as a continuation of Tsarist policy is ridiculous. Bourgeois writers who do so have not grasped even the purely external manifestations of this policy. It used to be an axiom of Tsarist policy that it should strive by every available means to gain possession of the Dardanelles and of an ice-free port on the Pacific. Not only have the Soviets not attempted to seize the Dardanelles, but from the very beginning they have tried to establish the most friendly relations with Turkey; nor has Soviet policy ever had as one of its aims the conquest of Port Arthur or of Dairen. Again, Tsarism, or any other bourgeois régime in Russia, would necessarily resume the struggle for the conquest of Poland and of the Baltic States, as is doubtless clear to any thoughtful bourgeois politician in those countries. The Soviet Union, on the contrary, is most anxious to establish friendly relations with these countries, considering their achievement of independence a positive and progressive historical factor.

It is silly to say that geography plays the part of fate, that it determines the foreign policy of a state. Tsarist policy originated not in geographical conditions, but in the privileges of the Russian nobility and the demands of young Russian capitalism. The questions raised by geography are dealt with by each social formation in its own way; that way is determined by its peculiar economic and political aims.

II

We are thus led to the first fundamental question: What are the aims which may and must be pursued by a society which is building up Socialism and which is based on Socialism?

I shall not attempt to give here a historical survey of the foreign policy of the Soviet Union. Suffice it to recall that when the Soviet Government came to power it set out promptly to rescue the country from the conflagration of the World War, and that having achieved this purpose at a heavy price it was forced for about three years to defend its independence against the intervention of the leading imperialistic nations, an intervention due partly to the desire of these to drag the Soviets back into the World War and partly to their desire to destroy the first government of the workers, which the capitalist world looked upon as a gross provocation to the capitalist system. This fact compelled the Soviet Union to give a preliminary solution to the problem of defense which had been forced upon it by the aggressive tendencies of the capitalist nations. But even in this early period Soviet foreign policy displayed clearly its fundamental lines, which are fully in harmony with the foreign policy of the Socialist system.

The main object for which Soviet diplomacy is fighting is *peace*. Now this term "peace" is much abused. There is no diplomat whose official pronouncements do not use this term reverently over and over again, even though he is a representative of one of those imperialistic nations which are most active in preparing war. But those who are incapable of understanding the specific place occupied by the struggle for peace in Soviet foreign policy are altogether incapable of understanding that policy in whole or in part. Why is the struggle for peace the central object of Soviet policy? Primarily because the Soviet Union—to use the expression of Lenin—"has everything necessary for the building up of a Socialist society."

As early as 1915 and 1916 Lenin, then preparing the struggle for the seizure of political power, maintained that it was possible to build up Socialism in Russia. He saw the country's vast size, its immense natural resources, and that it possessed a degree of industrial development which would insure, on the one hand, the leadership of the working class and, on the other, provide the required minimum of technical knowledge which was necessary for starting Socialist construction.

In Lenin's lifetime the Soviet state, having victoriously ended the war against intervention, took up the work of reconstruction, rebuilding the industry that had been destroyed and establishing normal relations with the peasantry. These normal relations assured the proletariat the supply of raw materials and foodstuffs necessary for the expansion of industry, as well as the support of the peasant masses. Lenin's successor at the helm of the Soviet ship of state, Stalin, deciding the course of this ship, set as its object the building up of Socialism within the borders of the former Empire of the Tsars. This object seemed utopian, not only to the capitalist world, but also to a group inside the Communist Party which followed Trotsky and rejected the fundamentals of Lenin's policy.

In this inner party struggle the policy of Stalin was victor; and his victory found its realization in the Five Year Plan. This plan has already been put into practice. Its achievement consists in the creation of an industry on such a large scale as to provide the solution of three problems. In the first place, it allows the Soviet Union to proceed independently with the further development of its industry, that is to say, in case of necessity, without importations from abroad, because under the Five Year Plan the Soviet Union has acquired a powerful heavy industry and machine-building equipment of all sorts.

Thanks to the solution of this first problem, the working class can now—and this is the solution of the second problem—provide the peasantry with a number of machines sufficient to prove to even the most backward groups of peasants the advantage of collectivization. On the basis of collectivization it became possible to liquidate those classes of the peasants which were pushing agriculture in the direction of capitalism. The economic annihilation of the kulaks and the creation of an agriculture which has for its chief driving power the products of large-scale machine industry—tractors, reapers and other agricultural machines—owned by the workers' state, has created a situation in which the peasantry can and must develop in the direction of Socialism. The peasant today is still in an intermediate stage between the position of a small owner and that of a member of a society carrying on a collective enterprise with the help of means of production owned by the society. But it is already perfectly clear that as a result of the advantages of tractors, electricity and oil over horses, ploughs and scythes, the well-being of the peasantry will depend in increasing degree on the productive forces of the Socialist society and not on labor arising from privately-owned means of production. Within the peasant ranks, too, differentiations in productive and economic standards will be abolished, and the peasantry will gradually be transformed into a uniform Socialist mass. The economic lot of the peasants will continue to improve and year by year they will grow closer to the proletariat. This result is guaranteed not only by the increasing industrialization of the countryside, but also by the fact that industrialization is a means for raising the cultural level of the village to that of the urban proletariat. The solution of this second problem—the collectivization of farming—in conjunction with the solution of the first problem—industrialization—makes possible the accomplishment of the third object of the Five Year Plan, namely the creation of conditions which assure the national defense of the Soviet state.

This capacity for national defense is based on the creation of a heavy industry which provides the country with all the means of defense essential to success in modern war, and on the disappearance of all social classes hostile to the up-building of Socialism. These classes have been defeated, even though remnants still survive and even though the psychology of the small owner, inimical to Socialism, cannot disappear in all groups of the population at once. But if we ask the question, what is the general trend of development, it is clear that the fulfillment of the Five Year Plan and the development of the program of reconstruction in the Second Five Year Plan have proved that the Soviet Union, having laid down the foundations of Socialism, is capable of proceeding to build up the complete structure of Socialism, the integral Socialist society, that is, a classless society which bases itself on all the discoveries of modern technique and that assures to the masses of the population social and cultural conditions of a type which capitalism cannot possibly achieve.

Does the Soviet Union need war in order to build up Socialism? It does not. Certain capitalist circles have stubbornly asserted since the Soviet Union was founded that it would seek a solution of its difficulties in war; these assertions are repudiated by the history of the Soviet Union during its sixteen years of life. Even at the moment when we were particularly ill-equipped to undertake the building-up of Socialism, immediately after we had assumed governmental responsibilities, we readily accepted the heaviest sacrifices in order to give peace to the country. We deeply believed—and this was of great importance—that we had in our hands everything necessary for building up a Socialist society. Now we know that the problem of building Socialism in the Soviet Union admits of a practical solution and that a considerable part of the problem has been already solved. The peace policy of the Soviet Union therefore rests on the granite foundation of triumphant Socialist construction.

The enemies of the Soviet Union attempt to undermine the importance of this fact from two directions. Some of them accuse the Soviet Union of having given up its international aims. These aims, in their opinion, would demand military intervention by the Soviet Union to aid the emancipation of the international proletariat and of the colonial peoples. Others, on the contrary, maintain that, because the Bolshevik Party which controls the Soviet Union is inherently an international party, all the peace declarations of the Soviet Union are purely provisional and hence that having reached a certain economic level which enables it to wage an aggressive war the Soviet Union will repudiate its peace declarations and assume the initiative in a war. The best way of answering both these accusations is to quote the statement made by Stalin in December 1926:

This is what Lenin actually said: "From ten to twenty years of sound relations with the peasantry, and victory on the world scale is assured (even despite delays in the growing proletarian revolutions); otherwise from twenty to forty years of sufferings under the White terror." ("Leninski Sbornik," Vol. IV, p. 374.)

Does this proposition of Lenin give ground for the conclusion that "we are utterly incapable of building up Socialism in twenty or thirty years?" No, it does not. From this proposition we can derive the following conclusions: (a) provided we have established sound relations with the peasantry, victory is assured to us (that is, the victory of Socialism) within ten or twenty years; (b) this victory will be a victory not only within the U. S. S. R., but a victory on the world scale; (c) if we fail to gain victory within this period this will mean that we have been defeated, and that the régime of the dictatorship of the proletariat has given place to the régime of the White terror, which may last twenty to forty years.

And what is meant by "victory on the world scale?" Does it mean that such a victory is equivalent to the victory of Socialism in a single country? No, it does not. Lenin in his writings carefully distinguished the victory of Socialism in a single country from victory "on the world scale." What Lenin really means when he speaks of "victory on the world scale" is that *the success of Socialism in our country, the victory of consolidating Socialism in our country, has such an immense international significance that it (the victory) cannot be limited to our country alone but is bound to call forth a powerful movement toward Socialism in all capitalist countries,* and even if it does not coincide with the victory of the proletarian revolution in other countries, it must in any event lead to a strong proletarian movement of other nations toward the victory of world revolution. Such is the revolutionary outlook according to Lenin, if we think in terms of the outlook for the victory of the revolution, which after all is the question in which we in the Party are interested.[1]

Such are the fundamentals of the Soviet peace policy.

III

The Socialist society which is being built up in the Soviet Union has foundations already well established and its completion assured. It does not need war. This fact found ex-

[1] J. Stalin: "Ob oppozitsii" ("On the Opposition"), articles and speeches, 1921–1927, State Publishing House, 1928, p. 465-466.

pression in the Soviet proposal for a general disarmament by all the capitalistic Powers, first advanced at the Genoa Conference while Lenin was still alive. It has subsequently been the axis of the peace policy of the Soviet Union at the Disarmament Conference. This Conference required years of preparation and already has been engaged on its sterile deliberations for two years. Its fate magnificently proves the truth of Lenin's thesis that "under capitalism, and especially in its imperialistic phase, war is inevitable."

Immediately after the capitalist world recovered from the postwar commotion and achieved provisional economic stabilization, a new wave of armaments came into being. All nations began developing feverishly those methods of warfare which the war had proved important, such as aviation, chemical warfare and tanks. The mechanization of armies and the modernization of fleets have been taking place universally. The attempt to keep these armaments at least within certain limits is frustrated by the action of the law which Lenin formulated as follows in his work "Imperialism as the Highest Stage of Capitalism:"

> Financial capital and the trusts do not diminish but emphasize the difference in the tempo of growth between various parts of the world economy. But if the balance of forces has been broken, what can be used under a capitalistic system to bring about a settlement of the conflict except violence? [2]

And again:

> Under capitalism no other basis is thinkable for the division of spheres of influence, interests, colonies, etc., except an estimate of the strength of the parties to the division, their general economic strength, their financial and military strength, and so on. But the strength of the parties to division changes unevenly, because an even development of separate enterprises, trusts, branches of industries, countries, is impossible under capitalism. Half a century ago Germany was a mere nonentity, if we compare her capitalistic strength with that of contemporary England; the same was true of Japan in comparison with Russia. Is it "thinkable" that one or two decades hence the relation-

[2] Lenin: "Sobranie sochineni," Vol. XIX, p. 149.

ship between the imperialistic Powers should remain unaltered? Utterly unthinkable.

Under conditions actually prevailing in the capitalist world, therefore, the "inter-imperialistic" or "ultra-imperialistic" alliances—irrespective of the form these alliances might take, whether that of one imperialistic coalition against another imperialistic coalition, or that of a general alliance of all the imperialistic Powers—will necessarily be merely "breathing spaces" between wars.[3]

The opinions expressed by Lenin in 1916, in the midst of the World War, have been fully corroborated by postwar history. They explain why the capitalist world is incapable of obtaining any effective limitation in armaments and is therefore inescapably moving toward a new world war for a new redistribution of the world.

Germany, having strengthened her industry with the help of American, English, Dutch and Swiss loans, and confronted with a shrinkage of the world market, cannot exist within the narrow limits assigned to her by the Treaty of Versailles. In seeking equality in armaments she is seeking the possibility for preparing a war for the revision of the Versailles peace.

Japan, who developed her industry first on the basis of an inhuman semi-feudal exploitation of the village population (which still continues), later with the help of billions of war profits, and who is half-strangled in the knot of surviving feudalism which, in an even stronger degree than the laws of imperialism, prevents the development of her domestic market—Japan, who understands that the United States is compelled by the entire course of its economic development to deepen and expand its struggle for economic influence in China—Japan, fearful that as a consequence of the industrialization of Siberia she will lose her monopolistic position as the only industrial country in the Far East—Japan tears up the Washington and the London agreements, occupies Manchuria, and gets ready to occupy China before the economic domination of the United States has been fully established there. She raises the question of her hegemony over

[3] *Op. cit.*, Vol. XIX, p. 167-168.

Asia. This objective has been openly proclaimed by Japan's Minister of War, General Araki.

Italy, "offended at Versailles," seeks a redistribution of colonial lands in her favor.

The relations between the United States and England have suffered a fundamental change since the United States has risen to the position of being the first industrial Power in the world and has claimed equality in the control of the seas.

The uneven development of postwar capitalism has created a situation in which all the imperialistic Powers will seek to redistribute the world in accordance with their own interests.

The Soviet Union is opposed to imperialism. It is opposed to an imperialistic war. It recognizes as equitable only one war, the war for the defense of Socialism, the war of the enslaved peoples for their liberation. This point of view determines our attitude toward imperialism, as a system, and toward the consequences of its policy which find their expression in the preparation of a new war. It also dictates our attitude toward imperialistic alliances which evolve during the process of preparing a new war for the redistribution of the world.

The Soviet Union takes no part in the struggle for the redistribution of the world.

The words of Stalin at the Sixteenth Congress of the Communist Party of the Soviet Union—"We do not want a single bit of foreign land; but at the same time not an inch of our land shall ever be yielded to anyone else"—these words are the exact expression of the policy of the Soviet Union.

In the struggle for the new redistribution of the world the Soviet Union does not share. Taking account of the solidarity of the workers of the whole world, it can take no part in the plundering of foreign lands. Moreover, it does not need foreign land to carry on the work of constructing Socialism. This policy found expression in the Soviet attitude toward the struggle in Manchuria. Defending its economic interests in connection with the Chinese Eastern Railroad, the Soviet Union never accepted the partition of Manchuria into spheres of influence. It followed a similar policy in Persia, even though this rendered its relations with British imperialism somewhat more difficult. Non-participation in imperialistic alliances having for their purpose the plundering of foreign lands is the second leading principle of the foreign policy of the Soviet Union.

But the preparation of an imperialistic war is a fact, the existence of imperialistic alliances is a fact, and the Soviet Union can not limit itself to a mere expression of its negative attitude toward the objects of imperialism and toward imperialistic alliances. The Soviet Union must do everything to protect itself against the attack of the capitalist Powers who intend to conquer a portion of the Soviet territory or to overthrow the political framework of the Socialist state.

The peace policy of the Soviet manifests itself not only in the struggle for disarmament, the struggle for the maximum reduction in armaments, but also in nonaggression pacts. In any given concrete case such a pact means a guarantee of Soviet neutrality in conflicts which may arise among the capitalist nations, conceded in exchange for the undertaking by the latter to refrain from attacking the Soviet Union or intervening in its domestic affairs. There is nothing surprising, therefore, in the fact that the first nonaggression pact concluded by the Soviet Union was with Turkey, for friendly relations between the two countries had developed from the early help offered by the Soviet Union to Turkey in her struggle for independence. Nor is it surprising that the next state with which the Soviet Union entered into a pact equivalent to a nonaggression pact was Germany (April 24, 1926). In its fight against the Treaty of Versailles, Germany tried to establish friendly relations with the Soviet Union as the only Great Power which opposed the enslavement of one nation by another. The nonaggression pacts with Afghanistan, in 1926, and with Persia, in 1929, were results of the policy of the Soviet Union which bases its relations with the eastern peoples on the idea of equality and respect for their national independence.

It is not mere chance that for many years all attempts to conclude similar nonaggression pacts with the western neighbors of the Soviet Union remained fruitless. Those western neighbors for a long time participated openly or indirectly in the alignment of the victorious imperialistic Powers which had not given up the idea of intervention against the Soviets. Only experience—the experience which proved to these western neighbors of the Soviet Union that this policy not only does not protect their independence but might even weaken their position at the same time that they have to face the growing demand for the restoration of German imperialism—it was this experience only which developed their tendency toward peace with the Soviet Union and led to the conclusion of the nonaggression pacts between the Soviet Union, Poland, Latvia, Estonia and Finland. A similar change in the general situation on the Continent, Germany's growing desire to revise the conditions imposed upon her by the Treaty of Versailles—peacefully if possible, forcibly if necessary—proved to be one of the factors which induced France to enter into a nonaggression pact with the Soviet Union. Italy had been among the first to resume normal relations with the Soviet Union. It was her desire to strengthen her position with reference to France which influenced her to join the Soviet Union not only in a nonaggression pact but also in a pact of friendship. Soviet attempts to conclude a similar pact with Japan have up to the present time produced no positive results; this seems merely to indicate the existence in Japan of very strong tendencies to preserve complete freedom of action in case of conflict with the Soviet Union.

The Soviet Union is confronted both in Europe and the Far East with hostile camps which are preparing war against one another. It holds toward them a position of neutrality, and endeavors to guarantee its own peace by a policy of noninterference in their affairs and by entering into mutual obligations of nonaggression with all sides. These obligations have been stated concretely and precisely in the pact containing the definition of the aggressor. The Soviet Government has definitely undertaken not to move its armed forces by land, sea or air across the frontiers of states which have assumed similar obligations, and also not to intervene directly or indirectly in their domestic affairs. All this indicates to the world that the policy of peace and neutrality on which the Soviet Union has embarked is not a mere diplomatic gesture, but a concrete political obligation the earnestness of which should be beyond question.

The Soviet Union enters into pacts of nonaggression with any country which is willing to sign such a pact, that is to say it is ready to enter into nonaggression pacts with countries which may eventually be at war. It therefore must take into consideration that while its pledge of peace and neutrality strengthens one of the belligerent countries it may be disadvantageous to the other side, which in consequence may attempt to repudiate its nonaggression pact, violate its obligations, and attack the Soviet Union. Besides, of course, any action is possible on the part of the Powers which have refused to sign nonaggression pacts. It goes without saying that the Soviet Union's reply to any attack on it would be military action fully commensurate with the statement of Stalin that "not an inch of our land shall ever be yielded to anyone else." But then a situation might arise when the Soviet Union would carry on action parallel with the enemy of its own enemy, or would even coöperate with him in a joint action. The policy to follow in such an eventuality was foreseen by Lenin during the discussion of the Brest-Litovsk peace negotiations. Under quite different conditions, for then the Soviet Union was weak militarily, Lenin outlined the fundamental solution of the problem. This solution remains today one of the guiding principles of Soviet policy. "From the moment of the victory of Socialist construction in one of the countries, the question must be settled not from the point of view of the desirability of this or that imperialism, but exclusively from the point of view of the best conditions for the development and strengthening of Socialist revolution, which has already begun," wrote Lenin in his theses on the conclusion of a separate peace, on January 7, 1918.[4]

[4] *Op. cit.*, Vol. XXII, p. 195.

In his article "O chesotke" ("About the Rash"), of February 22 of the same year, Lenin, criticizing those who objected as a matter of principle to the conclusion of an agreement with the Allies against German imperialism, wrote as follows:

> If Kerensky, representative of the dominating class of the bourgeoisie, that is of the exploiters, enters into an agreement with the Anglo-French exploiters under which he obtains arms and potatoes, but conceals from the people other agreements which promise (in case of success) to one robber Armenia, Galicia, Constantinople, to the other Baghdad, Syria, and so on—then is it difficult to understand that the transaction is a dishonest, disgusting and revolting one from the point of view of both Kerensky and his friends? No. It is not difficult to understand. Any peasant will understand it, even the most backward and illiterate one.
>
> But what if the representative of the exploited class, of those who suffer, after that class has overthrown the exploiters and has published and annulled all secret and grasping agreements, is the object of a treacherous attack by the German imperialists? Is he to be condemned for dealing with the Anglo-French robbers, for accepting their arms and potatoes in exchange for timber and so on? Should such an agreement be called dishonest, shameful, unclean? [5]

By giving a positive answer to the question of the feasibility of an agreement between the Soviet Union and an imperialistic Power which, for the sake of its own imperialistic interests, was willing to help the Soviet Union in its struggle against other attacking imperialistic Powers, Lenin at the same time answered the question as to the possible expansion of the policy of the Soviet Union beyond the stage of neutrality in case of a struggle between the imperialistic Powers.

The Soviet Union does not close the door to the possibility of a deal, an agreement, with imperialistic Powers which are waging a struggle against other imperialistic Powers, if the latter attack the Soviet Union; but in entering into such an agreement the Soviet Union would not accept any responsibility for the specific purposes pursued by

[5] *Op. cit.*, Vol. XXII, p. 273.

the imperialistic Powers parties to the agreement. Never and under no conditions would it participate in the plundering of other nations, because participation in such a plunder would be contrary to the international solidarity of the workers. But against attacking imperialism an agreement is permissible with any opponent in order to defeat an enemy invading Soviet territory.

I think I have named the fundamental principles of Soviet foreign policy and have explained their interdependence. They are all derived from the basic fact that imperialism is unable to solve the great problems which mankind has to face today. A new imperialistic war will not solve them. It will lead to an immense destruction of productive forces, to unexampled sufferings among the masses of the people, and will achieve nothing except a new reshuffling of the possessions of the capitalist world.

The Soviet Union is an enemy of imperialistic wars which arise from the fact that capitalism is no longer in a position to develop the productive forces of the human race, but that it is still capable of attempting to seize a piece of land which is being reserved for the exploitation of a given national bourgeoisie. That is how the world is pushed toward immense new upheavals. We are therefore certain that the masses, thrust into the turmoil of new wars, will seek a way out along the same road that was followed by the Soviet proletariat in 1917.

The object of the Soviet Government is to save the soil of the first proletariat state from the criminal folly of a new war. To this end the Soviet Union has struggled with the greatest determination and consistency for sixteen years. The defense of peace and of the neutrality of the Soviet Union against all attempts to drag it into the whirlwind of a world war is the central problem of Soviet foreign policy.

The Soviet Union follows the policy of peace because peace is the best condition for building up a Socialist society. Fighting for the maintenance of peace, accepting obligations of neutrality toward the struggling camps of the imperialists, the Soviet Union has at the same time raised the military preparedness of the country to a level which answers the demands of national defense and the requirements of modern warfare. Its neutrality is a positive factor which the imperialistic Powers which have not yet lost the sense of realities will not fail to appreciate. Those of them which are unable to realize the importance of Soviet neutrality or are forced by the insoluble difficulties of their own position to risk an adventurous war against that huge country, with its dozens of millions of men united by a common desire for peace, a desire for peaceful creative work—to those Powers will be given the proofs that the generation which laid down the foundations of Socialism is also capable of defending them with iron energy. And we are convinced that, irrespective of what might be the course of the war and who might be responsible for its origins, the only victor that would emerge from it would be the Soviet Union leading the workers of the whole world; for it alone has a banner which, in case of a war, can become the banner of the masses of the entire world.

❖ ❖ ❖

NICOLAI BUKHARIN was one of the great theoreticians of Marxism, the author of "The A. B. C. of Communism" and "Historical Materialism," chief of the editorial board of *Izvestia,* one of Lenin's early colleagues in the Bolshevik movement and a member of the Politburo from 1918 to 1929. In this article, "Imperialism and Communism," published in July 1936, the Communist creed that war is simply a form of capitalist competition was given classic presentation. He was executed in March 1938.

Along with his command of Marxist theory, Bukharin—like most old Bolsheviks a European as well as a Russian—was a master of the art of pamphleteering. But though Soviet publicists no longer quote French and Latin, and the present fashion of vituperation is less beguiling than Bukharin's witty dogmatism, the major propositions of the argument nonetheless have a strikingly contemporary sound. Only the social and economic system of capitalism (of which the Fascist countries are exemplars) can be "imperialist." Tsarist imperialism was merely a product of Tsarist capitalism. The U.S.S.R. can by definition have no expansionist desires—in regard to the Baltic states or Turkey, for instance. If, however, these (or any) states became proletarian states, then they will logically join with the Russian proletarian state. Finally, in a "unified Communist society," the state will disappear and there will be peace. There is no possibility that Communism can be expansive and aggressive; but there is likewise no possible doubt that it can fail to embrace the world.

The contradictions of Communism seem not to have ended with the public confession of error which Bukharin made before he was shot. But westerners can hardly congratulate themselves upon their own perspicuity at that time. It was the era of appeasement of Germany. In 1935, Hitler had openly included in the Reichswehr the secret aviation force which the Versailles Treaty had forbidden. Great Britain's reply was the signing (without consultation with France) of the Anglo-German Naval Treaty of June 1935 which legitimized the construction of a German navy. The attempts to apply League sanctions against Italian aggression in Ethiopia, in 1935 and 1936, were a total fiasco, sabotaged in the last instance by Laval. In the offing were Hitler's occupation of the Rhineland, the policy of "nonbelligerency" toward the Fascist conquest of Spain, and the capitulation at Munich.

❖ ❖ ❖

IMPERIALISM AND COMMUNISM

By N. Bukharin

IT IS well known that people have sometimes talked prose without having the least idea what it is. This holds true not only of characters in French literature but also of professional politicians. Thus at the present time a regular epidemic of discussion is raging in certain sections of the capitalist press in the effort to find explanations for the acts of aggression which again threaten to rack the world with war. And they are being discovered in natural factors—territory, raw materials, growth of population. These are considered quite apart from the economic form of society and the political superstructure in which it finds expression. In this parlance, Germany, Italy, Japan are "nations without land." The natural growth of the population of these states necessarily leads to a hunt for new land and more raw materials. Here, according to this view, lie the roots of the future war. It is fate, historical destiny. And the only salvation lies in a redivision of territory.

A plan of this sort was proposed by the late Frank H. Simonds in an article entitled "The 'Haves' and 'Have-Nots' " in *The Fortnightly*.[1] *The Economist*[2] published detailed tables showing the distribution of land and raw materials among the various countries in order to prove Great Britain's right to the *status quo*. In France, the Fascist proponents of a rapprochement with Germany at the expense of Soviet Ukraine are highly indignant over the vast territories of the Soviet Union and the comparative sparseness of its population. In Germany itself, imperialism is frankly proclaimed as the sacred right of "Aryans" suffocating for lack of "space" (*"Volk ohne Raum"*). Needless to say, the re-

[1] London, June 1935.

[2] London, October 26, 1935.

quired "space" is sought in the Soviet Union, the government of which is, moreover, accused of continuing the foreign policy of the Tsars. In Italy and Japan analogous theories have become the creed of the ruling classes, which preach them *ex professo*. The basis of all these arguments—though most of their authors are unaware of the fact—is the so-called theory of "Geopolitik," now particularly fashionable in Fascist Germany. It is with this geopolitical "prose" that we shall commence our analysis.

I. "GEOPOLITICS" IN THEORY AND PRACTICE

It need hardly be said that the forerunners of geopolitics, *e.g.* the English historian Buckle, were in their day on a far higher level scientifically than their contemporaries who adhered to theological conceptions of the historical process; they were able to explain much by material factors that could not be explained by heavenly illusions. In Germany this peculiar brand of geographic materialism, or rather geographical naturalism, was developed by the founders of so-called "political geography," especially by Richthofen and above all Ratzel. The latter declared that the explanation of the historical process and of all politics lay in the size, position and frontiers of a given territory; in the form of the earth's surface and the soil, with its vegetation, water resources, etc.; and, finally, in the relation of the territory in question to other parts of the earth's surface. He maintained "that the attributes of the state are composed of those of the people and of the land" ("dass sich die Eigenschaften des Staates aus denen des Volkes und des Bodens zusammensetzen"). Before him, Richthofen had also introduced the race factor, in addition to factors of a geophysical order. The present-day school of "geopoliticians" (a name invented by the Swedish imperialist and political theorist R. Kjellén), who are grouped around the German magazine *Zeitschrift für Geopolitik* and its editor, Professor Haushofer, reiterate substantially the same ideas.

But while the views of Buckle (in so far as we are discussing the influence of climate, etc.) were progressive in their day, now, after the historical materialism of Marx, the writings of contemporary geopoliticians seem so much childish prattle (that is, logically; politically they are far from that).

In effect, geopolitics flatly denies all history. Relatively constant factors such as territory, soil, climate (and racial attributes which biological sociologists also consider as constant) cannot serve to explain historical and social changes. "Politics" does not grow out of the "land" at all, but first and foremost out of economic relations. The "land" undoubtedly influences the historical process; but it does so primarily through the process of labor and through economics, and these in their turn exercise a decisive influence on politics. The territory and the racial attributes of the British Isles have changed very little since the nineties of the last century, and they cannot possibly be made to explain, let us say, Great Britain's rapid change from free trade to a high protective tariff. The existence of a foreign trade monopoly in the U. S. S. R. cannot be explained by the "Russian steppes" or by the so-called "Slavic soul." But Great Britain's change to a high protective tariff can very well be explained by the transition of her economic system to monopoly capitalism, with its trusts and syndicates; and the foreign trade monopoly in the U. S. S. R. can very easily be explained by the peculiarities of the Socialist economic system, with its plan, and by the relationship of this system to the outside world. Arguments about space and territory *per se* remind one—if the adherents of these theories will excuse the remark—of people hunting for differential tariffs among crabs or for paper money on wheat fields.

But however ridiculous geopolitics is from the point of view of logic, it nevertheless plays a very active reactionary rôle *in practice*. It supplies an excuse for bellicose Fascism, a justification for war and imperialism; it preaches new conquests and wars of intervention. The essence of the matter lies here, not in the quasimoralistic poetized sophistry with which imperialists often veil their prose.

II. "PERPETUUM MOBILE" IN WARS

In his article which I have already mentioned the late Mr. Simonds, after sharply (and to a great extent correctly) criticizing the League of Nations, draws the conclusion that foreign territory and raw materials are indispensable to Germany, Italy and Japan; that any attempt to persuade these countries to the contrary would be absurd; and that the League of Nations must adopt the rule of economic parity and make an equitable distribution of the world's resources of territory and raw materials. This will avert a world tragedy.

Indeed? But what will come of this plan objectively, that is, apart from the subjective intentions of its authors? Let us analyze this plan of the new "levellers."

First. Who are to be the *subjects* of this deal? Alas! These do not include such countries as Egypt or China or India. Nor do they include any of the small independent states like Czechoslovakia. The subjects of the deal are to be the biggest capitalist powers.

Second. Who are to be the *objects* of the deal? Apparently the U. S. S. R. and a number of small independent countries such as Lithuania (for the author of the scheme seeks to justify German Fascist aspirations), China (for Japan's policy is similarly "justified") and the colonies (Italy's policy also finds "justification" in this scheme). Thus in effect it is proposed: (1) to cut up the U. S. S. R.; (2) to destroy the independence of small countries, such as Ethiopia; (3) to partition China; (4) to divide up the colonies again, like so much small coin thrown in to complete a bargain. In other words, the entire plan is aimed against: (a) the workers (the U. S. S. R.); (b) the masses in densely populated China (*i.e.*, the semi-colonies); (c) the colonial masses. *Cui prodest?* The biggest capitalist powers. Such is the scheme's "justice" and "morality."

Third. Let us assume that by some miracle or other the idea has been carried into effect. The great capitalist Powers have divided up the spoils among themselves (the others, as we have seen, are *quantités négligeables*) on a "basic principle" of superaristocratic world "parity." But what will happen the day after? That is the question.

It is not hard to answer. The mere fact that in different countries there are different levels of productive power, different quantities of skilled labor power, will lead to different results in the struggle for the world market. No amount of "autarchy" will save a country from having resort to this world market, the more so as the capitalist system will inevitably lead to overproduction. The search for new markets and spheres for capital investment will necessitate new re-divisions of land and resources. And since tariff barriers, trusts, armies and fleets will not disappear, the war song will break out afresh. Thus what is proposed is nothing more nor less than the continuing reproduction of wars, a *perpetuum mobile* of annihilating catastrophes. The picture is truly horrifying.

Fourth. Aside from all this, the plan recalls the verse about Roland's horse:

Wunderschön war diese Stute,
Leider aber war sie tot.

It is just another Utopia. The more powerful groups of capitalists wielding state power will not surrender their colonies for the benefit of their poorer relatives. If Germany, Japan and Italy cannot be persuaded to abandon their expansionist policy, then there is just as little expectation of philanthropy on the part of Great Britain, the United States or France. As regards the workers of the U. S. S. R., they can see absolutely no reason for surrendering their common property to their bitterest class antagonists.

Fifth. Capitalist states might ask themselves whether this levelling scheme does not have in it the germs of what Japanese diplomats would call "dangerous thoughts." For mankind is divided not only horizontally into states, but also vertically into classes. (By the way, this idea of a re-division, and of a blow at the maxim "Beati possidentes," calls to mind the whole class which is made up of the "possidentes." Here, however, it is not a question of re-dividing the factories and distributing the machines, among the workers, but of common ownership of the means of production. And this is the course which history will take.)

III. WHAT IS IMPERIALISM?

So we may put the question as follows: Is the present tendency to violent expansion now being displayed so strikingly in Japan, Germany and Italy a purely natural function of land and race, or is it a function of the social-economic system?

The question can be most easily considered by taking the example of Japan. The density of population in Japan is great. There is little land per capita. Emigration has always been very considerable. The German professor, Paul Berkenkopf, in his recent work "Sibirien als Zukunftsland der Industrie," uses the very fact of overpopulation ("Druck der japanischen Übervölkerung") to explain Japanese imperialist expansion, assuming, however, that this expansion will proceed primarily in the direction of Australia and the Philippines. And thus it would seem that here as nowhere else the bare laws of geopolitics are the determining factor. But in that case how can we explain the crisis of overproduction? And how can we explain the paradox that this strange profusion of products is constantly impelling Japan's ruling classes to more intensive expansion? What becomes, then, of all the primitive argumentation that where there is little land, nothing to eat, and too many people, *ergo,* new territory is needed? It simply goes to pieces. Obviously the matter is not at all so simple. In reality, it is a bastard form of *fin de siècle* monopoly capitalism coupled with considerable survivals of feudal barbarism: savage exploitation of the workers and peasants, land-hunger on the part of the latter, exorbitantly high rents, poverty, and consequently low purchasing power of the masses—all leading to the paradox of plenty and poverty, overproduction and the quest for new territories. And are not these things peculiar to capitalism as a whole? Is not the hunt for markets, coupled with overproduction and under-consumption, a characteristic feature of the special capitalist "mode of production?"

Or take Germany. We hear the chorus that it is absolutely essential for her to steal new territory from the U. S. S. R., since she, Germany, is starved for raw materials. We shall not speak here about the German war industry, which has swelled to gigantic proportions, which swallows up vast quantities of raw materials, and which does not in any way "grow" out of the properties of the German "soil." Nor shall we talk about the stocks of raw materials for war at the expense of consumption, nor about the sabotage on the part of the peasants. We only put the following elementary question: Why should not Germany *buy* raw materials from the U. S. S. R.? Does the latter want a high price? No, on the contrary. Many persons have shouted at the top of their voices that the U. S. S. R. is practising dumping—so favorable to the purchaser are the prices at which the U. S. S. R. has sold raw material. But German monopoly capital wants to have monopoly ownership of Ukrainian raw materials for military-economic autarchy, which in its turn is a weapon for further world struggle. "Territory," "space," (Fascist philosophers have raised the category of "space" five heads higher than that of "time") do not produce any policy *by themselves*. It is definite social-historical conditions that lead to wars.

Mr. Simonds quoted Signor Mussolini's dictum: "For us Italians the choice is between foreign expansion and domestic explosion." And he added: "And that is why Italy and Germany, like Japan, are preparing for war." About Germany he spoke still more clearly: either a war of conquest, or Communism.

Let us assume that this is so. But what does it signify? It simply signifies that Communism can live without wars, whereas the other social form, capitalism, through the mouths of its own politicians and ideologist, declares: Better a war of conquest than Communism. This only serves to corroborate the proposition that a war of conquest is a function of the social order, that it is not a non-historical category connected directly with geophysical and biological factors.

The structure of modern capitalism must be analyzed scientifically, soberly and without prejudice. The Italian Fascists claim that there is no capitalism in Italy, but a special kind of order which is neither capitalism nor Socialism. Herr Hitler's followers declare that in their country they have National Socialism. Mr. Araki and the other ideologists of Japanese aggression speak about the "imperial path," about Japan's peculiar traditions and her celestial mission: God himself points out definite strategic and tactical plans to Mr. Araki. Camouflage and juggling with words constitute one of the distinguishing features of profound social decadence. But fact remains fact. In none of the above-mentioned countries has one hair fallen from the head of the finance-capital oligarchy. Herr Fried in his book, "Das Ende des Kapitalismus," painted a very graphic picture of this oligarchy. But Hitler's régime has left it in complete immunity; these oligarchs have only been converted (in words) into "leaders of industry" on the basis of "public service." If we recall that Fascism's most outstanding philosopher, Spengler, considered the Hohenzollern Officers' Corps and the Prussian Government officials as the epitome of "Socialism" there is really no need for surprise. Has it not been said that "man was given a tongue to hide his thoughts?"

The same kind of camouflage is observable in another form even in capitalistic countries with democratic régimes. Not so long ago, for example, Mr. Thomas Nixon Carver, an indiscreet Pindar of "prosperity," proclaimed *urbi et orbi* that in the United States every worker is a capitalist. The subsequent spread of the crisis and of so-called "technical unemployment" have given a tragic refutation of this capitalist optimism.

What is in fact the real state of affairs? And why does this real state of affairs give rise to imperialist wars?

Since the eighties of the last century, as a result of the triumph of large-scale production and the centralization of capital, the form of capitalism has changed. From the previous stage of industrial capitalism, with its freedom of competition, its individualism, its principle of *laissez faire, laissez passer,* it entered the stage of monopoly capitalism (trusts, intergrowth of banking capital and industrial capital, monopoly prices). The partition of the world led to accentuated competition; to the policy of dumping (the losses incurred were compensated for by high monopoly prices in the home market); and to the system of a high protective tariff. In its turn, protectionism intensified the export of capital (in place of commodity exports, now hampered by tariff barriers). The monopolistic possession of markets, raw materials and spheres of capital investment, together with the whole system of monopoly exploitation, tariffs, etc., based on the already accomplished partition of the so-called "free lands" (which meant putting an end to the principle of the Open Door), led capitalist competition on the world market to acquire more and more clearly the character of forcible pressure (*Machtpolitik*). The diminished possibilities of "peaceful penetration" were remedied by the brutal policy of armed force.

Accordingly, the state power of capital, its "interference" in economic life, acquires increased significance. We witness the militarization of the economic system and an extreme intensification of the tendency to economic autarchy, which is also important militarily and politically in determining the *Machtposition* in the arena of world struggle. Here the inner motive is represented by the interests of profit, which on the one hand maintain the purchasing power of the working masses at an extremely low level (even in Ricardo's day it was a well-known fact that profit stands in inverse proportion to wages), and which on the other hand continually force commodities and capital beyond the bounds of the given state, compelling a constant search for fresh markets, fresh sources of raw materials and fresh spheres for capital investment. The greater the contradiction between the productive forces of capitalism and the mass impoverishment which is immanent in this system, the more intensive grows world competition, the more acute becomes the problem of war.

Imperialist war is an expression of the expansionist policy of monopoly capitalism. Such is the specific, historically limited, significance of imperialist wars. On the one hand, monopoly capitalism acts as a check on the development of the productive forces (the decay of capitalism); on the other, it leads to catastrophes of the most devastating kind.

Thus not every sort of war, not even every predatory war, is an imperialist war. Slave-owning forms of society waged wars for slaves; feudal lords fought for land; merchants and traders fought for markets and for exploitation through trade and plunder ("Handel und Piraterie," as Goethe called it); and so forth. Imperialism wages wars to extend the domination of one country's finance capital, for the monopoly profits of trusts and banks. Its wars are universal (for the whole world is already divided up); its wars confront all mankind with the dilemma: either death or Socialism. *Hic Rhodus! Hic salta!*

IV. IMPERIALISM AND THE U. S. S. R.

From the above it will be clear how senseless it is to talk about the "imperialism" of the U. S. S. R., as is done *con amore* by Fascist theoreticians and by "researchers" of the type of Herr von Kleinow. A phrase like "the imperialism of the U. S. S. R." is a contradiction in terms, like "dry water" or "square circles."

But it may be asked: Will not the U. S. S. R. pursue an aggressive policy, not in favor of finance capital, but against it? Will it not fight for the expansion of Socialism? Here again let us begin with an example.

As is well known, the Empire of the Tsars formerly occupied present territory of the Soviet Union, plus Poland, plus Finland, etc. It possessed even more territory and more "natural wealth" than does the U. S. S. R. But it was continually engaged in wars of conquest. On the eve of 1914 it dreamed of seizing Constantinople and the Dardanelles and of subjugating all Turkey, of seizing the whole of Galicia from Austria-Hungary, of dealing Germany a blow and of concluding a trade agreement with her on onerous terms; and so on. What, under Tsarism, drove not only the landlords but also the bourgeoisie (even before they had a share in the government) to these adventures? First and foremost, the weakness of the home market. The peasant was fleeced to the skin by the landlord, the worker's wages were meager. Hence the policy which the Tsar's minister Vyshnegradsky characterized in the words: "We'll go hungry but we'll export." Hence the Far Eastern adventure—and the Russo-Japanese War, during which, by the way, all sections of Russian society except the landlord aristocracy desired the Tsarist Government's defeat. Hence, too, Russia's participation in the World War, with a frenzied imperialist program (here the grain exporters played the biggest part).

Now let us take the U. S. S. R. One does not need to be a genius to observe that in the U. S. S. R. *the demand is not less but greater than the supply*. In our country we have a tremendously strong home market. Despite the enormous scale of production there is a shortage of commodities, there are still too few goods on sale.

The Socialist system contains within itself much greater possibilities for productive forces to develop, for labor to increase its productivity and for technique to progress. But in the Soviet Union, be it noted, this cannot result either in unemployment or in overproduction. Our national economy is conducted not with a view to profits for a capitalist class, but to satisfy the requirements of the masses. This means that when production of necessary articles is increased their consumption is proportionately raised, and not lowered into the sea like Brazilian coffee. If completely superfluous articles are produced—a highly improbable contingency—corrections can be made in the production process itself. Under planned economy it is easy to redistribute the productive forces; they can be transferred to new sectors, engendering new requirements and supplying the masses with new lines of production. There will never be any threat of unemployment, and a universal rise in labor productivity will only lead to a growth of plenty, shorten the working day, and leave more scope for cultural development.

Thus the motive inherent in the very nature of the capitalist system, which begets surplus value and prevents its realization—the motive which is most glaringly manifested in the era of imperialism and impels the ruling classes to war—is reduced in a Socialist society to absolute nonsense.

This was why beggarly Tsarist Russia, where the "upper ten thousand" of landlords and bourgeois lived in splendor while the masses starved, pursued a policy of wars of conquest. And that is why the U. S. S. R., which is rapidly growing rich in the sense that well-being is spreading throughout the entire mass of the people while social wealth is concentrated in the hands of the Socialist state, pursues an exactly opposite policy, the policy of peace. The U. S. S. R. is not interested in conquests in any direction whatever. But it is interested, very deeply and lastingly interested, in peace. What, then, remains of the celebrated argument that the U. S. S. R. "is continuing the policy of the Tsars?"

There is another piece of geopolitical sophistry in circulation which goes more or less as follows. Fact remains fact: in 1914 Russia was in conflict with Japan in the Far East; in 1914–18 she was in conflict with Germany; the same thing is happening again, *mutatis mutandis,* and the fundamental geophysical laws are again breaking their way through all obstacles.

What is the reply to this piece of sophistry?

First, even the facts themselves are distorted. For example, in 1914 and the years following Japan was in league with Russia against Germany; now Japan is in league with Germany against the U. S. S. R. The Japanese Samurai have even been proclaimed oriental Prussians of Aryan extraction.

Second, the question must be stated more clearly. What, in effect, is under discussion? What we are discussing is not the mere fact of a conflict (for a conflict presupposes at least two parties—our object in this case not being to analyze the inner struggles of a Hamlet), but the policy of one party and the policy of another. After this logical dissection the question becomes perfectly clear. In Japan power is in the hands of approximately the same classes as before, and Japan is continuing its policy of imperialist aggression, heading for war. The U. S. S. R. is not Tsarist Russia and the radical change of the country's economic system demands an exactly opposite policy, the policy of peace. Nevertheless war *may* break out, for the situation is not determined by the one-sided will to peace of the Soviets. War may be forced upon us. Contiguity of frontiers and territory certainly have an influence here, but not directly, and the war guilt will lie not with "the land" but with Japanese imperialism.

Finally, there is one other argument with which the opponents of the U. S. S. R. try to discredit Soviet foreign policy. It is trotted out regularly by Herr Hitler and his ideological agents. It runs, roughly speaking, as follows: National Socialism is based on "nationality" ("Volkstum," "Volksgemeinschaft"); its business is with the domestic, internal affairs of Germany; National Socialism is *national* socialism, and is not super- or supra-national. Accordingly it never meddles in "other folks' affairs," but speaks exclusively *pro domo sua*. Conversely, Sovietism—Bolshevism, Communism—has a super- and supra-national orientation; it is an international force, dreaming of world domination; it is the *spiritus rector* of all sedition and unrest.

Clearly this argument is intimately connected with our theme.

First of all, a few words about the Germany of Herr Hitler. The German Fascists, it is true, are idolaters of the fetish of so-called "race purity;" they even castrate those who are not pure Aryans and imprison people for the "crime" of sexual intercourse with non-Aryan men and women. They propagate economico-national autarchy, as a vessel containing the holy and precious body and blood of the "Nordic Aryan race." But it would be a childish absurdity to suppose that this leads to a policy of "noninterference." Quite the contrary. Fascist action is most energetic in all foreign countries. And this is easy to understand, for their very "national narrowness" is nothing more nor less than the clenching of the military-economic and ideological fist. Their orientation is towards world hegemony, entailing the crushing and enslavement of all other nations. No, to be sure, they are not internationalists. But they are potential nationalistic oppressors of all other nations (those of "low degree"). It is precisely from this point of view that the

Nazis meddle in the internal affairs of all other states. It is worth knowing, for instance, that even in the case of the United States the Nazis count on the millions of citizens of German blood to act against the Anglo-Saxon and other elements. In fact, it is to fear of a German revolt that Herr Colin Ross ascribes the unfavorable attitude of Americans towards National Socialism.[3] Setting out from the premise that "present-day America is tired and old, amazingly old" (*"das heutige Amerika ist müde und alt, erstaunlich alt"*) the author threatens a national upheaval of millions of "self-knowing" Germans. Approximately the same arguments ("salvation" of the Ukraine or of the Volga Germans) are employed by Herr Rosenberg in his appeals for war against the U. S. S. R. It is thus quite futile for the Nazis to pose as offended children, occupied in the washing of purely domestic linen. That argument is mendacious.

However, *revenons à nos moutons*. Do we believe in the world-wide triumph of Socialism? Of course we do. Moreover, we know for sure that this will undoubtedly come, as a result of the inner contradictions of capitalism, through the victory of the historically progressive forces within it. We know that our diagnosis and prognosis are scientific and exact. But does this mean that the U. S. S. R. should interfere in the affairs of other states or pursue a policy of conquest? Of course not. For the best "propaganda" of all is the very fact of the existence and uninterrupted development of the new economic relations and the new culture. It would be sheer stupidity to interrupt this process.

Hence it follows that not only from the economic but also from the purely political standpoint—not only from the standpoint of the U. S. S. R. proper but also from that of the ultimate world-wide victory of Socialism—it is utterly senseless to think of a policy of war being adopted by the proletarian state. And as regards the "last days" and the "world rule of Communism," history will settle this question. *"Que les destinées s'accomplissent!"*

However, in the interests of full scientific clarity we can-

[3] *Zeitschrift für Geopolitik,* XII Jahrg., 3 Heft. p. 135: "Idee und Zukunftsgestaltung der Vereinigten Staaten von Amerika."

not leave unanswered one further argument against the Marxist presentation of the question concerning the destinies of society. It is set forth in an article in *The Round Table* (No. 99) entitled "Economics and War." The author asserts that Marxism is wrong, because:

> If, as its disciples hold, the existing economic system leads inherently to the class war, which of its nature cuts across national boundaries, then surely it cannot also lead inherently to the war between nations, in which all classes are ranged side by side against their fellows of another country. . . . For experience amply proves that war is the great opportunity of the forces of the Left to overthrow the established régime. The calculating Communist, far more than the calculating capitalist, ought to foment war.

I regret to say that the author errs on every point. War "between nations" (or rather between capitalist states) formally unites classes, but only to aggravate class antagonisms still further later on and speed up the revolutionary process. So it was in Germany and Austria, so it was in Russia, where the revolutionary party was able to carry things through to the end. It is precisely for this reason that war enables "the forces of the Left" to "overthrow the established régime." But they are able to do so for the further reason that they rally the masses against war. It is as the force of peace, the only consistent force of peace, that they are victorious—not as the fictitious and silly-clever "calculating Communist" imagined by *The Round Table.* As regards the capitalists, they are driven on by the blind, supra-rational, elemental forces of an unorganized society. One of the characteristic features of this society is that people get results quite different from those intended: thus none of the capitalists wanted the crisis, but the crisis is the result of their actions. This is the so-called law of the heterogeneity of aims, characteristic of irrational (capitalist) society and non-existent in rational, organized (Socialist) society. Thus, the peace policy of the Socialist state is not just a passing "juncture" for it, not a temporary zigzag in policy, not an opportunist compromise. It expresses the very essence of the Socialist system.

We are not obliged to think for the capitalists. But, contrary to *The Round Table's* advice, we stand and will continue to stand for peace, peace and yet again peace. And precisely for this reason we shall conquer in a war if the imperialists force one on us.

V. THE SYSTEM OF PROLETARIAN STATES: COMMUNISM AND WAR

Now it will be easy to answer the question as to whether wars between proletarian states will be possible—wars for markets, for raw materials, for spheres of capital investment—and whether wars will be possible under Communism, *i.e.,* in the subsequent stage of mankind's evolution, after it has already taken to Socialism.

Basic actuating motives are represented by definite interests. The world economic system of the capitalist régime is broken up into "national" economic units with conflicting interests (we put the word "national" in quotation marks, for the term includes bourgeois states composing many nationalities). The most acute form of conflict in which this clash of interests finds expression is war between these states. War is a special form of capitalist competition, peculiar to the capitalist world as such. The question of relations between proletarian states is altogether different.

Logically: there is no clash of real interests between proletarian states whatsoever; on the contrary, their real interest is in maximum coöperation. From the very start this real interest is realized as the actuating motive of all activity, for it is commensurate with the whole system of rationally organized labor with the ideology of the revolutionary proletariat.

Genetically: the very process of the struggle waged by the proletarian states for their existence will knit them together in a still closer bond. There can be no doubt that after a certain stage of development tremendously powerful centripetal tendencies will be revealed—tendencies toward a state union of proletarian republics.

Empirically: the experience of the U. S. S. R. fully confirms these considerations. Tsarist Russia collapsed as an integral whole, and in those parts where the bourgeoisie remained in power (Finland, Estonia, Lithuania, Poland) it has split apart and now forms mutually antagonistic elements (*cf.* Poland versus Lithuania). On the other hand, in those places where the workers were victorious they have joined the Union of proletarian republics, united by a single economic plan and a centralized government, but organized in a federation. The constituent nations have full rights, and their various cultures, national in form and Socialist in content, are flourishing now as never before. This, of course, is far from being an accident; it is a manifestation of the most profound historical law, linked with a new social structure.

With the further flowering of proletarian states throughout the entire world, war will become unnecessary. War will be impossible in a system of unified Communist society, where there are no classes and even—*horrible dictu*—no coercive state power nor armies. This society will really "turn swords into ploughshares" and release gigantic masses of energy for national creative work for the benefit of all mankind. If even the first historical phases of Socialist development in our country have already produced such brilliant creative results as the Stakhanov movement, and the heroic feats accomplished by our youth in all fields of culture, then what abundant sources of social wealth will pour forth in the splendid fraternal society of Communism!

This, it will be said, is utopian. But we know very well that Aristotle was no fool, that he was one of the greatest men of all times. Yet he held that society was inconceivable without slaves. Not so long ago the planters of the southern states held that Negroes are innate slaves. So today the bourgeois and their little "Aristotles" hold that society would be as inconceivable without war as without wage slavery, and that the U. S. S. R. is a *lapsus historiæ*. Let them think so. *Qui vivra verra.*

❖ ❖ ❖

NOWHERE was the debate on the merits of different economic systems more intense, during the middle thirties, than in the United States, where the shock imparted by the "great depression" to accepted conceptions was greatest. Significantly, some of the most stimulating contributions to the interchange of ideas in this and other fields of thought in the United States came from men whom the Nazi totalitarianism had driven from central Europe. An example is "Politics Versus Economics," by Gustav Stolper, founder and former editor of the German weekly, *Der Deutscher Volkswirt,* member of the Reichstag and author of various books on economic subjects. His essay was printed in April 1934.

Everywhere in the world, the controversies of the era turned on one great question: the relation of the state and the individual. As concretely applied in the depths of the depression, this meant a searching study of the proper rôle of the state in economic processes. Hardly an aspect of American life, or of the values which were most characteristically American, escaped the examination which this central question provoked. Great words like freedom and democracy were discussed in seriousness again; hard times rubbed clean the tarnish which they had acquired in the twenties. What was freedom today for 12,000,000 men without work, it was asked? But what, it was rejoined, would be the value tomorrow of very nearly every democratic good that America had hitherto valued if the granting and withholding of livelihood were the prerogative of the state?

Answers to such questions were already written hard in the experience of men like Stolper in other lands; and as Americans sought answers for themselves, few of them were unaware that events in Italy, in Germany, in Russia had a bearing on their own decisions. By feeling and by reason, Americans sought a middle ground. But already, in this prelude to the debate on the question of intervention in the Second German War, it was becoming apparent that there would be no isolation for the United States, and no neutrality in the decisions which were remaking the world.

❖ ❖ ❖

POLITICS VERSUS ECONOMICS

By Gustav Stolper

POLITICIANS accuse the science of political economy of having failed. On the other hand, there are economists who see in politics nothing but a crude and undisciplined force which upsets their field of activity. The discussion would be more productive if only a little more effort could be devoted to arriving at an understanding of one or two cardinal problems affecting the relations between the state and economic life, and hence the relations between politics and political economy.

To the politicans I would suggest that, before accusing economics of having failed, they might first find out more about the recent results of scientific investigation in that field. Political economy is in a bad way. Although still a comparatively young science, it probably has made more rapid progress during the past few decades than has been made in any other branch of intellectual endeavor. But in the whole scientific domain progress always implies increasing complexity. Far from being simple, social life is infinitely complicated. How, then, can we expect to succeed in reducing the science of social life to a few simple formulas? In the field of natural science, the most ambitious layman readily admits that he does not understand the atomic theory or the quantum theory or the doctrine of relativity. But in questions of political economy anyone seems to imagine himself competent to pass authoritative opinions, even though he has never troubled to acquire the faintest idea of the many useful results of laborious economic investigation and reasoning. The worst of it is that there are even university professors in the ranks of these "laymen," a fact which tends especially to puzzle and confuse the non-specialist and the politician. It surely would be impossible today in a great university in any civilized country for anyone to teach physics if he knew no more about the atomic theory or the theory of relativity than the average newspaper reader—that is to say, nothing. But it seems to occasion no surprise that in every country there are professors of political economy who have never so much as heard of the new theoretic conceptions achieved in their own science during the past thirty years. There is no need to mention names. As a matter of fact, this science—or rather those representatives of it who know its modern significance—has never been so unanimous as it is today concerning recent economic events. If we consider the complexity of the questions here at issue, we must realize that such unanimity is no more a mere matter of course than would be the complete agreement of a number of physicians sitting in consultation on an exceptionally difficult case. Nor would the authority of the science concerned in either case be impaired by whatever differences of opinion might arise concerning diagnosis and treatment.

On the other hand, there are some scientists who approach their task too light-heartedly, treating politicians with the sovereign contempt shown by Archimedes toward the intruding Roman legionary at Syracuse. While a conscientious politician ought certainly to study what economic science says will probably be the results of a certain course of action before he embarks on it, the economist is arrogant if he expects political decisions to be taken exclusively on economic grounds. The economist, remaining within his own domain, simplifies his question—indeed, he has no other choice—by restricting himself to individual economic motives. He lives in the realm of economic reason and rejects any motives of an extra-economic, not to say anti-economic, nature. To mix these motives up with economics is, in his eyes, disturbing, senseless, criminal. To the politician, on the other hand, this world of extra-economic or anti-economic motives is his world, the world which it is his great task to master. In the mouths of many snobs and intellectuals the phrase "a clever politician" has a disagreeable flavor. But actually it is a title of distinction for any man in public life, provided he does not fail to measure up to legitimate intellectual and ethical standards. Just as in economic life the merchant has his place alongside the technician, so political life needs in addition to the scientifically trained official the politician who is well versed in his art.

II

The "new era," which really dates from the year 1914, is not defined by economic facts. This statement runs counter to current and customary ideas and therefore needs some amplification. The questions here at issue are of decisive significance, if a clear insight is to be obtained into the problem of the relations between the state and economic life. The most characteristic feature of this new era is the change in primary mental conditions. What I have in mind here may be discussed under three heads:

1. The ascendancy of politics over economics—an ascendancy which had seemingly been ended by the social developments in the last decades before the war—never was more pronounced than it is today. This is true in the field of foreign no less than domestic politics. Despite its absurdity, the thesis that the origins of the World War were economic still finds millions of adherents. The World War started in Vienna regardless of the fact that the former Austro-Hungarian monarchy represented the most perfect and the most satisfactorily balanced economic unit in prewar Europe. This did not prevent that old-established monarchy from falling to pieces, and concurrently reducing Europe to a heap of ruins, because the mere existence of such a half-absolutist and supra-national state was a negation of the democratic and nationalistic trends of the times. Nor had the antagonisms between Germany and France ever been economic in origin. From the economic point of view, indeed, France's recovery of Alsace-Lorraine was almost calculated to embarrass her, implying as it did increased competition in agriculture as well as important industries and thus adding to her economic worries. In the same way, economic considerations were never factors in the antagonism

between Austria and Russia. Nor was the economic value of the South Tyrol and Trieste for Italy ever great enough in itself to create her desire to own those regions; and today the maintenance of the ports of Fiume and Trieste, without any economic hinterland, is a very expensive affair for Italy. But such economic considerations were not enough to prevent the political antagonisms which had grown up from ending in armed conflict.

Similarly, the peace treaties show hardly a trace of economic considerations. The successor states to Austria-Hungary and Russia, viewed as economic units, are absurd and impossible, and constitute one of the elementary sources of the European crisis. Their economic absurdity is aggravated by the fact that, instead of joining forces, these small and medium-sized states have shut themselves off from one another. Evidently, then, they are prepared to pay a price for the enjoyment of their national self-consciousness. They do not adjust their political conduct to the laws of economic reasoning. Their principal goal is to consolidate themselves as nations and to acquire power; and they are quite willing to subordinate their economic interests and policies to those aims, even at a heavy sacrifice. The non-economic character of the grave international crisis now shaking Europe to its foundations is so evident that there is no need to dwell on it.

Though less obvious, it is nonetheless certain that the great domestic upheavals which have taken place all over Europe likewise spring from sources that are not economic in nature. Neither the Bolshevik nor the Fascist nor the National Socialist revolution can be explained on economic grounds. Any attempt to do so leads us astray. To say this seems paradoxical, especially in the case of Bolshevism, which parades before the world as a purely economic system. In pre-Bolshevik Russia literally all the economic and social premises for building a Socialistic commonwealth were lacking. There was really no question there of the dialectic transition by which, according to the Marxian doctrine, any highly developed industrial state is supposed to be forced into Socialism—for the simple reason that there was no such thing in Tsarist Russia as a highly developed capitalism with its attendant bourgeois and proletarian classes. Fascist Italy did not seek an economic revolution. Her chief aim has been to organize her national self-consciousness. Her whole creation of economic and social organizations, "corporations," is secondary and accidental. Nor is National Socialism to be explained by the economic crisis in Germany. The six millions of unemployed whom Hitler found when he came to power did not compose the army of his followers. On the contrary, the vast majority of the unemployed were in the Socialist camp, which Hitler proceeded to destroy. National Socialism can be explained only by its non-material factors; its economic program holds the very last place on the list of reasons for its success.

2. The war and its aftermath aroused the self-consciousness of the masses all over the civilized world. They had to be called upon for the accomplishment of the tasks imposed by the war, and this in turn made it necessary to provide for their elementary needs. In America this aspect of the war never gained anything like the significance which it had in Europe; in America the fate of single individuals was not affected by the war so deeply and so all-inclusively. All the same, no country has remained entirely unaffected by the moral and intellectual consequences of the war any more than by its political and economic effects. I will not attempt to depict "The Revolt of the Masses;" that has been done in definitive form by Ortega y Gasset. The only thing in which I am interested here is the profound and neglected truth that economic conditions had nothing whatever to do with the fact that millions and millions of men of all nations had to live for four years in the trenches, exposed to daily hazards; that during those four years they were forced back into primitive conditions of existence; that during those four years they were cut off from all their social, class and family connections.

The fate of the millions in the trenches was also decisive for the fate of the more numerous millions who remained at home. These were torn loose from their traditional moorings almost as completely as the soldiers at the front. Hardly a factory was able to carry on its customary production; in most cases new ways of manufacture had to be devised almost overnight, under new technical and commercial conditions. In the same way, with men fighting and women suddenly taking over the exhausting labor formerly performed by the men, social standards lost their significance. When marriages are sundered, families destroyed, friendships dissolved and professional connections broken, there is no room for purely traditional activities and ideas.

The new generation looks at every aspect of the world with completely changed eyes. This war generation is no longer conscious of class distinctions or class prejudices. It regards the blessings of technical civilization not with trusting eyes but skeptically. But while there can be no doubt that it has become brave unto death, it is none the less hungry for life. It is ready for anything. In its inmost nature it is revolutionary. This changed attitude towards life has opened up a breach between the older and the younger generation, in the democratic west no less than in Fascist Central Europe or in the Bolshevik east. And let me repeat and stress that this changed attitude is not due to economic causes; it represents the mental and moral effects of the war.

3. This changed mental and psychological disposition produced by the war encounters a change in the structure of the scientific spirit. Science today regards all problems as soluble by scientific methods. The inventor's genius has been replaced by the laboratory; daring conceptions have given way to the organized labor of the ant-hill. The aims of scientific reasoning, scientific planning, scientific willing, have advanced into the infinite, into the realm of the irrational; but the methods of scientific investigation have been rationalized down to the last detail.

If we would understand the crisis that has overtaken political liberalism we must grasp this phenomenon in its full meaning. The laissez-faire policy is in irreconcilable conflict with the restless mental attitude characteristic of the present time. The modern social consciousness finds it intolerable to let things go as they please in the political and economic sphere. It has become insufferable to be forced to face social and economic problems with resignation, while in all other spheres it has become customary to grapple with any problem whatsoever in a systematic way and to feel confident that it will be solved successfully. In short, this modern social consciousness resents it as an insupportable contradiction that man, who by adopting systematic methods can subject matter and natural forces to his will and press them into his service, should in economic and social life have to submit to the dispensations of a fate which he neither acknowledges nor comprehends.

III

Let us examine from this angle the changed aspect of the state and the equally changed aspect of economic life.

The state of 1934 is no longer the state of 1914. The present state has to deal with a different people and a different task. The state of 1914 had its place somewhere on the periphery of economic and social life; but the state of 1934 has been transferred to the very center, and it can never be pushed back again to the periphery. We shall therefore have to find ways and means to establish it permanently in the center. The internal unrest which has taken hold of all the great nations, and which in some cases has led to revolutionary movements, originates in an infinitely difficult and laborious process—the process by which the masses, with their newly gained self-consciousness and political power, are to be organized for the performance of the tasks and duties of the state, these tasks and duties, moreover, being more numerous and infinitely more complicated than ever before.

The war saw universal military service put into actual execution for the first time. Even in those countries where general service had been introduced as a matter of principle, it was of practical concern only to a minority of the total population able to bear arms. The war for the first time caused the entire nation to be called up for the defense of the state. It followed as a matter of course that political power was also distributed among the entire adult population. Even the Anglo-Saxon countries have known universal suffrage in the literal sense only since the war. When masses formerly excluded from political activity are given the vote in quiet times, they promptly become part of the traditional structure of national life. But if this happens at a moment when a political earthquake has all but buried tradition, a startling problem in political education is produced. So far it has been solved nowhere during the postwar period. It remains a momentous problem of our time.

The problem is also related to the new technical developments. Radios and movies have brought the masses nearer to politics, and political leadership nearer to the masses. A new type of political "leader" is needed—a leader able to capture the imagination of the masses, to whom he is now in a position to appeal directly and daily through the visual sense as well as by the spoken word; a leader who can explain the most complicated matters in plain and plausible language; a leader who claims liberty of action and knows how to defend it at any time, with the aid of the masses, against the political machine.

Up to this point—but no further—the problem is the same, whether in a democracy or in a dictatorship. That is why so many superficial observers in Europe are tempted to call President Roosevelt a dictator or to discern symptoms of a coming crisis for democracy in America—and this at a moment when the American democracy is probably furnishing the most incontestable proof of its power and competence in the entire course of its history.

IV

The transformation of the state is paralleled by the transformation of economic life. The capitalistic economy which dominated the century preceding the World War had been developing at a changing rate of progress, but continuously. "Today" was closely connected with "yesterday" and with "tomorrow." Thus, in adopting economic measures one was able to rely on an increasing store of tradition and experience. Freedom of movement was taken as a matter of course—whether of persons or goods or capital.

The direction of such movements depended almost exclusively on the capitalistic laws governing the market conditions. Year after year, millions of human beings emigrated from the crowded European countries with a low standard of living to the colonial countries in America and Asia. The stream of men was followed by a stream of capital, attracted by better-than-average chances of profit just as the immigrants had been attracted by the chances of attaining a higher standard of living. During the middle of the nineteenth century, Europe for a time was governed by free trade and liberalism. Its fundamental principles remained unshaken up to the war. An international economic system had thus developed which resulted in a real and steadily growing division of labor, bringing all nations the blessings of rapidly increasing wealth.

The war ended this continuity of economic development. The war destroyed traditions of international trade that had been built up in the course of more than a hundred years. All countries alike became hothouses in which industry was "forced" in one definite direction, namely to meet the needs of the war. The war in a few years transformed creditor nations into debtors, and debtor nations into creditors. The war succeeded in ruining the soundest currencies of the world. It paralyzed liberty of movement, not only of men but even of ideas. Thus it could happen, for example, that great technical advances were made in America during the war or during the first years of the postwar period about which Germany heard nothing whatever.

After the world had been reduced to chaos, tradition and experience were no longer of any avail. The fact that the two last decades witnessed the failure of so many old and conservative leaders in finance and industry, while upstarts and adventurers flourished everywhere, is to be explained simply enough by the circumstance that the compass-needle which during the quiet years before the war had guided the course of all economic endeavor had now ceased to function. Among all the various indices hardly a single one remained unchanged. Production and consumption, currency and credit, technical methods and habits of life, underwent a complete transformation—almost, one might say, overnight. Those who were not bound by any tradition, the daring adventurers, had their chance in those years. The old conservatives no longer could find elbow-room.

It may be quite true that, from the standpoint of economic theory, the crisis of 1929–1933 is in no way different from any of the crises of the past century—in its causes, in its progress, in the therapeutic measures to be taken. During each severe crisis of the nineteenth century contemporary observers were convinced that it was essentially different from all former crises, that it admitted of no comparison with any other, and that therefore any automatic recovery was out of the question. They believed, in short, that the past had to be buried, since in some sense or other a new era had been ushered in. And on each of these occasions the traditional economic system seemed finally to have been overcome. Today we are really justified in speaking of a new era. But it is not new in the sense that a crisis of capitalism has been brought about by any economic factors or developments, such as Karl Marx had in view when he spoke of the dialectic transition from capitalism to Socialism (in accordance with the immanent law of the system). Quite the contrary, what is really new is here again to be found in the extra-economic sphere. The war has created an economic situation which simply cannot be mastered without the aid and intervention of the state. The states, and they alone, were able gradually to reconstitute the world markets, which had been destroyed by political events and not by any economic crisis. The emergency bridges which had to be built across the trenches isolating one blockaded country from another were built by the states. The international debts represented in the main an accumulation of political debts. The freedom of movement of men, goods and capital, destroyed by the war, has not been restored to this day. Whether, or when, or to what extent it will ever be restored in the future remains an open question.

But the relation between the state and economic life has been radically changed, not only with respect to foreign intercourse, but also in the internal domain. Today the state has to deal with problems entirely foreign to it in the past. In all countries the war has bequeathed a financial problem bigger than any hitherto dreamt of; debts, normal public expenses and taxes everywhere have multiplied. And now the state finds that people no longer strive to exclude it from the economic and social sphere, as was the case in the nineteenth century, but on the contrary are determined and ready to invoke its aid at any moment, in any public emergency. The people have come to regard the state which organized the war as all-powerful. During the war the state made it its business to feed and clothe not only the army, but the civilian population as well; it also regulated the exchange of money and commodities and exercised a dictatorship over production and distribution. And while the state claimed this absolute power as a matter of course, it also did not hold back from acknowledging its own social obligations. Here is a fact pregnant with meaning; the state became for a time the absolute ruler of our economic life, and while subordinating the entire economic organization to its military purposes, also made itself responsible for the welfare of the humblest of its citizens, guaranteeing him a minimum of food, clothing, heating and housing. The famous cards for bread, fat, sugar, coal, underwear and shoes are not yet forgotten in Europe; and the wartime laws for the protection of tenants are still maintained, in one form or another, in many countries. This whole experience precludes even the wish to revive liberalism in the Manchester meaning.

V

Most people view the consequences of this crisis somewhat naïvely, in terms of the antithesis between capitalism and planned economy. I say "naïvely," because most of us picture capitalism to ourselves as a conservative, reactionary principle, and "planned economy" as a radical, progressive principle. Actually, it is just the other way around. Capitalism is inclined, for better or for worse, to liberate forward-driving forces; a planned economy is inclined to put artificial restraints upon those forces and to crystallize them at a given point. Such a statement will, I know, provoke a storm of protest and raise many doubts; but one has to take risks in sketching in rough outline a situation so vast and complicated. Suppose I try to make my meaning clear in the fewest possible words.

Any economy, and therefore a capitalistic economy, requires planning. Every businessman has to plan, and the larger his enterprise, the more careful and far-sighted must his planning be. A coal mine operator, in setting out to sink a shaft which at the earliest can be made ready in five years, must work according to a Five Year Plan that will take into account costs, possibilities of interruptions, and prices which are apt to prevail when finally the new coal reaches the market. A great electrical concern must try to estimate just how the demand for current is to develop over a term of years, in order to determine where to build turbines and how many. The same is true of all industries, almost without exception. The management of such an enterprise has to "plan" in the very same way that the "planning commission" of a Socialist community has to "plan," and it has very much the same data to work with—the birth rate, for example, the probable number of marriages, the foreseeable developments in technical methods, and so on.

The differences between the "planned" and the "capitalistic" system come down, rather, to the following:

1. Under capitalism, the businessman makes a miscalculation at his own risk; his mistake in the worst case spells economic ruin for him. The errors of a planning commission are paid for by the community at large.

2. If a hundred thousand businessmen are planning away, each on his own account, the mathematical chances that shrewdness and folly will offset each other to a certain extent are incomparably greater than is the case where the decision as to the economic fate of a nation is entrusted to one central brain.

3 (and most important). Capitalism functions under an objective law made manifest through the market—through prices and interest rates. The dictator, under capitalism, is

the consumer. In the long run, production is determined by what the consumer is willing and able to buy. Such a dictator is subject to human influences like any other, and, in principle, it does not matter whether the influence is exerted through advertising, persuasion, party-intrigues, or a pretty woman. No dictator lives in a vacuum; though a dictator, he is nonetheless a human being, responsive to all human motives. But he is also, nonetheless, a dictator. The capitalistic businessman can never escape the dictatorship of the market (the case of the monopoly we shall consider later on), and the market, at least in countries where oversupply rather than undersupply is the rule, is in turn determined by the consumer.

Under planned economy the dictator is not the consumer but the producer—the state—which prescribes how the consumer is to deport himself, what and how much he is to eat, what clothes he is to wear, where he is to live, what manner of life he is to follow. And the moment the Socialistic state acquires dictatorship over the consumer (in other words over the citizen who becomes forthwith a subject) it also assumes control over technical progress.

That, perhaps, may make clear why I view a Socialistically planned economy as embodying a conservative reactionary principle. An essential part of its very nature is a tendency to simplify things, make them "manageable," and therefore to crystallize everything at a given point.

To illustrate, one need only consider the parallel developments in technical invention and in manners of living during these past thirty years. Changes in dietary customs have revolutionized conditions in agriculture. The fact that women have come to wear lighter clothes has occasioned a crisis in cotton-growing. The radio and the talking-picture, which today play a leading rôle in the lives of the masses, were inconceivable 15 years ago. The use of the automobile as a commonplace vehicle has transformed the manners of living of the western peoples more profoundly than any other technical development of the last 150 years. The invention of the safety-razor should have put the barber out of business; instead, the switching of women from pigtails to bobbed hair has given the barber's business an importance no one could ever have dreamed it would have. For all such developments there would be no place whatever in a socialized "plan," for they have all been, as they will always remain, unforeseeable, owing their origin either to chance or to genius.

Differences of opinion are possible as to the importance to be attached to all such things. Here again the final judgment does not fall within the economic sphere. Recognizing the economic and technical superiority of capitalism, a person may still be a Communist because the Communist ideal as such, or the remedying of certain incidental defects in capitalism, may seem more important, more worth striving for. But that is not the decisive point. The decisive questions are whether individual freedom can exist apart from private property and freedom of consumption, and how highly one is to prize individual freedom. For even were capitalism incurably affected by all the evils ascribed to it by its opponents, it would still be a blessing to be defended to the last ditch if it were the only thinkable economic system under which individual freedom—freedom not only in the material sphere but freedom of thought, speech and movement—could be assured, and if a Socialistically planned economy precludes such freedom by nature and definition.

The real antithesis between capitalism and planned economy is therefore necessarily involved with the antithesis between democracy and dictatorship. And we have seen that this latter antithesis is unsolvable in the economic field.

VI

Fortunately, however, this antithesis is irreducible only in the domain of dialectic. As we have demonstrated, the capitalistic state has for a long time been located at the very center of business and it cannot and will not withdraw from that position. The problems with which it has to deal have ceased to be problems of ends: they are problems of means. How can the state meet the obligations that have been thrust upon it, without ruining business? How can it attain and preserve a maximum of social justice along with a maximum of economic efficiency? The state was gradually edged into the management of economic life at a time when it was not aware of doing any such thing and was far from wanting to do it. The problem that confronts it today is to make that management practical, to make it aware of its aims and purposes.

The question has to be considered along three lines: 1. Control of production. 2. Control of the distribution of national income. 3. Credit control and fiscal policy.

1. The scope of state control of production is relatively limited. It comes down, after all, to the problem of monopolies. For a generation or more the monopoly question has had a greater influence on political life in the United States than in any European country. The answer which the Americans found for it was to break up the monopoly and establish legal guarantees for free competition. The recent "codes" have to some extent taken the edge off this tendency in American political feeling, though it is apparent that the tendency as such is quite as strong as it ever was.

We must not forget, however, that another solution for the monopoly problem is possible: toleration of monopolies and governmental supervision of them. That has been the European solution, as developed more particularly in Germany. In most of Europe, railroads and public utilities are owned by governments, national or municipal. As regards control of industrial monopolies (in the form of trusts or cartels), practical results have been only moderately satisfactory. But the harm in that is not very serious; after all, the problem of industrial monopolies is far less important than the heated public discussion which it arouses might lead one to suppose. Even when there is no government interference, the limits within which the power of a monopoly can assert itself are very strictly prescribed. The monopoly or half-monopoly is commonly regarded as economically dangerous not only because the consumer may be exploited, but more especially because the excessive earnings of those who enjoy monopolies stimulate over-capitalization, which in the end represents economic waste. I do not believe that

that view is sound, or at least I do not consider it very important. I can think of no important case, either in America or Europe, where any real misdirection of investment is to be attributed to earnings from monopolies. But in any case, the fact that such-and-such an investment was wrong can ordinarily be determined in an objective sense only when the crisis resulting from it, real or apparent, has long since been overcome. Not till the next boom period does it become plain what has been rational or irrational in a given economic scheme.

Agriculture does not follow the law which business follows. Experiments like the A.A.A. may therefore be ignored in this connection. Agriculture turned to state control of production earlier and more generally than industry. There were so many causes for this, economic and non-economic, that I can hardly touch upon them here. In the farming world the technical revolution affected an especially conservative class of people, more than ordinarily resistant to change, and less adaptable to new circumstances. In agriculture, therefore, the state is promptly called in to halt or attenuate the working of economic laws. The state is now fulfilling that function by sheltering agricultural products—in different ways and to differing extents—from the law of supply and demand which rules the open market. Everywhere the farmer is winning the special treatment which he demands.

2. But the system of production is not (except for out-and-out Communists) the central point in the struggle in the political field. More and more the main way to drag the state into interference with business is through controlling the distribution of national revenue. Continuously greater and more varied needs of the masses are forever demanding and finding collective satisfaction. The great pot into which private initiative throws its product is being divided up more and more along collective lines. The state is pushing its activity in this connection further and further afield, and is assuming more and more of the responsibilities which used to be entrusted to private individuals. In this respect the United States has still much further to go than Europe,

where it is taken for granted that educational institutions, hospitals, theaters, picture galleries, should be maintained by the national or local government and not by private organizations. Actually, whether railroads or electrical plants are in private or public hands is much less important than the apostles of either system are inclined to pretend. In America, generally speaking, both those utilities are under private control. In Germany, electricity and railroad transport are both under public control. Fundamentally, nonetheless, the problems for both countries are the same. But the manner in which the state applies its policy of rate fixing is obviously becoming more and more important every day; for, both absolutely and relatively, the technique of traffic and of power supply plays a vastly more important rôle in social and economic life today than it did thirty or, say, fifty years ago. A much larger share of national income is being spent on railroads, automotive transport (in its relation to railroads, road-building, etc.) and electrical power than before, and to that extent a far larger proportion of this income is being made subject to governmental interference.

The housing problem will doubtless become even more important from this point of view in the years ahead. The rebuilding of the great cities of the civilized world is to constitute the great problem of the next decades. The masses of city dwellers live in buildings which do not in the least correspond to the technical and economic possibilities of our time. Strictly private initiative can hardly cope with the housing problem. The city of the future cannot be allowed to grow up wild; it has to be brought under a building plan. So far as one can foresee, this undertaking cannot be financed by private resources any more than the railroads or the schools can do without public support.

However, the most important and decisive step taken by the state in relation to the distribution of national income has been in the matter of unemployment insurance. This is the most typical product of the wartime conception that the state is called upon to guarantee a minimum subsistence to all its citizens. I doubt whether even the United States can very much longer avoid a system of organized public relief for the unemployed—whether it takes the form of insurance or some other form makes little difference. It is unendurable, both morally and from the standpoint of social utility, that millions of people who are out of work through no fault of their own should be abandoned to private charity. That is humiliating to giver and receiver alike, and the sense of humiliation, the feeling that hungry millions are dependent on the generosity of the rich, constitutes what is perhaps one of the greatest dangers to the capitalistic economic system. But however one looks at the matter, there can be no doubt that in guaranteeing subsistence to large numbers of its population the state is coming to apply a very considerable fraction of the social product to purposes which are determined by considerations not of an economic but of an entirely different order.

3. The problem of the unemployed drives the state to the last and most painful step. It cannot rest satisfied with dividing the pot which capitalistic production sets before it. The most urgent considerations force it to make sure that the pot is abundantly and regularly filled. And that brings us to the question that today overshadows all others—the question of state control over business cycles.

VII

The question as to whether and how far the state can control trade cycles and prevent crises must be put in the forefront of all current social and political thinking. The problem has very complicated and far-reaching ramifications. It may be said in the broadest sense to dominate the whole field of statesmanship in the latter's bearing on credit and finance.

Here again we must go back to the war days. The war gave governmental finance a quantitative significance that had never been dreamed of before. Public debts and public expenditures leapt into huge figures; and, since the war, state budgets the world over have taken on an altogether different structure. Two items which had played a subordinate rôle, or no rôle at all, have now come to constitute overwhelming and permanent burdens: interest on debts, and war pensions. Nowhere more conspicuously than in the domain of public finance has the state been forced from the border regions to the center of economic life. In most countries, in the old days, from five to ten percent of the national income had been sufficient to cover public obligations and expenditures. After the war the proportion rose in many countries to 50 percent, and even higher. So far as interest on debts is concerned, the state is undertaking nothing more than a redistribution of income, since the bondholders who collect their interest are also taxpayers. And the same is true, of course, of war pensions. But that makes the tax policy of the state and its credit policy only the more important—it is far from being a matter of indifference whether a government taps one source of income or some other in order to pay its debts. As things have turned out, the burden of debt which the war left in its wake has become unbearable, in the long run, for everybody concerned. For long years after the war there was a disposition in all European countries to play with the idea of a tax on capital in order to get free of part, at least, of the war debt. In some countries the thing was even put through.

But in the end all governments have followed the most practical road to a reduction of the war debt burden: devaluation of currency. The United States has been the last of the Great Powers to fall in with that policy, although in America the pressure of private debts played a more important part in bringing about devaluation than the public debt. But meantime the experience of the war has not been forgotten. The war showed to what unheard of lengths the state could go in controlling the capital market and in drawing on it for its own purposes; and it is altogether natural that once it has used that resource for war purposes it is tempted to use it also for the emergencies of peace.

Budget policy, tax policy, credit policy, currency policy—all go to make up one indivisible unit. Anything done in any one of those departments has its effect on all the others. As master of taxation, the state is in direct control of a large portion of the national income; as master of railroad and public utility rates the state is in indirect control of another large portion of the national income; as master of the credit markets the state has indirect command over investments; this state therefore cannot avoid taking currency under its control.

In broaching this theme I have no intention of touching on controversial matters connected with the recent currency policy of the United States. But ever since there have been centralized banking systems, the state has been coming closer and closer to control over currency. Since the war, we have seen the state everywhere taking charge of currency policy, however differently the formal and legal relation between government and central bank may be regulated in different countries. When important decisions have to be made, such formal differences count for little. Whether the Exchequer has the greater influence on the Bank of England or the Bank of England on the Exchequer is always a question of the individuals who happen to be in charge; but it is unthinkable that the Bank of England and the Exchequer could ever embark on conflicting policies. This is all the more true of France, to say nothing of Germany or Italy.

But once the state comes into possession of the decisive instruments of power in capitalistic economy—money and credit—it at once finds itself becoming responsible for prosperity and depression. That is an entirely new feature in the eventful history of the relations between state and business. It is, however, the logical consequence of an unmistakable development. Can the state assume any such responsibility and meet it—even halfway? That is the last and the most serious question which faces the state today. What it has been doing is nothing less than assuming responsibility for the whole economic fate of the nation.

I could not, within the scope of this article, even so much as allude to the theory of economic cycles. Whether the depression with which we are struggling is one of those normal cyclical developments that have been constantly recurring in the undulatory movement of capitalistic business ever since we have been able to follow its history, or whether it has an exclusively political background and so requires exclusively political remedies—that question I must leave aside. From the theoretical standpoint, the determining cause of the depression is a maladjustment between savings and investments. Every boom tends to drive investments above the savings' quota, and so to bring on a crash through an overstretching of credit. The readjustment takes place as the volume of credit is reduced, through the bankruptcy and shrinking of business, to the point where the supply of capital becomes more abundant, money becomes cheaper, and inducements are again offered to investors. The storm signal for a crash is the rapid rise of interest rates to abnormal heights (in 1929 call money reached 20 percent in New York). A sign of recovery is seen in a revival of the issuance of securities as a result of low interest rates on money. Whether this time this automatic recovery from depression through the cycle of credit expansion—credit restriction—new credit expansion, has failed we have no way of knowing, since everywhere, in Europe as well as in America, the impatience of governments has interfered with the "natural" course of things.

The forces which underlie that interference we have tried to lay bare in this article. State interference with the development of the cycle has not been voluntary, it has not been accidental, it has not been avoidable. But in saying that we have unfortunately said nothing as to its chances of success.

As long as the state handles itself as though it were a private businessman there is not much danger. The private businessman is on the lookout to keep a profitable relation between outlay and earnings. He will borrow money at three percent when he can use it in a business that promises four or five percent. If and so long as the state does nothing except replace private initiative, because the latter has been crippled by fright or inertia, it can do no great damage. But danger and damage appear in the offing when the state spends money for the mere sake of spending, regardless of economic purposes and returns. That means wastage of capital. In that case the state behaves like a spendthrift who enjoys himself for a longer or shorter period, but who some day stands face to face with ruin. The power of the state comes to an end at the point where the mechanism of the money and credit system begins to break down. The limit of the state's control of business is the line where inflation gets out of control. On that the mechanism of government itself breaks to pieces. Inflation may lead to the collapse of a governmental system.

(I must leave no room for doubt as to the fact that I see no such danger in Mr. Roosevelt's budget policy, provided it is really carried out to the end along present lines. The President does not seem to be contemplating the permanent replacement of private by public initiative. On the contrary, by concentrating the execution of great public enterprises in a short period of time, he merely is giving such strong encouragement to private initiative that the capitalistic machine will, so to speak, keep on running by itself. Danger will materialize only in case the impulse given to private initiative proves inadequate or merely ephemeral. In that case, the government will be faced with pressure from the masses and might have to carry on its program of expenditures on the original, or on an even larger, scale.)

VIII

Thus the problem of the relationship between political power and economic law becomes acute in a new and not yet sufficiently explored sense. A generation or more ago, science (in Boehm-Bawerk) had established the fact that inside the private capitalistic sphere the allotment (imputation) of national income to capital interest and wages can be only very slightly shifted by political pressure either from government or trade unions. But the state's present assumption of power over business becomes effective on a much higher plane. The state now claims the staggering prerogative of setting itself up as lord and master over the economic destiny of the nation, whereas in an earlier day it tried at the most to control conflicting group interests inside the economic framework. But here also the power of the state meets limits that are set by economic law. The conservative, of course, shudders at the mere attempt. He regards it as sheer insolence for the state ever to presume such a thing, for it ever to venture to interfere in the handiwork of God. And anyone who has enough imagination to appreciate the manifold and complicated nature of social processes can share that alarm. The conservative stands in awe and dread before the complexity of life. The radical takes things more lightly, partly because he does not know much about them, partly because he is not afraid of them so far as he feels himself a match for them. If the understanding and humble conservative finds himself involuntarily but unavoidably in alliance with inertia, the powerful ally of the aspiring radical is ignorance.

For the moment, however, the decision between the two does not rest with us, nor can we venture to prophesy what the future will be. Perhaps the conservative and the radical will join hands in the great and noble enterprise of political and economic education. Whether the state is to show itself equal to the gigantic task which history has thrust upon it is a question of the moral and intellectual qualification of leaders and masses alike. On this question hangs the destiny of capitalism and democracy.

❖ ❖ ❖

THE article "Nationalism and Economic Life," written by Leon Trotsky for FOREIGN AFFAIRS, was published in the issue of April 1934.

The barest facts of Trotsky's life are sensational: born in Elizavetgrad, Russia, 1879; exiled to Siberia 1898; escaped to England 1902; Chairman of the St. Petersburg Soviet in the revolution of 1905; again exiled to Siberia; again escaped; held an independent position between the Bolsheviks and Mensheviks, but joined the Bolshevik Party in Petrograd in 1917; Commissar for Foreign Affairs 1917–18; Commissar for War 1919–23; expelled from the Communist Party 1927; exiled 1928; banished 1929; assassinated in Mexico City August 20, 1940.

Trotsky was second only to Lenin in bringing to pass the triumph of will and doctrine that constituted the Russian Revolution, and when that act had been performed he could describe it, in "History of the Russian Revolution," in marvelous language. But all else was anticlimax. "Trotsky side-stepped the heritage of Lenin because he was inadequate to it," wrote Max Eastman, the American who knew him best. "Although incapable of saying so even to himself, he *felt* inadequate to it. He could command minds; he could command armies; he could sway masses from the safe distance of the platform. But he could not bring two strong men to his side as friends and hold them there."

He was one of the greatest men of words of our time, but he has likewise provided history with one of its supreme examples of intellect divorced from insight into human beings. The gift of tongues which so many of these Fathers of the Marxist Church enjoyed produced a "law" for every contingency. (Bukharin even included in his dialectical armory—as the reader will have noted a few pages back—the astonishing "law of the heterogeneity of aims"—in simple English, the law that anything can happen.) Only one thing is unprovided for in Trotsky's scintillating generalizations—the way in which men can alter the operation of blind historical forces by becoming aware of them. The third paragraph from the end of this article is a particularly interesting one for Americans who wish to test the validity of Trotsky's words against their own knowledge of his strengths and weaknesses, and their understanding of the forces with which Americans are confronted today.

❖ ❖ ❖

NATIONALISM AND ECONOMIC LIFE

By Leon Trotsky

ITALIAN Fascism has proclaimed national "sacred egoism" as the sole creative factor. After reducing the history of humanity to national history, German Fascism proceeded to reduce nation to race, and race to blood. Moreover, in those countries which politically have not risen—or rather, descended—to Fascism, the problems of economy are more and more being forced into national frameworks. Not all of them have the courage to inscribe "autarchy" openly upon their banners. But everywhere policy is being directed toward as hermetic a segregation as possible of national life away from world economy. Only twenty years ago all the school books taught that the mightiest factor in producing wealth and culture is the world-wide division of labor, lodged in the natural and historic conditions of the development of mankind. Now it turns out that world exchange is the source of all misfortunes and all dangers. Homeward ho! Back to the national hearth! Not only must we correct the mistake of Admiral Perry, who blasted the breach in Japan's "autarchy," but a correction must also be made of the much bigger mistake of Christopher Columbus, which resulted in so immoderately extending the arena of human culture.

The enduring value of the nation, discovered by Mussolini and Hitler, is now set off against the false values of the nineteenth century: democracy and Socialism. Here too we come into an irreconcilable contradiction with the old primers, and, worse yet, with the irrefutable facts of history. Only vicious ignorance can draw a sharp contrast between the nation and liberal democracy. As a matter of fact, all the movements of liberation in modern history, beginning, say, with Holland's struggle for independence, had both a national and a democratic character. The awakening of the oppressed and dismembered nations, their struggle to unite their severed parts and to throw off the foreign yoke, would have been impossible without a struggle for political liberty. The French nation was consolidated in the storms and tempests of democratic revolution at the close of the eighteenth century. The Italian and German nations emerged from a series of wars and revolutions in the nineteenth century. The powerful development of the American nation, which had received its baptism of freedom in its uprising in the eighteenth century, was finally guaranteed by the victory of the North over the South in the Civil War. Neither Mussolini nor Hitler is the discoverer of the nation. Patriotism in its modern sense—or more precisely its bourgeois sense—is the product of the nineteenth century. The national consciousness of the French people is perhaps the most conservative and the most stable of any; and to this very day it feeds from the springs of democratic traditions.

But the economic development of mankind which overthrew mediæval particularism did not stop within national boundaries. The growth of world exchange took place parallel with the formation of national economies. The tendency of this development—for advanced countries, at any rate—found its expression in the shift of the center of gravity from the domestic to the foreign market. The nineteenth century was marked by the fusion of the nation's fate with the fate of its economic life; but the basic tendency of our century is the growing contradiction between the nation and economic life. In Europe this contradiction has become intolerably acute.

The development of German capitalism was of the most dynamic character. In the middle of the nineteenth century the German people felt themselves stifled in the cages of several dozen feudal fatherlands. Less than four decades after the creation of the German Empire, German industry was suffocating within the framework of the national state. One of the main causes of the World War was the striving of German capital to break through into a wider arena. Hitler fought as a corporal in 1914–1918 not to unite the German nation but in the name of a supra-national imperialistic program that expressed itself in the famous formula "to organize Europe." Unified under the domination of German militarism Europe was to have become the drill-ground for a much bigger job—the organization of the entire planet.

But Germany was no exception. She only expressed in a more intense and aggressive form the tendency of every other national capitalist economy. The clash between these tendencies resulted in the war. The war, it is true, like all the grandiose upheavals of history, stirred up various historical questions and in passing gave the impulse to national revolutions in the more backward sections of Europe—Tsarist Russia and Austria-Hungary. But these were only the belated echoes of an epoch that had already passed away. Essentially the war was imperialist in character. With lethal and barbaric methods it attempted to solve a problem of progressive historic development—the problem of organizing economic life over the entire arena which had been prepared by the world-wide division of labor.

Needless to say, the war did not find the solution to this problem. On the contrary, it atomized Europe even more. It deepened the interdependence of Europe and America at the same time that it deepened the antagonism between them. It gave the impetus to the independent development of colonial countries and simultaneously sharpened the dependence of the metropolitan centers upon colonial markets. As a consequence of the war, all the contradictions of the past were aggravated. One could half-shut one's eyes to this during the first years after the war, when Europe, aided by America, was busy repairing its devastated economy from top to bottom. But to restore productive forces inevitably implied the reinvigorating of all those evils that had led to the war. The present crisis, in which are synthesized all the capitalist crises of the past, signifies above all the crisis of *national* economic life.

The League of Nations attempted to translate from the language of militarism into the language of diplomatic pacts the task which the war left unsolved. After Ludendorff had failed to "organize Europe" by the sword, Briand attempted to create "the United States of Europe" by means of sugary diplomatic eloquence. But the interminable series of political, economic, financial, tariff and monetary conferences only unfolded the panorama of the bankruptcy of the ruling classes in face of the unpostponable and burning task of our epoch.

Theoretically this task may be formulated as follows: How may the economic unity of Europe be guaranteed, while preserving complete freedom of cultural development to the peoples living there? How may unified Europe be included within a coördinated world economy? The solution to this question can be reached not by deifying the nation, but on the contrary by completely liberating productive forces from the fetters imposed upon them by the national state. But the ruling classes of Europe, demoralized by the bankruptcy of military and diplomatic methods, approach the task today from the opposite end, that is, they attempt by force to subordinate economy to the outdated national state. The legend of the bed of Procrustes is being reproduced on a grand scale. Instead of clearing away a suitably large arena for the operations of modern technology, the rulers chop and slice the living organism of economy to pieces.

In a recent program speech Mussolini hailed the death of "economic liberalism," that is, of the reign of free competition. The idea itself is not new. The epoch of trusts, syndicates and cartels has long since relegated free competition to the backyard. But trusts are even less reconcilable with restricted national markets than are the enterprises of liberal capitalism. Monopoly devoured competition in proportion as the world economy subordinated the national market. Economic liberalism and economic nationalism became outdated at the same time. Attempts to save economic life by inoculating it with virus from the corpse of nationalism result in blood poisoning which bears the name of Fascism.

Mankind is impelled in its historic ascent by the urge to

attain the greatest possible quantity of goods with the least expenditure of labor. This material foundation of cultural growth provides also the most profound criterion by which we may appraise social régimes and political programs. The law of the productivity of labor is of the same significance in the sphere of human society as the law of gravitation in the sphere of mechanics. The disappearance of outgrown social formations is but the manifestation of this cruel law that determined the victory of slavery over cannibalism, of serfdom over slavery, of hired labor over serfdom. The law of the productivity of labor finds its way not in a straight line but in a contradictory manner, by spurts and jerks, leaps and zigzags, surmounting on its way geographical, anthropological and social barriers. Whence so many "exceptions" in history, which are in reality only specific refractions of the "rule."

In the nineteenth century the struggle for the greatest productivity of labor took mainly the form of free competition, which maintained the dynamic equilibrium of capitalist economy through cyclical fluctuation. But precisely because of its progressive rôle competition has led to a monstrous concentration of trusts and syndicates, and this in turn has meant a concentration of economic and social contradictions. Free competition is like a chicken that hatched not a duckling but a crocodile. No wonder she cannot manage her offspring!

Economic liberalism has completely outlived its day. With less and less conviction its Mohegans appeal to the automatic interplay of forces. New methods are needed to make skyscraper trusts correspond to human needs. There must be radical changes in the structure of society and economy. But new methods come into clash with old habits and, what is infinitely more important, with old interests. The law of the productivity of labor beats convulsively against barriers which it itself set up. This is what lies at the core of the grandiose crisis of the modern economic system.

Conservative politicians and theorists, taken unawares by the destructive tendencies of national and international economy, incline towards the conclusion that the overdevelopment of technology is the principal cause of present evils. It is difficult to imagine a more tragic paradox! A French politician and financier, Joseph Caillaux, sees salvation in artificial limitations on the process of mechanization. Thus the most enlightened representatives of the liberal doctrine suddenly draw inspiration from the sentiments of those ignorant workers of over a hundred years ago who smashed weaving looms. The progressive task of how to adapt the arena of economic and social relations to the new technology is turned upside down, and is made to seem a problem of how to restrain and cut down productive forces so as to fit them to the old national arena and to the old social relations. On both sides of the Atlantic no little mental energy is wasted on efforts to solve the fantastic problem of how to drive the crocodile back into the chicken egg. The ultramodern economic nationalism is irrevocably doomed by its own reactionary character; it retards and lowers the productive forces of man.

The policies of a closed economy imply the artificial constriction of those branches of industry which are capable of fertilizing successfully the economy and culture of other countries. They also imply an artificial planting of those industries which lack favorable conditions for growth on national soil. The fiction of economic self-sufficiency thus causes tremendous overhead expenditures in two directions. Added to this is inflation. During the nineteenth century, gold as a universal measure of value became the foundation of all monetary systems worthy of the name. Departures from the gold standard tear world economy apart even more successfully than do tariff walls. Inflation, itself an expression of disordered internal relationships and of disordered economic ties between nations, intensifies the disorder and helps to turn it from a functional into an organic one. Thus the "national" monetary system crowns the sinister work of economic nationalism.

The most intrepid representatives of this school console themselves with the prospect that the nation, while becoming poorer under a closed economy will become more "unified" (Hitler), and that as the importance of the world market declines the causes for external conflicts will also diminish. Such hopes only demonstrate that the doctrine of autarchy is both reactionary and utterly utopian. The fact is that the breeding places of nationalism also are the laboratories of terrific conflicts in the future; like a hungry tiger, imperialism has withdrawn into its own national lair to gather itself for a new leap.

Actually, theories about economic nationalism which seem to base themselves on the "eternal" laws of race show only how desperate the world crisis really is—a classic example of making a virtue of bitter need. Shivering on bare benches in some God-forsaken little station, the passengers of a wrecked train may stoically assure each other that creature comforts are corrupting to body and soul. But all of them are dreaming of a locomotive that would get them to a place where they could stretch their tired bodies between two clean sheets. The immediate concern of the business world in all countries is to hold out, to survive somehow, even if in a coma, on the hard bed of the national market. But all these involuntary stoics are longing for the powerful engine of a new world "conjuncture," a new economic phase.

Will it come? Predictions are rendered difficult, if not altogether impossible, by the present structural disturbance of the whole economic system. Old industrial cycles, like the heartbeats of a healthy body, had a stable rhythm. Since the war we no longer observe the orderly sequence of economic phases; the old heart skips beats. In addition, there is the policy of so-called "state capitalism." Driven on by restless interests and by social dangers, governments burst into the economic realm with emergency measures, the effects of which in most cases it cannot itself foresee. But even leaving aside the possibility of a new war that would upset for a long time the elemental work of economic forces as well as conscious attempts at planned control, we nevertheless can confidently foresee the turning point from the crisis and depression to a revival, whether or not the favorable symptoms present in England and to some degree in the United States prove later on to have been first swallows that did not bring the spring. The destructive work of the crisis must reach the point—if it has not already reached it—where impoverished mankind will need a new mass of goods. Chimneys will smoke, wheels will turn. And when the revival is sufficiently advanced, the business world will shake off its stupor, will promptly forget yesterday's lessons, and will contemptuously cast aside self-denying theories along with their authors.

But it would be the greatest delusion to hope that the scope of the impending revival will correspond to the depth of the present crisis. In childhood, in maturity, and in old age the heart beats at a different tempo. During capitalism's ascent successive crises had a fleeting character and the temporary decline in production was more than compensated by the increase in production at the next stage. It is so no longer. We have entered an epoch when the periods of economic revival are short-lived, while the periods of depression will constantly become deeper and deeper. The lean cows devour the fat cows without a trace and still continue to bellow with hunger.

All the capitalist states will be more aggressively impatient, then, as soon as the economic barometer begins to rise. The struggle for foreign markets will become unprecedentedly sharp. Pious notions about the advantages of autarchy will at once be cast side, and sage plans for national harmony will be thrown in the wastepaper basket. This applies not only to German capitalism, with its explosive dynamics, or to the belated and greedy capitalism of Japan, but also to the capitalism of America, which still is powerful despite its new contradictions.

The United States represented the most perfect type of capitalist development. The relative equilibrium of its internal and seemingly inexhaustible market assured the United States a decided technical and economic preponderance over Europe. But its intervention in the World War was really an expression of the fact that its internal equilibrium was already disrupted. The changes introduced by the war into the American structure have in turn made entry into the world arena a life and death question for American capitalism. There is ample evidence that this entry must assume extremely dramatic forms.

The law of the productivity of labor is of decisive significance in the interrelations of America and Europe, and in general in determining the future place of the United States in the world. That highest form which the Yankees gave to the law of the productivity of labor is called conveyor, standard, or mass production. It would seem that the spot from which the lever of Archimedes was to turn the world over had been found. But the old planet refuses to be turned over. Everyone defends himself against everybody else, protecting himself by a customs wall and a hedge of bayonets. Europe buys no goods, pays no debts, and in addition arms itself. With five miserable divisions starved Japan seizes a whole country. The most advanced technique in the world suddenly seems impotent before obstacles basing themselves on a much lower technique. The law of the productivity of labor seems to lose its force.

But it only seems so. The basic law of human history must inevitably take revenge on derivative and secondary phenomena. Sooner or later American capitalism must open up ways for itself throughout the length and breadth of our entire planet. By what methods? By *all* methods. A high coefficient of productivity denotes also a high coefficient of destructive force. Am I preaching war? Not in the least. I am not preaching anything. I am only attempting to analyze the world situation and to draw conclusions from the laws of economic mechanics. There is nothing worse than the sort of mental cowardice which turns its back on facts and tendencies when they contradict ideals or prejudices.

Only in the historic framework of world development can we assign Fascism its proper place. It contains nothing creative, nothing independent. Its historic mission is to reduce to an absurdity the theory and practice of the economic impasse.

In its day democratic nationalism led mankind forward. Even now, it is still capable of playing a progressive rôle in the colonial countries of the east. But decadent Fascist nationalism, preparing volcanic explosions and grandiose clashes in the world arena, bears nothing except ruin. All our experiences on this score during the last 25 or 30 years will seem only an idyllic overture compared to the music of hell that is impending. And this time it is not a temporary economic decline which is involved but complete economic devastation and the destruction of our entire culture, in the event that toiling and thinking humanity proves incapable of grasping in time the reins of its own productive forces and of organizing those forces correctly on a European and a world scale.

❖ ❖ ❖

THE statement of "The Aims of Japan" made in July 1935 by Baron Reijero Wakatsuki illuminates the issue which confronted the people of the United States in the Pacific after 1931: to consent to the dismemberment of China or to fight Japan.

At the beginning of the thirties, China was unmistakably achieving nationhood. Japan dared wait no longer, and in 1931 she struck the first blow in Manchuria. The Stimson doctrine of nonrecognition of that conquest served notice that the United States would not abandon its policy of supporting the integrity of China; but there was no will to back words with action.

The series of naval conferences from 1922 to 1934 express in the peculiar hieroglyphics of ship ratios the painful adjustment of Great Britain and the United States to the realities of the postwar situation in the Pacific. For Britain, the essence of that situation was that her day as mistress of the seas was ended. The Washington Conference of 1922, which set a capital ship ratio of 5-5-3 for the United States, Britain and Japan, was in retrospect less significant for the scrapping of ships than for Britain's acceptance of the idea of parity with another Power. Once that hurdle had been taken, Britain and the United States moved on with relatively little delay, though with much talking at cross purposes, to their natural naval partnership.

For the United States the reality so painful to grasp was that Japan was prepared to fight for a Pacific empire. Japan's diplomatic objective, therefore, was so to limit the United States Navy that it could not contest this design, and she pursued it with increasing boldness in the conferences from 1927 to 1934. When the 1934 conversations were held, Japan demanded the end of all ratios and proposed limitation by total tonnage only. The upshot was the end of naval disarmament.

Baron Wakatsuki, twice Prime Minister, three times Minister of Finance and chief Japanese delegate to the Naval Conference of 1930, was a leader of the Japanese "liberals"—the amorphous group which Americans counted upon to rescue them from the logic of the choice confronting them. But the fact was that the assumption of the Japanese Foreign Office on the issue which would determine peace or war was precisely the same as that of the most fervid Japanese militarists. From the premise that Japan must expand overseas flowed the inexorable conclusions as to Manchuria, as to China, as to east Asia, and as to war with the United States.

❖ ❖ ❖

THE AIMS OF JAPAN

By Baron Reijiro Wakatsuki

IT IS with considerable diffidence that I venture to present briefly my views concerning Japan and her aims, for I am not at all certain that I can say anything which has not already been said many times. I do, however, welcome an opportunity of addressing American leaders in the world of thought and diplomacy. I should like to talk to them, as it were, in an informal, heart-to-heart fashion. That will serve best, I believe, the cause of Japanese-American friendship.

I am firmly convinced, as a large number of Japanese are convinced, that friendship between the United States and Japan is essential not only to both countries but to the welfare of the entire world. Perhaps I may be permitted to be somewhat personal. Towards the end of 1929, on my way to the naval conference which was then about to open in London, I spent a few days in Washington, where I had the opportunity of conferring with President Hoover and Secretary Stimson. What was then uppermost in my mind was how to advance Japan's friendly relations with the United States. To that end I considered it to be of the greatest importance that the two countries should come to an understanding on naval questions in advance of the London Conference. It was for that reason that I went to London by way of the United States. I recall with much pleasure and keen appreciation the hearty welcome given to me in Washington, and the friendly spirit in which both the President and the Secretary of State expressed themselves on various questions. Since then, whether as head of the Japanese Government, or as the leader of a political party, or merely as a private citizen, I have always done all I could to promote Japanese-American friendship. Naturally I have followed with constant and careful attention American public opinion towards Japan, as well as Japanese public opinion towards the United States.

II

The results of the London Treaty and more recently the Manchurian incident shocked public opinion considerably in Japan and in the United States. There were a number of Americans who criticized and condemned Japan's policy, just as there were a number of Japanese who held similar opinions about the policy of the United States. But I believe that before a nation passes any judgment upon another nation's conduct she should first consider what she herself would have done had she been in that nation's place. Therefore, I should like to ask you first of all to visualize clearly the situation confronting Japan.

I can readily enough see how difficult it must be for you to put yourselves in our place, as there are few points in common between the situation which confronts America and that which confronts Japan. The physical and geographical circumstances of the two countries are totally different, to say nothing of their histories or their customs and manners. Your country is compact, though vast in area; it is peopled rather sparsely, though the total population is great; and it is immeasurably rich in natural resources. In fact, America is almost entirely self-sufficient and self-supporting. Ours is a country consisting of many small scattered islands, extremely overcrowded, and so poor in natural resources that we must largely depend on imports for our supply of raw materials. The neighbors with whom you may have troubles are either small or militarily quite impotent. On the contrary, we are face to face with two great continental Powers—China, with an area 16 times as large as ours and a population of 400,000,000, and the Soviet Union, with an area 30 times as large as ours and a population of 160,000,000. These countries, by reason of the exceptional conditions prevailing in them, have been sources of constant anxiety to Japan.

In view of such an absolute difference in the situations of

Japan and the United States it may be too much to ask that you put yourselves in our place before you criticize our actions. But this you should try to do, just as we should try to put ourselves in your place before criticizing your actions. And I cannot help believing that, if you were in our place, you would be doing exactly what we are doing today.

III

As regards the domestic situation of Japan, we are faced first of all with a most pressing problem of population. We have at present a population of 90,000,000, and because of the smallness of our area Japan is one of the most densely populated countries in the world. This population, I must also point out, is increasing very rapidly, at the rate of eight or nine hundred thousand per annum.

Although it is only a few decades since we came into close contact with the Occident, Japan is an old country. We have long been known as an active and energetic nation. Marco Polo, who returned to Venice in 1295 from his travels on the Asiatic mainland, wrote of the "indomitable courage of the people of Zipangu." More than three hundred years after Marco Polo's time our country entered upon a hermit life, which lasted from 1636 to 1858. During that period the isolationist policy of the Tokugawa Shogunate suppressed the expansive vigor of the people. But as soon as the Meiji Restoration lifted the ban on foreign intercourse the long-pent-up energy of our race was released, and with a fresh outlook and enthusiasm the nation has made swift progress.

When you know this historical background and understand this overflowing vitality of our race you will see the impossibility of compelling us to stay still within the confines of our little island home. We are destined to grow and expand overseas. Well, then, whither? If Japan had, like America or Great Britain, immense and sparsely populated territories, it would not be necessary for us to go to Manchuria or anywhere else on the Asiatic mainland. The United States, Canada, Australia and New Zealand and other regions in the Pacific, with vast areas and scanty populations, where there is much room for emigration, are closed to us for no other reason than that we are Japanese. As for the question of Japanese immigration into the United States, while we resent strongly the discriminatory treatment to which Japanese are subjected, it is after all a question for the solution of which we consider it best to appeal to your sense of justice. Very recently, when an anti-Japanese movement arose in Arizona we relied for the settlement of the affair entirely upon the sense of justice and fair play of Americans. We do not wish to send our immigrants to any country where they are not desired. While we believe that the American law for the restriction of immigration is decidedly unfair to us, we are not disposed to demand the entry of Japanese into the United States against the wishes of the American people.

The path of our expansion lies, then, naturally in the direction of Manchuria, which is contiguous to Chosen. It was because of our concern for the peace of East Asia no less than because of our conviction that our only path of progress lay on the continent of Asia that at the time of the Manchurian incident our nation rose spontaneously as one man to grapple with the situation. The Manchurian affair was really a life-or-death struggle for Japan.

IV

Let us turn to Japan's industry. It is a fact that of late our industries have developed notably and that our country is being fast industrialized. In this connection I should like to call your attention to two points—first, that the industrialization of our country will contribute to the solution of our population problem; and secondly, that our industrial and commercial expansion has brought in its wake many serious international problems.

Westerners are in the habit of gauging the culture or civilization of a nation by its standard of living, and of vaunting their generous desire to bring the other peoples of the world up to their level of enlightenment. That is in a way true. Now we Japanese are doing our best to elevate our standard of living, which is not quite so high as that of some Occidental peoples. And it is to that end that we are developing our industry and commerce, which is practically the only way to increase our national wealth since our country is so poor in natural resources. We reorganized and improved our commercial and industrial methods. We worked patiently and tirelessly until we were in a position to compete in the world market with other advanced nations. However, we at once encountered a stupendous obstacle in the form of a boycott in China, the biggest market for our merchandise. When on February 24, 1933, the Assembly of the League of Nations adopted a report which declared that the Chinese boycott subsequent to the Manchurian incident was a legitimate means of reprisal in the light of international law, China was virtually closed to Japanese trade. There are those who accuse Japan of attempting to close China to other Powers, but as a matter of fact it was Japan who was shut out of China. We were forced to seek the outlet for our merchandise elsewhere. The flow of Japanese goods into various quarters of the globe was, though largely due to quality and price, traceable in part to the anti-Japanese agitation in China.

Great Britain and other Powers then began to adopt the quota system and other measures for preventing the importation of Japanese goods into their territories, despite Japan's protest that such action was a violation of commercial treaties. In view of the fact that Japanese articles, because of their good quality and cheapness, are welcomed by a large majority of the consumers in every country, and are in especial demand amongst the native populace of the European colonies in Asia and Africa, one cannot but conclude that the home governments are sacrificing the interests of large numbers of consumers in order to protect a few producers. It is questionable, however, whether a country can ultimately succeed in an attempt to protect its industries by artificial devices for the exclusion of foreign goods, without endeavoring either to improve its industrial organization and technique or to increase the efficiency of its workers.

Accordingly, I doubt very much if the prevailing economic nationalism, inaugurated by the European Powers, can continue indefinitely. At any rate, it is a regrettable fact that they are erecting various trade barriers to obstruct the free interchange of goods, and thus handicapping the cause of human happiness and progress. I believe that freedom of trade is essential for the promotion of the mutual interests and well-being of the nations. I hope, therefore, that all the Powers, casting aside shortsighted policies, will put international trade back upon the normal basis where it ministers to the wants of each and where it furthers mutual prosperity.

However, to return to my first point, the promotion of Japan's foreign trade is closely knit up with her international relations inasmuch as it directly implies the expansion of her industries. This in its turn advances Japan's culture and civilization by raising the standard of living, and offers an effective means of solving her population problem.

The world is moving forward constantly. But we cannot shut our eyes to the fact that the backward nations are moving at a much faster rate, in order to catch up with the more advanced nations in culture and civilization. Thus the Asiatic nations, now wide awake, are struggling to approach the level of European and American nations. It is necessary, then, in the interests of world peace and harmony, that the advancing nations be given adequate spheres of activity and expansion. Japan, which is forging ahead at a very rapid pace, is surely one of those nations.

V

Let us now examine Japan's environment.

Our relations with China date far back in history. Even during the period of isolation under the Tokugawa régime we continued to have friendly intercouse with China. But when early in the last decade of the nineteenth century she adopted an aggressive policy toward Korea, and threatened the peace of the Far East, we fought her (1894–95) and drove out Chinese influence from the peninsula. Following the Sino-Japanese War, China concluded a secret treaty with Russia, by which the latter was given the right to construct the Chinese Eastern Railway in Manchuria in return for a promise to come to China's aid in case of another war with Japan. Once entrenched in Manchuria, Russia launched out upon the conquest of the Far East. We fought her in 1904–5, and drove out Russian influence from South Manchuria.

In 1912 the Manchu Dynasty fell, and China became a republic. It was Sun Yat-sen himself, father of the Chinese Revolution and founder of the Kuomintang Party, who preached the doctrine of so-called "Great Asianism," urging the coöperation of Japan and China and declaring that China should abandon Manchuria as being the most likely source of Sino-Japanese friction. And it was the Canton Government, set up by Sun Yat-sen, which sent the expeditionary force under Chiang Kai-shek to the north and succeeded in establishing the present Nanking régime. But after the death of Sun Yat-sen the leaders of the Kuomintang, and later the authorities of the Nanking Government, adopted the ruthless anti-foreign policy called "revolutionary diplomacy." They attempted to check the Powers by playing off one against another. Hoisting the banners of "anti-imperialism" and "abrogation of unequal treaties," they clamored for the abolition of extraterritoriality, the return of foreign concessions at various ports, the cancellation of the Boxer Indemnities, etc. Now earlier, at the Washington Conference, we had made concessions to China which few other Great Powers similarly situated would have made. We had done this out of our growing sympathy with China and in the hope that after achieving unity and setting her house in order at an early date, she would redeem the various obligations which she had undertaken at that conference. It was such sanguine hopes and liberal beliefs which caused us to sign the Washington treaties regarding both the navy and China. These hopes were dashed by subsequent events. China failed to meet her obligations under the Washington Treaty. Indeed, our conciliatory attitude only served to increase her arrogance. In particular, our position in Manchuria became more and more precarious. There accumulated between Japan and China more than three hundred unsolved questions. It was in this tense atmosphere that the Manchurian incident occurred in 1931.

The split between China and Japan caused by the Manchurian incident lasted for some time. But of late the leaders of both the Chinese Government and the Kuomintang, realizing the folly of persisting in their antagonism toward Japan, and understanding better her real intentions, have been assuming a friendly attitude in harmony with the spirit of Sun Yat-sen's teachings. As a result, it seems to me, Sino-Japanese relations are now on the way to being restored to a normal basis. At the time of the Manchurian incident there were many critics in other countries, especially in yours, who severely censured our action. But now that Sino-Japanese relations are taking such a favorable turn European and American fears seem to have been groundless.

However, China has still to reckon with the Communists who have their strongholds in Szechuan and Kweichow. These are establishing contacts with their comrades in Sinkiang, across the Province of Chinghai which is practically a no-man's land. And there is the southwestern party which maintains an independent régime in Canton, and refuses to take orders from the Nanking Government. Such a state of disunity is directly or indirectly a source of concern to us.

VI

The Soviet Union is another neighbor of ours. The aggressive policy of the Tsarist Government brought on the Russo-Japanese War, as the result of which Russia was forced to withdraw from South Manchuria. The government of the Soviet Union was reported to have made a declaration in 1919 to the effect that it would abandon all the old Russian concessions in China; but it retained its rights in the Chinese Eastern Railway and held North Manchuria securely as its sphere of influence until the establishment of Manchukuo in 1931. Since then Moscow seems to have found it necessary to retire. However, in Outer

Mongolia and in Sinkiang the Soviet Union has consolidated its position. Although by the Sino-Soviet treaty of 1924 the Soviet Union recognized Outer Mongolia as an integral part of the Republic of China, Moscow had previously (in 1921) signed a separate treaty with "The People's Government of Mongolia," recognizing it to be "the sole lawful government of Mongolia," and the two Governments later exchanged plenipotentiary representatives. Today Outer Mongolia is virtually a Russian protectorate administered under a Soviet system. The present head of Sinkiang Province, Sheng Shih-tsai by name, is dependent on Russian support and the province is completely under Moscow's domination.

The aim of the Soviet Union is to bring about a world revolution and set up a proletarian dictatorship everywhere. The Soviet leaders have persistently worked to achieve their objective, though with varying intensity. For some years the Communist movement in China was widespread, and until very recently held Kiangsi and several other provinces in its grip. When the Union of Socialist Republics of China was established, with its seat of government at Suichin, the pamphleteers in Russia urged an alliance of the two Soviet unions of Russia and China. And they raged furiously over the advent of Manchukuo because it shattered a convenient link for that projected alliance.

VII

The policies and internal situations of China and Soviet Russia being what they are, these two great and close neighbors of Japan affect us both directly and indirectly. We once had to fight China, and then we had to fight Russia, at a great sacrifice of blood and treasure, for the preservation of the peace of East Asia. The peace of East Asia would not have been maintained, nor would the rights and interests of the Powers there have been secured, if Japan had not played the part of a watchdog. On the peace of East Asia hangs the fate of our nation. Other Powers may have important interests there, but these interests at most concern only their commercial prosperity, whereas the interests which we have are vital. I doubt if you have anywhere outside your borders interests so vital to you as those which we have in East Asia are to us. But supposing we did interfere in some question involving your vital interests, how would you feel about us? Our concern over affairs in East Asia is surely far more profound than any you ever have felt over questions touching your neighboring states. That is why we cherish so earnestly, and are ready to guard at any price, the peace of East Asia.

VIII

I feel I cannot leave the naval question out of any general discussion of Japan's problems.

The preliminary naval conversations opened in June of last year were adjourned in December, and the results are now being carefully considered by the respective governments concerned, with a view, no doubt, to paving the way to a formal conference in the near future. Those conversations served a useful purpose in that they clarified the viewpoints of the three major naval Powers as to their respective requirements, policies and intentions. Viewed in that light, the London parley was not a failure but a success, for naval accord is possible only when each of the interested Powers knows where and how the others stand. Since the findings at London are now being weighed by the three governments it would be inappropriate for me to go too far in detail into the subject at this time.

I was present as Japan's chief delegate at the London Naval Conference of 1930. The difficulties which that conference had to face at the outset were many, including not a few that seemed well-nigh insurmountable. I need not touch here upon the difficulties experienced by the delegates of the other Powers, but shall confine myself to our own problems.

To Japan, the most important question was whether or not the naval ratio of 5–5–3, which as you all know had been adopted at the Washington Conference of 1922 for the

American, British and Japanese capital ships and aircraft carriers respectively, should be extended to cruisers, destroyers and submarines. Japan took the stand that the same ratio should not be applied to auxiliary craft, and we submitted an alternative plan. Other Powers failed to agree to this plan on certain important points. It became obvious that our insistence upon our own formula would wreck the conference. We thought the consequences of a failure would be most unfortunate to all, and therefore, taking a larger view of things, we accepted, though reluctantly, a basis of deliberation that would lead the conference to success instead of failure. When I signed the resultant agreement on April 22, 1930, I issued a written statement, in my official capacity as Japan's chief delegate, in which I made it clear that the agreement was not to serve as a precedent in any subsequent naval conference. I stated plainly my hope and expectation that at the next conference, which was to meet within five years, the Powers would reconsider the whole question of ratio on a new basis. In spite of the unequivocal reservation which we made, it was, I must confess, an ungrateful task for us to sign the London Naval Treaty. We did sign it in the hope that it might materially contribute towards international harmony and particularly towards our friendly relations with the United States. However, as the years passed, the popular dissatisfaction in Japan with the London Conference and the London Naval Treaty grew in intensity, and manifested itself in one way or another upon various occasions.

Today there still remain a number of pending naval issues between Japan, Great Britain and the United States. As has been officially stated more than once, our proposition is that each Power should maintain such a navy as will not menace other Powers—a navy insufficient for attack but adequate for defense—and that the armament should be reduced to the very minimum required for defensive purposes so as to lighten the tax burden of the peoples.

A fundamental point in the naval problem, and one which I think Americans should bear in mind above all others, is that neither Japan nor any other Power on earth can effectively attack or invade their vast continent. Occasionally I read press dispatches from Washington reporting military and naval appropriations amounting to hundreds of millions of dollars. Of course that is an internal question for your country with which no foreigner should interfere. But you should keep in mind one thing, namely, that you are in a position in which no nation can attack you either from the Pacific or from the Atlantic, either from the air or from the sea. No naval Power can ever blockade you. The mere size of your territory and population, the magnitude of your wealth and resources, stand as an effective warning against any possible contemplation of foreign aggression.

In this respect Japan is the very opposite of America. From the standpoints of geographical position, topography, and size of territory and resources, as well as because of other circumstances, our country is not secure from external menace. We keep our navy for the sole purpose of defending our land. We harbor no aggressive designs against others, nor do we even contemplate sending our fleets near the waters of another country. We do not believe that a foreign Power should possess a navy capable of menacing another country.

IX

Following the Great War the nations, eager to secure a permanent peace and to dispense with the old world order which was based on the balance of power and under which one alliance was pitted against another, brought into being the League of Nations. The war-weary nations of Europe and all the other peoples rejoiced in the hope and belief that peace—a permanent and universal peace—had dawned upon the ruin left by the war. At the Washington Conference, held shortly thereafter, we made all possible concessions and signed the treaties concerning China, expecting that that country would forthwith set to work to restore order and achieve unity. We also signed the naval treaty which was to prevent a needless naval competition among the sea Powers. And subsequently for some years our government pursued a policy of drastic retrenchment not only on naval but also on military expenditure.

But the glowing hopes we had entertained for the new world order began to fade. In Europe the frail structure of international relations founded upon the various peace treaties quickly broke down. The entire Continent has long been plunged into a precarious state of instability and unrest. In the Far East, China not only failed to redeem the obligations and commitments she had made at the Washington Conference but embarked upon a campaign for the recovery of certain rights and interests and for the expulsion of foreign influence from within her borders. The Soviet Union had consolidated her position in East Asia, especially in Outer Mongolia, and at the same time expanded her military strength. Meanwhile, ever since the conclusion of the London Naval Treaty, which complicated and beclouded the naval situation, Japan had been seized with a growing feeling of uneasiness and discontent. Finally, there occurred the Manchurian incident, followed by the establishment of Manchukuo.

If we look on the brighter side, we see that very recently there have been signs that things are taking a turn for the better in our part of the world. Manchukuo has made rapid and healthy progress in all directions. Sino-Japanese relations are fast being restored to normal. The amicable settlement of the North Manchuria Railway question has served to relieve the tension between Japan and the Soviet Union, so that we may hope for a wholehearted tripartite coöperation and collaboration in the Manchurian region between Japan, Manchukuo and the Soviet Union. We are doing our best to promote these new hopeful tendencies in East Asia.

X

Finally, let us consider Japanese-American relations. From the very beginning of our intercourse some eighty years ago when Commodore Perry first arrived in Japan, our two countries have remained on the friendliest terms. These became most warm and enthusiastic during the years of the

Russo-Japanese War. But as Japan began to grow in power and prestige, somehow the United States began to show signs of apprehension. There arose between the two countries vexatious questions—the California question, the Chinese question, the Manchuria question, the naval question—which from time to time caused considerable irritation on both sides. Today there are still many questions pending. But they are all such as can be solved through diplomatic means. Certainly there are no pending issues that might possibly jeopardize our essentially friendly relations.

I believe that Americans will soon come to comprehend correctly the Manchurian question, and to appreciate fully Japan's position in East Asia. When you know exactly our position and our aspirations in East Asia you will readily understand our attitude and claims concerning the Chinese and the naval questions. I am confident that the sense of justice and fair play of Americans will in the end solve satisfactorily the immigration question. In the field of trade, I do not anticipate that we shall encounter any troublesome questions with your country such as we have with some other countries. Even if there should arise any difficulties, we surely should be able to adjust them amicably. If each of our two countries understands the other's position and aims and endeavors to promote peace and harmony by taking always a broad view, all the questions between us will be easily settled, and our friendship will grow more cordial than ever.

Japan is faced with many problems. Our path of progress is strewn with difficulties. But all we ask of the other nations is that they acquire a correct comprehension of our position and aims in East Asia. We do not care to meddle with the affairs of Europe or America. We are concentrating our efforts upon the stabilization of the situation in East Asia, as a nation with vital interests there. We have no intention to menace or attack our neighbor states, but on the contrary are endeavoring to carry out with them all a pacific policy based upon the principle of live and let live. Such are the obligations, as they are the aims, of Japan in East Asia.

❖ ❖ ❖

The following article, "The Evolution of Democracy," by A. Lawrence Lowell, President Emeritus of Harvard University, appeared in the issue of Foreign Affairs dated October 1938.

The eve of Munich marked the low point of democratic morale in the inter-war period. For 15 years the Italian, Japanese and German dictatorships had moved from aggression to aggression without a check, heaping unmeasured insult for democracy upon evident injury to the peoples espousing it. The Russian dictatorship, putting aside Lenin's virulent abuse of parliamentarism and his frank avowal of the incompatability of the Communist and western systems, had promulgated a constitution and proclaimed "Soviet democracy," and in 1934 the U.S.S.R. joined the League of Nations, in which body Maxim Litvinov preached collective security with ardor. There was no reason to doubt the sincerity of Russian fears of a Teuton attack in the west or of a Japanese attack in the east. But implementation of the new Soviet democracy by the time-honored methods of Russian absolutism—secret police, firing squad and Siberia—left western peoples highly uncertain as to the reality behind the change of terminology. They were inclined to lump the four dictatorships together as enemies of their way of life.

Furthermore, the U.S.S.R. was plainly building an industrial plant with remarkable speed; and Nazi Germany was proving the practicability of her special kind of autarchy. The people of the western democracies meanwhile had become uncomfortably aware of defects in their own economic system. These blows to western self-esteem led to a searching of values which had not been seriously questioned for perhaps a century.

It was as part of this reëxamination of first principles that Lowell published this paper. He had been President of Harvard University from 1909 to 1933, and was a hard-headed student of government, as evidenced by his standard work, "The Government of England;" and he took as his text the work of another student, his own close friend, Lord Bryce. The article is characteristic of Lowell's unexcited and acute mind. Democracy's destination he was to describe with an interrogation point; but he described with clarity the essence of the system. Democracy, he said, was the form of government that could correct its mistakes without indicting itself for treason. As was presently to be apparent, this was a more efficient weapon for security than any that the dictatorships were to disclose.

❖ ❖ ❖

THE EVOLUTION OF DEMOCRACY

By A. Lawrence Lowell

READING James Bryce's "Modern Democracies" a score of years after it was written, one is impressed by how far from the direction then expected the political currents of the world have run. Lord Bryce thought that the new states formed by the disintegration of Austria, by the liberation of subject nationalities from Germany and Russia, and by the extension of self-government through the system of mandates to peoples hitherto ruled despotically or as dependencies of European countries, would greatly increase the number of democracies in the world. He saw clearly the defects of existing popular governments. But he thought that the new ones could learn much from the experience of the old.

To help in this direction he undertook to study the actual working of democracy, and especially the distortions produced by the excessive growth of political parties and by their interference in matters, like local administration, in which they have no proper function. Recognizing that a man who has taken an active part in a political system is disqualified for judging it, he said little about England; but—with wide information gathered on the spot, and rare penetration—he discussed political conditions in France, Switzerland, the United States and the British self-governing dominions. All this he did with singular detachment; for his book is by no means a propaganda for democracy. On the contrary, it is a scientific study of actual conditions in the different countries treated, and an examination of the causes of the imperfections revealed. Incidentally, he considered Switzerland the least defective, largely because the activity of parties there is least extended beyond its appropriate sphere.

Not less interesting, instructive and detached than his description of existing governments were his speculations on the general nature of democracy, its origins and probable future. Here he showed the same open-minded skepticism of generalizations as in his studies of actual systems. He observed that popular government has usually been sought, won and valued, not as a good thing in itself, but on account of grievances endured or benefits desired; and that when the objectives have been attained, the interest in popular government has tended to decline. In some cases, he said, democracy may spring from a theoretical belief in its propriety; but, if so, that faith will show signs of fading when the result is disappointing. He noted the reasons for the loss of interest in forms of government in the Roman Empire, both eastern and western, and added: "Who can say that what has happened once may not happen again?" Later, he enlarged upon the same theme in commenting upon the idea that although democracy had spread, and no country that had tried it showed (at that time) signs of forsaking it, we were not entitled to hold that it is the inevitable form of government. "If it be improbable," he wrote, "yet it is not unthinkable that as in many countries impatience with tangible evils substituted democracy for monarchy or oligarchy, a like impatience might some day reverse the process." Referring to the strength of the Conventions of the Constitution in Switzerland, he remarked that it was largely through such means that the complex constitution of the Roman Republic had been worked. Such conventions fare well, he wrote, so long as their moral authority lasts, but in the long run they break down if unduly strained. He added that they had largely lost their force in England.

He recorded visible marks of discouragement with popular governments. "In 1914," he said, "there were signs of decline . . . but nothing to indicate in any country either a wish to abandon democracy or the slightest prospect that anything would be gained thereby. Disappointment is expressed, complaints are made, but no permanent substitute has been suggested." He recited what some of these signs were. Everywhere, he said, one is told that there is less brilliant speaking in legislative bodies than formerly; that the best citizens are less disposed to enter them; that the respect for them has waned; and although, as he judiciously remarked, one discounted all this, the allegation was too general to be passed by. He attributed it to the spirit of democratic equality; to the size of constituencies; and to a loss of personal dignity in legislators. Politics, he observed, had become more of a game. Party discipline had become more strict. Platform speaking had lessened the part played by parliamentary debates, as had the newspapers and the work of political organizations. In the other parts of administration, he added, democracy showed signs of decay. Local government did not advance, the sphere of the central power was extending—a natural result of changing economic and social conditions. And the larger the mass of citizens becomes, the more they tend to look to the executive, and especially to its head.

He recognized that the desire for self-government is by no means a universal trait in human nature. "When a people," he said, "allow an old-established government like that of the Tsars or the Manchus to be overthrown, it is because they resent its oppressions or despise its incompetence. But this does not mean that they wish to govern themselves. As a rule, that which the mass of any people desires is not to govern itself but to be well governed." To them, free institutions are artificial, regarded with indifference; and he quoted with approval de Tocqueville's remark that the love of equality is stronger than the love of liberty. Fraternity, he noted, had fallen out of sight. "This kind of Idealism has disappeared; it is material benefits that hold that place in the minds of the most recent advocates of change."

In fact, Lord Bryce saw very clearly the defects, the dangers and the uncertain future both of democracy and of the liberty that he loved; and he uttered something like a prophecy when he said: "There are times when under the pressure of some grave national crisis, such as a foreign or even perhaps a civil war, a nation resigns some of its liberties into the hands of the Executive, or adopts new methods of government calculated to strengthen its position in the world."

Democracy certainly has defects enough, some of them inherent, and others flowing from the way it is actually worked. An organization for industry, philanthropy or education managed like any of the large democratic governments would be doomed to fail. Imagine a bank, a factory or a university conducted on the principle of two parties, or a number of groups, one of which (or some combination of groups) directed affairs and strove to retain the control, while the other party (or another combination of groups) sought to take its place. Would not the waste energy, the diversion of power from attaining the institution's main objective to the struggle for its control, reduce the accomplishment far below that of a rival institution where the object of all the members was to agree and, by compromising differences, to make a common effort to achieve its purposes?

Moreover, while differences of opinion on public questions naturally arise, those which separate the parties in a large democracy do not accord with the natural division either on specific questions or in general tendencies of thought. In the main, these are really quantitative, not depending on whether something or nothing shall be done, but on how far to go in a given direction. Now, in such matters the divergencies of opinion normally follow the biological curve, the larger number of people being found near the

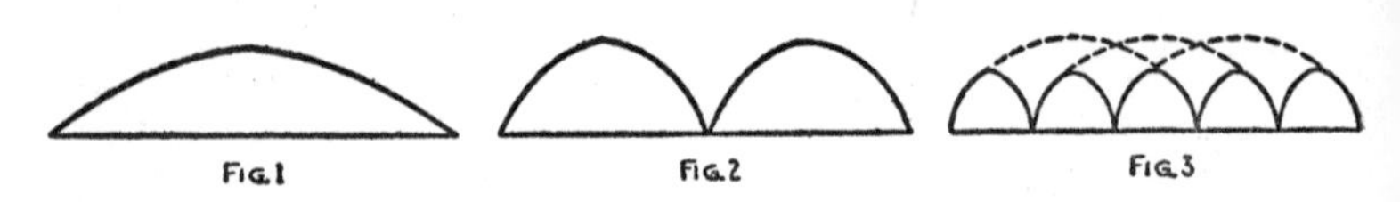

center, diminishing toward the extremes, as in Figure 1; whereas in a democracy with two parties the division is as in Figure 2; and in a system of many independent groups (as in France) the division is like that in Figure 3, the dotted lines representing the actual, but ephemeral, combinations supporting the ministry at any particular time. It may be noted that the Swiss system comes nearer than any other to the biological curve; for although the legislature is elected by parties, and the executive by it, the legislature is not divided into a ruling party and an opposition, while the executive is a committee representing all the principal parties, the object of whose members is to agree.

The chief reason for the division of all large democracies into two or more parties lies in the exigency of elections; for in these unorganized opinion has no strength. When the American Constitution was adopted the view of Rousseau was generally accepted that no people in which parties existed could be truly free. They were called factions and were regarded as pernicious. The Framers did not foresee them; and they devised a method of selecting the President, which the parties when they arose turned quickly into a fifth wheel of the coach. Parties did the same thing more gradually to constitutional monarchs under an effective parliamentary system.

Parties have their evils; and as a friend of mine remarked long ago, the inherent defect of democracy is that it is no one's business to look after the interest of the public. Yet so long as the contending parties oscillate about the center of gravity of public opinion, the system, though irrational, works fairly well. But not when the parties are too far apart. Then one of them becomes dominant; the other irreconcilable, and therefore to be crushed, by force if necessary. In such a case the conventions on which democracy is based are undermined, and chief among them the assumption that the divergent aims of parties, though mutually repugnant, are universally tolerable. In other words, parties seeking to supplant one another in control of the state are possible in a democracy so long as all of them agree that rule by a rival is better than disorder, and any legal method of deciding who shall rule better than civil strife. A striking example was the Hayes-Tilden contested election in this country where, amid the complex and irregular reports of the returning boards, the decision on counting the votes was very probably wrong, but where the general sentiment was that any method of determination was preferable to fighting. It is the obvious duty of every government, and especially of the party in power in a democracy, to avoid, if possible, carrying any policy so far as to weaken that sentiment or impair the conviction that the decision of the nation, legally made, ought to be obeyed and is better than strife. For the alternative is autocracy or civil war, and the belief on the part of any large fraction of a people that its government is autocratic tends to make it so.

Before seeking the causes of the recent rise of autocratic governments one must consider the conditions of the countries involved—how far they have been similar and how much they have differed. These countries were not alike in being all victors or all vanquished in the World War; for while Russia and Germany were defeated, Italy and Japan certainly were not. They differed also in their historic, political and cultural traditions. In fact, it would be hard to select any four peoples more unlike in these respects than those just named. Nor were they alike in their aspirations, as we see today in the sharp antagonism between the Communism of Russia and the Fascism of the rest.

On the other hand, there were strong points of resemblance. None of them had enjoyed a successful democracy—and here we are speaking of substance not form, for some of them had more or less ineffective popular institutions. And it is noteworthy that none of them is now wholly autocratic in form or in theory. The *Statuto* of Italy set up a parliamentary system, but it had become too feeble to cope with the prevalent disorders at the time of the Fascist march on Rome. Under the German monarchy the popularly elected Reichstag, though very influential, had by no means obtained the control of the government, and the Weimar Constitution was still experimental. Japan had not attained a consistent popular régime; Russia never had more than aspirations; while the Austrian and Russian succession states had just escaped from a condition of more or less subjection, and the Balkan countries had not long emerged from the same status. In all of them the conditions were somewhat chaotic, or at least unsettled; the older forms of government having either been destroyed or proved inept for coping with the problems following the war. Moreover, they had all been accustomed to strict subjection to military rule, not only in the army as in former wars, but as regards a large part of the civilians in much of their conduct and as regards all in some parts of their daily life. It is noteworthy that none of the European states that remained neutral—except Spain, where the issue is still in doubt—has shown a disposition to become autocratic in its form of government.

It is interesting to observe that the growth of autocratic rule has been associated with an increased interest in material welfare, a desire for a larger share of the world's goods both between the different elements in the population, and as against other peoples; nor should this be astonishing. Something of the kind has been observed after other great wars. The Napoleonic Wars were followed in France by an era when men turned their attention to amassing wealth. After the Civil War in the United States, the youth thought that having abolished slavery the time was at hand for removing all other human ills; but what actually came was the Tweed Ring in New York—the most barefaced corruption in the history of the country. It came because men were so occupied in restoring their own affairs that they had little time for public matters. This is perfectly normal. I remember in the last year of the World War a friend, who had a gallant son in the fight, saying that the young men had been raised to such a pitch of devotion that they would live on a higher plane than we had ever done; and I fear that I shocked him terribly by replying that this war, like every other, would be followed by an era of materialism. It is natural, because, like any physical strain, a great moral effort produces moral lassitude, in an individual and not less markedly in a people; and with the growth of organizations, of the power of united action for a common end, one may expect material objects to bulk large in national impulses. There is no novelty in the remark that the danger in the future lies less in individual than in coöperative selfishness.

Even by the time Lord Bryce wrote, law, instead of being a thing divine or natural in origin, and therefore in essence immutable, had become a matter of conscious human manufacture, and hence to be made for the benefit of the makers.

This has reduced the sense of permanence of law, and with it the sense of the rights, the obligations and the institutions which it has created. It has become arbitrary, to be remodeled both from philanthropic and selfish motives, and such an attitude toward it has obviously tended to increase the amount of regulation of human relations everywhere and in all matters. Men in control of legislation feel that they have a mission and an opportunity to enact laws for the benefit of those who need them, of those whose votes they need, and of themselves; and in practice it is difficult to distinguish between these motives even in the minds of the makers. But the result is an enormous increase in the amount of legislation, with a diminution in its moral authority. Not unnaturally, the same attitude has arisen in regard to international law, save that, there being no body authorized to enact it, the result is simply a lessening of respect for it and for the obligations it prescribes. This brings us to the question why the countries where these tendencies are most pronounced should have adopted autocratic forms of government.

The answer is that it was the only form they could adopt. In democracies there can be a peaceful change of the party in power within the framework of the government, because that is what modern democracy means. The loyal party opposition, which assumes the responsibility of ruling when a change of popular opinion occurs, is the great political invention of the last two centuries, and the essential principle of democracy on a large scale. But in countries where such a procedure is unknown, or the changes desired are too great, a shift of the ruling group must involve force—or the fear and threat of it—and therefore more or less autocratic methods. There can be no immediate reversion to a limited government after the conventions of constitutional procedure have been destroyed, for their destruction means rule by force in contrast to rule by general consent.

To put the matter in a different form: the crops have failed, kill the King! Economic distress causes discontent with the government. If a change of the party in power is customary, that may be enough to relieve the pressure; if not, a change in the form of the government itself may come. And such a change, being extra-legal, is highly likely to take the form of an autocracy that professes to bring more effective administration and prosperity. The French Revolution soon drifted into that road, and so have other political convulsions. But such a government has two dangers: first, it must, in order to endure, be economically and financially successful; and second it has usually no method of self-perpetuation. It is apt to be too largely based upon confidence in an individual who has nothing corresponding to the divine or customary right of a king, and who is a personality, not an institution. To speak of Russia or Japan in this regard would require a treatise by a scholar familiar with their conditions; but autocratic rule in Germany and Italy is apparently personal, and in the smaller countries where it exists it is subject to changes by intrigue rather than at the dictates of public sentiment.

However this may be, a system so established clearly cannot abide opposition. It must be militant and intolerant, because a changeable popular consent as a criterion of rightfulness has been obliterated. Ultimately all government is based upon the consent of those forces in the state that have power to maintain or change it; and, except for the use of armed force, that means a general consent, not to particular measures, but to the method of determining where that power shall lie, or a consent so nearly general that those who do not agree are for practical purposes impotent. This is the basis of any commonwealth. In a democracy the possibility of change in the persons in power and in the policy to be pursued is essential, for without that it would wholly lose its character. But an autocrat is the state, whose policy is assumed to be approved by the bulk of the people; any opposition must be directed against the state itself, and is therefore treasonable. That opposition must be suppressed; and to prevent its gathering headway all information about public affairs should emanate from the public authorities who know the facts. They choose such parts of the facts as they want popularly known, and by censorship of the press and exclusive control of the radio regulate the distribution of news. In all countries, democratic as well as autocratic, freedom of speech and publication is much restrained in practice during a war which calls for the utmost exertions of the people. In the former this is relaxed as soon as peace returns. But never can it be wholly abandoned by autocratic rulers without peril to their existence; and one excuse for its continuance now is that the world is still living under the terror of another general war.

The terror of another war, and the shadow of the one that is past!—for, since the ultimatum to Serbia, moral changes have come over the world. Shrinking from the infliction of suffering and death seems to have decreased in many countries. There has been a wane of belief in religion and in natural rights, a general decline in the sanctity of contract, and therewith of all other obligations, accompanied by a loss of mutual confidence among individuals and in international relations. These were the strands of which the fabric of civilization was woven, and one may well wonder how they will be restored or what will take their place.

The scope of human contacts seems to be contracting, the manifold loyalties of civilization to be compressed. One of the marked differences between the mediæval and modern world has been the great increase in points of contact among men, and each of these, in order to fructify, should give rise to a sentiment of fidelity, not inappropriately termed a loyalty. They relate to one's family, one's friends, one's neighborhood, one's church, one's party, one's nation, one's profession, one's business associates, one's comrades in every adventure, intellectual and philanthropic, and so on indefinitely. Such loyalties sometimes conflict, but less so than one might expect, because a principal aim of modern civilization has been to permit their coexistence; for the peaceful growth of highly complicated societies among men depends upon the strength of many independent loyalties in individuals. This gives the richness of personal, social and moral life.

Now the natural effect of the Great War was to subordinate or suppress some of these loyalties by the intensity of the effort for victory; so that the peace found the world poorer in the range of its loyalties, both in personal and international relations, and left those that remained more intense and more conflicting. Such a condition has not unnaturally fostered a tendency to make governments strive to keep the peace among inharmonious loyalties, and in autocratic countries to make loyalty to the state supreme over all others, which in fact become valued chiefly as they relate thereto. Yet with the growing interdependence of all mankind a multiplicity of loyalties is more important than ever for the world. The effect of war in the limiting of loyalties seems evident. Perhaps the effect of the limiting of loyalties in causing war may become obvious also.

Interesting questions about the future force themselves insistently on every inquiring mind. That the world will not return to its condition before the war may be assumed; but that does not imply an indefinite continuance of the present state of affairs. How far can we assume that autocratic government is the cause of an aggressive foreign policy, and how far a result of it? Is the rivalry between the "Haves" and the "Have Nots" in international relations genuine, or mainly a cry to interest and quiet peoples suffering from economic distress? What do the nations that have colonies with a lower civilization get out of them? Not revenues! Germany never made a profit out of her colonies, and is not likely to do so if they were returned. Nor, so far as one can see, does it seem probable that Italy will find Abyssinia profitable. Great Britain is getting less and less from India. She never received a direct revenue, but she obtained a market there for her manufactures, and occupation for her educated young men. Both of these are declining. France and England have drawn soldiers from their dependencies—a not too reliable resource. As for access to raw materials, in time of peace a nation can, as a rule, buy them if it can pay for them; and in time of war no nation can procure them that cannot command a military access to them by land or sea.

Is all this shifting of values and of decline in permanent convictions the result of forces that would have come into operation in any case, a change merely hastened by the war and therefore permanent? Or is it a product of the war and hence ephemeral? Or is it in part, and in what part, both? If not wholly permanent, when, how and to what extent will the process be reversed? If permanent, is the world to go back to a less civilized stage, or is there in store a high civilization of some sort, with a different basis for mutual confidence among men? That came in the case of the Roman Empire through a universal government which the world will not at present accept. More likely is a general recognition that the interest of all lies in mutual respect, giving what one would take and accepting what one would give. But before the opportunity for that comes, are we in for a desperate destruction of peoples and institutions, leaving wounds that may never heal? There has been an enormous increase in the effectiveness of modern weapons. Is universal destructiveness the final gift of the physical sciences to man?

❖ ❖ ❖

THE following article by Dorothy Thompson was published in April 1940, at the last moment before the shattering explosion of German power. The Soviet-German ten-year non-aggression pact was signed for the U.S.S.R. by Foreign Commissar Molotov and for the Third Reich by Foreign Minister Ribbentrop in Moscow on August 24, 1939. It was accompanied by a secret agreement dividing eastern Europe between the great Slav and Teuton Powers whose enmity for one another, and whose attraction for one another, had supplied the major design in the pattern of European relationships since the First World War. A week later, on September 1, Germany invaded Poland. Great Britain and France declared war on Germany on September 3, following the expiration of an ultimatum demanding the withdrawal of German troops from Poland. In a broadcast on the same date, President Roosevelt said to the American people: "You must master at the outset a simple but unalterable fact in modern foreign relations. When peace has been broken anywhere, peace of all countries everywhere is in danger."

On September 17, Russian troops entered Poland "to protect Russian interests." Polish resistance collapsed. Since Soviet forces did not reach the line of the Vistula, as contemplated in the secret treaty of August 24, a second secret agreement compensated the U.S.S.R. by including Lithuania in her zone. On October 6, Hitler told the Reichstag that he was ready to discuss peace, and declared that Germany and the Soviet Union would coöperate in the establishment of a new order in eastern and southern Europe. On October 31, Foreign Commissar Molotov praised the German effort for peace, criticized the United States for lifting the arms embargo, and denounced Great Britain and France for waging an ideological war against Germany. For five more months, the period of the "phony" war, the outward appearance of the old Europe remain unchanged. Then the German tank-plane team struck in the west and it disappeared forever. The merger of the Fascist and Communist revolts against European civilization had precipitated a world revolution.

The article has been called one of the best things Miss Thompson ever wrote, and one of the most perspicacious examinations ever made of the German character.

❖ ❖ ❖

THE PROBLEM CHILD OF EUROPE

By Dorothy Thompson

WHEN a drastic revolution occurs in a society the change in atmosphere and behavior is so overwhelming that one cannot believe one's eyes and ears. This is not the society with which one was familiar, the place where one felt so much at home. The old society had a face which one knew and trusted. Suddenly it is gone. Another face is there —a strange, foreign face. One thinks, "This is a nightmare." One closes one's eyes and pinches oneself, naïvely expecting that with another look the distorted vision will have passed, and the old familiar face will be there again. The first impression which a revolution gives anyone not a part of it is that it will certainly pass, and almost immediately. One says to oneself, comfortingly, "These people are not like that! I have known them for years!"

This attitude greatly contributes to the success and expansion of the revolution. For even the classes and groups hostile to it lend it collaboration, in the optimistic certainty that it is not really representative. This is inevitable, because all groups and individuals who have long enjoyed social power consider themselves, and themselves alone, as representative. They have a complacent conviction they can "handle" the situation. They need merely enter the revolutionary ranks, and in a short time the features of the revolution will conform to their own features. For *our* face, they argue, is the "true" face of this society.

The powers about to be dispossessed feel also that they enjoy an advantage in occupying a defensive position. They are fighting on home soil, against invaders. And actually, a drastic revolution does resemble a foreign invasion. I was in Germany when the 1933 Nazi revolution occurred. I remember standing with a fellow-journalist on the Grosse Stern in Berlin in April of 1933, watching a regiment of Storm Troopers march by. Their feet beat the ground rhythmically, their faces were grim, and in short, sharp barks they were repeating with a horrible monotony, *"Judah Verrecke! Judah Verrecke!"*—left, right—*"Judah Verrecke!"*—the cry giving the tact to their march. The sight of several thousand grown-up Germans marching in broad daylight to the words "Perish the Jews" seemed almost funny. One had, of course, seen these Storm Troopers marching before, but not in this manner of complete confidence. They had been mavericks, no more representative than the Christian Front in this country—merely more numerous. "Crazy people," was the usual comment, "when times are hard some people get like that."

Of course, what had happened was that a numerous but hitherto invisible class had risen to the surface. One thought, "Where, in heaven's name, did these people come from?" Yet possibly that man there had waited on you in the restaurant the night before; perhaps that one was the concierge who had unlocked the door to usher you to the elevator in a friend's house; that boy may have delivered the groceries in the morning. Hitherto they had been anonymous, the anonymous and indistinguishable mass. Suddenly they were very visible indeed. But still, one thought—or more accurately, felt—they are not representative. "They can't last."

By and by one begins to discern in the strange new mass-face of a revolutionized society certain familiar features. But they are distorted almost beyond recognition. One then has a feeling that society has gone insane. This realization is accompanied by a feeling of pity. A madman is a sad spectacle. Pity also assists the "madman." One must not treat the revolution too roughly. A revolution is like an hysterical woman. The best thing is to give her her way until she snaps back into normality. Normality, of course, is the previous society, the society to which one belongs oneself. One still feels sovereign and superior.

The Nazi revolution was assisted by this attitude, and the person of Adolf Hitler helped to cultivate it. The psychopathy of Hitler is obvious, and the Nazi revolution was made in his image. To the candid eye he is immediately inferior. Above all, of inferior race and breeding. His fulminations about the great superior Germanic, Nordic or Aryan race brought a smile to the humorous lips of any handsome, virile Jew. "Is this the face to launch a thousand ships in a race war?" one bantered.

It would have been more pertinent to inquire why this person had acquired such power over the masses. Clearly, he was a frustrated and even sick individual. Even a layman's eye diagnosed some pituitary disturbance, some masculine deficiency. The Leader of Men is not at all a masculine type. Then, all his talk about the masses being like a woman; his treatment of audiences—brutalizing and seductive, and culminating in orgiastic outbursts that were distinctly uncomfortable and embarrassing to the detached specator. What frustrations must be in this man, one thought—so sensitive, so cruel, so weak, and so aggressive! And those fantastic characters around him—perverts and adventurers, frustrated intellectuals who could not hold a job on any good newspaper or get their plays produced or their books published. And his own background—*"Lumpenproletariat"*—not even a casualty of the economic depression; one of the permanent class of unemployables, caught up briefly into the common adventure of war, taking refuge the rest of the time in a dream-world; a man whom nobody "understood," full of envy, furtive hatred, frustrated creative power.

One dismissed him, still clinging to the concept of "normal," not wondering what might happen if such a man, surrounded by others with a capacity for organization, should come to the surface in a *society* which shared his own symptoms, a society which was also frustrated and sick. "Can the blind lead the blind?" is an open question. Do not societies make gods in their own images? The tendency of history to employ disreputable characters is lost sight of in "normal" times.

A psychopath is a person unable to exercise conscious discipline over his unconscious urges. A drunkard achieves release from inhibitions by means of a stimulant. But all psychopaths and all drunkards do not behave in the same way. Nothing comes out of the released unconscious that is not there. Some men are aggressive when they are drunk, and some are amorous; some are garrulous, and some morose. Many go crazy, but not everybody goes crazy in the same way.

Release from the inhibitions and disciplines imposed by habit, tradition, reason and fear comes also in dreams. Freud says, "Tell me what you dream and I will tell you what you are." It would seem that not only individuals but whole societies have an unconscious life, a dream life, which differs from the unconscious and dream life of other societies. A revolution releases the unconscious; it destroys inhibitions. The result is a caricature of the society, as an individual in a psychopathic state is an aberration of himself and no one else: as a drunk is a caricature of himself sober.

And so, gradually, one comes to observe in the distorted Nazi face of Germany certain familiar German features. The face is more representative than we thought in the first shock of surprise. The patient will be quieter one of these days; this is certainly not his permanent condition; he will recover. But meanwhile he has revealed more of himself than he ever would have shown us, sober. It is worth watching this society released from its inhibitions. For we hope to live on good terms with it when it is well again, if we are well ourselves. And we shall understand it better hereafter.

But we have also had an opportunity to watch revolutionary developments in an urbanized middle-class society in the twentieth century. In the distorted features of this case we can discern more than German features. The behavior is not German only; it is, in many ways, twentieth century. Let us try to separate two sets of symptoms: symptoms peculiar to *Homo Germanicus,* and symptoms somewhat characteristic of all decaying middle-class society. We may learn something from both.

II

The German revolution did not begin in 1933, with Hitler. It began in 1918, with the loss of the war and the collapse of the Hohenzollern state. It has gone through many phases and will go through more before it is over. In all its phases it is "German"—the Weimar Republic as well as the Nazi dictatorship. The German revolution and the Russian revolution coincided at their births, and, for a brief time, collaborated. It is not certain that they will not end in a close embrace.

The German revolution of 1919 occurred after a lost war in a world in which the middle class was the most representative class, and bourgeois values generally accepted. It occurred, however, in a society in which middle-class civilization had never had the authority that it has exercised in France or Great Britain. Germany was a country where the social and political ideas of the French Revolution did not take permanent root; and it had escaped almost entirely the English Revolution which preceded the French. The belief in the individual and in democracy lacked the authority which the spilling of blood for a cause lends to it. Germany had no Magna Charta, no Declaration of the Rights of Man, no Declaration of Independence, no popular cult of Liberty around which a moral unity could be built.

The ideal of individual autonomy had never had a real hold in Germany. There was a feudal Germany, an industrial Germany, and a workers' Germany. Feudal Germany was already in conflict with industrial Germany, and in that conflict seemed to come out on top. Actually, feudal Germany was closer to proletarian Germany, which was not democratic and individualistic, but Socialist.

Although radical Socialism was given no official encouragement and much official suppression under the monarchy, the form of the German state encouraged the tendency to Socialism rather than the tendency to individualism. The German state, from Bismarck's time on, was a *"Fürsorgestaat"*—literally translated, a "caring-for-you state," the state in the rôle of Providence. By the close of the war the economic organization of Germany had already brought about a strict social dependency. In the ensuing years Germany became urbanized to the point where only about a third of the population lived on the land; and in the east these lived on great estates as tenants and laborers. A quarter of the population lived in small towns, 40 percent in large towns, a fourth of these in cities of over 100,000. A breakdown of the population into social classes would have shown that only a quarter of the population could be regarded as economically independent; three-quarters of all of them were tied to the "system." The basis for liberal democracy—the democracy of individualism, thrift and middle-class morality—was not there. The drift toward Socialism, Communism, National Socialism, or some other expression of an urbanized, industrial, socially dependent society was inevitable.

The revolt against middle-class values had started before the war, especially in the Youth Movement. This movement of twentieth century minnesingers was anti-bourgeois, anti-respectable, against pedantry, materialism, and what they called "tradesman morality." It was a revolt against all conventions, including those surrounding sex. But it was not a revolt in the direction of economic liberalism. It was a search after a more coherent social life, not dominated by the idea of personal profit. It affirmed the war, for the war represented heroism, sacrifice and the spirit of the front—comradeship and mutual affection in danger.

The solidity of the Hohenzollern structure rested upon the Army, the Bureaucracy, the Church, the Junker Estates, the Great Industries. The organization was impressive and powerful. The Benevolent State could point with pride to the fact that Germany had no slums like those of Glasgow and Birmingham, no slaughtered forests as in the United States, no plutocratically controlled culture, but order, discipline, and strength. The organization was so impressive and powerful that it held the world at bay for four years. Then it collapsed. The world's best army lost the war; the All-Highest fled to Holland; the masses of the people were hungry. At a blow Authority had been destroyed, the authority of the Emperor and his caste.

The fall of Hohenzollern Germany was a psychological shock to a generation of Germans from which they never recovered. One must bear in mind that Germany, in the modern sense, the Germany created by Bismarck, had never fought a great war until 1914, and had never lost any war. England and France had waged many and lost several—and still lived and adjusted themselves. The lost war confronted Germany with a reality for which she was unprepared by previous experience. It was the incredible. If that could happen anything could happen. It made no difference that the Weimar Republic put down mob risings, dissolved Bolshevism, and restored order in a remarkably short time. Gone was Faith in an Order. What had happened once could happen again.

The shock gave enormous impetus to the idea of historic relativism. Obviously there were no enduring values. Nothing was permanent except change.

The second shock to which the German mind was subjected was the Inflation. This cannot be overrated. In the Inflation money *disappeared*. It simply vanished. It became utterly and completely valueless—a dollar was worth a billion marks. The effect of the total collapse of all money values upon an ill-founded and already weakened middle-class society cannot adequately be described. The German youth, who had lyrically denounced money values in the days when those values were very solid, saw that they really could disappear in the course of a few weeks. Germans ceased to believe in money. Ceasing to believe in money, they ceased to believe in thrift, or in any kind of individual security. The entire economic structure of society came into question. If wages, the savings of a lifetime, pensions, bonds, the most gilt-edged securities could all disappear overnight, were not the standards which had encouraged those savings worthless also?

The Inflation brought about rapid changes in classes. A whole breed of parvenus and *nouveaux riches* speculators cropped up to become the targets of hatred. The spendthrift and the speculator were rewarded, the sober man punished. To be rich was contemptible.

Two such overturns of values in the course of five years induced an acute feeling of crisis. But people in some curious way managed to survive. Life, then, was not the Emperor, or the finely organized caste-state, or the financial and economic system. Life was—life. A new money was made, the *Rentenmark* based on grain and not on metal. But why try to hold on to this money, either? Perhaps it too would go. Foreign money began pouring into Germany. It was welcome. Entire urban districts were rebuilt with it, industries rationalized, there was an era of intense economic activity in which Germany built the finest civil aviation service in Europe and launched the best and fastest ships on the sea. But the feeling of crisis never diminished. "This, too, will pass," was in everyone's mind. Since it will pass, let us live while we live.

The sense of living in a crisis induces a feverish self-analysis. A society that constantly analyzes its own symptoms becomes hypochondriac. The Communists saw in everything a prophecy come true. Since the next thing to come would certainly be Communism, the wisest thing to do was to push the careening society further along the escalator. The Social Democracy was loyal to the Republic, but in a half-hearted manner, for what the Socialists desired was not liberal democracy but Socialism. The Republic represented no ultimate value, but only a bridge to something else.

This concept of the existing order as only a stopping place on the road to something else—something ahead or something behind—was reflected in all the political parties. The idea that political parties are one means of approximating that balance of interests which is called "the General Welfare" never existed in Germany. The Socialists and Communists were not interested in the General Welfare. Marxian and class-conscious, they sought the welfare of the industrial proletariat alone. The German Nationalists were wholly interested in the reëstablishment of the caste state. The Democratic Party was liberal in the interests of the capitalists. Each party was a sort of sovereign state representing a specific interest and all coalitions were precarious. The party system tended to eternal divisions rather than to the repeated striking of an average. The political structure was therefore brittle, not elastic.

In 1929 came the third great shock, and again within five years: the world-wide depression. The over-expanded plant, over expanded on borrowed money, poured out, not goods, but wageless workers. The Providential state fed them, but at a table that became increasingly meager. The solidarity of the workers was broken. For there was not one working class of the proletariat, but a working class and an out-of-work class of the proletariat. The more privileged, the skilled, and those protected by the strong trades unions, were better off than the twice-dispossessed small bourgeoisie, and excited their envy and hatred. The Social Democrats, defending the Republic, held on to the privileged workers. The unemployed and the desperate small tradespeople, peasants, and white collar workers joined the Communists or the Nazis, looking for a radical solution. The Youth sat in employment offices, or took their various insurance cards to be punched. They had time on their hands—time to go to meetings, or march in parades. Soothsayers arose and the crop of mystic prophets who perennially rove the German countryside increased, to tell the people from crystals or stars or cabalistic books or out of their own visions that the world was going to collapse or that the Redeemer was at hand.

Characteristic of this time was that almost no one—but, precisely, almost no one—believed in capitalism. The little capitalists went broke for the second time in five years; the big ones also went broke but were salvaged by the state, which in instance after instance became the chief shareholder. The sons of all the Thomas Lamonts were Corliss Lamonts.

Marxian Socialism preached materialism, and it failed to excite the youth because they had long since ceased to believe in material values. To a great extent, Communism is based upon envy. But can an unemployed man really envy a bankrupt capitalist? Hitler offered to youth fellowship in a mystic community. "No one else wants you, but I want you. I need you. And I promise you that as long as I live you shall belong to me and I shall belong to you." In the ranks of the Storm Troopers there was a uniform and fellowship. It was the "front spirit" all over again, the front spirit of which the youth had heard their elders talk, but which they had missed.

The next phase in the revolution was Hitler's dictatorship. It cannot be wholly or even chiefly attributed to the Treaty of Versailles. It was the response to the 1929 depression, to the third shattering psychological shock in half a generation.

The revolution was gathering momentum, in a kind of psychological vacuum from which all values had been obliterated—belief in the old régime, belief in the economic order, belief in the present régime, belief in middle-class morality, belief in Communism. There was belief in *nothing*. If there is belief in nothing, one cause is as good as another. The most amazing thing about the success of the Nazi revolution is that most of its followers did not believe in most of its dogmas. In the years of 1930–1934 I met scores of members of the Nazi Party but I never met a 100-percent Nazi in my life—except Hitler. They only believed in the crisis, and in the certainty that "Something Must Happen," that "It Can't Go on Like This."

Those who followed Hitler did not believe, they did not have convictions; they had faith. They *had* to have some faith. Only the very strong can bear to live in a world utterly devoid of absolute values, which was what the bourgeois middle-class world had become. The rock-bottom of faith in life is "blood and soil."

Hitler came, mind you, as the Redeemer of precisely that middle-class world. But he could not save it. It was in the Euphoria of death when it elected him.

III

I have what the Germans would call *"eine unglückliche Liebe"* for Germany—a frustrated love. Germany is the only foreign civilization in which I have ever attempted to plunge myself. The word "plunge" slipped out on the typewriter and is revelatory. One would not think of "plunging" oneself into France. One enters the life of France step by step, and has to undergo an examination before every new door. The French tolerate foreigners but they do not welcome them. One has to prove oneself, by sheer merit. One would not dream of trying to "plunge" oneself into England. It would be a very uncomfortable experience.

But Germany invites the plunge. The German mind, the German psyche, has about it something oceanic and boundless. Despite the xenophobia that rules under the Nazis, despite all the talk about "German art," "German science," "German this" and "German that," the odd fact is that no people seem constantly to pursue the universal and to seek the generality as do the Germans. It is a much less compact society than the French, and there is nothing of the finely differentiated hierarchical structure of the British. The German mind seems constantly to struggle between a tendency to be open to all the winds that blow—open on all borders, north, south, east and west—and to make convulsive gestures to close those borders and dam the ocean between rigid dykes.

Whereas the French and the British social structures represent a fine equilibrium between freedom and order and seem to have some organic cohesion, German society always seemed to me to represent an attempt to enclose chaos in the straitjacket of a rigid organization. This chaos exercises an enormous attraction. It is something like the primordial chaos out of which came Creation. It gives one the feeling that something great might come out of Germany, something greater than anything that has ever been, if only for the reason that it might be *anything*.

The German mind has never been able to make itself up. Most importantly, it has never been able to choose, once and for all, between the east and the west. Dominant Prussia undoubtedly pulls it north and east; Bavaria and the Rhinelands pull it south and west; Austria and the new Slavic territories acquired will pull it south and east. If there is anything in the call of the blood, then that call comes from all directions too. For Germany is a land of the most mixed bloods—Slavic, Tartar, Nordic and Danubian, the latter being itself a description of mixture.

It is characteristic of the German that he is likely to find his spiritual home somewhere else. Goethe and Nietzsche both despised Germany. Goethe, however, loved the Mediterranean and western civilization. Nietzsche's blood pulled him eastward, for he was of Polish ancestry. Yet he incorporates the German longing for the west, the longing for form; and because he is paradoxical he is the more German. The desire of Germans to escape from themselves may account for the fact that they make first-class colonists. Germany has to keep their loyalty to the Fatherland by all sorts of propaganda and organization. But it still is easier to make an American out of a German than out of a Frenchman.

The Nazi leaders, who insist so strongly on Germanism, were to a quite remarkable extent born abroad. For them Germanism seems to be a kind of Zionism. Hitler was born in the Austria of the Hapsburgs and loathed it. He looked wistfully across the borders into the German promised land. Hess was born in Cairo; Darré was born in the Argentine; Rosenberg was born in Estonia. Ernst Bohle, head of the "Service for Foreign Germans," was born in England. I am sure that there is something significant in this. For to these men Germany is not a place, an existing organized society, but an idea. And that also is along the German line, for the Germans are the most idealistic people on earth, with a passion for the abstract.

The thinkers whom they have accepted, the men who have most strongly influenced their intellectual life, were idealistic philosophers and deductive thinkers, or else chaotic and explosive poets, like Wagner and Nietzsche. Hegel, who elevated the state into an ideal of total order and total virtue, is hardly more characteristic than Nietzsche, who was the total nihilist as far as the state is concerned, despising all forms of bureaucratic society as the enemy of the creative will. This polarity of the German soul (which

Nietzsche said was a chronic indigestion) accounts for a great deal, particularly the German discipline and the pedantically organized order. The German does not accept discipline because of a neat love of order. He accepts it the way a drunkard delivers himself into a sanitarium. He wants someone to impose it on him, because he cannot impose it on himself. He is anguished, divided, at loose in the cosmos. Even prison, since it means four walls and a routine, may be attractive to him. But inside the four walls he wants to get out again, into the cosmos. It was probably a great mistake to put Hitler into prison, for in prison he dreamed of *"Lebensraum,"* and in his fevered imagination the needed space became the whole world, which he would conquer and dominate.

Goethe said "Zwei Seelen wohnen ach, in dieser Brust," and Goethe probably understated it. At least two souls dwell in the German bosom. The polarity accounts for the amazing German sentimentality. German feeling is to an immeasurable extent *imagined* feeling, and the German temperament unreckonable. Germany is the only country where I have seen "strong" men weep for what would seem to an Anglo-Saxon the most trivial reasons. Observers under the Nazi régime have been amazed to see Germans cruelly beat some poor Jew one moment and pick up and comfort a stray kitten the next. It may also account for the curious lack of what other peoples consider loyalty. *"Deutsche Treue"* (German loyalty) has been a very odd thing from the Nibelungen onward. In twenty years we have seen the whole German people desert from the régime of the Kaiser to the régime of the Republic to the régime of the Nazis with a unanimity that is amazing. Each time they desert they have a plausible rationale for doing so.

But the Germans are also one of the most purely rational of peoples. It is a rationalism unhampered by common sense, a quality that the Germans, in their duality and profound inner individualism, possess less than any European people. They are rational but not reasonable. There is no "common" sense in Germany. The Germans do not speak of common sense or even of common aim, but of a common destiny.

The lack of empiricism leads them to the rationalization even of their vices. Other societies have homosexuals; it remains for the Germans to make a systematic apologia for homosexuality. Xenophobia exists almost everywhere, and anti-Semitism. It remains for the Germans to make a rationale of anti-Semitism and elevate it into a cosmic explanation of the world. This in no way prevents Nietzsche, who loathed Christianity as a "slave religion" foisted upon the human race by the Jews, from greatly admiring the Jews for denying their own child. Nor did it prevent him from proclaiming the Jews to be the most aristocratic of peoples, since they had learned how to live dangerously.

The German duality of feeling finds expression in many words in the German language. Take *"Schadenfreude."* There is no one word to translate this; it means literally "injury-joy"—joy in the injury of someone else. Now, this combination of emotions is known to all of us; it is the basis, for instance, of slapstick comedy. But some instinct warns other peoples to separate the concepts into different words. The fusion is dangerous. We see the same fusion of opposites in the word *"Liebestod"*—love-death—love, the assertion of life and creation, and death its opposite!

The very structure of the German language seems to indicate the desire to escape limitations. It is the greatest language in the world in which to express emotions. It is also the most useful in which to avoid an issue. French compels intellectual precision. English, the preëminent language of the verb, impels to action. The French language constantly pulls us back to reality. The German language pushes us out, if we are not very careful, into a no man's land. In the French, English and Italian languages the noun—the thing or the concept—is tied as closely as possible to the verb, the word that acts. We say, "Father has built us a beautiful home." The Germans say, "Father has us a beautiful home built." You have father, the concept of beauty, and home, before you know what father has done about it—whether he has built it or set it on fire. It is a language of unsigned or revocable treaties. The German passion for the concept and the abstract is equal to the German fear of the fact. The verb postponed is the fact postponed—the fact being reality.

This plurality and boundlessness, so attractive and so repellent, so intemperate, immoderate and profoundly unclassical, gives German spiritual life its vitality and its anguish. The one thing that no German poet could ever have written about his race and his nation are the words of John of Gaunt in Richard II: "This *happy* breed of men, this *little* world." To be German is to be divided, perplexed, longing for form, aggressively saying "I am" because one is not quite sure whether one is; and one is sure that, whether one is or not, one is something-beyond-Germanism. With all this goes a remarkable notion of world mission, but a remarkable uncertainty of what that world mission may be.

IV

"Mein Kampf" is one of the most illuminating books ever written. In it can be read the content of the German mind in a degenerate and plebeianized form. There is nothing at all in "Mein Kampf," except the description of propaganda, that has not been part of German intellectual wares for a long time. I do not mean to put Mr. Hitler's scholarship at issue. It is of no consequence whether he ever read Hegel or Nietzsche, or Marx or Luther. These four men have so influenced the German mind that their ideas have become part of the German collective unconscious, including the unconscious of Hitler himself.

Martin Luther made a Protestant church divorced from the idea of political freedom, commanding complete obedience to the state in everything but theology. His counterpart today is the Reverend Martin Niemoeller, who, being imprisoned for his defense of the rights of the Church in theological affairs, nevertheless, and from prison, offered his services to Hitler as a submarine commander.

Hegel saw the glorified state and the possible total sweep of its character. He gave it a moral and intellectual meaning that nobody before him had thought to contribute. The concept of the state as encompassing all of life was never reached more clearly than in Hegel.

Nietzsche, who hated the state and thought of life as torrential creative power, in which good and evil each had polar and equal functions, affirmed force, youth and violence.

Marx, who was a great deal more of a German than he was a Jew, was profoundly influenced by Hegel; he was a Hegelian scholar and took his famous dialectic intact from Hegel, using it, however, in the economic rather than the philosophical field. He is enormously important to the mental life of Germany, for Germany is the only country in the world in which the entire industrial proletariat was to some extent intellectualized, and in which all of it has been dominated by Marx. What Marx conveyed to the German workers was the *inevitability* of revolution, revolution according to inescapable law. Marxism combines the idea of will with the idea of predestination. It is therefore exceedingly powerful, for it puts a guarantee of success behind the will of men. The processes of history are inexorable and apart from human will; the human will can, however, expedite the processes. To be a Marxist is to be convinced that one is in an active alliance with inexorable history.

To hold these four men responsible for Nazism is, of course, absurd. Hegel, a profound moralist, must be turning in his grave at the thought of a frame such as the state which he conceived, filled with such bestial power. Nietzsche must be exploding in his, at the sight of *bureaucratized* violence. A "boiling soul of the people" organized to boil at the pressing of a button! And Marx's revolution is not going as he plotted it, either. That pedantic and embittered soul must be having one of his interminable arguments in purgatory.

But these men enlarged the psychological boundaries of the German mind. Nazism has usurped its content, and, of course, has indigestion. It is a fusion of perhaps unfusible concepts. The Nazi state is totalitarian and in that sense Hegelian, but it is also dynamic; and German "dynamism," which has direct roots back to Nietzsche, is rapidly turning the totalitarian state into totalitarian and perpetual revolution, which is another way of saying perpetual war. The word "state" is connected with the Latin "stet;" so are the words "status," "stay" and "static," which mean something that stays put. Hitler's state is a runaway state, which would seem to be a contradiction in terms. He has turned the state into a *"Bewegung"*—a movement—and even adopted as its symbol the Swastika, the wheeling cross. Instead of the Movement coming to rest, with the conquest of power, in the state, the state has become an enormous juggernaut to propel the Movement. The state and the Movement are in the relationship of the body of a motor car and the engine. All Germany rides in the body of the car (the state), but passively. The Movement is the propelling power, and the chauffeur is the Leader, who chooses the roads arbitrarily. This is the totalitarian state in one sense, but it is certainly not Hegelian.

Hegel is one of the most abstruse of philosophers. He is quoted as saying, "One man has understood me and he has not." It is pretentious for someone not a philosophical scholar to discuss him. But what is important is the residue of his philosophy in the minds of the intelligentsia, who have passed it on in a sloganized form to the masses. The idea of the *Volkstaat* is certainly to be found in Hegel. He conceived the individual as finding himself only in the society of which he is an organic member; religion was not universal, but the spontaneous development of the national conscience; the artist was not an individual but a concentration of the passion and the power of the whole community. The deformation of these ideas is part of Nazism. The organic state is the Nazi ideal, in spite of the fact that Nazism destroyed what is organic. For one cannot create an organism by *Gleichschaltung*—switching into line—an idea not derived from biology but from mechanics.

Reading Hegel, and observing the relationship in Nazi Germany between state and Movement, one can see how easy would be a jump to the conception of the state as a proselytizing church, an idea which possessed Byzantium and the Eastern Church, and which is given expression in Dostoevski's novels. In "The Brothers Karamazov" he makes Father Paissy say: "The Church is not to be transformed into the State. That is Rome and its dream. On the contrary, the State transformed in the Church will ascend and become a church over the whole world—the glorious destiny ordained. . . . This star will rise in the East."

I quote Dostoevski here because the sympathy between the German idealistic philosophers and the great nineteenth century Russian novelists is constantly apparent. The Russian Communist state is certainly not the state dreamed of by Dostoevski who, at the end of his life at least, was deeply Christian; but it is a state that is, at the same time, a secular religion with a mission of world salvation. And so is the Nazi state. And with this it stops being a state in any western sense of the word.

The attraction between Germany and Russia is enormous, and always has been. The Russian revolution was made in Germany—it grew out of German idealism via Marx—and Russia has contributed to it, and to the German mind as well, the spirit of Byzantium. That these two revolutions, the German and the Russian, would one day merge has been anticipated by many people. It is interesting that in 1931, two years before Hitler, the German Kaiser gave an interview at Doorn in which he expressed his scorn for any pan-Europeanism that would link Germany in an economic and spiritual alliance with western Europe, above all with France and England. In fact, he made the statement, startling from a conservative at that time, that Germany's next of kin was Russia. "Western culture has reduced itself to mere utilitarianism, but the pendulum of civilization is switching to eastern Europe and its way of life. We are not westerners. . . . We cling with all our roots to the east."

The German belief that the west is decadent reached its clearest expression in Spengler. Utilitarianism is interpreted as a sure sign of decadence. Except in the east—to which Germany belongs—idealism is dead. The west has lost its biological vitality, its will to life and power. So run the arguments. The Nazis' revolt towards paganism as a spring from which Life can be renewed, and their systematic anti-intellectualism, are both reflections from Nietzsche, who denounced the concepts of "the good, the true, and the beautiful" as arresters of Life. Good, true, and beautiful, are only relative. They are the values of impotent, humble, feeble men with slave minds. The morality of bold, vigorous, healthy men is different. Their ethic is an ethic of strength, cruelty, combativeness, vigor and joy. Caution, humility, cleverness, pacifism, are only virtues for slaves, who can best advance themselves by the cultivation of these qualities.

Every one of Hitler's ideas of the "master race" is in Nietzsche, who, like Dostoevski, prophesied what has happened. "The democratization of Europe is an involuntary preparation for the rearing of tyrants." "A daring ruler race is building itself up on the foundation of the intelligent mass." "Man's fate depends on the success of its highest types." "The twentieth century will be a classical era of great wars and revolutions." "There is no moral code for the generality of men. I am a law only for my own." That this master race should be bred according to a stud farm formula, as Walter Darré has conceived it, and that it would be formed in a society where fierce pride is more likely to land you in a concentration camp than anywhere else, was certainly not in Nietzsche's mind, any more than that the master-race idea should be made actual in a régime headed by a man overcompensating for severe inferiority. But Nietzsche himself foresaw "unwanted disciples."

The point is that the idea of a total transvaluation of values occurs over and over again in only two literatures: the German and the Russian. It reaches its summit in Nietzsche and Dostoevski. The latter, in the scene of the Grand Inquisitor in "The Brothers Karamazov," makes the most brilliant defense of Satan against Jesus, demolishing the idea of freedom and substituting for it the idea of equality, and affirming the "spirit of the earth," which demands bread and not freedom. Dostoevski was obsessed with the idea that the masses crave equality, that equality must mean slavery, and that the élite, the lovers of freedom, must rule as a priesthood and as vicarious sufferers taking upon themselves the sins of the masses. The idea is completely formulated in the description of Shigalovism in "The Demons." Both Dostoevski and Nietzsche could face and affirm nihilism—the return of civilization to primordial chaos, its rebirth in slime and corruption, and the emergence of a new society. In Dostoevski, a society "redeemed."

Even Marx with all his intellectualism has something apocalyptic about him. Social and economic power is to be centered in the "Dictatorship of the Proletariat." The state is to be an executive committee for managing the affairs of the proletariat, and for crushing their opponents. This accomplished, it is to wither away. Wither away into what? One asks—and comes again to the idea of the state as a Church or as a Movement. In Communist Russia as in Nazi Germany essential functions of the state are supplanted by the Party. In this sense, the state has already withered away in both countries; its power has withered. It does not legislate, it does not plan, it does not direct. It does not even judge, except in minor matters. Power in Russia is not in the Council of Commissars but in the Politburo; and in Germany also the direction and decision regarding crucial affairs are not in the state at all, but in the Party. And the Party—whether Communist or Nazi—is built along the lines of a religious order. It is a Leader and a following, a priesthood and a flock. To call either of these phenomena the super-state is false. They represent the anti-state.

But these parties came into being in both cases as instruments of war—of class war or race war. The Party is at once a proselyting and a fighting body, a flaming sword and a missionary society. It is concerned with the Propagation of the Faith, and obviously must place enormous importance upon the Propaganda Ministry, which in Germany as in Russia is attached to the Party not the state. The Party's purpose is to administer a war which has no foreseeable end, since in the one case the superior race, and in the other the class whose time has come in history (the proletariat) must first obtain their sway over the whole world.

For a long time the western world made the mistake—a mistake that may be fatal—of believing that there was no possible synthesis between the Russian and German revolutions. The possibility of synthesis was implicit from the beginning. Hitler always spoke of Germany as a "proletarianized nation." This slogan was invented by the German Communists, and stolen by Hitler. It was they who first said that Germany was the coolie of international finance capitalism. Marx believed that Germany would be the first workable Communist state, and the natural Communist Mecca for good Marxians ought to be Berlin. The idea of the Master Class and the idea of the Master Race that embodies and leads that class are not incompatible. We are already getting hints from Dr. Robert Ley, leader of the Nazi Labor Front, who is advising the workmen of the world to unite, throw off their chains, and, obviously, accept German leadership.

Western civilization, so runs the argument, is commercialistic, utilitarian, bourgeois and decadent. Karl Marx himself denounced the Jews and said they could be emancipated only when they were freed from *Judaism,* which he identified with commercialism. Translated into terms of "Communazism," the war against the Jews is therefore a war against commercialism and the west, especially England. When the Nazis say that England represents world Jewry, only the more gullible among them mean it in the sense of an Elders of Zion plot. The others mean it as a concept—that recurrent German abstraction! They mean that Judaism = Commercialism, that Commercialism = England, and that since things equal to the same thing are the same, England stands for Judaism.

One can imagine a slogan for the merged revolutions: "Proletariat of the world and all have-not nations unite under the Stakhanovite workers of Germany, and with your pure blood unspoiled by bourgeois marriages made for money, and your vital instincts to will and power uncorrupted by Christianity and Jewish Commercialism, throw off your chains! *Rot Front! Sieg Heil!*" This is not said as a joke.

V

In Nazi Germany and Communist Russia, the Party, having caught up into itself the powers of the state, is, at the same time, a caricature of the ugliest forms of the state—arbitrary force, which is terror, and arbitrary and self-appointed leadership, which is tyranny. The Party-state does not govern, because it is incapable of directing its actions by law. The state does not make laws, and the Party cannot make them. The state merely executes the aims of the Party, according to criteria which neither have predictability nor offer any security. That this condition of affairs will, in time, produce its own antithesis and new synthesis, one is compelled to believe, whether according to Hegelian dialectic or according to historic experience.

But it is a mistake not to recognize certain things that will probably remain in Germany, whatever new synthesis may take place. One is forced to conclude that whatever changes occur, Germany will remain, in however modified a form, a Socialist society. The nineteenth century middle-class order based upon individual economic liberty never had strong roots in Germany, and the roots and the plants have died or been destroyed. That flower will not grow again in German soil.

Furthermore, as long as the west represents what to average Germans is a dead or rapidly dying middle-class civilization, it will exercise no attractive power for them, just as it exercises none for the Russians. Herein lies the greatest weakness of the French and British approach to the German people. For the French and British representatives of middle-class economics and morality are trying to sell the German people something that they have lived through or given up, whether they are Nazis, or Communists, or neither. The whole of Germany is convinced that the epoch represented by the economics, moral values, and social forms developed since the eighteenth century is over. They never liked it much, and they believe that the future does not belong to individualism and bourgeois ideas, but to some form of coherent and organic community in which the vitalizing forces rise from the masses. The German mind was already groping in this direction before the war, and the German revolution through all its phases has emphasized the tendency.

Actually, moreover, this German and Russian tendency exercises an attraction for the west, for the west has already discovered in itself advanced symptoms of the decay of middle-class forms and values and also has become conscious of explosive forces rising from the masses, the unemployed and the youth. This attraction over the west exercised by Nazi Germany and Soviet Russia is, to be sure, a kind of horrible fascination. But it is a fascination. The problem of the west is to effect the transition from one form of society to another without the appalling aberrations and boundless exaggerations and horrors of the Russian and German experiences.

The growing crisis of western middle-class civilization is one of the greatest assets possessed by Hitler and Stalin, and they both count shrewdly upon it as a war potential. It is Hitler's "secret weapon." For he and Stalin know that the war will enormously accelerate that crisis. At present it is being pushed ahead in Great Britain and France by the policies of the most conservative middle-class society left on this planet—that of the United States of America. Our credit policy toward the Allies in the present war is forcing them into economic totalitarianism faster than they need otherwise go. The fact, curiously, is unobserved by our political representatives of capitalism, who preach laissez-faire domestically and simultaneously egg on state-controlled economics throughout the world.

Nevertheless, Hitler and Stalin probably exaggerate the results upon the conduct of the war of the rapid transition being made in France and Britain to a controlled economy and a form of military-Socialist organization. (I am compelled to use the word "Socialist" in a rather loose sense, as the opposite of individualism.) There is far more inner unity and spontaneous patriotism in England and France than there ever was in Germany. If in the business of winning the war they find that they must dispense with capitalism, in the nineteenth century meaning of that word, they probably will simply accept the fact and pay the price. Even if they find they must erect the Moloch totalitarian state they will accept it and plan that it will be temporary and that after the war they will be able to make an adjustment closer to their own traditions and genius. The very fact that the war is going on will produce collaboration until the war is over.

And whatever changes occur in the organization of social and economic life in the western democracies, the pattern that will emerge will not be the same as the German and Russian—unless the Germans and Russians win the war and impose it by force.

The German and Russian phenomenon that has emerged is military, messianic, despotic. It has a mass base. Its sources were latent in German and Russian thought and society. Both the Nazi and the Russian Communist movements are fusions between the army and the masses, forced by the Party. One must never forget that the modern German Reich—the Reich founded by Bismarck—was to an enormous extent the creation of the Prussian Army. Under the Hohenzollerns, the army had a symbolic value and moral authority that it does not have in France or in England. The French and English societies are civilian, and the army is their instrument. Soviet Russia is also very largely the creation of the Red Army, which established the Communist régime in the civil wars and the foreign invasions following the Great War. Russia never had had a middle class of any strength, and feudalism was extirpated by the Bolsheviks. The Party state which emerged is, like the Nazi Party state, despot-led—army plus masses.

By a succession of purges, both in Russia and Germany, the army has been transformed more and more into an instrument of the Party, that is to say of the Movement. Hitler had Roehm murdered for wanting precisely this function for the army. But the fact that a man is murdered does not necessarily mean that his policies will not be adopted by his assassin. Stalin exiled Trotsky and executed Tukhachevsky, but he adopted ideas from both.

To what extent the German Army actually has become one with the Party is still disputable. Some of the strongest moral values in postwar Germany were there, and it is difficult to believe that they have been wholly obliterated. The Elite Guards and the *Gestapo* may render the Army politically impotent. But there are grounds for believing that it still has a primary loyalty to the German nation rather than to the Nazi Party, that it differentiates between them in its mind. Nobody can say that its aid may not one day be a factor in rehabilitating Germany and restoring to her an organic social order.

At any rate, the eastern and Mohammedan-like concept is foreign to the whole spirit of western civilization. We certainly shall have a form of military Socialism in France and England during the war, but one cannot conceive of it as permanent. The social and economic structures of both countries, and indeed of all western countries, including our own, will certainly be profoundly modified before this great revolutionary period is over. But though German dynamism and Russian messianism have much in common, nothing in the tradition of England or France indicates a corollary there to the German and Russian experience. One can imagine a more controlled state economy there, and Socialism, and even dictatorship; but one cannot imagine oriental despotism or a mystique of despotism. One cannot picture the dictator in a halo, elevated to Godhead. The French had Jeanne d'Arc, but they burned her, and canonized her only when she had been dead a long time.

Because freedom in Germany was never so well rooted in political institutions as it was elsewhere in the west, and because it was never so universally associated with economic liberalism, is not proof that the Germans do not love freedom. They merely love it in a different way. The German universities, before Hitler, were as free as any on earth. Nothing so eager and paradoxical as the German mind can be wholly regimented and subdued. And the violent expression of the many ill-digested elements in that mind may bring about a great catharsis. The fact of another war, and within a generation, confronts the Germans with a check to that sense of illimitability which I have spoken of as so characteristic. A moving body moves until it meets an obstacle. The war is that obstacle. Germany cannot move now with the exuberance of a year ago. There must be something sobering for her in the recognition that other people also have force and that they can apply it. The German mentality is compelled again to recognize that there are limits, and if Germany is to belong to western civilization that is the lesson she has to learn. With the recognition of limits will come the possibility of making a truly organic and civilized society.

Docile acceptance of the unquestioned authority of the state, traditional in Germany, may be broken when Germans have had a sufficiently long and intimate experience of what the state, transformed into a militant messianic Movement, can become and do. Whatever may go on in the national mind, individual people remain individuals. They want to breathe and eat and make love according to their own tastes, have children and keep them around them, and die, eventually, in their beds. The Gestapo, the terror, the strangling red tape, the unceasing and horriby boring propaganda, the profound psychological insecurity of a country without law, the thousand and one petty irritations which this kind of system requires of the individual, may pull Germany out of the maze of abstractions and back to some simple realities. Freedom in the western democracies dominated by the middle class has been institutionalized in bourgeois forms, and is so wholly taken for granted that it is tarnished. Quite possibly it may find its rebirth in a Socialist Germany in the form of something as real, intimate and necessary as daily bread, deeply personal, alive and human, and founded not on middle-class economic ideas but on a profound and religious respect for the human soul. With the German transition into humanism the German prophecy may come true: "An Deutschem Wesen soll die Welt genesen" (The world will be redeemed by Germany).

If the state is to be transformed into the church, in Dostoevski's sense, then it must rest on moral foundations, and (since no one yet has invented anything approximately as aesthetically perfected and humanized) upon *Christian* foundations. Dostoevski came to this conclusion before he died; and Nietzsche died mad, trying to avoid the same conclusion. Satanism is not a permanent religion. The life of love is the affirmative life, releasing every creative instinct. The ethical content of Communism and Nazism is beneath contempt, and certainly beneath that great moralist Hegel. It was the German poet Schiller who said, in the words of the Marquis Posa to Philip II, "Man is greater than you esteem him." Germany is greater than Hitler esteems her to be and Russia is greater than Stalin esteems her.

One cannot avoid recognizing that the west confronts the greatest danger in her whole history. But the recognition should lead us to the realization of what a renascence is demanded. If the west is to survive it must throw off, in its own way, the musty and outworn values of nineteenth century individualism. It was a great century, but it is over.

If the west is to be true to its eternal spirit, it must transform these values, if need be under a changed economic and social system, into the humanist and personalist values which have always been the source of its greatest strength. I use the word "personalist" rather than "individualist" to indicate that a civilized society requires that the natural man, born an individual, develop into a person, a socially conscious and coöperative human being, whose "rights" are in direct ratio to his obligations. The west must find the way simultaneously to feed men and to liberate them, to adjust the social system to the reality of social interdependency without reëstablishing slavery. When it has achieved this, the pull of the German soul will be westward again. Or, if Germany finds the solution first, the pull of the west will be towards Germany.

Meanwhile, the west must save itself from destruction. Its awakening may accompany or follow the war. It has not yet come. But we who love the west, and yearn for a Germany integrated with the west, have faith that it will.

❖ ❖ ❖

WHY did the League of Nations fail to prevent the Second World War? There is no chapter of world history after 1919 which does not contribute to the answer, but the core of it is laid bare in Marcel Hoden's "Europe Without the League," published in October 1939, a factual record of events from 1934 to 1938, when the League made its bid to break the advance of Fascist aggression, was repulsed, and collapsed. It will repay a reading by those who want to apply the lesson of the League to the advantage of the new world organization.

In the perspective of a dozen years, the salient facts stand out plainly enough. By 1935, Germany and Japan had left the League, but Russia had joined it. Germany was only partially rearmed, and had not yet moved into the Rhineland. Militarily, the two Fascist Powers were at the mercy of the member states of the League. When Italy attacked Ethiopia, the issue of right and wrong was unmistakable, and the 50 states of the League recognized it at once. There was no doubt that Mussolini had violated treaties; there was no doubt that his action constituted aggression; there was no doubt that Article XVI of the Covenant provided a clear procedure to stop the aggression. There was no doubt, furthermore, that Italy and Germany both were frightened at the possibility of the imposition of sanctions by the League. But the fact was that effective action by the 50 member states of the League depended upon action of the two Great Powers. It also depended on the attitude of the United States, which of course was not a League member. Washington tried to adapt its policy to the League's, but could give no assurance that it would continue to do so effectively, for example in the matter of withholding from Italy a crucial commodity, oil. If France and Great Britain had been willing to risk a fight in 1935, there might perhaps have been war then and there. Perhaps there would not; perhaps the League would have lived, and with it European civilization.

Marcel Hoden, the author of this article, was a member of the Secretariat of the League of Nations from 1921 to 1938, and during the last eight years of that time was Principal Private Secretary to the Secretary General.

❖ ❖ ❖

EUROPE WITHOUT THE LEAGUE

By Marcel Hoden

THE suggested epitaph—"Died at the age of twenty!"—is not correct, for actually the League of Nations did not live even that long. Born in 1919; denied at birth by the United States; nevertheless flourishing for a time; but later neglected by France and Great Britain, and then abandoned by them outright, it finally succumbed at the end of September 1938 under the repeated and unresisted blows of the totalitarian aggressors. The destruction of the League signified more than the decline of a political system in which Great Britain and France had played the dominant part. That would have been dangerous enough. But in addition it meant the collapse, for the time being at least, of the most powerful barrier which men had ever sought to erect against war. Without it Europe lacked its most promising instrument for preventing the overthrow of civilization and a return to chaos.

Some authorities, particularly in Anglo-Saxon countries, attribute the League's downfall to its weakness in the Manchurian affair, or to its failure to solve the disarmament problem, or to its lack of any effective procedure for the revision of treaties. These were all important matters, though they were connected with imperfections in methods of operation (responsibility for which lies at the door of the Great Powers) more than in any basic principle. The writer gives it as his opinion, formed after participation in League activities from the very start, that its faults in procedure were far from dooming it to death. As a matter of fact the League never seemed more flourishing or more powerful than it did in 1934 and 1935.

The destruction of the League was an integral part, indeed the most important and necessary part, in the deliberate design of the totalitarian states—Germany, Italy and Japan—to divide, weaken and immobilize the peace forces in the world and thus to open the door to domination of the world. In the following pages the writer proposes to trace the origin, the underlying causes and the principal phases of this struggle—which in less than three years (1936–1938) brought the project of the totalitarian states to success.

I. THE FUNDAMENTAL CONFLICT BETWEEN THE LEAGUE AND THE TOTALITARIAN STATES

The League as given shape at the Peace Conference in 1919 was not a pacifist utopia. It represented an attempt to establish international relations on a juridical and contractual basis, and to give the people of the world practical and effective means for expressing and affirming their will to peace. In its preamble the Covenant set forth the principles which henceforth were to govern relations between the member states of the League: "In order to promote international coöperation and to achieve international peace and security by the acceptance of obligations not to resort to war, by the prescription of open, just and honorable relations between nations, by the firm establishment of the understandings of international law as the actual rule of conduct among Governments, and by the maintenance of justice and a scrupulous respect for all treaty obligations in the dealings of organized peoples with one another."

Thus the League of Nations brought to the world a basic law, a code of obligations, methods for the peaceful settlement of international disputes and agencies for putting those methods into practice (the Assembly and the Council). Under this system all states had the same rights and the same obligations, if not the same responsibilities. Respect for the sovereignty, independence, individuality and dignity of each state was proclaimed and established. Under this system no state had the right to take the law into its own hands; resort to violence was prohibited; problems were to be studied and discussed so as to solve them fairly; and provision was made for mutual assistance against aggression.

For fifteen years the League worked and developed. Its achievements were respectable and it seemed gradually to be winning a position as an indispensable element in modern international life. Then came the decline. This was caused by the impact of National Socialism and Fascism.

The doctrines, aims and practices of the totalitarian states are in direct conflict with the purpose and actions of the League. Achievement of its hopes and aims is certainly not less desirable or necessary today than when President Wilson stated them over twenty years ago. But it is by nature incompatible with the hopes and aims of the totalitarian states. The dictators do not respect international pledges because the nature of their aims are such that they cannot. They scorn the independence of states just as they scorn the liberty of individuals. They refuse to discuss their claims on equal terms with other states because it is an essential part of their thesis that states and races are not equal. They proclaim instead their supreme "right to existence" in the form of a vital "living space." They countenance no limits on their "natural aspirations." They cannot renounce the use of force, for it is their accepted mode of action. The only negotiations which they will carry on are those with a single other Power, because in such circumstances the advantage lies with the stronger. They reject every restraining action because their success depends on surprise and intimidation. They repudiate any and every form of collective security because it would make them vulnerable.

Besides their instinctive and natural hatred of the League, both doctrinal and practical, they also feared the strength which association with it gave to Britain and France. Japan and the Third Reich were the first to resign from the League. Japan announced her intention to withdraw on March 27, 1933, after having flouted successfully her obligations under the Covenant in her dispute with China and having escaped the application of sanctions. The Third Reich promptly followed suit. Germany resigned from the

League on October 21 of the same year, in order that the Nazi leaders might proceed with rearmament free of all restraint, preparatory to embarking on their determined course of treaty violations and *coups de force*. Both countries broke with the League so that they might without hindrance carry out their plans for conquest in Asia and in Europe and throughout the world.

II. THE LEAGUE: CENTER OF RESISTANCE TO THE TOTALITARIAN STATES

Despite the withdrawal of Japan and Germany, the League continued to be a center of considerable attraction for the nations which desired peace, and of resistance against the would-be aggressors. The admission of Soviet Russia to membership, the condemnation of German rearmament, and the application of sanctions to Italy are three striking evidences that it retained great vitality and power.

In 1934, Louis Barthou, Minister of Foreign Affairs in the Doumergue Cabinet, decided to utilize the League as the mainspring in a positive plan of political action. His Eastern European Pact, based on the Covenant and renewing the tradition of the Franco-Russian alliance, aimed at rallying within the League framework all those nations which were firmly determined to make a stand against the imperialism of the Third Reich. On French instigation Soviet Russia was invited in September 1934 to become a member of the League and to occupy a permanent seat on the Council. This move was of capital political importance, for it marked the return of Russia to the European community at the moment Germany was leaving it. It was a victory for France and her friends, and it was a victory for peace, because Soviet Russia was an international factor for peace rather than for war. For Germany it was a resounding defeat, as was also the conclusion of the Franco-Soviet Pact in the following year. Admission of Soviet Russia to the League was the signal for Germany and Italy to begin their campaign of propaganda against the League's "Bolshevization"—a line of argument, incidentally, which they subsequently used successfully to tar other good institutions and causes.

In March 1935, Germany denounced the disarmament clauses of the Treaty of Versailles. On April 17, on the motion of France, the League Council condemned this violation of a treaty. At the same time the Council decided to study "measures to render the Covenant more effective in the organization of collective security." Indignation ran high in Berlin. Germany had secured an important specific goal; but longer-range German calculations seemed to have misfired. In abandoning the League the Third Reich had intended not only to create a large military force free from outside supervision, but to make sure of being completely free to use it however she might choose. The resolution of April 17 was an unpleasant warning. The shot found its mark; for a year thereafter, until March 7, 1936, the Nazi Government refrained from breaking the Covenant or any individual treaties.

Italy voted for the resolution condemning Germany's violation of the treaty. But the successful German example was persuasive. Within six months the Fascist Government had invaded Ethiopian territory, thereby not only violating the Italo-Ethiopian Treaty of Friendship, but also the Briand-Kellogg Pact, the Statute of the Permanent Court of International Justice and the League Covenant itself. The world thereupon witnessed an unprecedented phenomenon—the spontaneous formation of a coalition of fifty states against an aggressor state. The League furnished this coalition with its means of action. In the forefront stood England, where public opinion had just expressed itself, in the famous "Peace Ballot," as being overwhelmingly in favor of enforcing the collective security clauses of the Covenant. On June 26, the day before the final results of the ballot were announced, Prime Minister Baldwin, anticipating this striking victory for the supporters of the League, had declared that "The Covenant of the League of Nations is the sheet anchor of British policy."

It was on October 3 that Italian troops crossed into Ethiopian territory. Swiftly, on October 7, the League Council denounced this as aggression. At its meeting four days later the Assembly took the same course, and also decided to apply sanctions. This was a unique moment in the short life of the League, and indeed in modern history. Those of us who lived through it hour by hour felt that at last an international conscience, a collective soul, had been created. Gravely and with a full sense of their responsibilities, each of the delegates to the Assembly went to the rostrum to affirm his country's intention of remaining faithful to its pledges under the Covenant and of upholding whatever decisions the League might take. Immediately after the Assembly vote, a Coördinating Committee (really a conference of states members of the League) met to consider applying Article XVI of the Covenant. Between October 11 and 19 the Committee adopted four proposals aimed to deprive Italy of certain products and raw materials indispensable for waging war and to limit her financial resources. November 18 was set as the date for imposing sanctions. In the interval Great Britain had obtained from the smaller Mediterranean states assurances of their naval support in those waters.

Thus it took the League Council only four days to decide and declare that aggression had taken place. In four days more, a coalition of the member states had been formed. And five weeks later sanctions were put into force.

The reverberation of these events was extraordinary. Intense fear was aroused both in Germany and Italy, as we know now for a certainty from numerous witnesses, diplomatic, military and other. Mussolini has never been able to forgive or forget the deep anxiety which descended on his people, while in Germany, too, the impression made on the public by the League's prompt and vigorous action was profoundly disturbing to the Nazi Government. From that moment the two dictators realized that they had no choice: the influence of the League must be destroyed.

Even so, the Covenant had not really been fully applied, either in letter or in spirit. Although faced by an undoubted (indeed avowed) war of aggression, the member states had refused to demand the severance of diplomatic relations with the aggressor and had continued the Council in its rôle of conciliator. They rejected the most important of all sanctions, that on oil. And they deliberately avoided military sanctions. In other words, they limited sanctions to economic measures which would make themselves felt in Italy only after a considerable lapse of time. They thus mutilated Article XVI and thwarted the mechanism for applying it.

Chief responsibility for these fatal errors, which in the end were to lead to Mussolini's victory over Ethiopia and over the League, rests on the government of Pierre Laval. His policy was a personal one, and it was contrary to the treaties, traditions and interests of France. His blows against the League, keystone of French diplomatic policy, came, moreover, at the very moment when the British people and their government were in process of being converted to the French view on collective security. After long years of effort, a Prime Minister of France at last had an opportunity to obtain Britain's promise of automatic aid in case of a threat of war. In this crisis Laval wavered, reserved French liberty of action, and ended up by favoring the aggressor.

The effects of Laval's behavior on British opinion were clear and immediate. As early as October 16, Sir Austen Chamberlain had declared in an interview in the *Paris-Soir:* "If the Covenant triumphs, our confidence in it will be fortified, and Great Britain will have created a precedent which will govern her attitude in other crises to come. If, on the other hand, other nations which have signed the Covenant, which have repeatedly declared their loyalty to it, and which have sometimes accused the representatives of Great Britain of being lukewarm in their support of it, now default on their engagements in this decisive hour, then Great Britain will consider that she has been released from her obligations."

In spite of this and many similar warnings, Laval stuck to his chosen course. On December 8, he obtained Sir Samuel Hoare's consent to certain proposals for settling the Italo-Ethiopian conflict. The plan, which in effect would have rewarded aggression, aroused the indignation both of British public opinion and of the British Parliament. It forced Sir Samuel Hoare to resign and obliged Prime Minister Baldwin to make humiliating excuses in the House. But although the Council of the League discarded the Hoare-Laval plan, the damage was done. Laval's policy had estranged England from France, paralyzed the League, and headed the whole system of collective security towards the abyss.

III. THE DESTRUCTION OF THE LEAGUE BY THE TOTALITARIAN STATES

Thereafter events came thick and fast. In April 1935 the League had condemned German occupation of the Rhineland in violation of treaty obligations. In October 1935 the League had voted limited sanctions on Italy for her attack on Ethiopia. By September 1938 the totalitarian states had definitely worsted the League. Through each of the Italian, German and Japanese adventures which now took place the main objective can be easily discerned. As in the reoccupation of the Rhineland and the Italian war on Ethiopia, so in the war in Spain, the Sino-Japanese "incident" of 1937, the debates on the "reform" of the League Covenant, Mr. Chamberlain's experimentation in European settlement outside the framework of the Covenant, Germany's annexation of Austria, the dismemberment of Czechoslovakia, and Italy's seizure of Albania—all were stages marking the League's decadence and final destruction.

Let us look back briefly at the chief of these events. In January 1936 Anthony Eden, new head of the British Foreign Office, strove sincerely and with youthful energy to rally the dispersing League forces and to assume moral and political leadership at Geneva. At the Quai d'Orsay Laval was succeeded by Flandin. For France, the change was merely a jump out of the frying pan into the fire. Flandin continued Laval's policy by refusing to accept Eden's proposal for an oil sanction, alleging that he had received threats from Rome that "the oil sanction means war" and that Mussolini would leave the League (*sic*) if this new and effective measure were taken against him. Thus once again France refused to run the risks of collective security and headed toward the alternative risks of war.

This brings us to March 2, 1936. Less than a week later, on March 7, Hitler denounced the Treaty of Locarno and sent the Reichswehr into the Rhineland. Hesitating to resort to force, the French Government swung round towards the League. Here, now, it was her turn to find herself abandoned. The League Council met at London. A wave of Gallophobia had enveloped Parliament, the City, society and the press. Hitler had been clever enough to follow up his violation of the Locarno Pact by presenting a "Peace Plan." British public opinion swallowed it and demanded negotiations with Germany. Some League members saw in all this a just reward for France's policy in the Ethiopian conflict. But most of them were as much dismayed by French passivity before the new German menace as by the menace itself. It was impossible to obtain more from the Council than moral condemnation. Attempts to form a "second coalition" met with a cold hostility in Britain and produced only confusion in the other countries. The League functioned poorly because France had been discredited, because she had become estranged from Great Britain, and because all the nations of Europe had consequently fallen prey to suspicion and fear.

If in the closing days of the Italo-Ethiopian conflict the League managed to save its honor by upholding the law, this was thanks mainly to the courageous stand of the smaller countries and the Soviet Union. Three times during 1936—in April, in June and in September—Mussolini tried in vain to make the League withdraw its condemnation of his aggression and accept the *fait accompli* in Ethiopia. By May the defeat of the Negus had been complete and in July sanctions had been lifted. Yet to each Italian demand the Council or the Assembly replied by repeating the declarations and the decisions they had previously made. The League thus emphasized its intention not to reconsider its earlier condemnation nor to recognize the conquest of Ethiopia.

In September, in particular, the Italian Government (encouraged by a much-criticized visit made to Rome by the Secretary-General of the League) sought to prevent the League Assembly from seating the representatives of Ethiopia. Notwithstanding pressure from various sources, the Assembly allowed the Ethiopian delegates to take their seats. The steadfast attitude of the League delegates reflected not only their desire to protest against Italy's violation of the Covenant, but a feeling of betrayal and anger on the part of the smaller states toward the Great Powers. This was especially evident as regards Great Britain. The smaller states felt that after having won them to the policy of collective security, British statesmen had left them (and especially the Mediterranean states which had agreed to naval coöperation) to the tender mercies of Italy.

We now come to the Spanish war. London (in the lead) and Paris (reluctantly) adopted the principle of "non-intervention." Heedless of the requests of the Spanish Government, long a loyal member of the League, neither the Council nor the Assembly was willing to recognize that Italy and Germany were guilty of aggression in Spain. To contrary proofs they shut their eyes.

In the Sino-Japanese "incident" which began on July 7, 1937, the League evinced the same hesitations, and in the end refused similarly to act, even though the Chinese Government formally informed the Council that Japan's action was "an aggression against the territorial integrity and existing political independence of China, a Member of the League of Nations." In both the Spanish and Chinese cases a sense of caution, if not of impotence, seemed to have affected the British and French Governments. Their fear of "irritating" the totalitarian states spread through the entire League.

Despite all these blows the moral force and the potential strength of the League remained considerable. The feeling that they belonged to an international community still persisted among the member states and preserved the basis for concerted action whenever leadership should appear. Though they showed signs of timidity in putting the Covenant into effect, the nations still thought of it as a reserve fund of security for future use. In Paris and London there were men who understood this situation. Though handicapped by the injury done Anglo-French solidarity by Pierre Laval, the Blum Government sought to revive confidence in France and in the League. "France boldly declares," said the Premier in the Chamber on July 1, 1936, "and will attest by her acts, her loyalty to international law. She will put far from her mind at this hour all thought of disappointment or discouragement. She gives her word; she will keep it. Her wish is to make the idea of collective security a reality. She will contribute by all the means in her power to revive within the League and around it that outburst of enthusiasm and faith which threw a lustre on certain great days: in 1924, at the time of the Protocol; in 1932, when the Disarmament Conference opened; and again last autumn, when the associated states proclaimed their unanimous resolve."

In London, Anthony Eden and Lord Cranborne remained sincere advocates of collective security, despite their inability to follow an always logical course in supporting it on specific occasions; for though they understood the League's value, the same could not be said for the British Governmen of which they were a part. The Prime Minister and his most powerful colleagues had decided to draw a lesson from the defeat suffered in the Italo-Ethiopian affair and to go a separate way regardless of France and the League. They were determined that, since apparently the Covenant could not be applied, it should be amended by lessening its obligations, notably those concerning sanctions in Article XVI. Furthermore, with Berlin making overtures to London, many British Tories began to envisage the return of Germany to a modified League and the resumption of Italy's collaboration "without obligations or sanctions."

This was the genesis of the idea of reforming the Covenant, as put on the League agenda by the British Government as early as July 1936. It was an artificial question, for, as Titulesco once remarked, "If the League has miscarried, the fault lies not in the Covenant, but in man." The question was full of dynamite, too, for to discuss the Covenant might jeopardize the high purpose of the League and was almost certain to shake its unity.

At first there was considerable resistance to the idea: France, Soviet Russia, and the members of the Little Entente and the Balkan Entente decided that any new study of the Covenant undertaken should aim at "reinforcing the authority of the League" and "increasing the true efficacy of the guarantees of security which the League offered its members." They purposely adopted a slow procedure. But at the end of May 1937 Stanley Baldwin retired and was succeeded as Prime Minister by Neville Chamberlain. He retained Eden as head of the Foreign Office, but with the tactic of "imprisoning" him and at the same time using his presence in the Cabinet to reassure the Opposition and the French Government. In the past Chamberlain had rendered at least lip service to the League, and had campaigned on a League platform. But he neither liked the League nor really understood it. He had come to think of it as not merely useless but positively dangerous. He allowed Eden to affirm the British Government's fidelity to the League; but in his own mind he had chosen another policy, that of direct negotiation for the defense of limited British interests as he understood them. He discouraged the little nations from appealing to Geneva. He preferred Franco to win in Spain. He sought personal contact and reconciliation with the dictators. At the end of July he sent a personal message to Mussolini; in November, profiting by Eden's absence in Brussels, he sent Halifax to Berlin.

Meanwhile, what of France, rent by domestic dissension? After the advent of M. Chautemps to power in June 1937 she followed the lead of Great Britain. Her allies in eastern Europe forsook her; her best friends were in disgrace. Poland, with the approval of England, drew steadily closer to the Third Reich and let the Nazis assume a dominant position in Danzig. Belgium, under van Zeeland and Spaak, slipped gradually into what was called neutrality. In Rumania, Titulesco had already been removed from power. Jugoslavia, where Premier Stoyadinović had fostered German economic penetration, concluded a political agreement with Italy after consultation with London. The Little Entente was shaken to its foundations. Czechoslovakia, against which a German campaign had already begun, slowly became isolated. Henlein started his series of trips to London and Berlin and Berchtesgaden. Soviet Russia, prey to an intense and bloody domestic crisis, withdrew within herself. The Franco-Soviet Pact became a dead letter.

In November 1937, MM. Chautemps and Delbros went to London. Neville Chamberlain did not hide from them his scorn for the League. The French ministers heard him out. For the first time in seventeen years the communiqué issued after Anglo-French conversations did not mention the League. To Eden's surprise the French ministers did not object. They accepted Chamberlain's formula reaffirming "the desire of their Governments to coöperate with all countries in the common task of promoting international appeasement by methods of free and peaceful negotiation." Downing Street had won. Eden was beaten on his own ground. He resigned soon thereafter.

The great "Chamberlain experiment" had already begun, and we must note in fairness that it had at heart the tacit approval of the French Government. It was to continue for many months at the expense of both Great Britain and France, as well as of Europe and the League. We all know into what terrifying territory it eventually led us.

The consequences for the League of the Anglo-French communiqué of November 30 were soon evident. Earlier that month an Anti-Communist Protocol had been signed at the Chigi Palace in Rome by Ciano, von Ribbentrop and Hotta, Japanese Ambassador to Italy. This pact became the nucleus of the totalitarian coalition against the League at the very moment that Great Britain and France deserted it. On December 11, 1937, Mussolini announced to the world, on a great flood of publicity, that Italy was withdrawing from the League; on the next day the official Nazi press bureau published a communiqué in which the German Government solemnly declared that "a return to Geneva will never be considered." These reciprocal assurances gave birth to the "Axis." It was not coincidence, we might note, that this expression became a part of the world's political vocabulary simultaneously with the first overt steps against the League. "We are withdrawing from the tottering temple where they do not work for peace but prepare for war," declared Mussolini in a speech on December 11. The German press followed suit and warned the smaller states that the League was merely "a war machine" and that "to adhere to the Covenant is to enlist."

Never had arguments of doctrine, used to show the inevitability of the conflict between the League and the totalitarian states, been so clearly and vigorously expressed. Never had the attack on the Anglo-French political system been so direct or so frank. According to the totalitarian spokesmen, the German-Italian-Japanese alliance was undertaking a task even more universal than that of the League —to put an end to "obsolete positions of monopoly" and to "create a world-order in which the really vigorous nations can live together." The warning to the western democracies thus was clear: the goal of the new confederation was a world domination. The totalitarian states had set out by promise and by threat to tear the League asunder, thus isolating France and Great Britain for the final *Machtprobe*.

Faced with this menace, London and Paris came to life. They had two opportunities to reply to the dictators: the one hundredth session of the Council, which met at Geneva on January 26, 1938; and the meeting of the Committee of 28, created to study the reform of the Covenant. In the Council, the French and British delegates answered Mussolini's speech of December 11 and the German communiqué of December 12 by reaffirming their loyalty to the League. All the other members thereupon followed their example. Said Mr. Eden: "His Majesty's Government in the United Kingdom does not think it inappropriate, at a moment when it has to acknowledge the repudiation in some quarters of the League of Nations, to declare that its faith in the aims and ideals that inspired the League remains unchanged." "The Government which I represent," declared M. Delbos, the French Foreign Minister, "desires to reaffirm its loyalty to the League of Nations and its continued faith in the future of that organization." The Soviet representative boldly approached the ideological problem and cleared up misconceptions created by totalitarian propaganda. "But there is another kind of ideology," he said, "the essential principles of which are respect for the integrity and independence of all existing states, inviolability of their frontiers, renunciation of war as an instrument for settling international disputes, recognition of the equal rights of all peoples, great and small. The League of Nations undoubtedly, if it wishes to be true to its aims, cannot but be a bloc of that kind of international ideology."

In late January and early February 1938, 17 states represented on the Committee of 28—Finland, Argentina, Czechoslovakia, China, Soviet Russia, Iran, Turkey, Colombia, Canada, Spain, Mexico, Greece, Bulgaria, France, Rumania, Great Britain and New Zealand—announced that for the time being they were opposed to any reform or to any modification, either unilateral or collective, in the articles or the application of the Covenant, and that as regarded the future they were against any decision which might weaken the Covenant or circumscribe the League's authority and its field of action. The representatives of the Netherlands, Switzerland and Sweden, while they would have liked the Committee to recognize formally that under existing conditions Article XVI could not be applied in its entirety, nevertheless emphasized that their governments rejected the idea of neutrality, that they intended to remain faithful to the principle of collective security, and that they hoped some day to be able to reëstablish the obligation to impose sanctions.

The offensive against the League was thus for the time being repulsed. The small states, reassured and appeased, stayed within the fold; at heart most of them were glad that nothing had been done to Article XVI, a source of anguish and yet of comfort to them all. At this juncture it would still have been possible for France and Britain to draw the other countries firmly within the framework of the League. But this would have required the adoption of a resolute stand by France and Britain themselves—and for this neither showed any inclination.

On February 20, 1938, Hitler delivered an insolent and threatening speech before the Reichstag. On the same day Chamberlain parted company with Eden, who had remained till then in the Cabinet as the champion of collective security even though his initiative had been extremely circumscribed. In order to dispel any doubts as to his true sentiments and the direction of his policy, Chamberlain in a speech in the House two days later deliberately rejected "the imposition of sanctions and the use of force," and, sounding the knell of collective security, warned the little states clearly not to count any longer on the League.

Almost at once came Germany's invasion and annexation of Austria, whose independence had been guaranteed by the League. When Britain and France failed to offer any resistance, terror and confusion overtook the League's smaller members. On April 16, Chamberlain went a step further by signing the Anglo-Italian agreement and exchanging cordial messages with Mussolini.

The policy of appeasement and reconciliation with the totalitarian Powers appeared to observers in the smaller states of Europe as a mixture of egoism and weakness. Thenceforward the idea of neutrality made rapid and steady progress in Scandinavia, the Netherlands and Belgium. In May, the Swiss (on special grounds, to be sure) decided to resume their full and unconditional neutrality. A burst of energy shown by Britain and France at a moment of crisis in Czechoslovakia in May was not followed up. In July, Chamberlain reaffirmed his intention of pursuing the "policy of appeasement," condemned anew the system of sanctions, and preached the transformation of the League into a union of nations devoted to "consultation and conciliation." Enlightened beyond all peradventure as to Chamberlain's intentions, the states in the "Oslo group" met in July and agreed to demand of the next League Assembly that it state authoritatively the discretionary character of sanctions. "This," gloated the *Giornale d'Italia,* "means the end of collective security. . . . Henceforth the powerful armaments of the democracies cannot be excused on the ground that they are for the use of the League of Nations."

This brings us down to August 1938. By that date Hitler's intentions toward Czechoslovakia were no longer a mystery to anyone. Everybody therefore expected that the French Government, bound by a treaty of assistance to the Czech Government, would shortly be seeking to induce the League Council to declare that a German aggression had been committed against Czechoslovakia, a member of the League, and would demand that sanctions be applied. The Franco-Soviet Pact, like the Franco-Czech Pact, could come into force only within the framework of the League.

The League Assembly met on September 12 in an atmosphere heavy with anxiety. The totalitarian states had of course exerted every possible effort to frighten the smaller League members and obviate the danger of sanctions. Would France and Britain stand firm, reassuring the anxious ones, rallying the laggards and restoring cohesion by determined leadership? Once more the fate of the Covenant, the very existence of the League, rested in the hands of Great Britain and France. But could the spirit of 1935 be reawakened? Could the coalition for peace be reëstablished?

On September 26 and 27 President Roosevelt sent his famous messages to Beneš and Hitler. A day later the League Assembly gave its support to President Roosevelt's lead. The following day the Prime Minister of Great Britain and the Premier of France—ignoring the initiative taken by Roosevelt and the Assembly, brushing aside the Covenant of the League of Nations and disregarding the Franco-Czech Treaty of Mutual Assistance and the German-Czech Convention of Conciliation and Arbitration—went to Munich, as Chamberlain had already gone to Berchtesgaden and Godesberg.

President Masaryk once said: "Jesus and not Cæsar, that is the essence of democracy." He might have added "and of the League of Nations." At Munich the British and French Governments deserted Jesus to make a sacrifice to Cæsar. On October 1 the Assembly broke up. Nothing was left of the League of Nations.

IV. THE NEED FOR A LEAGUE

Between the League of Nations, a free association of states determined to observe certain principles in their relations with one another and prepared to submit to certain rules, and the totalitarian states, which cannot and will not accept any limitation but that of force, conflict was inevitable. But the conflict need not have ended as it did.

In 1935 the League seemed headed for ultimate victory. But victory was denied it, and for this a large measure of the fault lies with the French Government and another large measure lies with the British Government. The final triumph of might over right and the collapse of the League in the general "save-yourself" flight of frightened peoples stemmed directly from the conciliatory overtures made to the totalitarian states, now by Paris, now by London. Resistance to aggression by the dictators required the existence of an "international ideology" and the resolute will of those who accepted it to defend it. Such an ideology did, in fact, exist in the Covenant of the League. Around it men of good will, who regarded it as the highest expression of international right and justice so far achieved by man, should have gathered determinedly and confidently even in days of greatest stress.

After Munich the world was confronted with this dilemma: either to restore the reign of law among nations, which meant to revive the League, or to accept the life of slaves in a universe directed by primitive instincts and dominated by force.

Deceived and betrayed by Hitler and Mussolini, the British and French Governments decided to act. After having allowed the League, their best instrument for action, to be smashed under their very eyes, they began striving, at the price of countless difficulties and much haggling, to reëstablish a peace coalition, to reawaken the spirit of 1935, to revive an international conscience. Would it not have been better to have enforced the Covenant in the first place? Much would have been saved—much that was of value spiritually as well as much that was worth saving materially.

When our western democracies have at last imposed peace on the totalitarian states, France and Britain will have before them the task of reawakening the good will, the confidence, and the support of other peoples, both in Europe and beyond the seas. They must revive that cult of liberty, equality, law, justice and honor which inspired those who prepared the Covenant of the League and gave it shape and life. When peace is restored, they must, this time let us hope with the help of the United States, reconstruct the world in accordance with the League's original principles. The League is dead. Long live the League!

❖ ❖ ❖

A GREAT many Americans were seriously looking at maps for the first time in their lives in April 1941, the date of the publication of "The Myth of the Continents," by Eugene Staley, then Professor of International Economic Relations at the Fletcher School of Law and Diplomacy. Hitler controlled Europe from the Carpathians to the Atlantic. The Soviet-Nazi alliance was still in force. In the Far East, with the connivance of the Vichy régime, Japanese troops were soon to pour into Indo-China. The might of the Rome-Berlin-Tokyo Axis seemed irresistible. Of the Great Powers, only Britain fought back, and British troops were to be driven from Greece, their toehold on the Continent, at the end of April. Moreover, the effort to save Greece had disastrously weakened General Wavell's forces which were guarding the North African approach to the Suez.

What in these circumstances were the nature and extent of the interests of the United States? That was the question which sent Americans to the geography books. But the maps they saw were, more often than not, the familiar Mercator projections, which showed the familiar flat world—the oceans in their accustomed broad proportions, the American continents satisfactorily isolated by stretches of blue ink from danger to the east or west. If America must take a posture of defense, isolationists argued, it should be the one designed by nature. That is to say, the United States should reserve its strength for use in the compact zone where lay its essential interests—the western hemisphere.

Look again, urged Professor Staley, and, since the world is round, look at a globe! See, for example, that the spot in the North African desert called Bengasi, where the British Commonwealth troops were fighting to protect the crossroads of the world from a new world conqueror, is nearer Madison, Wisconsin, than is Buenos Aires; and so, in the opposite direction, is Manchukuo. That the world is indeed round, that United States interests are world-wide, and that bodies of water are avenues of communication not barriers to it, need no further demonstration for an era which saw Nimitz's fleet and MacArthur's and Eisenhower's armies in action.

The true dimensions of the problem of Pan American solidarity is seen only with the admission that the peoples of the western hemisphere who, for profoundly important strategic, economic and psychological reasons, must be good friends are for the most part distant neighbors.

❖ ❖ ❖

THE MYTH OF THE CONTINENTS

By Eugene Staley

IN earlier writings as well as in his latest book Charles A. Beard reads from (or into?) American history the lesson that "continentalism" represents the predestined course of our foreign policy. Jerome Frank, writing a chapter on "Disintegrated Europe and Integrated America," argues that the basic issue in Europe, and the cause of unfortunate developments in Germany and Italy, has been "the absence of continental integration." In America, he continues, we have continental integration, "and therefore the possibility of relative self-sufficiency." Stuart Chase embroiders still further Frank's theme of "disintegrated Europe, integrated America," collects figures to explore the possibilities of various "continental economic units," and, in the last sentence of his book, urges the United States to avoid economic and political entanglements in the affairs of other nations which, "in the nature of their geographical deficiencies, must quarrel, until some day they too achieve continental unity." [1]

The western hemisphere complex, so conspicuous in discussions of American foreign policy, has often been associated with ideas of "continental" unity and "continental" solidarity. A noteworthy instance occurred in a symposium at the meeting of the American Political Science Association a year ago where Clarence Streit's plan for Interdemocracy Federal Union was up for discussion. A distinguished political scientist—a student of municipal government—based his criticism on the view that the natural political and economic

[1] Charles A. Beard, "A Foreign Policy for the United States" (New York: Knopf, 1940); Jerome Frank, "Save America First" (New York: Harper, 1938); Stuart Chase, "The New Western Front" (New York: Harcourt Brace, 1939).

grouping is the "continental" one. He therefore favored solidarity with Latin American countries as against overseas countries.

There is, of course, a tremendous literature on the theme that "Europe" must unite. Coudenhove-Kalergi's magazine *Pan Europa;* the efforts of practical statesmen like Briand, Herriot and others to promote European union; and more recently a new flood of books, articles, plans and speeches advocating a "United States of Europe" or some sort of European federation all carry a continental emphasis. Sometimes there is an explicit argument to explain why continents, as such, must be united. Thus, H. N. Brailsford writes, "Air power has made inevitable the unification of continents." More often than not, however, this point is simply taken for granted.

On the other hand, there are strong trends in current political action and thought, as well as existing economic and political connections, which cut directly across continental lines. Public opinion and official policy in the United States are today influenced very decidedly by the realization that our own ability to defend ourselves depends in no small measure on what happens in Europe and Asia. The British Commonwealth of Nations, so long as it stands, will continue to be a practical challenge to the thesis that continental units are the natural ones. The war emergency has publicized the fact that the economic affiliations of much of South America, as well as the cultural affiliations of Latin America in general, are with Europe—distinctly un-continental. In the realm of thought about the future, particularly in the discussion of war and peace aims, continental lines are being as regularly disregarded by some as they are being emphasized by others. Proposals like "Union Now," and the more moderate proposals of those who, while doubting the feasibility of complete federal union, nevertheless envisage some kind of a permanent bond between the United States and other democratic nations, reject the continental principles in favor of an ocean-linked unity.

One general theme runs like a red thread through most of these discussions, by continentalists and non-continentalists alike. That is the conviction that the day of the small, completely independent, sovereign national state is past. There will be in the future—and ought to be—*larger* politico-economic units of some kind. This, in the view of the present writer, has to be accepted as unquestionably sound. But is the natural progression from small, sovereign states to *continental* groupings? There is reason for making an examination of this question now, for the words "continent" and "continental" seem to be acquiring strong emotional and symbolic values which may even affect policy. Is this a well-founded development, or have we here an instance of the fascination (not to say the tyranny) of certain words? What are the general characteristics that mark off continental from non-continental, overseas, or maritime groupings? What is to be said for permanent supra-national groupings of a continental sort as compared with non-continental, maritime, or oceanic groupings? With respect to the defense problem of the United States, what are the relative virtues of a policy which stresses "continental" defense lines (admitting aid to Britain largely because it buys time for preparation), as against a policy which allies us with overseas friends in all-out resistance to the totalitarian challenge and in joint maintenance of dominant world sea power? [2]

II

There is only one universal characteristic which distinguishes continental from non-continental groupings—the existence of land connections (or barriers) instead of sea connections (or barriers) between the members of the group. What political or economic consequences, if any, follow from this difference?

Distance has human significance only in terms of the barriers it interposes against the exchange of messages (communication), the movement of persons (travel), and the

[2] Wherever "sea power" is mentioned in this article the term must be understood to *include* the necessary complement of air-power required under modern conditions in order to hold command of the surface of the seas and in order to defend the bases—military and industrial—on which sea power rests.

movement of goods (transport.) How does *over-land* distance compare with *over-water* distance in these three respects?

Obviously, the answer depends on the character of the particular lands and seas involved (land areas differ more than sea areas in the obstacles they offer) and on the technology of the times. Nowadays, communication, which permits exchange of intelligence, impressions and feelings, takes place over water and over land with practically the same speed, cost and convenience. Radio waves and the air mail pay little attention to continental lines. So far as travel is concerned, surface travel on land today is swifter where there are good railway lines and highways than surface travel by ship, and it is hard to generalize about the differences in expense and convenience. But if one travels by air —and that will surely be the standard method of long distance travel in the future—there is no important difference even today between over-land and over-water distance. Stratosphere flying will probably soon abolish what little difference does now exist. This leaves land and water distances about equally significant, in human terms, except for transportation of goods.

The transport of goods (freight) should certainly not be ranked below communication or travel in its fundamental importance for determining the "naturalness" of economic connections between different places. If freight can move easily and cheaply between two regions their economies are much more likely to become integrated, interdependent and complementary than if the movement of goods between them is difficult and costly. Now, it happens that for heavy, bulky goods, which are the staple items of inter-regional trade, water transport is much cheaper than land transport over equal distances. This has been true for centuries. It is one of the reasons why the great trading centers of the world are typically located on rivers, or lakes, or on the seacoast. It is still true today. Rumanian oil, in time of peace, moves to Germany by the long overseas route around Spain to Hamburg, instead of over the much closer "continental" connection. Italy, though linked by several railway lines to continental Europe, imported 20,000,000 tons of goods by sea in 1938 and only 4,000,000 tons by land. Coal from Germany moves overseas to Italy when there is no blockade. South American international trade, even to places on the same continent, is largely by sea.

Let us compare, in practical terms, the cost-distance from such a center as New York City to inland "continental" points and to overseas points. Using prewar rates in all cases (effective as of August 1, 1939), the "wheat-distance" between Kansas City and New York, expressed as the cost of shipping 100 pounds of wheat in carload lots, was 33½ cents to 42½ cents, while it was only 13 cents from New York to Liverpool. In mileage, Liverpool was three times as far as Kansas City; but Kansas City was nearly three times farther than Liverpool when it came to economic relations in wheat. The overseas route from Singapore to New York is more than twenty-five times longer, in miles, than the rail route from New York to Akron, Ohio. Yet the distance measured in freight cost for transporting a 240 pound bale or case of crude rubber was $1.50 from Singapore and $1.03 to Akron. In other words, Akron was two-thirds as far away from New York as Singapore, in "crude-rubber distance."

In summary, for two places a given number of miles apart it makes very little difference under modern conditions whether land or water stretches between them, so far as communication and travel are concerned. For the transportation of heavy goods, however, which is a major aspect of economic connections, the two places would be effectively closer to each other, measured in "cost-distance," if there were water between them than if there were land. *Given the same separation in miles, there is less economic distance across water than across land.*

But are not places on the same continent or in the same "hemisphere" closer to each other in miles than places on different continents or in different "hemispheres"? It is a temptation to suppose so. Ex-Governor Philip La Follette of Wisconsin warned his countrymen not long ago to beware lest we find ourselves fighting "not in this hemisphere where we can be supreme, but fighting with expeditionary forces four thousand miles away in Europe and six thousand miles away in Asia." Will the reader at this point be good enough to examine a globe? Attach a string to a pin at Madison, Wisconsin—Governor La Follette's home town—and measure how far from home he might have to go if he were sent to defend important points "in this hemisphere where we can be supreme," as compared with other points on the supposedly distant continents of Europe and Asia. Note the following facts:

It is farther from Madison to Buenos Aires in a direct line ("great circle" distance) than from Madison to Bengasi. Ankara is about as far as Buenos Aires. Actually, by the regularly travelled routes, Buenos Aires is considerably farther away than either of these points in Africa or Asia, because of the "bulge" of Brazil.

No capital in Europe, including Moscow, is as far from Madison as is Buenos Aires, and only one European capital (Athens) is as far as Rio de Janeiro. Again, this is direct-line distance, and by actually travelled routes Europe is relatively closer.

Gibraltar is closer to Madison than is the capital of Bolivia, closer than Tacna or Arica, and closer than any major city in Brazil or any place at all in Argentina, Chile, Paraguay or Uruguay.

Gibraltar, incidentally, is not merely closer to the entire South Atlantic coast of South America than is Madison, but is closer by sea than the *nearest point* in the United States (Miami). In the same way, advanced European bases at Dakar, Bathurst and Freetown on the coast of Africa are nearer to southern South America than our most advanced Caribbean bases.

If the Nazis were to capture the British naval base at Scapa Flow in Scotland they would be closer to Madison than if they were established at Lima, Peru.

As for Asia, Manchukuo is closer to Madison than is Buenos Aires. For those to whom "continental" land connections seem especially important, it may be added that a Japanese flying over the shortest route from Manchukuo to Madison (a great circle via Bering Strait) need hardly lose sight of land.

Points on the same land-mass may be as far apart in miles as places on opposite sides of an ocean, and may be still farther apart in economic distance measured by transport costs. On the other hand, there is likely to be a greater continuity of human habitation between them than between the overseas points. How shall we weigh this characteristic in appraising the significance of continental as opposed to overseas politico-economic groupings? One might argue that the continuity permits conquest and culture to spread by easy stages, and hence that each land-mass could be expected to have more political and cultural unity, more history and tradition in common, than would exist between places on separate continents. Actually, every continent has natural barriers—deserts, mountains, swamps, jungles—which are almost uninhabited and which may be more difficult to cross than the ocean. The sea, especially in earlier centuries, has offered one of the main means of contact between peoples on the same continent, so that the peripheral areas often developed more traits in common with each other and with other continents than with land-locked regions. Thus, the political and economic system of the coastland states of Europe spread more effectively to relatively vacant areas like America and Australia than to parts of eastern and southern Europe.

It is no accident that early civilizations developed in river valleys and that the great center of ancient times is spoken of as "the Mediterranean world" and not the European or the African world. Nor is it without significance that Europe, having the most broken coastline, best adapted for sea-borne traffic, became the originator of modern world culture and world politics, while Africa, most "continental" of all land areas because of its smooth contours and difficulty of access by sea, remained the "Dark Continent."[8] In short, land connections, which would appear to establish easy contact between peoples on the same continent, may be barriers as well as connections, while the bodies of water, appearing superficially on the map as barriers, may actually be most important connecting links. Because this has been

[8] For each mile of coastline Europe has 289 square miles of surface, North America 407, Australia 534, South America 689, Asia 763, Africa 1420. Derwent Whittlesey, "The Earth and the State: A Study of Political Geography." New York: Henry Holt, 1939, p. 308.)

so distinctly true in the past, the existing patterns of culture, tradition, political affiliation and economic interdependence which confront us in the world of today are as often oceanic as they are continental.

III

We in this country can give the "continental" doctrine an immediate and practical test by applying it to the grand strategy of United States defense. In general, the same people who talk about "continental integration" draw a line around the so-called western hemisphere and refuse to concede that the United States has any vital interest outside—except that limited aid to Britain may be desirable in order to gain time for perfecting defenses within the "hemisphere." It should be noted, however, that our relations with the western hemisphere countries to the south of us are not really "continental" in any significant practical sense. A land connection is afforded by the Isthmus of Panama, but no one ever travels, or sends messages, or transports goods between North and South America *overland*. In fact, all Latin America, not merely South America, is overseas to us, with the partial exception of Mexico. Latin America is susceptible of defense by the United States only if the United States controls the sea routes, including routes which are problems of high-seas defense.

If the western hemisphere, then, is to be considered as one unit for defense purposes, or for other purposes, it provides an instance not of continental but of *maritime* solidarity. The practical issue today, in reality, is between two kinds of maritime solidarity. Some would make our area of maritime solidarity quasi-continental—that is, confined to North and South America and their immediate vicinities—while others would team up with Britain in a world-girdling maritime defense group.

Which grouping offers us the best line of defense? The technology of warfare and the nature of the enemy's strategy in attack have an important bearing on that question. Recent developments in warfare include far more than the efficient use of machines. The "extended strategy" of the Nazis—to use their own term—involves: (1) isolating the opponent by outmanœuvring him on the chessboard of international politics, placing him, without allies, in front of vastly superior economic and military force; (2) creating confusion and fomenting an uprising from within; (3) undermining the enemy's will to resist, by propaganda stressing the goodness of Nazi purposes, the hopelessness of resisting, and by fear—the "war of nerves"; (4) last of all, outright military attack. Against this strategy there must likewise be an "extended defense"! What grouping is best for the purpose?

Certain basic facts about the problem of defending the western hemisphere are now fairly well known. The American people have realized with a shock that the Monroe Doctrine has rested in the past not merely on our own power, but on the existence and the friendliness of the British Navy. If the British Navy were to be captured, or sunk, or scattered, we would face a combined Axis naval superiority that might amount to two or three to one against us. The "two-ocean navy" our Congress has voted cannot be completed before 1946. Furthermore, can we assume that a victorious Axis would be unable to match our new vessels, or to outmatch them? The estimated annual shipbuilding capacity of countries now under Nazi rule (Germany, Norway, Denmark, Holland, Belgium, France), plus that of Japan, plus that of Italy, was about 3,200,000 gross tons at the outbreak of war. In the event of a Nazi conquest of the British Isles, additional equipment rated at an annual capacity of about 2,500,000 gross tons would be in the hands of the totalitarians. The grand total so amassed is 5,700,000 gross tons, as of September 1939. It seems reasonable to assume that since then new installations and destruction by bombing may have offset each other. Over against this annual capacity of nearly 6,000,000 gross tons the United States had an estimated shipbuilding capacity (including navy yards) of perhaps 800,000 gross tons at the outbreak of war, and this had been pushed up to 1,500,000 gross tons as of January 1, 1941. Experts hold that by building new yards we can probably increase this capacity at the rate of about 1,000,000 tons a year. If that is a good estimate, it would take us more than four years to overtake totalitarian shipbuilding capacity, *supposing that they stood still.* In the meantime, we should start with something like a 4 to 1 shipbuilding ratio against us. This must be a most disquieting fact if we hope to defend, single-handed, distant overseas areas like the South Atlantic coast of South America.

The power of a naval force decreases with the distance it must operate from its bases. Recall, then, what was pointed out above: that the sea-distance from the southeastern coast of South America (including important cities like Rio de Janeiro and Buenos Aires) is shorter to Gibraltar than to Miami, shorter to Dakar than to our most advanced Caribbean base at Trinidad. Furthermore, look on the globe at the British islands in the South Atlantic—Ascension, St. Helena, Tristan da Cunha, the Falklands—which might become Axis outposts in case Britain lost control of the seas around Europe.

But why plan to defend southern South America, since it is so far away? If Britain should be conquered, why not "write off" that part of the western hemisphere, let the Axis take it if they want it, and retire to a shortened defense line running across the continent at the equator or at the level of the "bulge"? We might actually have to give serious consideration to this scheme of "quarter-sphere" defense if Britain were defeated. But there are grave weaknesses in such a defense line.

First, the tradition that the Monroe Doctrine applies to the whole of both Americas is so strong that it might not be feasible to reconcile public opinion in the United States to such a policy.

Second, this retreat from our often-announced intention to keep trespassers off both the Americas would be a psychological defeat of the first magnitude, important in the war of nerves.

Third, we should be abandoning as potential allies the most developed and progressive countries in South America, the only ones capable of contributing largely to a common defense.

Fourth, these countries exercise important leadership throughout Latin America. By abandoning them we should forfeit whatever good will and friendly coöperation we might otherwise expect from Latin American countries closer home, and we should present the Axis with unexcelled political and cultural outposts for penetration into the vital Caribbean area, which everybody agrees we must defend at all costs. This is important, in view of the fact that the most effective "secret weapon" of the Nazis thus far has been internal dissension and fifth-column activities.

Fifth, strategic raw materials like Brazilian manganese and Bolivian tin lie south of such a "quarter-sphere" defense line, and this would be an important consideration if the world oceans were closed to us—which we would have to expect, unless we yielded to Axis demands.

Sixth, and finally, if we allow the Axis to establish strong positions "below the bulge," connected to Europe by the sea-lanes of the South Atlantic which they would control, aviation bases could be pushed northwest across the continent to threaten directly the most vital and vulnerable link in our ability to defend North America—the Panama Canal. Already, in fact, Axis-dominated "commercial" companies are pushing in this very direction, into remote areas that offer little commercial traffic, but might provide numbers of secret landing fields. Relatively small Axis forces, hopping over the jungles in the air, could conceivably establish such a serious menace to the Canal that we would be forced to send an expeditionary force to root them out. And what permanent security would this bring us, supposing we were successful, unless we were prepared to maintain forces throughout a large part of South America?

In sum, South America is overseas to us, and important parts of it are farther from our bases than from the bases of European powers. The problem of defending South America is a *maritime,* not a continental problem, and if command of the seas in the South Atlantic passes to hostile powers we could neither establish bases there ourselves nor prevent them from ensconcing themselves on the Continent. Once they were there, only a major expeditionary force could root them out or prevent them from gradually working northward by successive jumps overland. Those soporific calculations about the number of ships an invader would have to have in order to send an expeditionary force from Europe to the United States, and about the perils to which such a force would be exposed from land-based defenders, *would apply to us in reverse, once command of the South Atlantic had passed to the Axis.* For strategy of the Nazis could place us before the dilemma, either of trying to drive them out of South America, or of letting them work northward to the Canal. In fact, the Nazis would know how to create a situation, after taking over important Latin American countries by "consent," without using any military force at all, where we would have to be the attackers.

Colonel Lindbergh testified before the House Committee on Foreign Affairs that aviation has increased the vulnerability of any country to attack from forces on the same continent, but has decreased the vulnerability of a whole continent to attack from without—that is, by way of the seas. Presumably, this was intended to support the isolationist thesis that the United States has little to fear regardless of who wins in Europe. The hollowness of the argument is exposed by the considerations advanced above. The advantage of land-based aviation against sea attack would be our advantage only if we can assume that the United States can count on getting and holding and supplying bases in that distant overseas territory on the east coast of South America, and that we can prevent the Axis from doing so. This is a most unlikely assumption, if control of the high seas, and especially of the South Atlantic, passes to the Axis by the defeat of Britain. In other words, once control of the high seas passed from our friends to our enemies we would eventually be exposed to land-based, *continental* attacks by relatively small units of the Luftwaffe on the Panama Canal region, which is vital to the naval power on which defense of our own coast depends. On our side, we could find a remedy only by a major effort involving probably the transport of troops a long distance *overseas* in an area where the advantage of established positions and nearness to bases might be all against us.

These doubts about the security of a defense system limited to the western hemisphere are strengthened by consideration of the economic problems of defending against totalitarian attack. The great bargaining weakness of a western hemisphere economic bloc as over against an Axis-dominated world would arise from the surpluses of products competitive with our own which are produced in Latin America, especially in the temperate climate of southern South America. In 1937 continental Europe and the United Kingdom absorbed considerably more than two billion dollars' worth of western hemisphere exports, principally petroleum, cotton, wheat, copper, meats, corn, tobacco and linseed. Important Latin American groups depend for their income on selling such goods abroad. It is easy to write glibly about diverting production to products needed in the United States, disposing of surpluses by hemisphere stamp plans, raising living standards throughout the hemisphere by fostering industrial development, and creating cartels to limit production and to barter with Hitler. These are the things we must try to do if Britain collapses and we have to make a stand on the line of hemisphere defense. Some of them are worth doing anyway. But rechanneling of production takes time, and it meets social and political resistances. By stimulating Bolivian tin-mining or Brazilian rubber production we would not automatically reëmploy the gauchos of the Argentine pampas, or the wheat farmers of Alberta and Saskatchewan, or the tobacco growers in Virginia and North Carolina.

It is not at all clear that the Latin American countries would feel inclined to undergo difficult economic readjustments for the sake of fitting into the defense plan of the United States and thereby antagonizing the Axis. Hitler, if he had defeated Britain, could probably offer them more than we could, while demanding less from them in the way of readjustment of established patterns of production, and he could also threaten them more effectively.

If Britain can be kept in the picture, on the other hand, even if Hitler manages to hold what he has in Europe (in some kind of a stalemate or truce), the economic problem of defending the Americas becomes much more manageable. The reason is that a large volume of foodstuffs and raw materials of a sort competitive with United States production, and which we therefore do not care to import, regularly flows from such countries as Argentina and Uruguay to Britain, to be paid for by goods and services which Britain furnishes to Empire countries and to others. Some of these countries in turn sell large export surpluses in the United States (for example, rubber and tin from the East Indies), and the United States sells more than it buys in Argentina. Britain is the pivot of this triangular and multiangular trade on which the disposal of a considerable part of South American surpluses depends. Let Britain's economic life be destroyed, or let it come under the domination of Hitler's New Order, and the effect on the economic defense of the Americas is analogous to the effect the sinking or capture of the British fleet would have on the naval defense of the Americas.

A defense area limited to the western hemisphere has another important economic disadvantage as compared with a world-girdling defense area based on joint British and American sea power. *We* would be the blockaded party. The Nazis, controlling the overseas trade routes of the world, except those in the immediate vicinity of our bases, would have on their side the quiet, undramatic but steady weight of advantage in economic power for defense or aggression conferred by the ability to draw upon the best and cheapest sources of materials in Europe, Asia, Africa, Australia, and the islands of the seas, and probably portions of South America. We, and not they, would have to waste part of our productive power making substitutes and adapting our industry to inferior materials. To be sure, the United States, together with the adjacent areas that our navy could protect, is better equipped than any other region to withstand a siege. But the engineers, mechanics, machine-tools, materials and inventors used to build synthetic rubber plants, or to establish our own tin smelters, or to develop *Ersatz* materials could not be used at the same time for producing planes and tanks, nor for producing civilian goods. The side which controls the world oceans, and which thus enjoys access by sea to allies and neutrals alike, has an inestimable long-run advantage in the scales of economic power.

Recently the editors of *Fortune* captioned a pair of world charts: "U.S.A.—Compact, Easily Defended; British Empire—Diffuse, Vulnerable." The theory implied in these captions has certain commonly accepted elements of truth. But in them may also lurk a dangerous fallacy—particularly dangerous under new techniques of warfare used so skillfully by the totalitarian Powers. The "diffuse, vulnerable" area, *if its communications can be maintained by dominant sea power,* is in a position to unite its allies and divide its enemies. It can nip in the bud, so to speak, threats to its position which may arise from any one of many different quarters—provided it acts resolutely and in time. The "compact, easily defended" area, on the other hand, may not be able to take action against the increasing power of a potential enemy until every ally has been "mopped up," until the enemy has gathered his forces without interference and has chosen the most advantageous moment for attack. The "diffuse-vulnerable" area, always supposing it holds command of the seas, can base its military effort on the economic resources of most of the world, including the materials and the industrial manpower of allied and non-belligerent countries far out of reach of the adversary. Finally, compactness may be no particular advantage, and even a great disadvantage, in the psychological phases of modern warfare. There is an important psychological as well as material difference between surrounding the enemy and being surrounded by the enemy. In the case of the United States, this is the difference between joining with allies from all the rest of the world to help keep Hitler caged in Europe and trying to resist a Hitler who controls all the world except our immediate neighborhood. "Compact—easily defended; diffuse—vulnerable" tacitly assumes that the land connects, that the sea divides. Such a slogan dramatizes inaccuracies of thinking that might prove as dangerous to us as the "Maginot mentality" proved to France, as little conducive to survival as the rigid strength of the mastodon in competition with the flexibility and adaptability of other animals and man.

Incidentally, if we were forced to defend the western hemisphere against attack by an Axis-dominated world, and if we were successful in fighting off the attack, what would be the next move for us? Would we ever again feel secure? Would we ever again be able to organize our life on anything but a military basis from top to bottom? Would we ever be able to devote less than a quarter or a third or a half of our national income to defense purposes, unless we were able to put the enemy back across the water, to reconquer the strategic strong-points commanding access to the seas of the world, and, in effect, to reconstitute the command of the world's oceans which we now have if we act together with Britain?

The western hemisphere defense plan is a static plan, and either the hemisphere or the "quarter-sphere" defense lines would, on the whole, be weak compared with the maritime defense line available to us so long as Britain survives. The United States should regard western hemisphere defense lines as distinctly secondary, to be prepared for emergency use if the first line breaks and we are forced to fall back for a last-ditch stand. It is less risky to stand now for all-out defense, together with Britain, of the seas and the strong-points commanding the seas of the whole world—Singapore, Hawaii, Panama, Gibraltar, Suez, and Britain itself—than to let Britain go down and then to try to defend the western hemisphere practically alone.

❖ ❖ ❖

THE British Government was in flabby hands and the French Government was in the hands of a scoundrel in October 1935 when Italy invaded Ethiopia and the League of Nations made its great and abortive effort to bring Fascist aggression to a stop. But it would be unbecoming for Americans to omit a further element in assessing responsibilities for the supine behavior of the democracies then and in the years down to 1939. For about 15 years the majority of Americans, including an overwhelming majority of the members of Congress, had been telling Englishmen and Frenchmen that if they took part in another war, the United States would wash its hands of the whole affair. In other words, no program of resistance to Fascism was to count on any help from the most powerful of the democratic nations.

In the Neutrality Acts of 1935, 1936 and 1937, the United States made a series of efforts, each more intense than the last, to prevent involvement in the war which had ended in 1918. As late as January 1940, our Government was protesting to Great Britain against the measures of blockade she was trying to enforce against Germany, and the American Republics were insisting that British warships could not interfere with German merchantmen within a "security zone" 300 miles around the Americas. And in August 1941, the House of Representatives by a majority of but one vote renewed the Selective Service Act and thereby decided not to disband the United States Army four months before Pearl Harbor.

Behind this American weakness of will was more than the propaganda of xenophobes like Hearst and McCormick or of Communists who from the signing of the Soviet-Nazi Pact to Hitler's attack on the U.S.S.R. proclaimed the undesirability of opposing the Fascist Powers; or than the belief that American participation in the First World War had been a mistake, and that a better peace would have resulted from a stalemate than from an Allied victory. An even more profound cause of the American weakness of will was the belief of many good but foolish people that since a democrat hated militarism he must be a pacifist. Such a confusion of values was democracy's greatest danger, for it rendered nerveless the hands of many of the very people who should have been dedicated to its defense.

This was the issue to which the French philosopher Julien Benda, famous author of "The Treason of the Intellectuals," addressed himself in July 1941 in his article "Pacifism and Democracy."

❖ ❖ ❖

PACIFISM AND DEMOCRACY

By Julien Benda

IN ALL countries there are democrats who maintain that a democratic state must, because it is democratic, refuse any kind of war—a war of defense just as much as a war of conquest. Their thesis is that a democracy must abstain from any international action which is liable to cause war. In short, it must be for peace at any price.

Those who take this position do not always say so frankly. They are embarrassed to admit that they refuse even a defensive war. They therefore claim that what is being presented to them as a defensive war is really an offensive war, planned by politicians or industrialists who expect to derive power or profits from having men kill one another. I once asked one of them whether he thought that the Greeks were right to have stood out against Xerxes rather than become his Helots. He did not reply. If he had stuck to his thesis he would have had to answer that they acted wrongly. Not long ago a citizen of a certain great democracy exclaimed: "This policy of our President means that we shall have war, and one out of every four of our sons will be killed." He should have been told that his own policy meant that all four of them risked becoming slaves. Maybe subconsciously he really preferred this prospect; but he probably would not have admitted it, even to himself.

Others are more outspoken. They endorse a slogan which a group of French Socialists adopted a few years ago: "Servitude rather than war!" Or one that we used to hear from certain French intellectuals: "In our eyes *nothing* justifies war." [1] In most cases this position is based simply on a

[1] Manifesto sponsored by Alain and signed by a group of students of the École Normale Supérieure at the time of the Italo-Ethiopian war.

desire to avoid fighting, camouflaged as well as possible under doctrinal reasons. The desire is normal enough, and especially today when war has become the thing we know it to be and when the whole nation is involved in it. Sometimes, however, the position is based on sincere ideological convictions. Those who adopt it often are veterans of the last war.[2] It is the position of these perfectly sincere people which we shall consider here, particularly the ones who maintain that the theory of peace at any price is an integral part of the definition of democracy.

II. DEMOCRACY'S "HIGHEST GOOD"

The mistake of thinking that peace at any price has anything to do with democracy comes from a confusion of essential values. It is imagined that democracy's paramount concern is human life, whereas it is human liberty. Human life deprived of liberty is worthless. Therefore the democrat, in order to preserve the advantages of democracy for his children, admits and sanctifies the sacrifice of life.[3] Over and over again in the course of history democracy has proved this to be its supreme law. If our pacifists were consistent, they would have to condemn the French revolutionaries who were willing to shed human blood to win their liberties, and the Americans who preferred war to remaining the servants of George III. As a matter of fact, some of them do. The question is how they can then pretend to be democrats.

They should meditate the words of George Washington, who was not a bad democrat. In his Farewell Address he weighed the advantages, in various circumstances, of neutrality, and did not hesitate to say that "we may choose peace or war, as our interest, guided by justice, shall counsel." We shall be told in reply that war has become something very different from what it was in 1796. But the question of principle has not become different.

[2] For example, Alain, who was a volunteer in the First World War.

[3] Jean Giono declares distinctly that the supreme value, the only one, is human life. "There is no glory," he says, "in being French. There is only one glory: it is to be alive." ("Jean le Bleu," p. 303.) But Giono makes no pretense of being a democrat.

The mistake also arises from a confusion between the *fact* of war and the *love* of war. Democracy may accept the one and condemn the other. War may be imposed upon men who have no love for it whatsoever.[4] The ideal of democracy is, certainly, to suppress the fact of war. But the effective way to attain this goal is to hold in check the people who worship war. This entails accepting the fact of war, under the democratic slogan "War on war."

III. SAVING PEACE AND ESTABLISHING PEACE

There is a distinction, though it is scarcely ever made, between *saving* peace and *establishing* peace. To save peace is to ward off war in some particular moment of great excitement. There is no leading motive, no general idea. To establish peace is to act deliberately to prevent war in accordance with a thought-out plan, in a time when no particular fear of war exists because those who might wish to disturb the peace have been temporarily deprived of the power to do so. At Munich in 1938 the British and French ministers saved peace. We all know that they did not establish it. At Versailles, the victors of 1918 were in a position to establish peace, maybe because four years earlier they had been willing not to save it.

Two profoundly distinct conceptions of peace are here involved. According to one, peace is based on respect for contracts between nations and on sanctions against violators. This is the *legal* conception. The other, the *sentimental* conception, expects love between men to bring about peace, all idea of contracts or sanctions aside. The first conception puts justice before peace, or at least states that it is respect for justice which must bring peace. This is displeasing to the sentimentalists who, naturally, place love above justice. At the time of the Italo-Ethiopian war, the Archbishop of Canterbury startled some persons by declaring that he, a churchman, favored the use of sanctions against the aggres-

[4] "What does one condemn in war?" says St. Augustine. "Is it the fact that it kills men who all must some day die? Faint-hearted men may blame war for this, but not religious men. What one condemns in war is the desire to harm, implacable hate, the fury of reprisals, the passion for domination."

sor. When told that sanctions were liable to cause war, he answered: "My ideal is not peace, but justice." He was only repeating the words of his divine Master: "I came not to send peace, but a sword"—*i.e.*, to make war against evil.

A few examples of the purely sentimental conception of peace might help my readers to measure its intellectual worth.

A famous author, I read recently, was visiting in the Engadine. As he stood looking at the landscape he uttered some words which were much admired by the newspaperman who reported them. "Facing so much beauty," he said, "how is it possible not to think that men ought to love and not hate one another!" Laments of this sort seem to me quite childish. Men should be loved when they deserve to be loved, when they show justice and loyalty and respect for the rights of others. I am under no compulsion to love them when they violate elementary rules of moral conduct. Instead, I have to protect myself from them—even if, later on, I try to change them. Landscapes have nothing to do with it.

Recalling pleasant memories of his youth, my compatriot Jean Guéhenno writes: "We were twenty years old. It was a serene July and the sun shone over Europe. . . . Our thoughts, like the earth, were ripening. . . . And then, all of a sudden, there was war, because an Austrian Archduke, whose name no one remembers any more, had been killed at Sarajevo." What does all this signify? It may also have been a beautiful morning at Marathon, at Valmy, at Saratoga. Would that have been a reason to give in to Xerxes, to Brunswick, to Burgoyne?

Again, many of my readers probably saw a film depicting the wife of a German peasant who had been killed in the war giving a kind welcome to an escaped French prisoner. She lets him stay in her house several weeks and watches him depart with regret. The film's name, "Grande Illusion," obviously was chosen to show the error of believing that war between nations implies hatred between peoples. But this question is not related to the question whether or not France in 1914 was right to resist the German invasion.

The really significant thing, however, is that many of my readers will be disgusted that, confronted with such touching pictures, I persist in continuing to use my powers of reason.

IV. NOT DEMOCRATS, BUT ANARCHISTS

One of the ways the absolute pacifists have of arguing is to challenge their opponents: "You call yourself a democracy, that is, a government of the people by the people, and yet you send me to war without consulting me, in spite of myself." Thus we find a character in Roger Martin du Gard's book "The Thibaults" declaring that if the French people had been consulted in 1914, 80 percent of them would have rejected war. This statement rests upon the hope—apparently justified, I must admit—that most men, even in most democracies, still have so little political education that, if consulted individually, they will refuse to make the sacrifices necessary for the preservation of the whole. Now it is arguable that no true democracy as yet exists—in the sense of being completely a government of the people and by the people. But is not the reason precisely because men find such difficulty in forgetting their individual conveniences in favor of the collective good? If they were consulted separately, how many citizens would offer spontaneously to pay taxes? Yet even "absolute democrats" probably admit that taxes are indispensable for the state.

"Absolute democrats" also contend not only that there should be a referendum on war, but that only those who voted "yes" should then have to go to war. This is a denial of national solidarity. Yet such people certainly accept some of the advantages of national solidarity. If they are civil servants, for example, they want to be paid salaries which some (perhaps many) of their fellow-citizens might, if they were consulted, refuse to grant. If they are interested in art, they might find that many tax-payers, consulted in the same way, would veto appropriations to maintain the museums. The fact is that these intellectuals would be more truthful—or, let us say, more enlightened about their own natures—if instead of pretending to be pure democrats they called themselves pure individualists or pure anarchists.[5]

Another sophistry often is uttered in the name of democracy. It consists in rejecting even a defensive war on the ground that it will require the surrender of full powers to the governing body, and that this surrender will spell "the end of democracy." They forget that among the basic democratic principles it is formally inscribed that in exceptional circumstances a nation may grant full powers to the governing body. During its famous meeting of September 9, 1793, the Convention declared that it accepted the idea of dictatorship for times of crisis. This doctrine meant, of course, that popular control would be suspended only temporarily and that it would be restored as soon as the emergency had passed. "Revolutionary France," says the historian Mathiez, "would never have accepted the dictatorship of the Convention if she had not been convinced that victory was impossible without the suspension of her liberty."

Two occurrences in French history show democracy accepting dictatorial powers because it is necessary, and discarding them as soon as the necessity is past—the rise and fall of Robespierre, and the rise and fall of Clemenceau. The fall of each occurred when victory was at hand and the danger which the dictatorship had been created to repel seemed safely over. I say "seemed" because France was far from being out of danger on November 11, 1918, and it would have been better for the country if the war government had continued for a while longer.

V. FORCE, BUT FOR JUSTICE

This is still another side to the argument of the "absolute democrats." They say that when democracy resorts to force it denies its essential character and becomes similar to the very systems which it affects to despise. This is a formalist argument. It forgets that one can inquire on whose behalf

[5] The American States, though always jealous of their autonomy, conferred upon the Federal Government, as early as 1787, the exclusive power to declare war and the right to promulgate the laws necessary for the "common defense."

force is to be used. To use force on behalf of justice is not the same thing as to use it for aggression. This being so, the democratic system which uses force for justice cannot be assimilated to opposite systems which use force for aggression.

There also seems to be a widespread conception that democracy is a sort of celestial body, aloof and, by definition, scornful of mundane necessities of self-defense. This idea, like the total condemnation of force regardless of the purpose for which it is used, plays straight into the hands of those who wish to use force for aggression. It thus becomes itself an agent of immorality.

At the bottom of these erroneous conceptions of democracy we discern what some would call a Christian idea, namely that it is the fit and necessary lot of the righteous to be weak and to suffer. If the righteous ever becomes strong enough to demand justice, apparently he ceases, for this school of thought, to be righteous. If Socrates had resisted his executioners, for example, he would no longer symbolize righteousness. Carry the argument one step further, and it will be the executioners who, having become the victims, incarnate righteousness. This obviously was the sort of feeling which obsessed many persons in 1918, when a violent nation had at last been compelled to cease from violence and listen to reason.

In such matters, democratic doctrine, like the doctrine of one great school of Catholic thought,[6] considers that the righteous are entitled to "the right of the sword" when they use it in a just cause and without regard for personal profit. Democracy merely remains true to its dogma when it reminds absolute pacifists that there are angels who go armed; and that because Lohengrin draws his sword and strikes the felon down, he is not thereby any the less Lohengrin and has not become Attila.

Pascal said: "Justice without force is powerless." I should like to add: "It is essential for democracy that justice shall

[6] The so-called scholastic doctrine of war, enunciated by Thomas Aquinas. See my "Trahison des Clercs" (edition in English, entitled "The Treason of the Intellectuals," p. 130).

have power so long as there are men determined to ignore it." Contrary to those who pretend that, by very reason of its democratic principle, the democratic state must be deprived of arms, I contend that by very reason of its democratic principle it must be better armed than any other state, in order that it may be respected by states which might otherwise be tempted to ignore justice and strike across its borders.

VI. HOW ABSOLUTE PACIFISM EVADES THE ISSUE

To be consistent, non-resisters must accept the prospect that their country may be annihilated. André Gide wonders: "What would have happened in 1914 if France had offered no resistance to Germany?" Everyone knows what would have happened. When he says that France would have been invincible if she had used only spiritual force against Germany, instead of opposing force to force, he forgets to inform his fellow-citizens that there is nothing incompatible between the "invincibility" which he speaks of and the erasure of their country from the map.[7]

Others go even further and find that non-resistance to evil is a practical doctrine, the only one which will bring peace to the world. Tolstoi in his "Intimate Diary" says that when a wall stands up to blows it causes the aggression to continue, whereas if it gives in it "absorbs the movement" and causes it to stop. By analogy, war would be suppressed if people never resisted any group which was greedy to expand at their expense. Tolstoi omits, however, to tell us that in "absorbing the movement" the wall ceases to exist, that is to say, loses its life, which, oddly enough, it might wish to keep.

VII. NON-INTERVENTION

It is absolutely contrary to the democratic ideal to watch from a distance, without interfering, while a strong nation crushes a weaker one and deprives it of its liberty. Non-

[7] "Journal," p. 1320-1321. The author adds that though Germany "could swallow France, she could not have digested her." There are no grounds for this assertion. Moreover, it is a most cruel experience merely to be swallowed.

intervention may be forced upon democracies because they happen not to be strong enough to give material help to the nation which is being abused and oppressed. But if they are true to themselves, they must deplore their weakness and inertia. To some extent they must feel disgraced, as a European minister felt disgraced when, in answer to a call for help from a small country whose independence was being threatened, he replied: *"Flere possumus, juvare non."* To set up non-intervention as a principle, to feel almost proud of it, is to undermine democratic morality. Selfishness may be a necessity. It cannot be a democratic dogma.

A democracy which rejects the idea of intervention usually declares that it has adopted this attitude in order to "save peace." The truth is that its passiveness encourages the aggressor. He not only attacks the state which has appealed in vain for help, but some day he will perpetrate an act which even the laggard democracy cannot condone and which therefore causes war a second time. Thus the war of 1914 was brought on by the inertia of the democratic governments which did not care to interfere with Austria in Bosnia-Herzegovina in 1908. A statesman of one of the Central Empires told us in 1920: "It is you who were responsible for the war. You yielded to us for so many years that you led us to think that we could do anything with impunity." It is unnecessary to cite more recent examples.

It is not by accident that those who disturb the peace of the world are almost always the heads of autocratic states. A man who mocks ordinary standards of justice at home sees no reason to act differently abroad. For that reason democracy should be prepared to intervene within a foreign state when its head flagrantly violates the rights of his people. This is what Mr. Herbert Morrison, a member of the British Parliament, meant when he said on November 27, 1939: "We must cling to an ideal of government, whatever its actual form, as something which exists to serve peoples and not to dominate them; and we must remember that this is no mere internal question, since the governments which dominate at home are often the peace-breakers abroad." In the past few years the democracies have usually refrained from this kind of intervention. But their course has not been determined, as some would like to have us believe, out of regard for democratic principle, but simply because democracy has come to worship peace and quiet. So far as I know, there is no principle inscribed in its statutes providing for, or excusing, that form of worship.

VIII. OF "DEMOCRATIC ANTI-MILITARISM"

Another aspect of the pacifist democracy which we are here discussing is that democrats often display a sort of systematic hostility to their country's military institutions. They haggle over the number of men there ought to be in the army, the number of years they should serve, how much money should be voted to cover their expenses. They claim that this "anti-militaristic" attitude suits the real spirit of democracy.

In a true democracy the military element should be subordinate to the civilian. Once this principle has been established, we need merely see to it that the military machine is powerful enough to perform its tasks and so to enable the democratic state to survive. One looks in vain through the great declarations of democratic principle, in any time or country, for a single text advocating a weak army. There are plenty of statements about the ideal future world in which this kind of institution will no longer be required. But there is no statement that makes weakness a virtue.[8] Once again we find that an idea which never had any connection with democracy has been added to its concept and has falsified it.

We saw in France, a few years ago, what harm the doctrine of peace at any price can do to democracy. Its devotees maintained that the best defense against a neighbor's greed was disarmament. They even went so far as to advocate a general strike in case war came. Recently in several countries the enemies of democracy exploited the doctrine of

[8] In his "Histoire de Belgique" the great historian, Henri Pirenne, shows how systematic anti-militarism made it impossible for Belgium to avoid war in 1914.

peace at any price in order to prevent a war which, though necessary for the salvation of the state, menaced the interests of their particular class. In France men of this sort who for years had berated the working class for their pacifism, suddenly found that same pacifism beautiful and called on labor to oppose the war which lay ahead.

Pacifism, in the sense I have described it here, is a parasite on democracy. It has nothing to do with democratic doctrine. Democracy must repudiate it.

❖ ❖ ❖

ONE who sought the exact content of the term "liberal," often used so loosely, might do worse than examine the history of the English weekly, *The Economist,* whose present editor is the author of the following article, "Freedom and Control," printed in FOREIGN AFFAIRS in January 1944.

The Economist was founded in London in 1843 by James Wilson, partly to promote the effort for free trade, which at the moment was coming to a climax in England in the campaign to repeal the corn laws, but also as a journal of public affairs in the broadest sense—"a Political, Literary and General Newspaper, as well as the Weekly Commercial Times, Bankers' Gazette and Railway Monitor." Wilson, besides being a banker and publicist, was a Member of Parliament and Financial Secretary to the Treasury. Surely no journalist has ever launched a publication with two young assistants such as he had the foresight to engage: Herbert Spencer and Walter Bagehot. Bagehot succeeded him as editor in 1860.

The tremendous influence of *The Economist* on English thought in Victorian days was the product not only of exceptional editors, but of a new idea—the simple yet revolutionary idea that argument in all fields was to be referred to fact for verification. "Sound practice never could be secured by ready-made rules," wrote Bagehot. He was interested in the evidence, not the theory. Objectivity, independence, and free play of mind were the distinguishing characteristics of *The Economist.* It is this tradition of concentration upon the search for a workable solution to concrete problems that carried English liberalism from the allegiance to *laissez faire,* which characterized the early Liberals, to the position which Geoffrey Crowther took, in 1944, in this discussion of the highly-charged issue of "planning" versus "free enterprise." It is interesting to note the method no less than the substance of Crowther's analysis—a scrupulously fair statement of the problem, a disinclination for a doctrinal solution, an effort to detach a single aspect of the general question and to propose a practical next step.

FREEDOM AND CONTROL

By Geoffrey Crowther

AT THIS stage of the last war, friend and foe alike knew the main general principles of the world order that would follow on an Allied victory. The world would be made up of self-determined, independent, sovereign states, linked together by a League of Nations founded on the principles of collective security, arbitration and disarmament. The normal pattern for a state would consist of a two-chamber legislature elected by universal suffrage, a responsible executive, an independent judiciary and guarantees of the civil liberties. Financial relationships between nations would be regulated by the gold standard, buttressed by central banks. Commercial policy would permit only moderate protective tariffs and would frown on such expedients as quotas, discriminations, dumping and official trading. Internally, every state would be dedicated to the principles of free individual enterprise, with a minimum of state interference or control.

It is beside the point that these principles were not completely applied and that some of them which were applied were unsuccessful. In 1918–19 that all lay in the future. The point is that, at the end of the last war, the world knew what an Allied victory would mean. The "triumph of democracy" then had a fairly detailed intellectual substance as well as an emotional content.

But who knows today what an Allied victory would mean? Of the four major Allies, two are democracies, but, apart from the general conviction that people should be allowed to settle their own affairs, how much of the formulae of democracy do the Americans and British regard as articles of export? To take a specific case, should we recommend the Germans to set up a replica of the Weimar Republic, or the French to restore the Third Republic—supposing that our advice were asked for in either case? And, if not, what do we recommend? Moreover, the other two major Allies do not, in their own affairs, practise anything that we should recognize as democracy. Some allege that the real preference of the western Allies is for legitimist, conservative, monarchist governments in Europe. One may think that it is not so. But can anyone of us say, of full knowledge, that it *is* not so? We want governments to be democratic, yes. But we want them to avoid the mistakes that were made in the name of democracy after the last war. And where does that leave us? Does anyone know?

The confusion is hardly less in the sphere of international organization. The League of Nations is still alive, and the many small nations of the world will not abandon without a very fierce struggle the doctrines of sovereign equality and equal sovereignty on which the League was founded, or the principles of arbitration (*i.e.* willing submission to arbitration), collective security (*i.e.* security by the consenting coöperation of all) and disarmament (*i.e.* equalization of advantages and burdens) by which it hoped to secure peace. But there has been much talk of other conceptions. Much has been heard of the international police force. Some conceive it as a genuinely international body, responsible to a world agency, to which, consequently, the essential attributes of sovereignty would have to be ceded. Others conceive it more in the light of a continuance into the peace of the concept of the present major allies. This latter has become almost a majority concept; and even most of those who criticize the idea of an Anglo-American alliance (should anyone propose it, which no one in authority has done thus far) are usually content if it is enlarged to cover only four of the nations of the world. Does anyone know whether the system to be created will be a "Great Power system" or a generally collective one? If a compromise, will it lean more one way or the other? And do we believe in disarmament, for ourselves, in the practically foreseeable future?

Our economic principles are equally indefinite. Do we still

believe in free individual enterprise as the basis of economic activity? Many Americans—probably the majority—say they do, though the vehemence and frequency with which they say it seem to suggest the existence of a doubt. (It was not necessary to make any such profession of faith in 1919.) Most Englishmen have very serious doubts whether private enterprise can any longer be regarded as the sole, or even as the principal, determinant of economic activity. And the Russians have no doubt at all that it cannot. In this supremely important aspect of human society, what would an Allied victory mean? Do we believe in the gold standard? In the old sense, clearly not (for the minority of the faithful is very small). But do we believe in the possibility of universal currency standards in any sense? It is the question that has underlain the recent international discussions, and no answer that is given can be more than experimental. Do we believe in a return to a commercial régime of moderate tariffs only, with the abolition of all the other obnoxious obstructions to world trade that have grown up in the last generation? The American and British Governments share some hopes, but not much confidence. The Russians have not been heard from. And if we do not believe that the international economy of which free trade and the gold standard were the chief symbols can, or should, be recreated, what do we believe in to take its place?

II

This is a formidable list of questions, and if there is any one of my readers who can answer any one of them—answer it, that is to say, not for himself alone, but as expressing the dominant view of the United Nations, or even of the two democratic Great Powers—then he is a far bolder man than I am. It has often been pointed out that there has been nothing in the present war to compare with Woodrow Wilson's magnificent series of definitive and expository speeches in the latter phase of the first World War. The Atlantic Charter was very vague, and subsequent pronouncements have been even less precise. But this is a very small part of the story. It was easy for President Wilson to make his speeches because he knew what to say and he knew that it would command general agreement. He knew this because the western democratic world knew in 1918 what it was after. Last time, we knew what our ideas were. We were putting the finishing touches to a triumphant program. The war of 1914–18 was to be the means of plucking good out of evil, an opportunity to finish off the job on which the western democracies had been engaged for more than a century. The Armistice and the peace were to register the final victory of everything in which the nineteenth century liberal believed. Wilson and everybody else knew what the ideas were because a hundred years had been spent in working them out.

Now nobody knows for sure. We have not yet made up our collective mind (and not many people have made up their individual minds over the whole range) whether there is life in the old dogmas yet, or whether our problems are so different that they cannot be handled by the former body of doctrine, however amended. Is the twentieth century an extension of the nineteenth century, or something different? We do not know, and it is very foolish to cavil at Mr. Roosevelt and Mr. Churchill because they have not taken an afternoon off to tell us. They do not know either. The western democratic world is perilously close to a vacuum of faith.

It is the thesis of E. H. Carr's influential book, "Conditions of Peace," that the dominant ideas of the nineteenth century are dead—or at least that they no longer have sufficient validity to serve as our guiding lights. He defines these dominant ideas as being, in domestic politics, representative democracy; in economics, free individual enterprise; and in international affairs, the sovereignty of self-determined nations. For myself, I would not admit that either representative democracy or free capitalism was dead. But even in our domestic affairs, it seems to me to be very difficult to affirm that they are still the sole or the dominant principles. And as articles for export they are even more doubtful, while between nations it has become clear that national sovereignty, so far from being the only valid principle, is the only certainly disastrous principle. In general, though I would differ from Mr. Carr in matters of degree, I find it impossible to refute the substance of his charge. The twentieth century is *not* simply an extension of the nineteenth. The problems of the postwar world will not be those of the nineteenth century. In many respects they will be directly opposite (*e.g.*, the pressure to create maximum employment rather than maximum income, the need to curb the freedom of nation-states rather than to create them), and in every case they will be different.

Moreover, the people who will face them will be different. Hitherto, the world has been run by men and women who were born in the nineteenth century. Only one man born in the twentieth century has yet sat in an American or British Cabinet. The Russians and Chinese leaders are nineteenth-century-born. So are the chief Nazis. It happens that the children of the nineteenth and twentieth centuries are divided by much more than the accident of a numeral. The eldest child of the twentieth century—a man who was born on January 1, 1901—was within a few weeks of the draft age when the last war came to an end. He stands just on this side of that great dividing line—a borderline of much greater psychological importance than any that will be created by this war, for all but the very youngest of those who fought in the last war had been brought up to a world of security. They had come to accept a set of absolutes which crumbled in front of their eyes, while the children of the twentieth century have never known what a secure world is. In Britain, though not in America, there is also the great chasm of the "missing generation" dividing the children of the twentieth century from their fathers.

This is not the only accident of history that sets them off. The great technical inventions of the nineteenth century were industrial processes, which the individual rarely saw; they were ways of producing familiar objects in greater numbers and at lower cost, ways of providing for the poor what had formerly been the prerogative of the rich. They extended the spread of comfortable living, but they did not greatly change its content. Round about the turn of the century, however, technical progress began to have a direct impact on social customs and modes of thought. The men and women born in the twentieth century are the first generation to have been familiar, for the whole of their lives, with such revolutionary molders of thought and custom as air travel, individual transport on land by means of the automobile, the moving picture, the radio. They have been influenced by the decline in formal religion. They are the first generation in which it has been more than an impiety to think that the human race could or should control its numbers. In America, they are the first generation in which high-school education has been universal and college education general. In England, the creation of a complete educational ladder from bottom to top dates from 1902.

The historians of the future will have to judge whether these changes were, on balance, for good or evil. My present point is that they make for a greater cleavage of instincts and of instinctive ideas between old and young than has perhaps ever before existed. And just when this strange new generation would in any case be beginning to push its way into the driving seat, there comes the vast catastrophe of the present war to accentuate still further the difference between its environment and that of its fathers. In view of all these facts, I do not believe it is an exaggeration to say that we stand at one of the grand climacterics of world history. If there is any carry-over of dominant principles from the former age to the latter, it will be a matter for marvelling.

My quarrel with Mr. Carr is not, then, that I wish to refute his main thesis but that I do not like being left where he leaves me. The dominant doctrines of the nineteenth century, if not dead, are so battered that they will not serve us any longer as our main props. We are, indeed, living in a vacuum of faith. But the trouble about a vacuum is that it gets filled, and if there are no angels available to fill it, fools—or worse—rush in. Let us, then, take Mr. Carr's threefold division of politics, economics and international relations, and consider in each case the alternatives to the old principles which he condemns. What are, not merely the theoretical alternatives, but the actual enemies that have been pushing them off their thrones?

The trend away from liberal democracy has been a trend towards totalitarian dictatorship. The trend away from individualist capitalism has been a trend toward rigid state control exercised in the interest of a war economy—or at least of a war-minded economy. The trend away from the sovereignty of the nation-state has been a trend towards the concentration of aggressive strength in the hands of a few Great Powers. These are not, of course, the only conceivable alternatives; but they are the alternatives that the pressure of the age has been forcing upon us.

That pressure, it will be objected, is about to be lifted by a victory for the United Nations. I am not so certain. I have the suspicion that the Nazi alternatives, diabolical though they are, have far too much of the logic of events in them to be brushed aside by the military defeat of Hitler. If we are realistic, we shall recognize, even though it increases the difficulty of our task, that there is a great deal in the circumstances of our century that leads straight to Fascism. The enormous development in the technique of propaganda and advertising, in the power to sway the minds of people in the mass, plays straight into the hands of the would-be dictator or any other manipulator who, for large ends or small, seeks to muddy the waters of democracy. The growth of large-scale industry, the need for gigantic aggregations of capital, the implications of a maximum employment policy—all these create the danger of a concentration of economic power. The technique of modern war, with its emphasis on the possession of certain complicated weapons which only a handful of highly industrialized states can produce, makes the small nations, or even the league of small nations, quite helpless, and compels the Great Powers to devote quite unprecedented proportions of their resources to the barren purposes of war. We cannot abolish these things, we cannot dodge them. We cannot cancel the invention of the radio and aircraft or unlearn the technique of mass production. But if we accept their existence, we must also accept their consequences. Propaganda *plus* the concentration of economic power *plus* Blitzkrieg technique add up to Fascism; or they may be made to add up to something new that will be compatible with democratic ideals. But whatever else they add up to, they certainly do not add up to the sort of democracy that our fathers thought of. The plain truth is that Hitler has an answer to the problems of the twentieth century and we, as yet, have not. It follows that whatever happens in the present war, Hitler will be hot on our heels for the rest of our lives. We shall have to think very fast, and run very fast, to keep ahead of him. One slip, one stumble, and he will be on our necks.

The central dilemma of the present age is that we can no longer rely on the old principles alone, but that we abominate the alternatives that time and tide, if it is left to them, will produce. This dilemma can be solved in only one way, by the birth of a new faith, adjusted in its instrumentalities to the needs of the new century, but preserving the ultimate objectives of the old. The only way to avoid the murder of nineteenth-century Liberalism by twentieth-century Fascism is through the birth of a twentieth-century democratic faith by the new out of the old. The biological analogy with the conflict of the sexes is exact. If one kills the other, no continuing life is possible. This is what would happen if the crude, raw impact of changed conditions were merely to remove the tried doctrines of an earlier age. Nor is the future to be secured by some hermaphroditic compromise, in which the two elements are so much in conflict that the result is, as Disraeli said of the mule, "without pride of ancestry or hope of posterity." No, the only solution is to take what is strong and good and lasting in the new ideas, to mate it with the old and to conceive something that has elements of both, but has its own life, is new, harmonious, growing, integral. What we need is not a compromise between the old ideas and the new, but a fusion; not a mixture but an amalgam. The nineteenth century, before it dies, must take what is virile in the hostile movements and give birth to something new. Only then can it die in peace.

III

To state the need for such a new democratic faith is one thing. To meet it is another. The task of developing the thesis here presented in every sphere of public policy, political and economic, domestic and international, is probably beyond the power of a single pen; and certainly far beyond the reach of a single article. It may, however, be permissible to proceed a little way further in one particular direction, that of economic organization. What I have to say is chiefly directed to the internal economic problems of nations such as the United States and the United Kingdom—though it is, of course, impossible to treat of these problems in isolation from their international implications.

The air is full at present of wordy warfare on the relative merits of unhampered private enterprise and of government planning of economic developments. Both are being argued in extreme and absolute terms—that is, as principles capable of being applied universally and in unadulterated form. Possibly the protagonists have reservations and modifications in mind, but, if so, they escape but rarely into print or speech. Not often does an advocate of private enterprise make the admission that there are certain economic problems (and among the largest) which must either be tackled by the organizing powers of the government or else left untackled. Still less frequently does an advocate of "planning" pause to concede that over a vast range of industries and occupations either the mainspring of activity will (in any easily foreseeable future) remain that of individual enterprise and ambition or there will be no mainspring at all. No, the argument proceeds in absolutes: the free enterprise party has no use for "bureaucracy" anywhere at any time; and the planners will not admit that a businessman, by serving the interest of his own profit, can ever serve the general interest.

It is, of course, a sham fight. I do not mean that the contestants are not sincere; many of them doubtless (and unhappily) are passionately sincere. It is a sham fight because there is not the slightest chance of either side winning its fight. In the circumstances of the twentieth century, there is no prospect whatever of an industrial democratic state basing its affairs on the principle of unrestricted individual enterprise to the exclusion, or even to the subordination, of other principles. Even less can an industrial democracy contemplate governmental "planning" of the bulk of its activities—at least it cannot do so and remain a democracy.

Perhaps it is worth while pausing for a moment to justify these dogmatic statements. The reasons why unrestricted private enterprise is insufficient by itself are perhaps clearer to a British observer than to an American. The United States, after all, is still in the period of rapid expansion. It is wholly reasonable to suppose that by the end of the present century the American national income may be at least double what it is now—that is to say, at least three times what it was in the late 1930's. And the frontiers of possible achievement are more distant still. The supreme necessity of the American economy remains that of expansion and there is an almost automatic source of demand for great masses of capital. The pioneer is no longer, perhaps, the American archetype—but he is still a socially necessary type, and it is, of course, in a pioneering environment that unregulated private enterprise shows to maximum advantage.

In Great Britain, on the other hand, the end of the rising national income is in sight, owing to the imminence of a stable and even a falling population. It is unlikely that the British national income will ever be more than 50 percent higher than it is now, and even that moderate increase requires optimistic assumptions on the trend both of population and of individual productivity. The peak will be reached in about a generation from now, and thereafter the national income will be preserved from falling only if the rise in individual productivity succeeds in outpacing the fall in total numbers. Clearly, this puts the pioneer and the builder at a discount and the administrator and allocator at a premium. Moreover, there are other problems, hardly more important but possibly more urgent. Britain needs her foreign purchases to live, and the war has knocked a series of holes in the credit side of what was at best a somewhat precarious balance. The task of the postwar years will be not merely to get back the prewar trade, but to find markets for something like a 50 percent increase in the prewar volume of exports. No one but a fanatic would believe uncoördinated private enterprise capable of out-facing these difficulties.

Thus there are reasons why there is less talk in Britain than in America of the sovereign virtues of unregulated individualism. But this does not mean, in my judgment, that there is the slightest possibility of a return to laissez faire even in America. For one thing, I remain obstinately skeptical about the possibility of making any appreciable headway against the menace of recurrent depressions except by the road of government action. The present attempt, sponsored by the Committee for Economic Development, to demonstrate that a regular and adequate flow of savings into physical investment can be organized by business itself, is a gallant rearguard action. I wish it well, but my money is on the other horse. Secondly, I remain even more obstinately skeptical about the ability of a free-enterprise economy—that is, of an economy where the requirements of free enterprise have priority over other objectives—to bring about any substantial improvement in the unequal distribution of wealth and welfare. Yet if there are two things in the sphere of economic policy that the electorate is going to impose as categorical imperatives on its representatives, regardless of party, they are contained in the current expressions Full Employment and Social Security. Walter Bagehot, the great apostle of the free economy, wrote nearly eighty years ago that "the coöperative, if not the compulsory, agency of the state ought to be used far more than now in applying to our complicated society those results of science which are new to our age." He was thinking, in the main, of physical science. But his remark applies with even greater force to those results of social science (and of social experience) which are new to our age and which must be incorporated into our economy and policy without damaging delay. There are certain objects that society can attain—it has been demonstrated—by means of "the coöperative, if not the compulsory, agency of the state." The Russians have shown that it is possible to secure a very rapid increase in the national income; the Germans have shown that it is possible for a highly industrialized state to remove within a few years one of the largest masses of unemployment known to economic history. We may abominate the methods by which these achievements were secured. But we cannot pretend they do not exist. On the contrary, the electorate is going to insist on emulation of the results, if not on imitation of the methods. Employment of "the coöperative, if not the compulsory, agency of the state" is an inescapable consequence.

But if the wholly free economy is an impossibility, the wholly controlled economy is no less unacceptable. There are two main reasons for this. In the first place, experience seems to show—and common sense would confirm—that it is considerably less efficient in the production of wealth for consumption. The planned economy has had its triumphs. But none of them, I think, has been a triumph in supplying in large quantities at low prices consumption goods of the kinds and in the variety that people want. Yet that must remain one of the fundamental and co-equal objects of any democratic economy. There are examples of planned economics where the strength of the state has been increased, where the capital equipment of the community has been enriched, where mass unemployment has been avoided. I do not know of a wholly planned economy where the consumer has been satisfied. And, in the second place, a wholly planned economy is incompatible with any degree of political freedom. The possibility of a man's earning his own living in his own way, without let or hindrance, is the essential condition of there being any freedom of discussion, any freedom to oppose. If more than a fraction of the electorate come to depend for their livelihood upon the temporary masters of the mechanism of the state—that is, upon the politicians—then democracy is at an end.

It follows from this discussion that the economic system of the next few decades will inevitably have elements both of individual freedom of enterprise and also of purposive direction by the state. This conclusion, by now, is almost a commonplace. What is not so generally realized is that it matters most vitally how the two elements are combined. Neither can, it is true, remove the other; democratic society is not going to be either wholly planned or wholly unplanned. But each opposing principle can very effectively obstruct the other. A society which is based on an active coöperation of the two principles will be a vastly different place from a society based on a deadlock between them.

Deadlock is what the western democracies have been threatened with in the past thirty years. It is easy to see how the desire to plan economic development, the desire to make it follow motives more socially respectable than the incentive of profit, the desire to ensure security in an insecure world—it is easy to see how these desires have clogged and frustrated the free economy. Over far the greater part of the economy, the businessman is still left with the responsibility of initiating activity. He has to make up his mind whether an enterprise is worth the risks involved in it, and unless he gives the word to start the wheels turning, no one else will or can. But the risks of loss have been increased by the great load of prior charges that has been put upon him in the way of rigid wage-rates, wasteful labor practices, social security contributions and the like, while his incentive to take these risks has been dulled by heavy and differential taxation, and his arm has been jogged by all manner of inspectors, controls, regulations, inquisitions, prohibitions and indictments.

The impact on our economy of the idea of planning and of the motive of social welfare has hitherto been almost wholly negative. Few industries have been planned, but a vast number have been bedevilled by planning. In many cases, the approach has been more than negative, it has been punitive, and the entrepreneur has been abused and penalized precisely in proportion to his success in performing his duty of running economic activity at a profit. To date, we are certainly far more planned against than planning.

The other side of the medal is very similar. Wherever the state has tried, by the use of collective methods, to make headway against the problems that beset it, it has been held back by a hundred visible and invisible strings of timidity and orthodoxy. If it wishes to close the deflationary gap by deficit financing, it can do so only within the very narrow field that runs no risk of competing with private enterprise. And every step is taken to the accompaniment of charges ranging from corruption and dictatorship to red ruin.

IV

The result has been deadlock, and if we sometimes wonder why it is that our economy seems to have lost its elasticity, its power to respond to opportunity, if we complain that only in wartime are its potentialities realized, the reason is that we have been busy putting brakes on both the two possible springs of initiative. We make it difficult for the profit motive to work lest it should be anti-social in its effect, and we make it difficult for the social motive to work lest it be too wasteful.

In this struggle, neither side can win. It follows that the most urgent task for all economic statesmen is to work out means by which the two principles of organization can live side by side. If there is to be activity of any sort, there must be some incentive to activity. For a generation or more, we have been hard at work whittling down all incentives, and trying to work out a compromise between freedom and organization on the basis that we shall have as little as possible of either. That is wrong. The right course is to have as much as possible of both, to take the brakes off both the profit incentive and the social incentive.

This is not the place to discuss how this can be done. But the method clearly lies along the way of sorting out the economic activities of the community that are to be powered by each incentive. There are no absolute rules for determining where the line should be drawn, and no doubt it will be drawn in different places in different countries, and at different times in the same country. There are some activities that every country puts on the "organization" side of the line and makes no attempt to run on a profit-earning basis—justice, education and war-making, for example. There are others that every democracy will put on the "freedom" side—the press, entertainments and most luxury trades. Between these extremes, the people will draw the line as they choose and the location of the line is a fit and proper subject for party controversy. What is essential is that, on either side of the line, the dominant incentive should be left as free as possible to stimulate activity. Neither one can be quite exclusive: profit-minded enterprise cannot be allowed to be anti-social, nor can social-minded activity be undertaken without any regard to its economic cost. But in each sphere the interloping considerations should be adjusted to interfere as little as possible with the dominant incentive. The businessman, for example, cannot be relieved of taxation; but his taxes can be designed to interfere as little as possible with the earning of profits.

There will be those among the critics of this doctrine who will shake their heads and say that it cannot be done. They will quote Abraham Lincoln to the effect that a nation cannot live half slave and half free. If so, then the prospect is black indeed for all of us; because, for the reasons given above, it seems to me inconceivable that we shall ever be able to pin our faith on either of the alternatives. If they are so instinctively and inevitably antipathetic to each other that they cannot live in peace, side by side, then we must conclude that democracy is incapable of resolving the contradictions to which it gives rise and must surely perish. I take a more optimistic view. It is true that the opposing principles of economic freedom and of economic organization have, in fact, generated frictions which have perceptibly slowed down the progress of the democratic economy. But this is because they have been stupidly handled and the frictions would not arise if the object of all parties were to avoid them, instead of, as at present, to seek battle on all occasions. Both the British and the American democracies have, each in its own way, over the past 150 years resolved the very similar conflict between freedom and order in the political sphere. I see no overriding reason why the same success should not be achieved in the economic sphere, provided the same essential moderation is shown.

There are those also who hold that there is some inevitability of conflict in the international sphere between nations which draw the line between freedom and organization in different places. This seems to me to be even purer defeatism than the former objection. No state is wholly without compulsory organization in its economy and none is wholly without freedom. The differences are of degree, not of kind, and our affairs are in a sorry posture if differences of ideological degree are going to cause irreconcilable conflicts. The battle, it is said, will come on the management of international trade; a country that exercises conscious management of its trade relations will necessarily have an unfair advantage over one that does not, and thus controlled economics are inevitably aggressive. But if there is anything at all in this objection, the way to meet it is directly, by securing agreement on the definition of unfair practices and putting a ban on them, whether perpetrated by governments, by cartels or by individuals.

V

This economic argument, as has been said, is intended only as an illustration of the wider thesis that, if western democracy is to confront its twentieth-century problems with any hope of success, there is an urgent necessity for hard thinking on first principles. It is not enough either to demonstrate the inadequacy of the old liberalism or to expatiate on the abomination of the Fascist alternative. Both are destructive exercises, necessary as preliminaries perhaps, but contributing nothing to the positive task of construction. That task involves nothing less than the creation of a new faith, a newly articulated set of principles by which the imperishable objectives of a free humanity can be sought by techniques appropriate to this century. And the first step is to realize that it is not only the theses of the nineteenth century that are dead or dying, but the antitheses also.

I am not one of those who holds that a vacuum of faith will be much handicap to us in winning the war. War is fought mainly by material means, and though it would be an advantage to know what we are fighting for, it is enough to know what we are fighting against. It is after the fighting is over that the trouble will begin. For when material force is removed, it is only the force of ideas that can prevail. At present, in the realm of ideas, we are almost completely disarmed. Rearmament, with modern weapons, cannot begin too soon.

❖ ❖ ❖

By April 1944, when the following article by Wendell Willkie appeared, military victory for the United Nations in the Second World War was a foregone conclusion. The open question was the shape of the peace—above all (so it then seemed) the question whether the United States Senate would ratify American membership in a world organization. In the debate, the overshadowing word was "sovereignty." It had been in defense of American sovereignty that Lodge and his band in 1919 attacked Article 10 of the League Covenant (which undertook to protect member states against external aggression), alleging that Congress would be deprived of its constitutional right to decide whether or not the United States would go to war. Now once again the decision as to American membership in a world organization threatened to depend on the implications of this term.

Scarcely two authorities agreed what the term meant. On the one hand, it was said that sovereignty was so sacred a concept that not even by a two-thirds vote of the Senate could the American people join an international organization and thus divest themselves of a degree of this impalpable presence: only a constitutional amendment would sanction such a step. This was the argument that was intended to make participation in the organization impossible. On the other hand, some advocates of world government could see no virtue in any international organization not preceded by total renunciation of sovereignty.

Wendell Willkie said bluntly that such ratiocination was nonsense, that if sovereignty meant anything it meant the power of directing one's own destiny, and that in order for us to do this we must use our sovereignty and not merely worship it. Willkie's article, "Our Sovereignty: Shall We Use It?", was perhaps the single most effective blow struck in the campaign which deflated the balloon of the concept of unabridged sovereignty. In the end, the tremendous drive for ratification of membership in the United Nations turned out to be a push against an open door.

The debatable question now is whether the American people might at that time have used their sovereignty even more boldly. Throughout the time when Willkie was preparing this article, and in many other conversations in the office of Foreign Affairs in those last months of his life, he urged a foreign policy of boldness, and always more boldness.

❖ ❖ ❖

OUR SOVEREIGNTY: SHALL WE USE IT?

By Wendell L. Willkie

SINCE the turn of the century we have lost the power of directing our own national destiny. We must regain it. To show how much we have lost control over our destiny I need only point to our unwilling participation in two world wars and to the instability of the American economy during the period between them. We have sought to escape war and to maintain our economy as a separate entity in the world by jealousy guarding our sovereign rights. I am forced to the conclusion that something is wrong with what we have meant by the term "national sovereignty" if it produces Hawley-Smoot tariffs; the banking failures, depressions and misery of 1929 and ensuing years; highly nationalistic economic policies, with consequent deficit financing and violent discords among groups within our own society; agrarian unrest and farmers' strikes; and, finally, two decades after we brought our boys home from one war in Europe, the loading of transports to take their sons across submarine infested seas to fight in another.

I believe that if we are to avoid the same disastrous cycle when the present war in Europe and Asia has been won we shall have to give up the idea that sovereignty is something simply to be conserved, like the talent which was laid away in the earth in the biblical parable, and accept the idea that it is an active force to be used. That is the thesis of what I have to say here.

I want to see our Government and people use the sovereign power of the United States in partnership with the sovereign power of other peace-loving nations to create and operate an international organization which will give better protection to the rights of all nations, on a wider political, economic and social basis, than has ever yet been attempted in history. To my mind, mutuality of responsibility and service represents more real freedom, in the sense of freedom from wars and economic disaster, than can be gained through adherence to all the sterile formulas of exclusive national sovereignty written into all the books of international law ever published.

This means that we must expand the use of our sovereignty to the extent that other nations will expand theirs to accomplish the common purpose. If we decide to do this, we may succed in turning the page of history which we fumbled at but failed to turn 25 years ago. If on the contrary we decide to continue the same static, passive and essentially frightened isolationist policy which we adopted after the last world war I feel sure we shall be heading into a third one.

II

"It will be a long time, I venture to believe, before there will be any necessity or any justification for the United States engaging in a foreign war." The statement was made in January 1934, one year after Adolf Hitler took control of the destinies of Germany. It was made by the late William E. Borah, Senator from Idaho and Chairman of the Senate Committee on Foreign Relations, a man greatly respected, profoundly sincere and, in matters of foreign policy, tragically shortsighted. "Internationalism," continued Senator Borah in the same address,[1] "if it means anything more than the friendly coöperation between separate, distinct and wholly independent nations, rests upon a false foundation. And when undertaken, it will fail as in the name of progress and humanity it should fail."

Ultimate proof of a nation's freedom, Senator Borah saw, resided in its ability to choose freely between war and

[1] Made in New York before the Council on Foreign Relations, January 8, 1934.

peace. He also knew that peace was the fundamental condition of all useful activity by the people of the United States or by their Government. The primary aim of governmental policy, then, was the preservation of peace. Near the end of his life he stated the sort of policy which, in the light of the nation's experience, he considered most likely to achieve that aim. It would have to be one which "offers peace to all nations, trade and commerce with all nations, honest friendship with all nations," but it should be based, he thought, on "political commitments, expressed or implied, with none." Only if the United States pursued that sort of policy did Senator Borah think it would have freedom of action—the freedom "to remain aloof or to take part in foreign wars."

Today open-minded and alert Americans are drawing a different lesson from our national experience. They perceive that the United States has not been free to choose peace or war in the twentieth century. Our area of decision has not extended to whether or not we would go to war. We have only been able to decide that temporarily we would postpone going to war.

In 1914 we approached a "foreign" war in a spirit of determined neutrality. In 1939 we did the same, armed with a specific program designed to make us immune to any external shock. Both times we were forced, contrary to our desires and efforts, to abandon our neutrality, point by point. Both times we found that our national existence was at stake. Both times we had to fight to defend it. In the present war, the very hour and minute at which we had to resort to arms was dictated to us by our enemies.

In the modern world, an American foreign policy which assumes that nations are "separate, distinct and wholly independent" is a foreign policy which permits other nations to make decisions affecting vital American interests at *their* convenience and when *they* choose.

Our loss of the separate power to control our own separate destiny in economic affairs is scarcely less striking. We have faced the fact with reluctance. For a century—thanks, in part at least, to the fact that our country within itself was largely an undeveloped world—we prospered magnificently on the assumption that we needed to consider only our own wants, our own resources, our own energy—and the enjoyment we took in putting all three to use. Yet even in the nineteenth century the cotton growers of the South discovered important exceptions to the rule that the American economy was self-contained. In 1915 the farmers of the Middle West and West discovered their close relationship to countries 5,000 miles away.

This discovery of the farmers was pleasant at first, for the prices of farm products shot upward under the demand of Allied buying, and 40,000,000 additional acres were put to the plough to meet the world's cry for food. But then came the drastic postwar deflation and the emergence of the 20–year "farm problem." The memorable McNary-Haugen Bill, twice passed by both Houses of Congress and twice vetoed by President Coolidge, represented a first attempt to find a solution for the farmers' problems in terms of the international situation. It was an effort to devise a special kind of farm tariff which would free agricultural prices from the deflationary pressure of surplus production. Perhaps it was not scientific. But it showed that the western farmer was coming to realize that his own well-being was closely connected with policies and actions in other parts of the world.

When the depression began the country turned to extreme protectionism in the search for economic security. The Hawley-Smoot tariff of 1930 raised our duties on imports to the highest level in history. Retaliation followed in the form of discrimination against our products by Spain, Italy, Switzerland, France and a score of other countries. In 1932, Great Britain and the dominions instituted their system of "imperial preferences." Which was cause and which effect in the economic chaos of the depression years need not be argued here. The war debts, the reparations tangle, the foreign loans, the speculative mania, the panic of 1929 on the New York Stock Exchange, the collapse of the Kredit Anstalt bank in Austria, Britain's abandonment of the gold standard—these were only high spots of the general debâcle. All the events were interrelated and the effects of all were world-wide. The United States found out with a vengeance that it was not exempt from those effects, that it was, in fact, an integral part of the wide, wide world.

Our Government, faced with this stubborn fact, pursued contradictory policies. Our only consistency, indeed, was that we stuck to nothing long. One Administration attempted to revive foreign lending and stimulate international trade by pressing for a suspension of reparations payments and placing a moratorium on war debts. But at the same time it raised the tariff. The next Administration initiated a program looking to international currency stabilization and dropped it, spectacularly, soon after its own emissaries had gathered with those of other nations in a World Economic Conference. It then attempted to institute a program of planned economic nationalism of its own, supported by heavy deficit financing.

This program and its inevitable results accelerated the decline of the economic structure of the European democracies which were then beginning to feel the pressures of totalitarianism (a system of political action and economic organization growing, in part at least, out of the nationalistic policies almost universally practised by the nations of the world). Winston Churchill in 1937, on the floor of Parliament, pointed out that, "Those who are keeping the flag of peace and free government flying in the Old World have almost a right to ask that their comrades in the New World should, during these years of exceptional and not diminishing danger, set an example of strength and stability. The well-being of the United States may spell not only the well-being but the safety of all sorts and conditions of men. . . . A prosperous United States exerts, directly and indirectly, an immense beneficent force upon world affairs. A United States thrown into financial and economical collapse spreads evil far and wide, and weakens France and England just at the time when they have most need to be strong."

All this is recalled to emphasize one point: our experience demonstrates that we are not "wholly independent." As Senator Capper said on behalf of the farmers back in 1927:

"Wherever we turn we find the Middle West and its economic woes entangled in the elusive 'foreign situation' with which it used to concern itself very little."

Some farmers again show signs of being misled into thinking that high protectionism will give them security after this war. I do not believe that many of them will wish, on second thought, to resume the hopeless effort to "lock up" wheat prices on a purely national basis. The price of wheat in the United States is not a "separate" affair. Similiarly, the price of cotton will continue to be determined, not solely in the United States, but also in Egypt and India and Manchester and a dozen other cotton-producing and cotton-processing centers. Conditions in Argentina and Australia will continue to affect the livelihood of cattle and sheep raisers in North America. Our businessmen and our farmers alike know in their minds, if not yet fully in their hearts, that the economy of the United States is irretrievably intertwined with that of other nations.

III

Congress and the press have been discussing the steps which should be taken to bring the peacetime foreign policy of the United States into harmony with twentieth century realities. Much of the talk has centered about the term sovereignty.

In the whole literature of political theory no word has occasioned more disputes. Students of politics hold generally, I think, that few countries have contributed more significantly to the development of political institutions than the United States. But since the days when Madison, Hamilton and Jay wrote for *The Federalist* we have made few notable contributions in the realm of theory. Perhaps we should be grateful that Americans are traditionally interested in finding out, not the fine shadings in a word's meaning, so much as the essence of the thing it represents. Even so, we cannot dismiss the conflict in opinion over the term sovereignty as mere juggling with words.

The word sovereignty does represent a most important

idea. And it is of additional practical importance for us now because some of our deepest emotions and loyalties, our pride in our country's past and our concern for her future, are associated with it. But we had best be aware also that it often gets into the forefront of our thoughts for other and less legitimate reasons. Often it is deliberately invoked to create confusion. And often, as with other words which receive a lot of attention, it becomes a catchword, a slogan. Many people now feel the necessity of putting the word "sovereign" into any sentence describing our relationship to other nations in the postwar world as automatically as they put on a necktie when they dress in the morning. I believe it is much too important a word to be used as a mere convention of speech.

The word has had many meanings in the course of humanity's long effort to perfect the idea and instruments of self-government. Only comparatively recently did it come into use as a specific name for the source of power and authority within a state. Toward the end of the Middle Ages it described the position of the feudal chief to whom allegiance was due. There were then layers of "sovereign lords," beginning with a very small "sovereign" who controlled the lives and property of a miserable handful at the bottom of the heap, up through somewhat more impressive sovereigns who ruled over several small ones, to a group of great barons who recognized no superiors. In the course of time and much fighting these many sovereigns yielded to one, and the nation-state emerged with all power in the hands of one ruler, the king.

The story of how the absolute authority of the monarch yielded in turn to the authority of the community—that is, of the people—is the story of the development of democracy, the great theme of modern history.

The line of development was by no means straight. Sometimes it doubled back—as in the Fascism of our own time. There have been variations in the theory designed to widen the base of popular authority in the state or to narrow it, to keep things as they were or to make way for change, to restrict the electorate or to extend it—as when the franchise for women was debated. It is sufficient for us to note about these theories simply that they were developed in response to the pressure of practical circumstances—political, military, economic or social.

Some ardent theorists have endeavored to separate sovereignty from reality altogether in their search for a completely logical system built up out of words. Sometimes the search for a mystical point called the ultimate source of sovereignty has turned into a game for special devotees, as in the studies which find the ultimate pinpoint of sovereignty in the sub-section of the Constitution which provides for the amending of the Constitution. I have no quarrel with those who enjoy such academic pleasures. But there need be no confusion regarding the central fact of the matter. Sovereignty within the United States resides in the people of the United States. The people of the United States exercise the supreme power of the state. They are sovereign.

IV

What, then, is the difficulty? It comes from the effort to extend the sovereignty concept beyond the purpose for which it was developed and apply it in the field of relations among nations.

Does the sovereignty of the American people extend throughout the world? The question has only to be put to be answered: obviously not. Two states, at the moment, pretend that they have a right and duty to enforce their will throughout the world. They have dressed their claim up in fancy and most offensive theories based on blood, race and mythology. It is now in the course of being put down. The idea of the absolute sovereignty of any nation in international relationships is as impractical in operation as the idea of the absolute separateness of any nation.

To the extent that the term sovereignty is taken to mean that we have the right to do exactly as we please in dealings with other nations, and that what we choose to do is not properly of concern to any other nation, it is out of date. During roughly 125 years of our national existence we assumed that this conception of sovereignty was valid. We even got into the habit of believing that it was an essential part of national freedom. Its invalidity was brought home to us only with the development of modern communications. To try to defend it against the facts of modern life would be unrealistic and dangerous. Nor would we thereby be preserving freedom.

Many of us remember when there were so few motorcars that each driver was left free to make his own rules of the road. It was generally understood that a good citizen behind the wheel of a two-cylinder runabout would slow down on corners and either stop or make as little noise as possible when he encountered a horse. Beyond that, if he didn't deliberately run into people, "reckless driving" meant only that he would break a spring or his own neck. But as the roads became filled with powerful automobiles there had to be traffic lights and motor cops. A man could no longer make his own rules of the road. Today if there were no traffic laws no one of us would dare take his car out of the garage. The red and green lights give us freedom to use our automobiles.

Let us face the analogous situation in the relationships of nations. The highways of the world now are crowded. From Hong Kong to Narvik, and from the North Pole to the South, there are no empty seas, no air spaces which are not traversed, no land where rights and interests of many peoples do not meet and may not conflict. The United States or any other nation cannot make the rules of the road all by itself.

In this matter I think we must prepare to revise our ideas even further. Nations cannot as a matter of principle refuse to arbitrate international disputes which arise from domestic policies. Speaking on this question, one of the most distinguished statesmen of our day, Secretary of State Charles Evans Hughes, later Chief Justice of the Supreme Court of the United States, said in 1923 in a speech before the Canadian Bar Association: "In these days of intimate relations, of economic stress and of intense desire to protect national interests and advance national opportunity, the treatment of questions which, from a legal standpoint, are domestic, often seriously affects international relations. The principle, each nation for itself to the full extent of its powers, is the principle of war, not of peace."

Understand, I am not suggesting the abolition of sovereignty. I am merely following out logically what seems to me an obvious line of reasoning. Senator Austin of Vermont recently expressed it when he said: "In order to save sovereignty we must use sovereignty in joining other nations for security."

Sometimes the suggestion that sovereignty be used causes unnecessary alarm lest thereby sovereignty be lost. I think these fears are based on nothing more serious than a misunderstanding of method. "As I speak of sovereignty," said Senator Wiley of Wisconsin in a recent debate in Congress, "I speak of something which is precious. I speak of that which my grandfather obtained when he came to this country. Although he still could not understand the English language, he could obtain 160 acres of land, and he never forgot that that was his soil. . . . After he came to this country he became inspired with something called American sovereignty, and he was a part of the national sovereignty. I say that I do not think we, as trustees, can barter that thing away—the sovereignty of the state or the people."

Each of us shares the feeling for the American soil expressed so movingly by Senator Wiley. Each of us values the backbone which the feeling of self-reliance he extols has given the American people. Each of us, with him, gets angry at the suggestion we might "barter away" something which we hold so precious. But this, it seems to me, is another example of the way in which shades of meaning can obscure the essence of what a word stands for. The actual proceeding of give and take described by the word barter has nothing unworthy about it. Indeed, the phrase "enter into a contract to do such-and-such on such-and-such terms," which might properly be substituted in this connection, carries only honorable and businesslike implications.

I think that if we wish to establish relations between nations based on law instead of force the method which must be followed is the one employed when men enter into a contract of partnership. This has been developed over the years as a practical device for advancing the interests of civilized persons. A proper partnership involves clear rights and equivalent duties for all the partners, proportionate to their respective stakes in the common enterprise. The rights do not exist apart from the duties. This means that anyone who wants to enjoy the advantages of a partnership must give up some of his individual freedom of action. This voluntary limitation on his own future action constitutes the advantage which his partners gain in return for giving up some of their freedom of action in his favor.

It is a simple fact that we have often contracted to limit our theoretically absolute right to do as we liked in dealings with other nations, in return for something which we thought of equal or greater value. Let me cite a single example which we have come to take so much as a matter of course that many people will be surprised to be told it *is* an example. In 1874 we bartered away our "right" to require that inhabitants of other countries who wished to mail a letter to the United States must abide by postal rules fixed independently by the United States. Did we "lose" any of our sovereignty in joining the Universal Postal Union which set standard weights and rates for letters exchanged between Americans and people in other parts of the world? A hundred other equally elementary examples could be given—the rules of safety at sea of 1889, the international sanitary regulations of 1903, the international regulation of radio wave lengths of 1927. Together they show beyond dispute that in the world today no single state which wishes to have friendly relations with other states is able to exercise *all* its rights independently of other states.

The subject which therefore ought to be debated now is not whether we should join in any sort of give and take with other nations but what the items of give and take should be.

Let me indicate by a simile the sort of thing I have particularly in mind. Visualize several big apartment houses which touch one another in a single city block or occupy adjoining blocks. Is it sensible and profitable for each to depend for protection against fire exclusively on a fire-fighting organization composed of its own dwellers and employees? Or is it better for the owner of each to make agreements with the others as to the conditions under which he will allow his stand pipe to be used and under which fire brigades from neighboring houses may use his roof in fighting a neighborhood fire? Going one step further, should the owners not agree to pay taxes at agreed rates to maintain a fire department which will serve them all?

Common support of a common fire department does not affect the individual titles of ownership to individual properties. The point is that, unless the owners do arrange for common support of some kind, they will wake up one day to find that their title deeds are indeed perfect and without a flaw but that what they apply to are piles of rubble and charred beams. A title deed in a safe deposit box does not afford protection from fire and many other forms of trouble and loss. Only the wise and proper exercise of the rights and powers inherent in the title deed can afford protection. So with sovereignty. The proper exercise of sovereign rights protects sovereignty; the failure properly to exercise sovereign rights puts it in jeopardy.

Much of the current confusion over the term sovereignty comes, of course, from those who are willing from considerations of apparent personal or party advantage to promote discord between the United States and other nations. Usually the nations they seem to hate most are our two chief allies. One of their methods of argument recently has been to shout that they will never permit a "mongrel flag" to be substituted for the Stars and Stripes and to say that the Moscow Agreement was "a victory for the Axis." Senator Reynolds, who contemptuously opposed the measures which put this country in a position to resist Germany successfully, assumes to defend our sovereignty now by managing to imply, in the most insulting language, that we should not have diplomatic relations with Russia.

It is true that today as we try to find the right road through the complicated problems raised by this war we sometimes feel baffled by various aspects of British or Soviet policy. But when that happens we should not be surprised or discouraged and we should not feel unfriendly toward either of them as a result. We do many things which are baffling to them, too. Under our constitutional system, for example, our Government is not permitted to make commitments regarding future action to the same extent they are allowed to do under their systems. Let us remember that none of us can read the future exactly and that what we all are searching for is a means to safeguard our nations from future shocks in unpredictable situations. It would be a sad commentary on the human intelligence if three such great peoples allowed irritations caused by temporary uncertainties to make them cynical. They must not despair. They must not give up the search for a thing they all three want in common—a thing I believe they can find if they have the faith to act in common.

None of the arguments used against necessary international coöperation really pretends to be addressed to reason. One of the chief organs stirring narrow nationalistic emotions in this country is the *Chicago Tribune*, the newspaper which published the most secret military plans of our army and navy high command for national defense on the eve of Pearl Harbor; which tries to make martyrs of warped and twisted Americans who have been indicted for conspiracy to undermine the morale of the armed forces; and whose proprietor recently announced his heroic action in saving the United States, some years back, from an invasion by a British Army. The hurt surprise of that particular individual when his activities are described as harmful to his country's welfare reminds me of a tag-line popular in my boyhood. It was taken from Owen Davis's famous play, "Nellie, The Beautiful Cloak Model." In the first act the villain pushed Nellie under a descending elevator. In the second he threw her off the Brooklyn Bridge. In the third he tied her to the tracks of the elevated railroad as a train was approaching. In the last act he climbed through her bedroom window in the dead of night, and, as the poor girl drew back in alarm, demanded reproachfully, "Why do you fear me, Nellie?"

Only a very small group of Americans, however, live in those shadowy caverns of the mind. For most of us who look at the problem of sovereignty without personal or party bias the question that arises is simply: What specific actions are necessary and wise for the extension of the use of our sovereignty?

Here opinions can and will differ. Given the premise that some action is proper, and that many forms of action may be necessary, disagreement is natural and healthy. Agreement in such cases can be reached by argument and mutual give and take. As the war enters its final phase, proposals as to how the peaceable nations of the earth should organize to prevent new conflicts will multiply and take more definite shape, and we shall begin to examine and discuss them in detail. Let us enter upon this great debate with the object of coming to an agreement and not, as once before at a similar moment in our history, in an irreconcilable spirit and the determination to vindicate a particular point of view.

V

In the League of Nations debate of 1919 and 1920 the sharpest differences of opinion within this country arose over the question whether the United States should commit itself to the use of force in upholding international agreements. Friends and foes alike of the proposed international organization saw that this would be the test of its usefulness. Persons who wished to prevent the United States from joining any world organization at all inflamed emotions and awakened prejudice by proclaiming that such a commitment would be "treason." Those who wanted to make the organization the instrument for preventing a second world war saw that it would succeed or fail according to the willingness of member states to pledge themselves to the use of force to maintain the rule of law, by an agreed procedure and in agreed circumstances.

Today this is still the core of the decision which we must take. Are we willing only to talk when any situation arises which plainly threatens war? Or are we willing, in agreed circumstances, to act?

Two episodes gave Hitler his cue and made the present war certain—the unchecked Japanese aggression in Manchuria in 1931 and the unchecked Italian aggression against Ethiopia in 1935. The chief reason why the Powers now joined together as the United Nations did not check those aggressions was because none of them believed that any of the others was prepared—psychologically or militarily—to do more than talk.

The growth of that state of mind can be traced all the way back to 1919. Apportionment of blame for it among the various countries concerned is not at this moment important. What is important today is that unless the American isolationism which we are now putting out the door is to fly back through the window, we must preface any discussion of details of the international organization which we expect to help create by a clear statement that we are prepared in principle to join with other members of that organization in using force to sustain its decisions.

Would the creation of a joint instrument of force threaten our sovereignty? Or would it, on the contrary, represent a useful extension of our sovereign powers in an effort to protect our vital interests?

First of all let us consider the immediate and concrete postwar situation which will make an international armed force necessary. Obviously, it is the requirement that Germany and Japan be policed to make sure that they do not again acquire the military power to wage wars of aggression. The idea of "policing" parts of the world outside the boundaries of the United States is not a new one for us. Acting unilaterally—that is to say one-sidedly and by ourselves—we have used our armed forces for police work in other parts of the world more than 50 times in our history. (In this connection, incidentally, we might remind ourselves that certain of our one-sided expeditions into Latin America were part of a policy which we now believe to have been unwise and which by agreement with the Latin American countries has now been renounced in favor of coöperative action in cases where police work in this hemisphere may be necessary.)

Besides these instances of unilateral action, we have on 25 or more occasions taken police action in coöperation with other nations. The agreements which we entered into with Great Britain in 1891, and with Russia in 1894, to patrol the Bering Sea against illegal fur sealers might be cited as examples of such international policy. These agreements gave both Russia and Great Britain the right to seize suspected fur hunters and their ships, even if they were American citizens sailing under the American flag. Both those countries in turn gave us a similar right to seize ships and men, of whatever nationality, including their own, if we suspected them of illegal activities. Those agreements were not destructive of our sovereignty or of British and Russian sovereignty. They represented a constructive use of sovereignty, mutually advantageous to all three parties.

This established principle of coöperative international policing gives us the foundation on which to build for the future. No dramatically long step is required. I can see the practical difficulties in attempting to create a closely integrated internationalized police force. But I do not have any difficulty in conceiving of an agreement between the peace-loving nations to the effect that each will maintain certain land, sea or air forces and that each will use them collaboratively, in agreed situations and within agreed limits, to prevent aggression.

This seems to me the minimum requirements to ensure that international disputes which are clearly covered by international law shall be submitted to courts and judges, and that those which are not shall be settled by conciliation and compromise. For such a procedure to work successfully, the members of the international organization must say plainly, in advance, that if peaceful methods fail the aggressor state will encounter sufficient armed forces to ensure his eventual defeat.

In planning how this force would be operated as a practical matter we have a model in the combined chiefs of staff with which this war has made us familiar. Such a staff would make the necessary technical preparations for effective collaborative action in the event that should ever become necessary. I would hope that the mere preparation for action would forestall the need of ever taking it. But if the time should come when collective action had to be taken, it certainly is in the interest of the United States and of all other peace-loving states that it be taken promptly and decisively.

To repeat once more: I think that our use of our sovereignty to create an effective instrument of peace is the best way of protecting our sovereignty. If this is called "bartering," I would say that it is a profitable transaction, and I would rather see the United States enter into it than pursue its own aloof way into a third world war.

After this war we shall face many tough problems which can be met only by international action. Some will be scientific or technological, some cultural or educational. Some will be economic—our struggle, in partnership with our allies, to use the raw materials and the markets of the world to increase living standards everywhere. Some will be political—the delicate and hazardous adjustment to freedom and self-government of millions of people who have now heard those magic words and will need our help as they grope dangerously for a way to turn them into reality.

In an international organization which was backed by the machinery needed to enforce its decisions the United States for the first time in history would be in a position to deal boldly and effectively with the problems which will confront it. In coöperation with our allies, we shall still be leaders by virtue of the strength and ingenuity of our people. To use this leadership, for our own enrichment and that of mankind, will not be to weaken the sovereign power of the American people; it will be to widen it and make it more real.

❖ ❖ ❖

To get the full flavor of Sir Halford J. Mackinder's perceptive and original mind, the reader should look up (if by chance he is not already familiar with it) Mackinder's little book, "Democratic Ideals and Reality," published in 1919, to which the following article, printed in FOREIGN AFFAIRS in July 1943, is the already famous supplement. "The time has at last come to take larger views," he wrote on page one of that prophetic volume. Seldom in our day has there been a book so capable of opening men's minds to the long view of history; and seldom in history has a great prophecy been so crowned with irony. For Mackinder's warning to his own countrymen on the morning of the triumph of Allied sea power—that land power can conquer sea power by outflanking it, that is to say, by capturing the bases from which the sea power must operate—was disregarded by both Britain and the United States. Instead, the theory was made the foundation of a new effort of world conquest by Germany. It was upon a too literal acceptance of Mackinder's concept of "geographical causation," and of the potential might of the Heartland, that Karl Haushofer founded his school of geopolitics.

Few who today look at Mackinder's little maps in "Democratic Ideals and Reality," or grasp the significance of his concepts in this essay, will fail to find their own thoughts starting on a long voyage outward. The world is indeed round, he says, and the center of it is the Continent—the one Continent—not Europe, but the world-island of Asia, Europe and Africa. North and South America are two of its satellite islands, inferior in population, in resources, and in strategic position. The Heartland is Russia, linked by the "isthmus" (the region from the Baltic to the Black Seas) with Germany, which lies in the neck of the "Latin Peninsula" pointing into the Atlantic. To the south is Macedonia, in the neck of the Greek Peninsula pointing into Egypt. Control of this area by a single Power could mean control of the world.

When Mackinder died on March 7, 1947, at 86, the prospects of building the "unshakable" dykes east and west, which would cleanse the German mind of its black magic were far less promising than they seemed when he published these pages. Few would dare assume at the present time "the fresh start" that was the premise of 1919; but the hard core of fact which he inserted in his formulation of the ideal is now almost a commonplace.

❖ ❖ ❖

THE ROUND WORLD AND THE WINNING OF THE PEACE

By Sir Halford J. Mackinder

I HAVE been asked to carry further some of the themes with which I have dealt in my past writings, in particular to consider whether my strategical concept of a "Heartland" has lost any of its significance under the conditions of modern warfare. In order to set the concept into its context, I must begin with a short account of how it took shape.

My earliest memory of public affairs goes back to the day in September 1870 when, as a small boy who had just begun attendance at the local grammar school, I took home the news, which I had learned from a telegram affixed to the post office door, that Napoleon III and his whole army had surrendered to the Prussians at Sedan. This came as a shock to Englishmen, who still moved mentally in the wake of Trafalgar and the retreat from Moscow, but the full effect of it was not realized until some years later. Britain's supremacy on the ocean had not yet been challenged, and the only danger she saw at that time to her overseas empire was in the Asiatic position of Russia. During this period the London newspapers were quick to detect evidence of Russian intrigue in every rumor from Constantinople and in every tribal disturbance along the northwest frontier of India. British sea power and Russian land power held the center of the international stage.

Thirty years later, at the turn of the century, von Tirpitz began to build a German high seas fleet. I was busy at this time setting up the teaching of political and historical geography at the universities of Oxford and London, and was noting current events with a teacher's eye for generalization. The German movement meant, I saw, that the nation already possessing the greatest organized land power and occupying the central strategical position in Europe was about to add to itself sea power strong enough to neutralize British sea power. The United States was also rising steadily to the rank of a Great Power. As yet, however, its rise could be measured only in statistical tables; although in my childhood someone had already been impressed with American resourcefulness, for I remember in our schoolroom a picture of the battle between the *Merrimac* and the *Monitor,* the first armored ship and the first turret ship. Thus Germany and the United States came up alongside of Britain and Russia.

The particular events out of which sprang the idea of the Heartland were the British war in South Africa and the Russian war in Manchuria. The South African war ended in 1902, and in the spring of 1904 the Russo-Japanese war was clearly imminent. A paper which I read before the Royal Geographical Society early in the latter year, entitled "The Geographical Pivot of History," was therefore topical, but it had a background of many years of thought.

The contrast presented by the British war against the Boers, fought 6,000 miles away across the ocean, and the war fought by Russia at a comparable distance across the land expanse of Asia, naturally suggested a parallel contrast between Vasco da Gama rounding the Cape of Good Hope on his voyage to the Indies, near the end of the fifteenth century, and the ride of Yermak, the Cossack, at the head of his horsemen, over the Ural range into Siberia early in the sixteenth century. That comparison in turn led to a review of the long succession of raids made by the nomadic tribes of Central Asia, through classical antiquity and the Middle Ages, upon the settled populations of the crescent of subcontinents: peninsular Europe, the Middle East, the Indies, and China proper. My conclusion was that,

> . . . in the present decade we are for the first time in a position to attempt, with some degree of completeness, a correlation between the larger geographical and the larger historical generalizations. For the first time we can perceive something of the real proportion of features and events on the stage of the whole world, and may seek a formula

which shall express certain aspects, at any rate, of geographical causation in universal history. If we are fortunate, that formula should have a practical value as setting into perspective some of the competing forces in current international politics.

The word Heartland occurs once in the 1904 paper, but incidentally and as a descriptive and not a technical term. The expressions "pivot area" and "pivot state" were used instead, thus:

> The oversetting of the balance of power in favor of the pivot state, resulting in its expansion over the marginal lands of Euro-Asia, would permit of the use of vast continental resources for fleet-building, and the empire of the world would then be in sight. This might happen if Germany were to ally herself with Russia.
>
> In conclusion, it may be well expressly to point out that the substitution of some new control of the inland area for that of Russia would not tend to reduce the geographical significance of the pivot position. Were the Chinese, for instance, organized by the Japanese, to overthrow the Russian Empire and conquer its territory, they might constitute the yellow peril to the world's freedom just because they would add an oceanic frontage to the resources of the great continent.

At the end of the First World War, my book, "Democratic Ideals and Reality," was published in London and New York. Clearly the "pivot" label, which had been appropriate for an academic thesis at the beginning of the century, was no longer adequate to the international situation as it emerged from that first great crisis of our world revolution: hence "Ideals," "Realities" and the "Heartland." But the fact that, even when additional criteria were brought to bear, the thesis of 1904 still sufficed as the background for an estimate of the position fifteen years later, gave evidence that the formula sought had been found.

II

We turn now to the main object of the present article—the drafting of an interim estimate of the value of the Heartland concept in a survey of the world preliminary to the coming settlement. It must be understood that I am dealing with strategy, which, of course, is effective in peacetime no less than in wartime. I do not presume to join in the wide-sweeping debates already in progress which look forward over generations to come; I center my thoughts on the years during which the enemy is to be held down while, in the language of Casablanca, his philosophy of war is being killed.

The Heartland is the northern part and the interior of Euro-Asia. It extends from the Arctic coast down to the central deserts, and has as its western limits the broad isthmus between the Baltic and Black Seas. The concept does not admit of precise definition on the map for the reason that it is based on three separate aspects of physical geography which, while reinforcing one another, are not exactly coincident. First of all, we have in this region by far the widest lowland plain on the face of the globe. Secondly, there flow across that plain some great navigable rivers; certain of them go north to the Arctic Sea and are inaccessible from the ocean because it is cumbered with ice, while others flow into inland waters, such as the Caspian, which have no exit to the ocean. Thirdly, there is here a grassland zone which, until within the last century and a half, presented ideal conditions for the development of high mobility by camel and horse-riding nomads. Of the three features mentioned, the river basins are the easiest to present cartographically; the water divide which delimits the whole group of Arctic and "continental" rivers into a single unit does isolate neatly on the map a vast coherent area which is the Heartland according to that particular criterion. The mere exclusion of sea mobility and sea power, however, is a negative if important differential; it was the plain and the grassland belt which offered the positive conditions conducive to the other type of mobility, that proper to the prairie. As for the grassland, it traverses the whole breadth of the plain but does not cover its entire surface. Notwithstanding these apparent discrepancies, the Heartland provides a sufficient physical basis for strategical thinking. To go further and to simplify geography artificially would be misleading.

For our present purpose it is sufficiently accurate to say that the territory of the U.S.S.R. is equivalent to the Heartland, except in one direction. In order to demarcate that exception—a great one—let us draw a direct line, some 5,500 miles long, westward from Bering Strait to Rumania. Three thousand miles from Bering Strait that line will cross the Yenisei River, flowing northward from the borders of Mongolia to the Arctic Ocean. Eastward of that great river lies a generally rugged country of mountains, plateaux and valleys, covered almost from end to end with coniferous forests; this I shall call Lenaland, from its central feature, the great River Lena. This is not included in Heartland Russia. Lenaland Russia has an area of 3,750,000 square miles, but a population of only some 6,000,000, of whom almost 5,000,000 are settled along the transcontinental railroad from Irkutsk to Vladivostok. In the remainder of this territory there are on the average over three square miles for every inhabitant. The rich natural resources—timber, water power and minerals—are as yet practically untouched.

West of the Yenisei lies what I have described as Heartland Russia, a plain extending 2,500 miles north and south, and 2,500 miles east and west. It contains 4,250,000 square miles and a population of more than 170,000,000. The population is increasing at the rate of 3,000,000 a year.

The simplest and probably the most effective way of presenting the strategical values of the Russian Heartland is to compare them with those of France. In the case of France, however, the historical background is the First World War while in the case of Russia it is the Second World War.

France, like Russia, is a compact country, as long as it is broad, but not quite so well-rounded as the Heartland and therefore with a rather smaller area in proportion to the length of boundary to be defended. It is encompassed by sea and mountain, except to the northeast. In 1914–18 there were no hostile countries behind the Alps and the Pyrenees, and the fleets of France and her allies dominated the seas. The French and allied armies, deployed across the open northeastern frontier, were therefore well defended on either flank and were secure in the rear. The tragic lowland gateway in the northeast, through which so many armies have surged inward and outward, is 300 miles wide between the Vosges and the North Sea. In 1914, the line of battle, pivoting on the Vosges, wheeled backward to the Marne; and at the end of the war, in 1918, it wheeled forward on the same pivot. Through the four years' interval the elastic front sagged and bent but did not break even in the face of the great German attack in the spring of 1918. Thus, as it proved, there was space within the country sufficient both for defense in depth and for strategical retreat. Unfortunately for France, however, her principal industrial area was in that northeastern sector where the unceasing battle was waged.

Russia repeats in essentials the pattern of France, but on a greater scale and with her open frontier turned westward instead of northeastward. In the present war the Russian army is aligned across that open frontier. In its rear is the vast plain of the Heartland, available for defense in depth and for strategic retreat. Away back, this plain recedes eastward into the natural bulwarks constituted by the "inaccessible" Arctic coast, the Lenaland wilderness behind the Yenisei, and the fringe of mountains from the Altai to the Hindu Kush, backed by the Gobi, Tibetan and Iranian deserts. These three barriers have breadth and substance, and far excel in defensive value the coasts and mountains which engird France.

It is true that the Arctic shore is no longer inaccessible in the absolute sense that held until a few years ago. Convoys of merchant ships, assisted by powerful icebreakers and with airplanes reconnoitring ahead for water lanes through the ice pack, have traded to the Obi and Yenisei Rivers, and even to the Lena River; but a hostile invasion across the vast area of circum-polar ice and over the Tundra mosses and Targa forests of northern Siberia seems almost impossible in the face of Soviet land-based air defense.

To complete the comparison between France and Russia, let us consider the relative scales of some parallel facts. Heartland Russia has four times the population, four times as wide an open frontier, and 20 times the area of France.

That open frontier is not disproportionate to the Russian population; and to equal the breadth of the Soviet deployment Germany has had to eke out her more limited manpower by diluting it with less effective troops drawn from her subject countries. In one important respect, however, Russia began her second war with Germany in no better position than France occupied in 1914; as with France, her most developed agriculture and industries lay directly in the path of the invader. The second Five Year Plan would have remedied that situation had the German aggression been delayed a couple of years. Perhaps that was one of Hitler's reasons for breaking his treaty with Stalin in 1941.

The vast potentialities of the Heartland, however, to say nothing of the natural reserves in Lenaland, are strategically well placed. Industries are growing rapidly in such localities as the southern Urals, in the very pivot of the pivot area, and in the rich Kuznetsk coal basin in the lee of the great natural barriers east of the upper Yenisei River. In 1938 Russia produced more of the following foodstuffs than any other country in the world: wheat, barley, oats, rye and sugar beets. More manganese was produced in Russia than in any other country. It was bracketed with the United States in the first place as regards iron, and it stood second place in production of petroleum. As for coal, Mikhaylov makes the statement that the resources of the Kuznetsk and Krasnoyarsk coal basins are each estimated to be capable of supplying the requirements of the whole world for 300 years.[1] The policy of the Soviet Government was to balance imports and exports during the first Five Year Plan. Except in a very few commodities the country is capable of producing everything which it requires.

All things considered, the conclusion is unavoidable that if the Soviet Union emerges from this war as conqueror of Germany, she must rank as the greatest land Power on the globe. Moreover, she will be the Power in the strategically strongest defensive position. The Heartland is the greatest natural fortress on earth. For the first time in history it is manned by a garrison sufficient both in number and quality.

[1] N. Mikhavlov, "Soviet Geography." London: Methuen, 1937.

III

I cannot pretend to exhaust the subject of the Heartland, the citadel of land power on the great mainland of the world, in a short article like this. But a few words should be devoted to another concept to balance it.

From Casablanca there came lately the call to destroy the ruling German philosophy. That can be done only by irrigating the German mind with the clean water of a rival philosophy. I assume that for, say, two years from the time the "cease fire" order is given, the Allies will occupy Berlin, try the criminals, fix frontiers on the spot and complete other surgical treatment so that the older generation in Germany which will die impenitent and bitter cannot again misrepresent history to the younger generation. But it would obviously be worse than useless to set alien teachers to work in Germany to inculcate the theory of freedom. Freedom cannot be taught; it can only be given to those who can use it. However, the polluted channel might be swept clear very effectively if it were controlled by strong embankments of power on either hand—land power to the east, in the Heartland, and sea power to the west, in the North Atlantic basin. Face the German mind with an enduring certainty that any war fought by Germany must be a war on two *unshakable* fronts, and the Germans themselves will solve the problem.

For this to happen it will be necessary in the first place that there be effective and lasting coöperation between America, Britain and France, the first for depth of defense, the second as the moated forward stronghold—a Malta on a grander scale—and the third as the defensible bridgehead. The last is no less essential than the other two, because sea power must in the final resort be amphibious if it is to balance land power. In the second place, it is necessary that those three and the fourth conqueror, Russia, be pledged together to coöperate immediately if any breach of the peace is threatened, so that the devil in Germany can never again get its head up and must die by inanition.

Some persons today seem to dream of a global air power which will "liquidate" both fleets and armies. I am impressed, however, by the broad implications of a recent utterance of a practical airman: "Air power depends absolutely on the efficiency of its ground organization." That is too large a subject to discuss within the limits of this paper. It can only be said that no adequate proof has yet been presented that air fighting will not follow the long history of all kinds of warfare by presenting alternations of offensive and defensive tactical superiority, meanwhile effecting few permanent changes in strategical conditions.

I make no pretense to forecasting the future of humanity. What I am concerned with are the conditions under which we set about winning the peace when victory in the war has been achieved. In regard to the pattern of the postwar world, now being studied by many people for the first time, it is important that a line should be carefully drawn between idealistic blueprints and realistic and scholarly maps presenting concepts—political, economic, strategic, and so forth—based on the recognition of obstinate facts.

With that in mind, attention might be drawn to a great feature of global geography: a girdle, as it were, hung around the north polar regions. It begins as the Sahara desert, is followed as one moves eastward by the Arabian, Iranian, Tibetan and Mongolian deserts, and then extends, by way of the wildernesses of Lenaland, Alaska and the Laurentian shield of Canada, to the sub-arid belt of the western United States. That girdle of deserts and wildernesses is a feature of the first importance in global geography. Within it lie two related features of almost equal significance: the Heartland, and the basin of the Midland Ocean (North Atlantic) with its four subsidiaries (Mediterranean, Baltic, Arctic and Caribbean Seas). Outside the girdle is the Great Ocean (Pacific, Indian and South Atlantic) and the lands which drain to it (Asiatic Monsoon lands, Australia, South America and Africa south of the Sahara).

Archimedes said he could lift the world if he could find a fulcrum on which to rest his lever. All the world cannot be lifted back to prosperity at once. The region between the Missouri and the Yenisei, with its great trunk routes for merchant aircraft between Chicago-New York and London-Moscow, and all that the development of them will stand for, must be the first care, for it must be the fulcrum. Wisely the conquering of Japan waits for a while. In due course China will receive capital on a generous scale as a debt of honor, to help in her romantic adventure of building for a quarter of humanity a new civilization, neither quite eastern nor quite western. Then the ordering of the Outer World will be relatively easy, with China, the United States and the United Kingdom leading the way, the last two each followed by its trail of a commonwealth of free nations—for though their histories will have been different the result will be similar. But the first enterprise undertaken in economic rebuilding will surely have to be in the area within the desert girdle, lest a whole civilization should deliquesce into chaos. What a pity the alliance, negotiated after Versailles, between the United States, the United Kingdom and France was not implemented! What trouble and sadness that act might have saved!

IV

And now, to complete my picture of the pattern of the round world, let me add, briefly, three concepts to the two already visualized. For the purposes of what I see described in American writings as "Grand Strategy," it is necessary to build broad generalizations in geography no less than in history and economics.

I have described my concept of the Heartland, which I have no hesitation in saying is more valid and useful today than it was either 20 or 40 years ago. I have said how it is set in its girdle of broad natural defenses—ice-clad Polar Sea, forested and rugged Lenaland, and Central Asiatic mountain and arid tableland. The girdle is incomplete, however, because of an open gateway, a thousand miles wide, admitting from Peninsular Europe into the interior plain through the broad isthmus between the Baltic and Black Seas. For the first time in all history there is within this vast natural fortress a garrison adequate to deny entry to the

German invader. Given that fact, and the defenses to the flanks and rear which I have described, the sheer breadth of the open gateway is an advantage, for it provides the opportunity of defeating the enemy by compelling him to make a broad deployment of his manpower. And upon and beneath the Heartland there is a store of rich soil for cultivation and of ores and fuels for extraction, the equal—or thereabouts—of all that lies upon and beneath the United States and the Canadian Dominion.

I have suggested that a current of cleansing counter-philosophy, canalized between unbreachable embankments of power, may sweep the German mind clear of its black magic. Surely no one is going to be mad enough to set foreign teachers to exorcise the evil spirits from the soul of the conquered German nation. Nor, after the first inevitable punitory years, do I have sufficient trust that the conquering democracies will maintain garrisons of the necessary spirit and number *stationed in the vanquished lands;* for there is no use in asking democrats to persist in an attitude contrary to the very spirit and essence of democracy. The cleansing stream might better be released to flow from some regenerate and regenerating *German* source, between the embankments of power I have named, the one within the Heartland and the other within the territories of the three amphibious powers, American, British and French. The two friendly forces facing one another across the flow of the canal would be of equal power and should always be equally ready for necessary action. Then Germany would live continuously under the threat of immediate war on two fronts should she be guilty of any breach of the treaties which prohibited either physical preparation for war or the misleading of youth which is another way of preparation for war. The democratic garrisons in their home countries would be, by force of example, the teachers.

On this proposal follows my second geographical concept, that of the Midland Ocean—the North Atlantic—and its dependent seas and river basins. Without laboring the details of that concept, let me picture it again in its three elements—a bridgehead in France, a moated aerodrome in

Britain, and a reserve of trained manpower, agriculture and industries in the eastern United States and Canada. So far as war-potential goes, both the United States and Canada are Atlantic countries, and since instant land-warfare is in view, both the bridgehead and the moated aerodrome are essential to amphibious power.

The three remaining concepts I shall do little more than sketch, and only for the sake of globular completeness and balance. Girdling the twin unit just described—Heartland and the basin of the Midland Ocean—there appears on the globe the mantle of vacancies, constituting a practically continuous land-space covering some 12,000,000 square miles—that is, about a quarter of all the land on the globe. Upon this vast area there lives today a total population of less than 30,000,000, or, say, one-seventieth of the population of the globe. Airplanes will, of course, fly along many routes over this girdle of wilderness; and through it will be driven trunk motor roads. But for long to come it will break social continuity between the major communities of mankind on the globe.[2]

The fourth of my concepts embraces on either side of the South Atlantic the tropical rain-forests of South America and Africa. If these were subdued to agriculture and inhabited with the present density of tropical Java, they might sustain a thousand million people, always provided that medicine had rendered the tropics as productive of human energy as the temperate zones.

Fifthly, and lastly, a thousand million people of ancient oriental civilization inhabit the Monsoon lands of India and China. They must grow to prosperity in the same years in which Germany and Japan are being tamed to civilization. They will then balance that other thousand million who live between the Missouri and the Yenisei. A balanced globe of human beings. And happy, because balanced and thus free.

[2] Some day, incidentally, when coal and oil are exhausted, the Sahara may become the trap for capturing direct power from the Sun.

❖ ❖ ❖

THE thesis that the diplomatist Jules Cambon put deftly in 1930 was beaten out again with hammer strokes in January 1945 by one of his friends and disciples, the French journalist "Pertinax"—André Géraud, the author of "The Gravediggers of France." Géraud, perhaps the leading journalist of Europe, for many years foreign editor of the *Echo de Paris* and then editor of *Europe Nouvelle,* was always an incorruptible foe of Pan-Germanism and appeasement of Hitler, and a powerful advocate of Anglo-French collaboration.

In the classic French view, definite commitments by a few Great Powers to use force to meet a definite menace is the bedrock for any structure of security and the precondition of the development of world law. As André Géraud makes plain, the concept implies a continual conscious adjustment of the interests of those Powers so that the alliance will be real and strong. In that most important respect, it is in harmony with the purposes of a world organization devoted to shaping the interests of nations as a means of laying the foundation for world law. But it places the responsibility for keeping the peace upon a few nations, not upon the concerted action of many. In this respect, of course, it conflicted sharply in the inter-war years with the popular disesteem for "power politics," and the neat division of foreign policies into the "old" and the "new." France, obsessed with her fear of Germany, it was said, was herself militaristic and the enemy of peace. The vigor of André Géraud's warning against the "new" diplomacy must be read against this background. The San Francisco Conference in the spring of 1945 put the decision as to the use of force against an aggressor state solely in the hands of a few Great Powers, as he argued it should be. Paradoxically, we soon thereafter saw the unwillingness of the Soviet state to enter into an alliance with the United States, Great Britain and France to meet the specific menace of another Pan-German aggression. Whether or not this marked the final collapse of the Great Power coalition upon which the San Francisco arrangement was predicated remains, in 1947, still to be seen. At any rate, comprehension of the classic thesis as stated by Géraud must be included in any understanding of two present problems of international affairs: How to form a Great Power alliance which can face any aggressor with overwhelming force? What shall be its responsibility to all the peoples of the world?

❖ ❖ ❖

DIPLOMACY, OLD AND NEW

By André Géraud
("Pertinax")

THE terms "old diplomacy" and "new diplomacy" have been in common use for twenty-five years or more. The system of alliance set up by France, England and Russia to ward off the German danger in the decade before 1914 is dubbed "old diplomacy." The system of so-called international security which took shape in the League's Covenant of June 1919, and afterward regulated or was supposed to regulate the relations of the fifty-odd states of the world, is labelled "new diplomacy." All the implications of the word "alliance" connote "old diplomacy." In the same way, "new diplomacy" connotes the twin ideas of replacing the bilateral alliances of the past with a universal or semi-universal association of states pledged to compliance with a set of general principles embodied in international law, and the abandonment of "power politics"—that is, the use of force to settle conflicts between nations.

It is difficult today to imagine the unbounded enthusiasm which burst out in most European nations when the American President landed in Brest in 1918. I shall always remember the remark of an eminent British political writer with whom I was taking a short rest in the country. A common friend was about to go to London as correspondent of the *Echo de Paris,* the newspaper of which I was then foreign editor. That friend, who was to make a great name as a playwright, had remarked that he was attracted by his new journalistic task but feared lest his scanty knowledge of history would prove a serious hindrance. "Do believe," said the Englishman, "that we are starting today with a clean slate and that the interests and the passions which formerly have determined the fate of the world will henceforth be of little weight." Such was the belief of many, perhaps of most—if not in France, at least in England, and, I am sure, here in America.

Those great expectations have been frustrated. The ambitious experiment started by the preceding generation of statesmen has ended in war—in an ordeal more terrible than the one old diplomacy had been unable to forestall. Was new diplomacy at fault? Numerous voices insist that it was not. New diplomacy, they say, was not given a fair chance. It was stifled in its very cradle by the men and the ideas it was to replace. This time, they conclude, we must make a complete break with the political tenets and practices which held sway in Paris, London and St. Petersburg when the present century was in its teens.

This article examines only the pattern of old diplomacy worked out by the Powers of the Triple Entente—France, Russia and Britain. They are the Powers that tried to preserve peace, and we are interested in defense, not in offense. It is meaningless to use the terms "old" and "new" diplomacy in reference to Germany. Germany, a persistently aggressive empire, had no more to do with new diplomacy than was necessary to disguise her program of revenge.

The danger at the present moment, with full victory within the grasp of the American, British and Russian Armies, is a fresh venture in the field of new diplomacy as it was understood at the termination of the First World War. For the common good we must rid ourselves of confusion of thought which, if continued, cannot but play into the hands of all disturbers of the peace.

My contention is that, to nip in the bud all forms of aggression, to curb any would-be disturber of the peace, to initiate any vigorous action in the international field, definite political and military commitments must be entered into. Political and military commitments are not likely to prove adequate if diluted into general pacts subscribed to by twenty, thirty or forty participants. To believe that such pacts suffice to maintain peace is to beg the whole question, to assume that the conduct of international relations can forever be divorced from the use of material force, that the rule of law has already been made secure throughout the world, that no secular arm is needed in support of law—in short, that the days of power politics are over. Clearly, no such assumptions are permissible. And as long as international relations involve questions of power, only the commitments which create a distinct solidarity of the few Great Powers can exorcise war.

Those few Great Powers must so closely adjust their respective national interests as to be equally determined to take up the challenge, whenever the challenge comes. And I doubt that such adjustment of national interests between the few is possible if too many signatories are gathered. Moreover, with a great number of signatories, the execution of the pledges will unavoidably lack the necessary decisiveness. In a convoy groping its way across the ocean, the pace is set by the slowest ship. Not very differently, collective enforcement of obligations binding dozens of states runs the risk of being adjusted to the gait of those which are the less determined to act and the most prone to entertain extensive reservations, if not, indeed, to play a double game. I do not imply that the Great Powers who must assume the responsibility for dealing with the disturbers of the peace are free to trample on the rights of the international community, and to ignore notions of justice and equity. By no means. Within the international organization, unequal functions ought not to generate unequal rights. In a well-ordered international polity, there should be procedures by which secondary Powers could mobilize public opinion against the leading states, should the latter become domineering. I wish to emphasize only that the leadership in the effort to maintain peace must rest with the principal Powers. That leadership must be founded upon their alliance.

II

Old diplomacy failed in 1914 because the counter-alliance it managed to set up in order to hold in check the Triple Alliance of Germany, Austria and Italy was not impressive enough and, consequently, did not deter the Central Empires from their sinister undertaking. New diplomacy failed in the thirties because, having brought about the dissolution of the Anglo-French alliance, it could construct nothing positive from the wreckage of its ideological schemes. History will hold that the sins of commission for which the new diplomacy is answerable outstrip the sins of omission laid at the door of the old.

The danger to European civilization and to the world in the German bid for supremacy which became visible in the opening years of the century cannot now be minimized by the wildest stretch of pacifist and humanitarian imagination. To its eternal honor, French diplomacy was first to detect it. The alliance of the United Nations in the present war as well as the system outlined in the Dumbarton Oaks proposals are the lineal descendants of the coalition pieced together some forty years ago.

On the day Théophile Delcassé took office as Minister of Foreign Affairs in June 1898, France undertook not only to unite Britain and herself in a common bond, but also to unite Britain and Russia, the ally of France since 1891–92. Indeed, Delcassé himself was not the original inventor of the Triple Entente. The scheme loomed large in the talk of Léon Gambetta, some eighteen years earlier, and the idea had been taken up by Paul Cambon and Camille Barrère, the most farseeing ambassadors any French government ever had in its service. Let us add to the small group of pioneers the names of Alexandre Ribot (the Minister who brought into being the alliance with Russia), and of Jules Cambon, who was not to be given an ambassadorial post until 1898. They are the statesmen who fully perceived the convergence of Franco-British interests, latent all through the nineteenth century in spite of superficial discords. The problem was to draw Russia and Britain together for the sake of European salvation. After Gabriel Hanotaux left the Quai d'Orsay for good in 1898, Delcassé let nothing interefere with his main purpose. A close adviser of Delcassé once told me of the Minister's deep emotion on leaving the room of Lord Lansdowne at the Foreign

Office in the spring of 1903. The Frenchman had come to London to further the progress of the contemplated convention on Egypt and Morocco which was to seal the Entente Cordiale the following year. All of a sudden Lord Lansdowne said to him: "You ought to open the way for some rapprochement between ourselves and Russia." "I felt," related Delcassé to my friend, "that my head was about to burst. But I did not show anything of the feeling those words had stirred deep in me. I was content to remark that I should avail myself of every opportunity to praise in the presence of Russian statesmen the satisfactory working of the Entente Cordiale. I could not promise to do more, at the outset, since great care had to be taken not to raise doubts, among Russian diplomats, as to our loyalty to the Franco-Russian alliance." The dream of Delcassé became true on August 31, 1907. On that day the Governments of London and St. Petersburg reached full agreement on Persia, Afghanistan and Tibet. The Triple Entente was born.

When put to the test, seven years later, the Franco-Russian branch of the system worked without a hitch. As unhesitatingly as Germany supported Austria, France remained loyal to her bond and unflinchingly accepted the terrible risks and sacrifices of the First World War. It was the Anglo-French branch which was slow to operate. Properly speaking, no formal alliance between France and England was in existence: only a mechanism for coöperation between the general staffs of the two countries had been set up.

The old diplomacy of the period was outdone by the warlike moves of the Central Empires. It took the British Government a full week or more to estimate correctly the far-reaching consequences of the ultimatum delivered by the Austrian Government to Belgrade on July 23, 1914. I vividly remember calling on Paul Cambon the morning of the next day, a few hours after the text, or a summary, of the ultimatum had been made public. Oddly enough, he knew nothing of it. Apparently no warning had reached him as yet from the Foreign Office or even from his own staff. He carefully perused the Ballplatz note and said: "It means war. I easily visualize what is about to happen. If the British Government put its foot on the whole thing today, peace might be saved. But Grey is going to wobble and hesitate. Meanwhile, the Germans will go ahead in the belief that England does not dare intervene. England is sure to join us in the end but too late!" Paul Cambon only too accurately forecast the British course.

To a great extent, the European tragedy arose from the fact that, instinctively, our British friends were still involved in the traditional concept of the balance of power. For ages that concept had done them good service. They clung to it against a mass of premonitory warnings. I ask the reader not to imagine that I find some wanton delectation in plunging into the recesses of the past, that I wander about unburying the dead for the sake of indicting the British Government. But the lesson implicit in those records of thirty years ago has a bearing on the present time and must not be missed.

The balance of power principle had a very peculiar significance for England. As used by a Frenchman, the expression meant that no single Power or group of Powers must be permitted to become a law unto itself, and that unless France was ready to forfeit her independence she had no choice but to band her resources with the resources of others as soon as she felt unable to maintain an equilibrium by her own might. But France was always to be at the center of the contemplated coalition, in the thick of the fight, with her land and sea forces. As the British Cabinet understood the balance of power, England, on the contrary, needed not be in the midst of the storm. Britain's control of the seas and the incomparable consequences of sea power, as appraised in London, made it possible for her to hold the scales on the Continent with a minimum contribution of her own substance. The necessary prerequisite of such a policy was, of course, that calculations of every nation's resources and purposes should be faultless.

In 1914, the British ministers were blind to many new international factors. Many of them did not rightly judge the strength and threat of the German Navy. The dynamism and the scope of the Pan German movement escaped their notice. As late as 1899, for example, Joseph Chamberlain favored the conclusion of an alliance with Germany. And British ministers failed to perceive the significance of the changes of structure in Austria-Hungary.

They could not shake off old connections and prejudices before it was too late. I doubt that more intelligent ministers ever sat around the Council table at 10 Downing Street than such men as Herbert Asquith, Edward Grey, R. B. Haldane, David Lloyd George, Winston Churchill. But they were imbued to the marrow with the optimism of the nineteenth century. A very charming girl of 13, close to one of them, once addressed a colonel of the Guards in the following words: "How extraordinary that you should spend your life preparing for emergencies which will never come to pass! Can you take yourself seriously?" The appeasement of Germany by the London Cabinet, from 1907 to 1914, makes a story which approximates the show of Munich. In those acts of surrender—the agreements initialed or even signed on Asiatic Turkey and the Portuguese colonies—the German Emperor and his counsellors found a convincing proof of the British resolve to keep aloof, and they went to war. Nothing less than a fully constituted military alliance might have dissuaded them. The Triple Entente was realistically planned but very inadequately implemented.

The French, British and Russian statesmen of the period have been charged with secrecy, and people in the United States are particularly apt to suspect them of shady machinations. I have approached many of the diplomats who then played an active part. Oddly enough, I was even a regular visitor at the German Embassy in London, and the counsellor and chargé d'affaires, Freiherr von Kühlmann, who was to take charge of the Wilhelmstrasse in 1917, spoke to me with little restraint. I can bear witness that it was no harder to follow whatever international negotiation was in progress than it is today. No press conference was held, it is true. But are press conferences of such great assistance? While knowing how to be discreet as to details, the protagonists never concealed their movements. Paul Cambon, held to be the very embodiment of old diplomacy, evinced utter frankness, a frankness never shown by such a man as Aristide Briand, for instance. I am at a loss to understand how Woodrow Wilson could have been caught unaware by the treaty intended to bring Italy into the war in April 1915, or by the territorial and political advantages simultaneously promised to the Imperial Government of Russia. It is true that neither the letters exchanged in 1891, 1892 and 1899 by the French and the Russian ministers and military leaders to define their countries' alliance, nor the correspondence between Sir Edward Grey and Paul Cambon in November 1912, which regularized the military consultations between the French and British general staffs, were ever made public. This was in accordance with the practice of the time. The treaties of Triple Alliance—incomparably more involved and detailed documents—were shrouded in mystery. It would not have helped our cause to give the potential enemy an insight into our very fragmentary arrangements. The content of the agreements negotiated with Sergei Sazonoff, the Foreign Minister of Tsar Nicholas II, and with Baron Sonnino, the Italian Foreign Minister, were not so very unlike the adjustments of national interests which today have to be made among nations.

III

The advent of new diplomacy can be dated from January 1920. Then the Council of the League of Nations met in Paris for the first time and a very numerous staff set to work under the guidance of Sir Eric Drummond (Lord Perth), Secretary-General of the League. Sir Eric Drummond was a regular Foreign Office diplomat, but of the weakest type. Later, he served as Ambassador to Rome. If the dispatches he sent from Mussolini's capital are ever made public otherwise than as excerpts from selected documents, his intellectual caliber and his strength of purpose will be evident to all. The French League officials under him were picked up very casually. Lord Robert Cecil (Lord Cecil of Chelwood) had forced upon Clemenceau's acceptance a French protégé of his, a businessman who had everything to learn about foreign affairs. "Since I do not care a brass for the League of Nations," said the French Premier, "I have conceded Lord Cecil's request." The old statesman was wrong. The League of Nations was out to destroy French policy as shaped in the Delcassé-Poincaré tradition, and it succeeded in this endeavor.

To listen to the talk current at the Geneva forum was a shocking experience. The adepts of the new faith believed that the political universe could be rebuilt on a set of very simple principles. For instance, they did not doubt that calculated economic interest would henceforward have greater weight with the mass of the people in enemy states and elsewhere than chauvinistic programs. Had it not been proved that victory did not pay? "Then why don't you let me have some little crumbs from your table?" retorted the German Foreign Minister Stresemann to an egregious lady friend of mine who had expatiated on that theme. The proponents of the League were convinced that public opinion crossing frontiers would surely assert itself in a tremendous volume against the government daring to violate the rules of the Covenant and retain its military establishments. The assumption was that the Weimar Constitution had turned the German people into peace-loving liberals.

It is a fact that during a period of some ten years, which opened with the defeat of Raymond Poincaré in the general election of 1924 and closed about two years after the death of Aristide Briand, everyone behaved as though the Covenant was indeed the regulator of international relations. The attempt of French diplomacy to resist the change which was fatally to weaken the enforcement of the Treaty of Versailles was overwhelmed. The Secretary-General of the Ministry of Foreign Affairs, Philippe Berthelot, was a strange person. He boasted that while paying tribute to the Geneva institution in high-sounding words he knew how to safeguard the long-tested concepts and positions of French foreign relations. That man has always baffled me. Whether he was more than an exhibitionist addicted to perpetual paradoxes, an opportunist, and a questionable connoisseur of exotic antiquities, remains a riddle. However that may be, his name must be linked with the disintegration of France's policy.

In theory, the Covenant of the League of Nations was consistent with the continuation of the alliances. Such is the meaning of Articles 20 and 21. But the spirit of that instrument was antagonistic to all separate groupings of power, and, except in special circumstances, favored general commitments entered into by all states, great and small alike. The American prejudice against old-fashioned political and military agreements also contributed to the decay of the alliances. And from the outset, the British Government shared to the full in the reaction against them. The Franco-British bond was the first to suffer. Then, under pressure from the United States, the London Foreign Office resigned itself to severing the alliance with Japan, though convinced at the time that Japanese nationalism and imperialism were thereby being given free rein. Alliance, therefore, gave way to a system of general engagements unrelated to any concrete situation. Its fundamental weakness has already been underlined.

Leaving aside problems of execution, can it be said that on paper, at any rate, the Covenant was a closely-woven document which made all acts of aggression punishable by the League? No. Preventive action by the Council? Article 11 provided for it. But the requirement for a unanimous vote sterilized the procedure. The solitary exception to the rule of unanimity was found in Article 15, dealing with the settlement of conflicts by the Council—conflicts which had actually broken out. Was Article 15 thus to be taken as an unshakable bulwark of peace? Let the reader ponder on paragraph 7 and enlightenment will come: "If the Council fails to reach a report which is unanimously agreed upon by the members thereof, other than the representatives of one or more of the parties to the dispute, the members of the League reserve to themselves the right to take such action as they shall consider necessary for the maintenance of right and justice." That, in fact, meant that governments with delegates on the Council could lawfully pass into the camp of the attacking nation! In the Covenant there was room for "lawful wars." Other gaps could be singled out.

Then, in what set of circumstances were the economic and military sanctions with which Article 16 dealt intended to become effective? Those sanctions were only to be enforced if the warmaker had not complied, before unsheathing his sword, with the long drawn out procedure before the Council (Article 15) or with the alternative method left to his choice—arbitration (Articles 13 and 14), if he had started waging war regardless of the three months delay (after the award by the arbitrators or the report by the Council) prescribed in Article 12.

None of the aggressors of 1931 to 1938, neither Japan nor Italy nor Germany, took the trouble to avail herself of the several loopholes which the Covenant afforded her to fight "lawfully." They struck their blows without bothering about Article 16 and its sanctions. They knew that the rule of unanimity stood in the way. (All the ingenuity, energy and brilliant intellect of Nicolas Titulesco had to be employed to get around that rule of unanimity in October 1935, when Fascist Italy invaded Abyssinia.) They knew also that economic sanctions carried out by fifty states—with no compulsory military sanctions to back them—could not hit the target. What a paradox that no permanent military committee should ever have had a lasting rôle in the Geneva framework, that the helpless permanent consultative military committee of 1920 faded away in 1928 without leaving a trace behind! Only a fully organized Franco-British alliance could have given vigor to the League in those great emergencies when war again threatened to engulf the world. It was not at hand. It was not to be revived in time. Moreover, in the tumult of ideas and men which followed the check inflicted on Poincaré's Ruhr policy in 1924, unscrupulous and perverse politicians—Laval, Flandin, Bonnet—came to the top and wielded an influence which would never have been theirs had not the traditional school been so drastically dismantled.

When the full history of the League is written, the most pathetic chapter will relate what was done from year to year to uphold the great illusions. Who first invented the idea of "pacts of non-aggression" whereby a promise to refrain from making war on one's neighbor without provocation was treated as a substantial consolidation of the European structure and rewarded accordingly? Was it not an open admission that there was such a thing as a right of aggression? The idea flowered in the futile Kellogg-Briand Pact of August 1928. What an ersatz for a guarantee of peace!

But the Treaties of Locarno of October 16, 1925, must be regarded as the most deceptive and dishonest instrument of the period. Article 4 in the treaty of mutual guarantee among Germany, Belgium, France, Great Britain, Italy (the so-called Rhineland Pact) and Article 1 in the arbitration treaties between Germany and Poland, Germany and Czechoslovakia, are worthy specimens of the whole compact. Article 4 is a contradiction in terms. On the one hand, England and Italy, the guarantors, were under the obligation immediately to come to the help of France in case of a flagrant violation by Germany of the clauses of the Treaty of Versailles on the demilitarization of the Rhineland. On the other hand, the guarantors undertook "to act in accordance with the recommendations of the League's Council," which implied procrastination. When the Rhineland Pact was bluntly challenged by Hitler in March 1936, the British guarantor remained inert. (It was out of the question, of course, that Italy should make good her guarantee.) And the Council of the League, on being called upon to intervene, coldly declared that the whole pact was *res inter alias acta* and that it was not concerned in the matter. Article I in the Locarno treaties of arbitration covertly ruled out territorial disputes. The said treaties did not apply "to disputes arising out of events prior to them and belonging to the past." It would not be easy to find a match for such trickery with words in the diplomatic records of the nineteenth century. After all, naked cynicism is to be preferred to hypocrisy. We were on safer ground before 1919. The true significance of treaties was not so well concealed behind a screen of make-believe.

The successors of Poincaré in France professed to trust

the trilogy "arbitration, disarmament, security;" nonetheless, they endeavored to get some reinsurance in the old style. But all the constructions between France and Poland, France and Czechoslovakia, among Czechoslovakia, Jugoslavia and Rumania, and among Jugoslavia, Rumania, Greece and Turkey, were mere castles of cards. Again, only the alliance of France and England could have given them some solidity; and that central pillar had long been pulled down.

An effective Franco-Russian alliance might have proved a substitute. But the contract to which Laval and Litvinoff appended their names remained a dead letter. The industrial and military growth of Russia frightened the French bourgeoisie out of their senses and the country was cut asunder. At last, in November 1936, after the Rhineland had been occupied by the Reichswehr, there was a general stampede toward the mode of international security deliberately destroyed fifteen years before. The London and Paris Governments formally undertook to stand together against a German attack; but British commitments did not extend beyond western Europe—a restriction which was not to disappear until the spring of 1939, six months after Munich. At this point the two great allies, with their eyes wide open at last to the impending peril, had to put up with the terrible consequences of their relative disarmament. The control of the air had slipped from the western Powers to Germany. The British Admiralty labored under an exaggerated sense of British impotence on the high seas. France had maintained an army, despite the bitter criticism which surged against her from the Anglo-Saxon world; but the all-pervading pacifism, born of the social schism, and an out-of-date High Command, made it an indifferent force. Salvation was tentatively sought in a policy of appeasement carried much further than in 1912–1914.

Making light of all Geneva formulas, Britain had once again played the game of the balance of power. Lord Lothian hailed Hitler's repudiation of the military clauses of the Treaty of Versailles in March 1935, and the reassertion of full German sovereignty over the Rhineland as healthy changes, harbingers of a well-poised Europe. So much for the achievements of the new diplomacy, in cursory review.

IV

The conduct of diplomatic business in the years between the two world wars deserves particular attention. The French and British Ambassadors lost a good deal of their importance in the great capitals. On the whole, they were abased to the level of ushers, messengers and mailboxes. Essential negotiations were no longer channelled into their care. The heads of government, or the foreign ministers who met in Geneva four times a year during the regular sessions of the League's Council and in the international conferences held outside Geneva, became the supreme negotiators. In wartime, when military and political problems are inextricably interwoven, this is inescapable. But, in wartime, the heads of government are more often than not men of outstanding stature, men who have successfully withstood the impact of tremendous events and proved their mettle. In peacetime, the ministers at the helm have won promotion in the electoral and parliamentary field. Most of them have not been tried elsewhere. They are not prepared to undertake tasks which call for a thorough knowledge of the political and economic forces at work in the Old and New Worlds, an understanding to be won only through many years of intense study and sustained observation.

It is true that in the interwar period career diplomats sometimes bowed more abjectly than their masters to the whims of uninformed public opinion. But their very mediocrity was the result of the new rôle assumed by the political chiefs. They were often selected because of their pliancy and servility. "Are you aware," said Jules Cambon to his brother Paul, "that nowadays we could not serve as ambassadors?" He meant that a diplomat more experienced in foreign affairs than the titular minister, and with definite opinions about his country's interest, was in honor compelled to revolt against a system where ignorance and foolhardiness had free rein.

The personal conversations Aristide Briand had with Stresemann, for instance, did not help international harmony. Philippe Berthelot was never able to find out from Briand what had really passed between him and the German leader in Thoiry in 1926. And what about Sir John Simon and Hitler, Ramsay MacDonald and Mussolini? I am told by an English friend who knows what he is talking about that the diplomatic correspondence pigeon-holed at the Foreign Office can never be printed. The archives issued in book form on the origins of the wars of 1870 and 1914 redound to the credit of the majority of the French diplomats concerned, even under the reign of Napoleon III.

This is not the place to discuss the functioning of the press in the era of emphatic idealism. Corrupt journalists in France and elsewhere have come in for their fair share of denunciation. But they did no greater harm than honest but naïve, ill-informed and wrongheaded editors. The speeches of Lord Lothian in the House of Lords and his articles in the London *Times,* signed and unsigned, are a sample. I hope they will be collected and published; they might convey a warning. Before the 1914 conflict, the press in western Europe probably gave its readers a more accurate picture of the political world than did the press during the period of the new diplomacy.

V

To sum up. The protective system created by France, Russia and England in the first decade of this century was in an embryonic state when Germany and Austria-Hungary resolved to force their hegemony upon the Continent by means of war. To deter them, a full-grown alliance of the three Powers was needed; and even such an alliance might not have kept the peace. The alliance remained a rudimentary one largely because British political thought had stagnated in the concepts of the Victorian Age. Nonetheless, the Triple Entente did not give way under the German onslaught. It was soon in full battle array, and but for the stupid policy followed toward Turkey and for the medieval structure of Russian society, it might have won through to victory without the full participation of American troops. It rested upon the convergence of French, Russian and British national interests. It was cast in the mold of political realism. The statesmen who brought it into being had assimilated the lessons of historical experience and were full of contempt for ideologies. Their task, as they understood it, was not to resettle the universe *sub specie aeternitatis* but to solve its problems empirically. They trusted that their successors of the next generation would meet new circumstances in a similar spirit and carry their work further. They believed that all panaceas were likely to make impossible the solutions which the problems of the near future required, and they considered any panacea positively dangerous.

The international system which came into its own in 1919–20 led the victors of the First World War to a new and more terrible ordeal, though the possibility of safeguarding European peace in 1934–36 was incomparably greater than in 1912–1914. A modicum of common sense and courage could have avoided the ordeal of the Second World War. But no success was possible unless the whole policy of the preceding fifteen years was abruptly reversed and the old alliances restored. In 1934, after Germany had slammed the door on the League, Louis Barthou did his utmost to precipitate the reversal. Perhaps a great opportunity was at hand. It vanished the day he was assassinated and Pierre Laval took office. Too many incompetent or unworthy men crowded governmental councils in Paris and in London to permit the great undertaking to be performed. Fools and knaves, in posts of influence, cannot but wreck the best conceived international system. And in 1935–1936 everything had to be assembled anew out of materials scattered on the lawns of Geneva.

The tentative proposals for a world security organization drafted at the Dumbarton Oaks Conference do not fall within the range of this article. However, it may be permissible to record that they conform to the lessons of the last thirty years and retain suprisingly little of the claims and the practices of the new diplomacy.

Disarmament was in the forefront of the program of the new diplomacy. The lasting military alliance of the Great Powers is at the hub of the organization contemplated at Dumbarton Oaks. The pretense of the new diplomacy was to rule the world on the basis of a set of universal principles embodied in a "covenant." No covenant has issued from Dumbarton Oaks. It was felt that the Atlantic Charter—which is in the nature of a geometrical limit—had better be retained. The grand alliance is centered on the enforcement, over many years, of the armistice conventions to be imposed upon Germany, Germany's satellites and Japan. Its feet are on the ground. And the national interests of the Great Powers are being submitted to an unbroken process of adaptation to make certain that centrifugal forces will not get the better of their concord. This makes for an experimental, yet well-defined system.

Does not even this brief glance at the recent past support the conclusion that only well-defined systems, geared to a concrete purpose and comparatively modest in scope, can take a firm grip on international realities? At the same time I think that this political world of ours will not always be denied, at any rate, the sort of stabilization which became the privilege of man under the Roman Caesars in the first three centuries of the Christian era.

In the pages above, new diplomacy has been dissected and found wanting. But it ought not to be inferred that we shall be confined to the narrow circle of possibilities within which old diplomacy moved before 1914. Whether and when the reign of undiluted international law will be made secure cannot be predicted. However, it is reasonable to stand by those two assertions.

Assuming that the grand alliance which emerged from the Dumbarton Oaks Conference is to withstand the test for the length of one generation, then some definite progress toward an international system built on more ambitious lines may well materialize. The ideology embodied in the 1919 Covenant did not have the flimsiest chance to succeed, 25 years ago. But let us rewrite history. Let us suppose that, 25 years ago, the war alliances had been continued and that all the revengeful preparations in Germany had broken upon that rock, between 1930 and 1940. In that case, is it so unreasonable to imagine that the tide of the time might have favored grandiose projects of pacification? The Covenant of 1919 could not be a point of departure. To some degree it might have been a point of arrival.

In the interval ahead, it will devolve upon public opinion to provide some of the checks and balances needed in the "security organization." To scorn and decry that kind of check and balance is only too easy. They cannot be relied upon at every turn and perhaps even on most occasions. Even so, it is fairly safe to lay down the general rule that no grand alliance of the Dumbarton Oaks model would prove capable of surviving many years against a rising volume of criticism in the principal democracies of the world. Against the eventual excesses of the system, this safeguard must not, therefore, be called inexistent.

❖ ❖ ❖

MILITARILY, politically and psychologically, a new chapter of world history began in the summer of 1945. Organized German resistance in Berlin ended on May 8, 1945. Two weeks before that, American and Russian troops had met on the Elbe River; three days later, they were to meet in Czechoslovakia. There were mountains of smoke and flame over Hiroshima and Nagasaki on August 6 and August 9—terrible exclamation points for the end of a page of history—and the capitulation of the Japanese homeland, without invasion and with 5,000,000 Japanese soldiers still under arms, took place on August 14. The San Francisco Conference which put into final form a plan for a new world organization had adjourned on June 26, 1945. The United States Senate ratified the treaty establishing United States membership in the United Nations organization, 89 to 2, on July 28. The period of American neutrality had ended.

John Foster Dulles' article "The General Assembly," published in October 1945, marks a divide in the history of the 25-year period which these articles from FOREIGN AFFAIRS outline. Dulles could speak with authority, for he had been one of the Advisors to the United State Delegation at San Francisco, and had a background of experience as Counsel to the American Commission to Negotiate Peace, 1918–1919, American representative at the Berlin debt conference, 1933, and the representative in 1944 of the Republican presidential candidate, Thomas E. Dewey, in fixing the basis for a bipartisan approach to foreign policy.

There was no disposition on any hand to pretend that the coming chapter opened with a clean white page. But the analysis of the past had (provisionally at least) been made, its lessons (it was hoped) learned. The machinery devised at San Francisco made action to enforce peace against the threat of an aggressor nation depend upon action by the Great Powers—in the first instance by the condition of Five Powers acting in unanimity; in the second instance (under Article 51) by "individual or collective self-defense" outside the Security Council if necessary. It was intended by this means that the peace would be kept, while agencies to change the conditions which produce wars set to work.

❖ ❖ ❖

THE GENERAL ASSEMBLY

By John Foster Dulles

"GOVERNMENT," said Alexander Hamilton, "ought to contain an active principle." Political institutions which advance the welfare of their human constituents achieve an internal state which is cohesive and dynamic and produce an external environment which is sympathetic and receptive. Those are the conditions needed for survival and growth.

The United Nations Organization is charged with positive tasks. That at least gives it a chance to be potent in the world. Whether the chance is realized will depend primarily upon the General Assembly. The rôle of the Security Council is predominantly negative. Its task is to stop the nations from public brawling. But it has no mandate to change the conditions which make brawls likely.

By contrast, the General Assembly, directly or through its Economic and Social Council, is charged: to promote international coöperation in economic, social, cultural, educational and health fields; to assist in the realization of human rights and fundamental freedoms for all, without distinction as to race, sex, language or religion and, in this connection, to establish a Commission on Human Rights; to promote higher standards of living, full employment and conditions of economic and social progress and development; to coördinate the policies and activities of what the Charter calls "specialized agencies," such as the World Bank and the Food and Agriculture Organization; to promote the development and codification of international law; to recommend measures for the peaceful adjustment of any situation likely to impair the general welfare or friendly relations among nations; to deal with colonial trusteeships for non-strategic areas; and, generally, to discuss any matter within the scope of the Charter—thus assuming the rôle of a "town meeting of the world," where public opinion is focused as an effective force.

The foregoing list is not complete, but it is enough to give an impression of the vast range of opportunities opened up to the Assembly. Also, it is enough to make apparent that the Assembly is given an invitation to chase rainbows.

The Assembly will have to pick its way carefully if it is to justify the responsibility which the Charter places upon it. It cannot afford the luxury of dabbling pleasurably in experimentation while looking to the Security Council to keep the peace. The tasks given it are, indeed, the primary means to peace. They must be undertaken with sober realization of such basic facts as these:

The Organization as now set up lacks the political powers usually relied upon to assure civic order. It would, therefore, be reckless to let peace depend upon the political functioning of the Organization. Its lack of political power is a semi-permanent fact. It is not due to an oversight on the part of the authors but to basic conditions which the Charter meritoriously reflects. Peace, accordingly, will depend primarily upon there being such fellowship among the member nations as will prevent the occurrence of a major war, while advancing the time when the Organization is made a more adequate political instrument.

Fellowship based on a war coalition usually disintegrates after the enemy's defeat. The way to prevent this from happening to the United Nations is to continue them in combat against the material and spiritual enemies of human welfare. To organize that combat is the primary responsibility of the General Assembly, and to do it successfully calls for a high order of statesmanship.

II

The political inadequacy of the United Nations Organization is obvious. Any political order which eliminates major violence over a long period of time must depend largely on laws defining, concretely and acceptably, what conduct is admissible and what is not. They need to be changed frequently so as to adapt the basic judgments they express to constantly changing conditions and so as to assure an acceptable balance among members of the society who incline to pull in different directions. The achievement of such a body of laws calls for a lawmaking process. And to enforce them there is required, in addition to the pressure of public opinion, a judicial system and a police force which will act automatically as the law directs.

At San Francisco these political goals could not be realized. The Charter itself does not establish rules of conduct which the Organization is committed to enforce. It does set forth certain general principles; but these are expressed as self-denying ordinances, not as law which the Organization enforces. The Security Council is under no injunction to move against violators. Some consideration was given to a possible prohibition of "aggression." But, as Mr. Eden observed at San Francisco, aggression is a concept without any precise agreed content. Some expansions and contractions of zones of national influence are reprehensible and some may be desirable. It is not easy to find words which would define and prohibit such exploits as the initial acts of Hitler and Hirohito and yet permit the expansion of the U.S.S.R. from the low ebb to which Russia fell under the Tsars and authorize Great Britain to "erase the sore spots in Europe" as now proposed by Professor Laski.

Of course, there are always people who would like to make change in the world illegal. Some are satisfied and selfish, some are morally shocked at the injustices which too often accompany change. That point of view prevailed in 1919, with the result that the Covenant of the League of Nations, by Article 10, went far toward identifying peace and morality with the maintenance of the status quo. Elihu Root, when he saw that proposed Article, said:

> It would be an attempt to preserve for all time unchanged the distribution of power and territory made in accordance with the views and exigencies of the Allies in this present juncture of affairs. It

would necessarily be futile. . . . It would not only be futile; it would be mischievous. Change and growth are the law of life, and no generation can impose its will in regard to the growth of nations and the distribution of power, upon succeeding generations.

The point of view thus expressed by Root prevailed at San Francisco. The Conference abstained from seeking to legislate perpetual peace by a single Article sanctifying for all time things as they are. Yet after that deceptively easy way had been rejected, the problem of legislating was seen as immensely difficult. The nations represented at San Francisco had not yet reached the position where they constituted a true community with common judgments about conduct. Also, many of them did not want the establishment of any law which would be superior to their own particular will and conscience. Wisely, then, the Conference did not attempt to write laws for the Organization to enforce. But it recognized that the omission to do this represented a grave inadequacy in the Organization as constituted.

The San Francisco Conference also failed to establish a body to make laws hereafter. There is to be an international court; but courts do not, or at least should not, legislate. The Assembly is directed to encourage the development and codification of international law. But neither it nor the Security Council is given any authority to enact law. The Security Council, although not intended to be a legislating body, might conceivably build up a body of international common law through its reasoned action in dealing with international disputes. In view, however, of the difficulty of the Security Council's taking any action at all, under its voting procedure, it is not likely that an adequate body of law could develop in this way in time to meet the necessities which will face the world.

Obviously, neither the Assembly nor the Security Council was qualified to be a legislating body. The voting procedure in both is so artificial that it could not be relied upon to reflect the predominant will of the world community. In the Assembly, where each state has one vote regardless of size, a small minority of the people in the world could impose its will on the great majority. In the Security Council, a single great state could block action desired by all the others. At San Francisco much was said about the inequity of a big Power like the United States or Soviet Russia having a right of veto. Very little was said about Liberia and Luxembourg, for example, having equal voting power in the Assembly with the United States and Soviet Russia. The fact is, the small Powers as well as the big ones are still tenacious of special privileges. So long as that is so, the Organization cannot be politically mature. This was a second grave inadequacy to which the Conference felt it must reconcile itself.

Since the San Francisco Conference was unable either to write rules of conduct into the Charter or to establish a lawmaking process, it could not establish any effective enforcement procedure. Neither courts nor policemen can do much without an adequate body of law behind them. A police force ought to work automatically, as previously instructed by law. With no laws, and with no body to make them, an international force cannot perform in the manner of a police force. No act of violence, however flagrant, will enable the military contingents of the World Organization to go into action immediately. In every case they must await the decision of the Security Council. The reaching of that decision is a quasi-legislative process, something like passing a special law which will be retroactive. Many political factors will have to be considered and, finally, the five Permanent Member States will have to concur.

In view of this, many persons at San Francisco felt that the Security Council might prove rather impotent so far as concerned its use of force. That was a third grave inadequacy to which the Conference felt it had to reconcile itself.

III

The political inadequacies described above are not of a kind that can be quickly remedied. It is not a matter of rewording the Charter. Underlying conditions caused the Charter to be what it is. Many went to San Francisco hoping for a Charter worded differently from the one which emerged. Few, at the end, would have had it very different from what it is.

The present Charter represents a conscientious and successful effort to create the best world organization which the realities permit. Of course, anyone who is free to disregard realities and to act only in the realm of theory can write a "better" Charter. A reasonably intelligent schoolboy could do that. The task of statemanship, however, is to relate theory to reality. Political institutions ought to come as close to theoretical perfection as is consonant with their vigorous survival in the existing environment. Orchids may be the perfect flower. But it is a waste of time to plant orchids in Iceland. That is what many peace planners would do.

The merit of the present Charter is not disclosed if one judges it merely as an abstract political document. That, as we have seen, discloses its inadequacies. The merit of the present Charter lies in the fact that its words correspond with the realities. What in the abstract are defects become in reality merits. The Charter was deliberately made to mirror the hopes and fears, the trusts and distrusts, the strength and infirmities of the human environment in which it must live and work.

Never before has such a project been tested on so tough a proving ground. The Holy Alliance was the exclusive handiwork of three rulers and their personal advisers. Its noble words bore no relation to realities. The Covenant of the League of Nations was essentially the work of five or six men. It was adopted after a committee of 20, made up of two representatives from each of five states and one representative of each of 10 states, had held 14 meetings. At San Francisco, 12 Committees, each composed of 50 delegates and about 100 advisers and technical assistants, met regularly over a two-month period. Literally hundreds of proposals were considered and every avenue of action was explored. The discussion took place in an atmosphere of freedom and in a spirit of responsibility. There was no compulsion and no veto except that imposed by the good judgment of the delegates.

The result is an honest document. Under present conditions it could not advantageously be made materially different. But some day it ought to be different. The delegates at San Francisco were almost unanimous about that. They gave much thought to how and when the Charter should be revised. Indeed, that was the most debated topic of the Conference. But the most earnest proponents of easy amendment did not want an immediate special Conference to review the Charter. About ten years should elapse, they felt, before a first review of the Charter could usefully be attempted. That was because they realized that what was needed could not be brought about by changing words, but only by changing the conditions which had made the present words inevitable. Such a change of conditions, they saw, would require well-directed efforts over a period of time.

IV

The present war has caused an unprecedented exhaustion, both human and material, and the end has not yet been reached. Even now that Japan has been beaten there may still be an aftermath of disturbances as peoples and régimes seek new equilibriums, internal and external. But the time will probably come when the dominant craving of men everywhere will be for a chance to recuperate and when no important group will tolerate a government whose policies risk a major war. During such a period even an inadequate organization can keep the peace. Exhaustion and fear will be its allies. But, judging by reason and experience, this will be merely an interlude between wars unless the time is used to good advantage.

The San Francisco Conference succeeded in transforming a war alliance into a political association containing the potentialities of growth. As we have seen, however, it was not able to establish an Organization possessing the political powers usually depended on to maintain civic order, because the United Nations are not yet sufficiently aware of their continuing interdependence, sufficiently homogeneous and sufficiently trustful of each other to delegate such powers to a new political organism.

We must not accept that condition as permanent. There are certain risks which only an adequate political institution will be able to eliminate. To seek the increased trust and sense of unity which will make the attainment of a more adequate political instrument possible should therefore be the major goal of the next era. Human nature is still such, however, that unity is achieved easily only through common effort for a common advantage. That is why external perils create coalitions and why those coalitions disintegrate when the common enemy is vanquished. That is why the present unity of the United Nations will vanish unless we find new enemies to fight together.

The great merit of the Charter is that it faces up to this reality. It creates an Organization which has "active principles." It brands intolerance, repression, injustice and economic want as common enemies of tomorrow, just as Nazi Germany and Imperial Japan have been the common enemies of yesterday. It proposes to its members that they stay united to wage war against those evils.

If this new call to battle arouses the enthusiasm of the peoples of the United Nations, and if they commit their best abilities to waging it successfully, the normal trend toward disintegration can be halted and a trend toward a greater sense of unity and greater friendship can be substituted. Thus can be gradually created the store of trust and confidence which must precede any adequate delegation of power to a world organization.

V

It is the General Assembly which will have to plan the campaign of the United Nations against their newly proclaimed enemies. The Charter offers many possible objectives, not all of which can be pursued immediately. The Assembly must make an orderly choice, and it must take into account not merely the relative merits of the goals themselves but the degree to which the pursuit of them will produce the by-products of increased fellowship between the member nations. Various considerations will need to be weighed in this connection.

It is very important, for example, particularly during the first years when the war coalition will tend to disintegrate, that the Assembly choose projects which are likely to succeed. The possibility of preserving unity between the United Nations will depend above all upon a quick practical demonstration that, by staying together, they can accomplish desired results which otherwise would be impossible. A joint success brings co-workers to a generous appreciation of each other, while a failure leads to recrimination and disunity. Therefore, it is of the utmost importance that the Organization in its early stages should embark on undertakings where success is likely.

It is important, too, that the goals first chosen by the Assembly should include some which will arouse popular interest and backing. Much technical work can usefully be done on an international basis, but the compilation of scientific data on meteorological and hydrographic matters does little to promote the fellowship of peoples. Though such tasks should of course continue to be undertaken, they are no substitute for activities which will develop the enthusiastic loyalty and support of the peoples of many lands and afford a peaceful outlet for their dynamic impulses. The Assembly should seek psychological substitutes for military warfare. It must do some things that will be dramatic.

The Charter recognizes in Article 55 that "conditions of stability and well-being are necessary for peaceful and friendly relations among nations." Economic distress and social maladjustments give evil men the opportunity to gain leadership and to menace the peace of the world. In choosing its objectives, therefore, the Assembly should utilize its grant of authority and act to ameliorate the economic and social conditions which help to breed war.

Future peace depends above all upon accord between the Great Powers. The Charter recognizes this by forbidding the Security Council to take any enforcement measures unless the "Big Five" are in agreement. But while this emphasizes the importance of harmony, it does not assure that harmony will exist. Of course, the Great Powers themselves will primarily determine the character of their relations with each other; but the Assembly can contribute to the accord between them which is necessary if the Security Council is to function. Negatively, it can refrain from using its privileges, notably that of discussion, in a way to exploit and magnify the minor differences which will inevitably arise among the Great Powers. Affirmatively, it can select tasks upon which the Great Powers can readily unite.

Since the smaller nations control the Assembly, there will be a natural tendency for them to organize its social and economic activities so as to benefit themselves at the expense of the larger members. Of course, the strong must help the weak, if only because their self-interest is served by preventing anarchy. But such help, of which UNRRA is an example, should be left to the initiative of the strong powers. The Assembly should consciously sponsor activities which bring the larger powers to like an international way of life and thereby promote harmony between themselves and the small powers. It will succeed in this if it chooses activities of a kind which will be affirmatively advantageous to all.

Other factors which the Assembly should consider in deciding on its initial program could be mentioned. But even the above tests show how hard its choice will be if it is to be successful. To illustrate:

One mandatory task of the General Assembly is to encourage the development and codification of international law. This is of extreme importance, since, as we have seen, lack of law is a principal weakness of the present situation. However, to achieve a body of written law enforceable against states as such is a most difficult project. "The Federalist" said that thinking men would at once dismiss it "as idle and visionary," and added: "The principle of legislation for sovereign states, supported by military coercion, has never been found effectual. It has rarely been attempted to be employed, but against the weaker members."

There is, however, an alternative to legislation for states, namely, the adoption of laws to operate upon individuals. This avenue of development is being explored today, when considerations of justice have brought the United Nations to postulate the existence of an international law enforceable against individual Germans. The time is thus propitious to begin to frame international law which will not be merely applicable retroactively but which will operate in the future to deter individuals anywhere from wilfully or maliciously plotting or inciting international disorder. Also, once individual duties are made a subject of international law, it becomes logical also to define the international aspects of individual rights. By promoting that development the General Assembly could begin to give practical content to the affirmation by the peoples of the United Nations of their "faith in fundamental human rights, in the dignity and worth of the human person."

If an effort were made to develop international law for individuals rather than for states, then the criteria we have mentioned could largely be met. There would be a good chance of some success. The effort would be dramatic and would awaken popular interest. A cause of war might be curbed. The effort would be one in which the nations, large and small, could be expected to work together in harmony. It was the sponsoring Powers which, at San Francisco, by one of their "four-power amendments," unhesitatingly and enthusiastically determined that a major purpose of the Organization should be to promote and encourage "respect for human rights and fundamental freedoms for all without distinction as to race, sex, language, or religion."

Another task for the General Assembly is the solution of international problems of an economic character. The conditions of trade and finance ought to be such that nations can acquire, on a fair exchange basis, the food, raw materials and other products which do not lie within their own resources and which they need for the maintenance of tolerable standards of living. The Bretton Woods plan for a World Bank and Monetary Fund is an effort to solve this problem primarily through its financial aspects. That approach alone will be inadequate, for neither credit nor monetary arrangements can permanently substitute for a near balance in the exchange of goods and services. The Assembly can undertake a broader and sounder approach. The effort probably would not arouse popular enthusiasm. Also it might frighten, even though needlessly, the more productive countries. Nevertheless, a practical success can be achieved along this line, and it ought to be possible to achieve it on a basis advantageous to all. A success here would do much to eliminate some of the underlying causes of war.

The General Assembly is authorized to promote international coöperation in the field of health. Of course, disease is not in a primary sense a cause of war. Indeed, a cynic might say that to reduce mortality from disease increases the risk of war from population pressures. On the other hand, a successful combat against disease, particularly the epidemics which inspire general dread, can arouse popular interest and give a practical demonstration of the advantages of international action. The Rockefeller Foundation, now in its thirty-third year, works in various fields—health, natural sciences, social sciences and the humanities. Its labors which have produced the most tangible results and have brought it world-wide good will have been those in the field of international health. The Assembly could, with advantage, consider that experience in deciding what lines of effort can be expected to produce a demonstrable success. The field is one where all the Powers could advantageously work together, pooling for peace the achievements of their scientists, as they pooled them in war to produce the atomic bomb

Such are some of the problems which the Assembly will face in planning its contribution to peace. The San Francisco Conference was, in a sense, the first meeting of the Assembly. It will now approach its concrete tasks with zeal born of a first success and with discretion born of responsibility. The meeting at San Francisco went far to assure a successful transition from the unity of war to a new unity of peace. Trust and confidence, somewhat in suspense during the early days of the Conference, developed strongly toward the end. Hard, competent work resulted in a good start being made. The Conference can be said to have done much to reverse the normal trend toward postwar disintegration.

It cannot be taken for granted, however, that future meetings of the Assembly will be like that of San Francisco.

Success there was due above all to the millions of individuals throughout the world who directed upon that Conference the power of their spirit. They put the immediate participants under the strongest possible moral pressure not to fail. Without that constant pressure the Conference might have broken up on any one of several issues, or it might have ended with merely perfunctory results.

The present danger is that the millions who compelled the achievements of San Francisco will now relax, feeling that the battle has been won and the Organization can carry on alone from this point. That would be disastrous. Organizations are incorporeal; they have no will, no mind, no soul. They live only through human beings who implement them. The individuals whose wills and brains and spirits will animate the Assembly of the United Nations will need the same sort of stimulus that made the San Francisco Conference a success. Their task will not be mechanistic. It will be to select, plan, organize and lead great works of human betterment. They can do that successfully only in response to the expressed wishes and demands of their fellows. Thus, in the final analysis, the peoples of the world will decide their own fate.

❖ ❖ ❖

It is instructive to note that the thought of the two great geographers of our time, the Englishman Sir Halford J. Mackinder, and the American Isaiah Bowman, revolves about the same central theme—the relationship of ideal and actuality in politics. Bowman, President of the Johns Hopkins University and for 20 years before that Director of the American Geographical Society, has taken a leading part in the practical tasks of peacemaking after two World Wars—as Chief Territorial Specialist of the American Commission to Negotiate Peace at the Paris Conference in 1919, as Chairman of the Territorial Sub-Committee of the State Department Committee on Post-war Problems, 1941–43, as Special Adviser to the Secretary of State 1943–1945, and as one of the Advisers to the United States Delegation at Dumbarton Oaks and San Francisco.

Both Bowman and Mackinder have exerted a great influence on the minds of many students, far outside the classroom, in addition to contributing to the shaping of political events. But there is likewise an interesting contrast between the two men. Mackinder's thought is most characteristic when embodied in a grand metaphor—in one of those poetic generalizations of geographical fact which have helped open the imaginations of the men of the twentieth century to a more accurate view of the round world, but which in other hands can also tend to dissolve into the gigantesque, or the cloudy. Bowman's thought centers on a point—human beings. It is in people that he looks for the synthesis of ideal and reality. The boundary line is "home;" the study of it embraces man's past history, current situation, future ideal. But the study has a specific purpose. "A boundary has to be here, not hereabouts." Bowman's thought is always concrete. This, too, is in a great tradition—that of Burke and Holmes.

The student who wishes to examine Bowman's writings in detail must be referred for the most part to specialized works such as "The Pioneer Fringe" and "Limits of Land Settlement." Some of his most interesting papers, however, are reports or speeches given on particular occasions, or occasional studies like the following, published in the January 1946 issue of Foreign Affairs under the title "The Strategy of Territorial Decisions."

❖ ❖ ❖

THE STRATEGY OF TERRITORIAL DECISIONS

By Isaiah Bowman

THERE is a profound psychological difference between a transfer of territory and a change in a trade treaty or pact of international coöperation. Territory is near and plain and evokes personal feelings and group sentiments. To a people conscious of its individuality, "how sweet the silent backward tracings." Such people endow the land itself with a mystical quality, hearing revered ancestors, the authors of past grandeurs and the doers of heroic deeds, speak from their graves in its soil. To all classes, landscape is an essential part of home. Enshrined in every national literature are the changing moods and compositions of river, mountain, plain, forest and shore. All the familiar techniques of living are involved in the complex of feeling, remembered experience and imagination surrounding place and home.

It is title to sentiments like these, and not merely to so-and-so many square miles of land, that is transferred when there is a change of boundaries and rule.

No such serious questions of sentiment or prestige are involved in writing a short-term military alliance or a commercial treaty dealing with goods and profits or a compact embodying the generalities of a world order; for these are not among the spiritual intimacies of life. The links between place and people are countless. The fact that one was born in a certain spot pursues one throughout life. The first question in most census schedules is, "Where do you live?" In common thought today, as in the earliest folklore, one's dwelling place is the center of the universe. Thus national leaders must be especially alert to territorial losses and gains, for they touch the main nerve center of popular feeling.

The dim curves of the future are more likely to be perceived correctly if we bring to the settlement of territorial issues a knowledge of sentiment, tradition and changing national fortunes of the past. Even so, such knowledge is inert and unproductive unless it is combined with judgments based upon a wider political sophistication than that created by mere possession of statistical data and formal historical training. In politics, action must be based on mixtures of right and wrong. The scholar says, "You must keep such-and-such facts in mind whatever you do." The busy official is tempted to ask simply, "What shall I do?" Neither is enough. Always and everywhere a decision about territory requires the examination of an existing situation respecting power. Behind that situation lies history, and ahead of it stretches the ideal of a fair solution. When a decision is to be made, three factors should be taken—past history, current situation, future ideal—and a judgment expressed jointly upon them. Such a judgment is neither more nor less than an opinion, based on experience with human nature, as to what participating leaders and nations are likely to do or may be persuaded to do in the interest of that recognized fairness which is one of the essential elements of a stable peace.

II. THE RISKS

However fair a given territorial solution may be, the seeds of trouble will generally remain. Risk can never be eliminated from territorial transfers; for the past will always be raked, in moments of potential change, to find arguments which sustain claims to the recapture of territory once held. A contemporary incident suddenly highlights an historic cause, or is made to do so. Population mixtures provide abundant opportunities for oppression; and the oppressed of yesterday, we have painfully discovered, often turns oppressor. Such mixtures are unavoidable in many border zones because national frontiers could not possibly be made to follow every ethnic and linguistic intricacy. Thus a boundary, however logically drawn, remains a thing of conflicting local hopes and fears. We have seen situations in which a man, to be secure, must have two houses, one on either side of a boundary, so that he can flee persecution wherever its source. The threat of a change in boundary or in the form of government has led hundreds of thousands to live, in a sense, on both sides of a boundary—their homes on one side and their bank accounts on the other. It is hard to improve on the child's school essay: "The Boundary is an imaginary line, drawn through Ireland, between the good people and the bad. If it were not for the Boundary, Uncle Joe would send us a goose for Christmas."

That there is a general lack of confidence in the territorial settlements which are made is shown by the general aversion to giving them guarantees of permanence. We suspect that we may be heading for the rocks and so leave the escape hatch open. This practically invites agitation for change from both sides concerned—or from several sides, when the interests of more than two nations are involved. Witness the general feeling in 1937 that perhaps it was right, after all, that Austria should be joined to Germany. We disliked the manner in which the change was effected, and we abhorred the agent who effected it; but some eminent men, including a few scholars, had favored the change for years; and anyway the world feared war if it acted against it. Witness, again, the still tangled skein of Palestine, where an interweaving of irrelevancy, bad judgment, personal differences, national election considerations here and in England, political whipsawing, fear, suspicion and *realpolitik* have all but excluded morality, fairness and reason. It is a major issue, yet virtually all leaders talk on both sides of the subject, as if the answer lay only in expediency, self-interest and compromise. The United States may be faced with the question whether it will undertake to guarantee the outcome of this play of passion and special pleading.

Consider the difficulty of dealing with remote peoples in any event. To prescribe for them as to forms of government, or to take away territory here and add it there, is to suppose a careful analysis of a people, their institutions, motivations, range of political experience, depth of sound traditions, solidity of character. This may seem easy when a people is far away. Our domestic experience should warn us of our limitations. What American can predict the moods and acts of even the United States? Who knows our country region by region well enough for that?

Rival social and political systems add to the complexity of the problem. Each former political satellite of Nazi Germany is now a house divided against itself. All nations join in proclaiming "democracy" but all are passionately divided as to meanings. A "democracy" set up with Soviet support does not look like American democracy at all. The situation of many countries is like that of a certain sequoia tree in the Yosemite National Park. Two hundred feet above the ground the crown was once knocked off by lightning, and upon the scarred and weakened main stem a new trunk began to grow and has now reached a height of at least fifty feet. It is vigorous and symmetrical, but its survival is conditioned by the old storm-broken trunk below. If there was ever a time to "think in things, not words," as Justice Holmes advised, it is now. The trunk and roots matter most, not the lovely crown about which it is so easy to write fine words.

Territorial settlements involve all the complexities of civilization—historical fitness, population mobility, resource distributions, tax bases, divisions of agricultural fertility zones, and a thousand other considerations. Territory is not an abstraction. Unfortunately, nations cannot be separated approximately. A boundary has to be here, not hereabouts.

Critics have said that the Paris Peace Conference failed because the peacemakers were preoccupied with boundaries when their minds should have been on essential economic arrangements. As a participant, I know of no such preoccupation. The economic arrangements were bad and the subsequent failure was inevitable, whatever boundaries were delimited. Not the fragmentation of Europe but the rise of economic autarchy was the root of the trouble in the 20's and 30's. The choice between economic advantage and political independence, moreover, was often made deliberately.

In many parts of Europe the feelings of two or more nationalities about the same piece of territory are irreconcilable. If there is to be peace in such cases, it must be imposed from without. Each will oppress the other if it has the opportunity. The overlapping sovereignties and remembered wrongs of the past feed the "eternal light," which burns not only to remind men of past heroisms but to light the pathway of the irredentists and would-be (in turn) oppressors. Sometimes, of course, boundary disputes are settled without bitterness. When, for example, the last boundary problem between Colombia and Venezuela reached the point of negotiation, the Colombian Minister of Foreign Affairs proposed that the matter be handled as between two gentlemen. Air photography had revealed advantages to both sides, because the streams ran in a way that neither supposed. In a rare spirit of give-and-take, a settlement was made. But there were few people in the district and none in the essential part of it. There were no local votes, no ideas afloat, no trends, no rival cultures. Only empty land permits of so neat a solution.

It is a grave error to suppose that there is one right and stable solution to every territorial problem, a solution to be found, adopted and forgotten. Time and life produce their unpredictable changes. At one point in a prolonged discussion in a recent conference, a fatigued member said to another, "Words, words, words!" to which the reply was made, "Yes, words, words, words; but underneath the words are meanings, and underneath the meanings is life." He meant changing and unpredictable life. As life and time surge forward, the meanings change and the words (the political agreements) change with them, logically or by free negotiation in a few cases, by force in many others.

The dream of many simple minds is that disputed territory can be divided according to some self-contained scheme of logic or set of generally accepted moralities. This notion overlooks the truth that life which has become static is death. Moreover, scientific discovery is a perpetually unsettling factor. No sooner has jet propulsion set tongues wagging about the need for a "completely new strategy" than the atomic bomb and the proximity fuse vastly extend the range of possibilities. Every time a new weapon is introduced or a new technique devised, a new appraisal must be made of every scrap of territory we own or may desire to control internationally or otherwise. It is fundamentally wrong, in my opinion, to think that a system of world coöperation or international defense can minimize the importance of territory. Ownership and hence boundaries remain scientifically valid and of first importance in a world not yet united—in fact profoundly divided—with respect to forms of social organization and control.

History warns us of the danger of overconfidence. In 1916, when we bought the Danish West Indies, we most unwisely relinquished rights based upon discovery and exploration in Greenland, though for years Peary had hammered on aviation possibilities with the persistence of a zealot. It will soon appear whether our occupation and use of Greenland in a time of temporary Danish helplessness will give us future standing (internationally or otherwise) in this part of the front yard of the hemisphere. Our painful experience with the Japanese mandated islands in the Pacific is so recent as to warn us that territorial dispositions call for the highest statesmanship we can command. The historical record of the judgments of prime ministers and parliaments, presidents and congresses, is not reassuring.

England's historic moat was crossed by enemy airplanes in World War I. Grave pronouncements followed: in a military sense the English Channel, it was said, had been obliterated. And in the spring of 1940 this conclusion seemed about to be confirmed. But Hitler did not invade England, and the moat had something, indeed much, to do with it. English ships with their unmatched fighting crews had control of the Narrow Seas and menaced every continental foreshore held by the enemy. The factors in what happened in the summer and autumn of 1940 were many, variable and complex, but there was one factor present in every new and swiftly evolving phase of the situation—twenty miles of salt water.

It is clear from examples dotting the pages of history that

some crucial territorial arrangements have been wise and others unwise from either the long-range or the short-range point of view. Critics of the Alaska Purchase, limited in outlook, wrote "Seward's Folly." British top leaders, officially advised, let go of Helgoland. Tricky in their effects on judgment are neat distributional maps, whether of oil, or the differentials of population growth, or the production of steel, or the location of rare and critically important minerals. An examination of technical data will never supply the key to wisdom. To reach a wise decision *a political composition* is required. If it proves correct we call it statesmanship. The cynic will ask whether any decision that will be tested by human behavior in the future is more than a guess. I suggest we are more likely to guess rightly if we are thoroughly at home with the possibilities.

III. SOME COMPONENTS OF POLITICAL JUDGMENTS

Territorial settlements usually are based less on principle than on political power judgments of the moment. Probably no major peace settlement came nearer the mark of principle than the European territorial settlements of 1919. The boundary network established at that time fitted the complicated patterns of speech, folk groupings and sense of nationality more closely than ever had been the case before in modern history. But judgments upon the 1919 boundaries, and upon those now in the making, are not like the judgments of a court rendered according to an accepted code of law. Decisions in this field are not based on abstractions of social experience or generally accepted moral theories. Their nature is political. Justice cannot weigh "historical rights" blindfolded and decree consistent action.

Negotiation has flexible limits and involves opportunistic appraisal to a high degree. If policy makers come to a conference unprepared to discuss social and political ideas which are in conflict within a given territory, they are unprepared to frame a decision respecting the transfer of such territory. The same sort of thing is true, of course, even of international conferences that deal with subjects like food, aviation and international organization. They are simple only by title; in reality, they deal with bundles of things, with overlapping and often contradictory forces and conditions. All international actions have in them a high degree of opportunism, called euphemistically "the logic of events." We proclaim principles and strive toward ideals; but events do not wait upon mature reflection. As a result, almost all broad international political decisions, whether upon territories or otherwise, are hurried, tentative and incomplete.

A new chapter in our domestic politics has been opened by our wider and more active participation in world affairs. In launching our barque upon a wider sea of responsibility we will do well to reëxamine the rigging of our national political processes. No sooner do officials take a position or make a decision than they begin to justify it, backed by the power of an official propaganda machine supported by the taxpayers, who thus pay to be told how right their government has been. The official attitude is defensive, protective and self-justifying. No one praises democracy or any other system more highly than those who are its salaried beneficiaries. In the case of territorial decisions, the scope of political dialectic is enlarged by the nature of the problems involved. As we have seen, they are characteristically gray, not white and black. As a rule there *is* something to be said on both sides. A thousand wait their turn at the public tribune for one who, looking for truth, delves quietly into the nature of a tortured situation. One thing only can be counted on—the brevity of public attention and interest. It is smart to be "on the beam" of current interest. No use talking about diplomacy as an art when the public wants to know who was responsible at Pearl Harbor.

A major factor in the political discussion of foreign problems is that many of our domestic racial groups offer support or threaten reprisals upon candidates for public office according as they promise to favor or oppose group programs for achieving some supposed benefit for distant homelands. In many local political situations such foreign groups hold the balance of power. We all want peace; but each group wishes its own kind of peace settlement. Besides their attachments to particular places, groups have preferences as to forms of government and social systems. Every political wind, especially at election time, brings into the arena of national debate the clamor of noisy minorities, with two loyalties, not one. War with Italy was a clean-cut affair for our Government by comparison with the subsequent tangles when, in the moment of victory, the problem of Italy was transferred from the military front westward to Chicago, New Haven and New York. Then the politician began looking over his shoulder.

Group dissension over every troublesome territorial problem weakens the public resolution to support the settlement of it. And the domestic consequences of these divisions will be closely watched abroad. We have become the mainstay of international organization for peace; but foreign observers know that the national tide, now running high in the direction of accepting world responsibilities, will surely recede if we put national power—which includes American bayonets—behind programs designed merely to capture the Italian vote or the Polish vote or the Jewish vote. We should sharply challenge a course of action that weakens the determination of the American people as a whole to support the world order. Unless the majority insist that their public servants rise above these group interests we risk losing by domestic political trading what we thought we, along with the other nations of the world, had won at the San Francisco Conference.

A new map of the United States would enable us to undertake a much deeper political self-analysis. The map would show the chief centers of foreign population and their voting habits. What has been the record of the Congressmen who represent such groups? What have been the decisive preëlection issues? What were the constituents promised? We cannot say that such conflicts of opinion in our democracy cancel out, on the ground that main national decisions are made upon higher and broader plateaus of interest. The democratic line known as the "diagonal of contending varieties" has not always been extended in the right direction. Prohibition proved this, and so did the events of December 7, 1941, only five months after Congress had continued selective service with not one vote to spare. The nature of the political process is exceedingly complicated. Now one force, now another, one guided by a wise leader, the other unguided and uncertain, moves the finger that writes our fate upon the wall.

We cannot expect largeness of vision and disinterested points of view from groups that act on the urge of remembered wrongs "over there." We wish those wrongs settled in the light of what we see, share and dream in free America. We expect the citizen to be rooted *here* and his passions to be poured out in the national interest of America. To be sure, the two promptings often coincide. But we participate in settling territorial problems not for the purpose of favoring a given group abroad, regardless of the rights of other groups, but for the purpose of establishing the fairest and most lasting situation attainable. Czechoslovak leaders recently oriented the policies of their nation in the direction of Moscow, and I suppose this to be wise. What is the preferred orientation of the 300,000 or more American citizens of Czechoslovak blood? The present government in Poland believes itself capable of digesting the troubles that will surely beset the country if it swallows all of the territory east of the Oder. When faced with the imperatives of a practical settlement, how far shall we support the sentimental "backward tracings"?

The paradox is that if we make boundaries stable by international agreement we may confirm the injustice of an arbitrary or careless decision, while if we make them mobile we invite every minority group to agitate continuously, often in specious terms. Over-all prosperity and stability and a free life within the framework of collective responsibility are objects that can be achieved in every corner of the world only *after* they are first achieved in the round or in general terms. We cannot achieve molecular peace and justice everywhere by a stroke of the pen or by any sort of organization or wisdom that we know. The touchstones of success for a world organization are that it shall have a workable structure and that it shall generate a coöperative will to see justice *become* paramount. If we are not alert to the danger, the territorial settlements ahead of us will tend to draw attention away from other main issues. I do not assert that every detailed decision will induce a step backward toward isolationism, but I fear it may be so. There is a risk that groups may attempt to capture the victory for objects different from those that only time and sustained coöperation will achieve. If we succeed as a united people in our big job in the world, particular boundaries and individual minorities will become, we hope, less and less important.

IV. THE STRATEGIES OF PEACE

The decision about Greenland referred to above was taken by a mind not alerted to aviation as an instrument both for keeping the peace and for making war. Without pretending that the list is complete, let us look at some of the things to which we should be alerted today. Pending territorial decisions will be made within the framework of some such composition of strategies of peace as the following.

The grand international strategy is to work for and win a peace of justice, buttressed by coöperative will and enterprise. The national aim of the United States should be to demand insistently the application of the *principle of fairness,* and to be its foremost exemplar. It is a principle understood in all languages; it is the white thread running through all systems of law. It is today's shining ideal, as it has been the ideal of sage and saint for millenniums past.

Are we up to a task set in these terms? Or will we allow trifles to steal in and monopolize our minds now that the immediate danger is past? Can the national will be sustained in the rare air of a universal humanity? We have set ourselves to perform a task of heroic proportions. The diversities of men and systems are not to be levelled by fine words or dissolved by concentrations of power appropriate for war. They are not merely differences of dress or manners, but include different systems of law rooted in profoundly different social experiences and environments, different codes of ethics, different degrees of inherent compassion, and wide and deep contradictions of purpose: élite vs. mass, colony vs. metropole, Communism vs. free-enterprise, democracy vs. totalitarianism. We have a long road ahead of us before the tentatives of our present collective will bear fruit in universal good.

There is not one strategy of peace but many strategies, and technology has recently multiplied them. It was so in war. "I know how to defeat Japan," said one top military commander in 1942. "Sink her ships!" We sank the ships, but this was only one of several routes to the heart of Japanese power. While the Charter of the United Nations is the chief instrument of our present hopes, the fact remains that territories are to be disposed of before proof can be provided that the United Nations have the will to implement the Charter. What tests of political democracy can be used to determine the will of a presently inert people? Whose scheme of social organization is to be adopted in the trusteed areas of the world? Tragic internal conflicts can arise among politically immature peoples if social and political experiments are inaugurated by outside powers of differing ideologies and aims.

Strategy based upon the military situation of the moment has proved disappointing. It was asserted repeatedly in the period 1939–1944 that territorial decisions must wait until the end of the war, when they could be resolved in a general settlement worked out in the calm atmosphere of peace. Events did not arrange themselves so conveniently. The successes of the Red Army had repercussions up and down the breadth of Russia and enlarged the limits of what it was practicable for Moscow to ask while contracting the limits of what it was practicable for Russia's allies to try to deny her. The Kremlin could borrow Clemenceau's words of 1919: Blood has given us the right to judge. It became the Curzon Line and nothing less! The world—including the Polish Government in London—could talk, but there stood the Soviet Armies, and they and they alone could advance into Poland. A long turning of thought followed, and the world was prepared to concede Polish claims to

East Prussia, provided population transfers could be made in an "orderly and humane" manner. Danzig and the Oder frontier followed.

In all this, who has given thought to the Polish capacity for self-government? Who has reviewed judicially the twenty-year acts, servitudes and party fragmentations of the *Sejm?* What difficulties were met in welding together the three Polands which had been thrown together in 1919? Now there is a fourth "Poland" in east Prussia and a fifth "Poland" east of the Oder. Will the Polish national temperament change overnight and permit the orderly evolution of local self-government, the wise and patient building of a democratic commonwealth? One hesitates to ask these questions for fear of being accused of satire. But we can understand the Russian side of the argument, for have we not also bought with our blood bits of territory over the vast expanses of the Pacific, and do we propose, other and peaceful means failing, to buy them over again at possibly greater cost? This is not sweet peace, if you will, but rather the military strategy of the outpost; but its purpose can be peace, and a coöperative peace if we can put our grand strategy through.

The strategy of minerals—occupying one of the larger areas of political interest—has been gravely neglected by our higher commands. In this field we back and fill because no one who has taken the time required to study the essentials possesses the authority to formulate a policy we can stick to. Most territories have mineral possibilities. Yesterday Saudi Arabia was a land of picturesque Bedouin; today it is an oil empire. Wherever there are rare and critical minerals, useful alike in peaceful industry and in war, there we are bound to inquire who owns them and to what political design they may contribute. Is access easy? Is the government stable? Would costs be reasonable? What are the alternative sources of supply? Are substitutes likely to be developed by scientific research? If the agencies of the American Government and American business are at cross purposes, neither can take the firm position in these situations which is desirable from the viewpoint of the national interest. American business in the foreign field has too often not known when it would be deserted by its own Government.

Population growths set the framework of another strategy. Bismarck's fear of the Polish mother is now shared in a wider sense by those concerned with the differentials of birth rates in the various nations of Europe. Will a possible rise in the standard of living in the Soviet Union, for example, have the expected effect of a drop in the present high birth rate there? We have been told that if Russia pays due attention to public health, she will have a population of more than 250,000,000 by 1970. If the projections of the experts are realized, the balance of population will shift drastically away from western Europe to eastern Europe. Granted the accuracy of the statistical facts and the prediction based upon them, what can be done about the situation? France and Great Britain will subsidize births, whatever the government in power or its social policy. But government assisted population growth is still in the experimental stage. Wrapped up in the experiment is a prior question: Shall an attempt be made to discriminate on a stock-selection basis, or will the worst stock inevitably be encouraged at the expense of the declining best? To breed for numbers, not quality, may be all that is possible. Thus it remains to be seen whether the policy of stimulating births spells strength or weakness for the nation practising it.

Closely tied with the strategy of population numbers is the question of migration. A free movement of peoples on a nondiscriminatory basis is persistently desired by allegedly overcrowded countries. The besetting fear of Australia serves as example of the other side of the argument. What shall be the choice between these opposite viewpoints? Has the United States a position in the dispute, now that its former policy of total Chinese exclusion is annulled in favor of a quota so small it does not matter? If the population pressure in China and India is so great, must the White Australia Policy be revised? There seems to be a fundamental error in the thesis that there should be a free and nondiscriminatory flow of population across frontiers, and since both theory and the actual conditions on which it is based now occupy places in the field of practical politics the problem is worth fuller analysis.

The theory of a mobile population has two grand divisions. The first is *Lebensraum,* in which space and culture are merged in a mystical relation that identifies force as a beneficent agent of fate. Once the higher culture prevails, who cares how it was made to prevail? In adopting the policy of *Lebensraum,* the Nazis rested their case both upon "the changing facts of life" and upon the theory that good ends justify the use of arbitrary means. Since the thesis inexorably implies the use of force, the seeds of tragedy are broadcast from the start.

In the present situation of the world, tragically divided as it is by hates and conflicting systems of government, the forced transfer of populations holds intensified dangers. Using an elaborate machinery based upon thorough research, the German Government before and during World War II moved nearly 500,000 people out of both marginal and distant territories and settled them within the bounds of the enlarged Reich. Since then, the worsening of health conditions, means of transport and food supplies, plus other changes, have made the lot of forced emigrants even more difficult. The ideal of tolerance is gone; attainment of the goal of "orderly and humane transfer" seems almost impossible. The bank of hatred will continually receive new deposits as the fury and woe caused by brutal transfers are fully experienced. The importance of boundaries will not be minimized by this procedure, but maximized; everywhere they will be thought to separate "the good people" from "the bad people."

The second grand division of the theory of mobility supposes that relief from home crowding will follow emigration. Clearly, however, there would be no appreciable relief for China if seven millions of Chinese out of four hundred million were to go to Australia. The population in Australia would be doubled but the crowding in China would be lessened hardly at all. The root of the trouble is not an insufficient land base but a high birth rate. The axe must be laid to that root if practical results are to be obtained. This means universal knowledge about birth control and universal access to the means of control. Only a general rise in the standard of living seems sufficient to bring these ends in view, and only accelerated industrial development seems likely to provide a basis for a higher standard. So far as we humans can now see, these are the only solutions.

The reverse of the medal must also be kept in view. A nation which neglects to promote national unity by sound democratic processes is selling its birthright. Our objective is not a flattened-out culture and opinion based upon either force or mass habit. A country cannot neglect a sound process of unification any more than it can afford to dam up the flow of general cultural diversity. Switzerland is a useful example of the way in which wide cultural diversity may accompany unity of political purpose; but the United States is an equally good one. Our protracted negligent attitude toward world affairs led our enemies to suppose that we had lost the power of unified purpose; it turned out to be one of our strongest weapons. North of the border, "Canadianization" has long been a conscious policy to overcome the internal diversities resulting from the block settlement of immigrants to that country. The soundness of the unifying processes which have produced such good results in these and other cases is beyond question. A nation is not an inchoate mass of people, but organization and purpose and cultural development, with freedom and will to choose and with knowledge to guide the choice. These are goals difficult to attain under any circumstances. Unrestricted migration would wreck both the means and the purposes of unity in freedom.

There are, as has been suggested, other and more promising methods. What can be done for China and India, for example, is to raise the standard of living through industrialization. All the world need not, like Belgium, possess a highly concentrated industry drawing large quantities of raw materials from abroad. But every country that has people with hands has aptitudes, developed or latent, which it can apply to raw materials, domestic and imported. It is better national policy to export a bale of goods than a man. The pyramiding of industry has limits, however; and it will be a special problem of the future to determine the best social balance between national production, importation, cheapening sources of power and population numbers. What concerns us in this connection now is that most countries have not reached the point of industrial saturation, so there is both room and time for experiment. Capital, enterprise and aptitudes, if suitably joined, will result in the surprisingly swift attainment of higher levels of living. In overcrowded countries there is a frontier in industry far more vast than any land frontier of history.

V. THE NEW RELATIONSHIPS

Among the strategies of peace and security is one we are next to try: the airing of threats to peace in the Assembly of the United Nations. The structure of organization, as finally accepted at San Francisco, provides for study of almost every conceivable major international problem. The world's confidence in the Organization may be expected to grow as such studies are impartially made and rationally interpreted. The wider the public knowledge and discussion of a problem the less likely that it is that a minority group will succeed in forcing a parochial decision.

What we have seen of aggressive national policies in the territorial field during and at the close of the present war raises a question of interpretation. If the national policies of Britain with respect to the southern shores of the North Sea form a 150-year-old tradition that deserves respect, how far is similar respect due to the Soviet desires at the Dardanelles and Gibraltar, in the Red Sea, the Persian Gulf and the Baltic? While we are making up our minds on this the Soviet Union acts. It has been urged that we act ourselves in the Pacific. We can note, however, without being sanctimonious, that when we speak of territorial acquisitions in that area we include references to a trusteeship system and that the populations involved (the Philippines excepted) are too small and primitive to give the issue local human meaning.

We have to lift our eyes from the map if we are to see the new form of relationship which is being imposed upon many areas of the world, big and little, by economic evolutions twice armed with efficient and expanding technologies. That neglected garden called the Amazon, for example, exports 80 percent of its production and imports 90 percent of its consumption. Thus its economy is dependent upon an outside market whose constant fluctuations are entirely beyond its own control, and it will remain in this condition so long as its people find it uneconomical to work up their products industrially. In the broad sweep of economic forces the smaller countries of the world are one by one caught up. Most of the 20 Latin American states, having narrow economies, depend for economic well-being upon three or four exports. Control is not governed by "full employment," as determined domestically, or by commendable human industry and resultant high production, but by prices fixed abroad. In the absence of world-wide rationing, country by country, of the production of such key products as coffee, sugar, cacao, tea, rubber and cotton, this fluctuates greatly. The resultant stresses in Puerto Rico, Java and Ceylon and many other dependent areas are well known; in all of them, the population problem is tied to economic policy. By contrast, the riches of the earth are at the disposition of the Bahrein Islanders, in the Persian Gulf, because of the handsome royalties on their oil reserves.

Small countries require a form of special consideration, therefore, when territorial changes are in view; at least some of them do. And since none of them has confidence that international economic arrangements will take its welfare and economic viability into sufficient account, all claim a right to share in the decision of the gravest global matters in both the economic and the political field on the principle of "sovereign equality." This principle, fully deployed, means that the little will decide what the big shall do. Clearly, the full future impact of a decision as to the Silesian coal fields is not alone of Polish concern. Since Poland was not developed industrially herself, the coal of Polish Silesia was a drug on the local market until the British general strike in 1926 provided an unforeseen opportunity for sales in Scandinavia. What are the new rationalities now that Poland possesses the whole of Upper Silesia?

The net result of the economic difficulties we have reviewed, and the likely play of political forces upon them, is to throw the responsibility for equalizing economic opportunity upon general arrangements evolved in the Economic and Social Council as a counterweight to any effort of the Great Powers to solve the problem through the medium of territorial arrangements. This will seem, to the small state eager to extend its frontiers, a distant and uncertain place to lodge reliance for vital benefits. The permanence of new and untried governments will be made to depend, not on local effort but on the nod of the powerful and the distant. It will take unbounded faith to make stability real in such circumstances.

Statesmanship means looking ahead. It also means wise appraisals and a wise choice among alternative possibilities. It is the duty of the statesmen to identify the factors one by one and give first consideration to those which are dominant; for not all factors have equal weight, or will have later. In doing this, statesmen must ever remember that any proposal for action is half ideal—"the intrusion of the eternal into time"—and half reality. It is fallacious to suppose that we can distil, by philosophical reflection upon a people's cultural value, a policy which will justify enlarging its territorial scope, nor is it necesary for us to do so. There is abundant room for all in the present world, where science and the inventive arts have given us a fourth dimension. However limited the territorial base may be, good social organization, developed aptitudes, and national unity and freedom can raise every national group to satisfactory levels of living.

The lesson of this is that a strategy of industrial expansion must be put beside the other strategies. It may be objected that an ultimate soution may escape us if all peoples are industrialized. But are there ultimates in this world?

The poet's phrase that "The end is forbidden" seems nearer the truth. There are too many unknown forces to justify self-confidence. Aptitudes vary almost as much as resources. Aptitude is a function of inherent powers, plus resources, plus education, plus energy, as conditioned by climate, biological setup and food supply. It often is too readily supposed that where a textile loom goes, there will originate competition in exported textiles. Will China continue to buy from us if we help industrialize her? One admits that Russia is a special case, for in that country overwhelming manpower is joined to industrial power in a system of political control that may spell danger. But here, as in all other cases and with all fears, the infinite varieties of nature in time will, in my view, surprise us. In any event, since industrialization is not consummated overnight, there will be time for adjustment—in social control, in relief from felt wants, in birth rates, and especially in the opportunity to strengthen coöperative will and action.

For the rest—and that rest has its full share of uncertainty—we must accept a fact of life, that all experience is a risk. Looking backward to 1919, for example, we see how immature we were as a nation, or as a government, when fate put into our hands the instrument suited to a new order of planetary living, and we rejected it. Yet, speaking in the round, the men of that time did the best they could. When the best devising and the highest resolution fail, we can only try again. A tough amalgam of historical and present-day interests, differing nation by nation, has to be fused and welded upon the main stem of the world's common interest in peace. The final strategy, we repeat, is that of coöperative international action. The highest patriotism henceforth will be to insist upon objective judgments and expressions of fairness all round.

If we can make a go of this, the grand strategy, all the other strategies will fall into place. Meanwhile, however, it is our fate, as we have seen, to be obliged to settle the problems of boundaries, minerals, migration and strategic bases *before* we have been able to put coöperative action to the critical test. Thus we are always compelled to take account of the possibility that coöperative hopes and endeavors may fail. This necessary division of faith and interest tends to weaken the will to coöperate.

We find ourselves, today, then, in a frontier zone of political living. Some of our friends of today may be among our enemies tomorrow. But life demands action in the present. We are obliged to reconcile the practical and the ideal. What I have tried to say is that their reconciliation, for example in the case of the territorial settlements that plague us, is almost infinitely difficult, but that it is not quite impossible. As a nation, looking up the long and steep road ahead, can we run and not be weary? Can we fulfull the pledge that we made when we wrote "We, the people" at the masthead of the Charter of the United Nations? Not if we listen to the small minds and the particularistic groups. Not if once again, as once before, we let trifles flood our minds. The struggle upon which we have embarked on the morrow of military victory is an eternal one. Weak and wrong as some of our decisions may in time prove to be, we must develop the stamina to face the consequences and try again and again and again.

❖ ❖ ❖

FOR the first time in history, at Nuremberg, Germany, in 1946, individual citizens of a state were convicted of the crime of planning and waging aggressive war. So great an advance in the field of international law of course produced differences of opinion. That the Nazi ringleaders had been brought to account for their crimes was accepted as wise and just by American public opinion generally and by most of the American press. Though some publicists sneered at "the Nuremberg novelty," most laymen saw in the Nuremberg trial welcome evidence that law had at last caught up with the sentiment of the civilized world.

For the most part, however, the controversy as to the justice of the trials was confined to legal experts, and in the main to one count in the indictment—that of crimes against peace. Thoughtful and responsible lawyers noted that, despite the Kellogg-Briand Pact of August 27, 1928, and other such formal documents as the Geneva Protocol of 1924 for the Pacific Settlement of International Disputes, the Resolution of the Eighth Assembly of the League of Nations of 1921, and the Resolution adopted by the 21 American Republics at the Sixth Pan-American Conference held at Havana in 1928, there was no plain statute on the books of law which could be cited by the prosecution at Nuremberg. Great popular movements can, after all, be in error; and some lawyers were uncomfortable, not doubting that justice in substance had been done but that the legal procedure had been impeccable.

It was to such doubts as these that Henry L. Stimson, Secretary of War under President Taft, Governor-General of the Philippines under President Coolidge, Secretary of State under President Hoover, Secretary of War under President Franklin D. Roosevelt, one of America's great public servants, and a great international lawyer, turned his attention in the following pages written for the January 1947 issue of FOREIGN AFFAIRS.

❖ ❖ ❖

THE NUREMBERG TRIAL: LANDMARK IN LAW

By Henry L. Stimson

IN THE confusion and disquiet of the war's first aftermath, there has been at least one great event from which we may properly take hope. The surviving leaders of the Nazi conspiracy against mankind have been indicted, tried, and judged in a proceeding whose magnitude and quality make it a landmark in the history of international law. The great undertaking at Nuremberg can live and grow in meaning, however, only if its principles are rightly understood and accepted. It is therefore disturbing to find that its work is criticized and even challenged as lawless by many who should know better. In the deep conviction that this trial deserves to be known and valued as a long step ahead on the only upward road, I venture to set down my general view of its nature and accomplishment.

The defendants at Nuremberg were leaders of the most highly organized and extensive wickedness in history. It was not a trick of the law which brought them to the bar; it was the "massed angered forces of common humanity." There were three different courses open to us when the Nazi leaders were captured: release, summary punishment, or trial. Release was unthinkable; it would have been taken as an admission that there was here no crime. Summary punishment was widely recommended. It would have satisfied the immediate requirement of the emotions, and in its own roughhewn way it would have been fair enough, for this was precisely the type of justice that the Nazis themselves had so often used. But this fact was in reality the best reason for rejecting such a solution. The whole moral position of the victorious Powers must collapse if their judgments could be enforced only by Nazi methods. Our anger, as righteous anger, must be subject to the law. We therefore took the third course and tried the captive criminals by a judicial proceeding. We gave to the Nazis what they had denied their own opponents—the protection of the Law. The Nuremberg Tribunal was thus in no sense an instrument of vengeance but the reverse. It was, as Mr. Justice Jackson said in opening the case for the prosecution, "one of the most significant tributes that Power has ever paid to Reason."

The function of the law here, as everywhere, has been to insure fair judgment. By preventing abuse and minimizing error, proceedings under law give dignity and method to the ordinary conscience of mankind. For this purpose the law demands three things: that the defendant be charged with a punishable crime; that he have full opportunity for defense; and that he be judged fairly on the evidence by a proper judicial authority. Should it fail to meet any one of these three requirements, a trial would not be justice. Against these standards, therefore, the judgment of Nuremberg must itself be judged.

II. PUNISHABLE CRIMES

In our modern domestic law, a man can be penalized only when he has done something which was authoritatively recognized as punishable when he did it. This is the well-known principle that forbids *ex post facto* law, and it accords entirely with our standards of fair play. A mistaken appeal to this principle has been the cause of much confusion about the Nuremberg trial. It is argued that parts of the Tribunal's Charter, written in 1945, makes crimes out of what before were activities beyond the scope of national and international law. Were this an exact statement of the situation we might well be concerned, but it is not. It rests on a misconception of the whole nature of the law of nations. International law is not a body of authoritative codes or statutes; it is the gradual expression, case by case, of the moral judgments of the civilized world. As such, it corresponds precisely to the common law of Anglo-American tradition. We can understand the law of Nuremberg only if we see it for what it is—a great new case in the book of international law, and not a formal enforcement of codified statutes. A look at the charges will show what I mean.

The Charter of the Tribunal recognizes three kinds of crime, all of which were charged in the indictment: crimes against peace, war crimes, and crimes against humanity. There was a fourth charge, of conspiracy to commit one or all of these crimes. To me personally this fourth charge is the most realistic of them all, for the Nazi crime is in the end indivisible. Each of the myriad transgressions was an interlocking part of the whole gigantic barbarity. But basically it is the first three that we must consider. The fourth is built on them.

Of the three charges, only one has been seriously criticized. War crimes have not greatly concerned the Tribunal's critics; these are offenses well understood and long generally recognized in the law or rules of war. The charge of crimes against humanity has not aroused much comment in this country, perhaps because this part of the indictment was not of central concern to the American prosecutor. The Tribunal's findings on this charge are significant, but not such as to raise much question of their legal validity, so I defer my comment to a later section of this article.

There remains the charge of crimes against peace, which has been the chief target of most of the honest critics of Nuremberg. It is under this charge that a penalty has been asked, for the first time, against the individual leaders in a war of aggression. It is this that well-intentioned critics have called "*ex post facto* law."

It is clear that until quite recently any legal judgment against a war-maker would have been absurd. Throughout the centuries, until after World War I, the choice between war and peace remained entirely in the hands of each sovereign state, and neither the law nor the ordinary conscience of humanity ventured to deny that right. The concept of just and unjust wars is of course as old at least as Plato. But in the anarchy of individual sovereignties, the right to fight was denied to no people and the right to start a fight was denied to no ruler. For the loser in a war, punishment was certain. But this was not a matter of law; it was simply a matter of course. At the best it was like the early law of the blood feud, in which the punishment of a murderer was the responsibility of the victim's family alone and not of the whole community. Even in 1914 the German violation of Belgian neutrality was regarded as a matter for action only by those nations directly concerned in the Treaties of 1839. So far indeed was this sovereign right of war-making accepted that it was frequently extended to include the barbarous notion that a sovereign ruler is not subject to the law.

In the face of this acceptance of war as a proper instrument of sovereign national policy, the only field for the early development of international law lay in restricting so far as possible the brutalities of warfare. In obedience to age-long instincts of chivalry and magnanimity, there were gradually developed international standards for the conduct of war. Civilians and neutrals were given protecting rights and privileges, the treatment of prisoners was prescribed, and certain weapons were outlawed. It is these long established and universally accepted standards, most of them formally included in the internal law of Germany, that are covered by the charge of war crimes in the Nuremberg indictment.

The attempt to moderate the excesses of war without controlling war itself was doomed to failure by the extraordinary scientific and industrial developments of the nineteenth and twentieth centuries. By 1914 the world had been intertwined into a single unit and weapons had been so far developed that a major war could shake the whole structure of civilization. No rules of warfare were sufficient to limit the vast new destructive powers of belligerents, and the First World War made it clear that old notions must be abandoned; the world must attack the problem at its root. Thus after 1918 repeated efforts were made to eliminate aggressive war as a legal national undertaking. These efforts reached their climax in the Kellogg-Briand Pact of 1928, in which 63 nations, including Germany, Japan and Italy, renounced aggressive warfare. This pact was not an isolated incident of the postwar era. During that period the whole world was at one in its opinion of aggressive war. In repeated resolutions in the League of Nations and elsewhere, aggression was roundly denounced as criminal. In the judgment of the peoples of the world the once proud title of "conqueror" was replaced by the criminal epithet "aggressor."

The progress made from 1918 to 1931 was halting and incomplete, but its direction was clear; the mandate for peace was overwhelming. Most tragically, the peoples who had renounced war were not sufficiently alert to their danger when in the following years the ruling groups of three great nations, in wanton denial of every principle of peace and civilization, launched a conspiracy against the rest of the world. Thus it happened that in the ten years which began with the invasion of Manchuria the principles of the Kellogg Pact were steadily under attack, and only as the danger came slowly home to each one of them individually did the peace-loving nations take action against aggression. In early 1945, as it became apparent that the long delayed victory was at hand, the question posed itself directly: Has there been a war of aggression and are its leaders punishable? There were many then, as there are some now, who argued that there was no law for this offense, and they found their justification in the feebleness and acquiescence of other nations in the early aggression of the Axis. Other counsels prevailed, however, and by the Charter of the Nuremberg Tribunal the responsible leaders of aggressive war were subjected to trial and conviction on the charge of crimes against peace.

Here we come to the heart of the matter. Able lawyers and honest men have cried out that this aggressive war was not a crime. They have argued that the Nuremberg defendants were not properly forewarned when they made war that what they did was criminal.

Now in one sense the concept of *ex post facto* law is a strange one to apply here, because this concept relates to a state of mind on the part of the defendants that in this case was wholly absent. That concept is based on the assumption that if the defendant had known that the proposed act was criminal he would have refrained from committing it. Nothing in the attitude of the Nazi leaders corresponds to this assumption; their minds were wholly untroubled by the question of their guilt or innocence. Not in their aggression only but in their whole philosophy, they excluded the very concept of law. They deliberately put themselves below such a concept. To international law—as to the law of Germany—they paid only such respect as they found politic, and in the end they had smashed its every rule. Their attitude toward aggressive war was exactly like their attitude toward murder—both were useful instruments in a great design. It is therefore impossible to get any light on the validity of this charge of aggressive war by inspecting the Nazi mind. We must study rather the minds of the rest of the world, which is at once a less revolting and a more fruitful labor.

What did the rest of us think about aggressive war at the time of the Nazi attacks? This question is complex, but to that part of it which affects the legality of the Nuremberg trial we can give a simple answer. That we considered aggressive war wicked is clear; that we considered the leaders of an aggressive war wicked is equally clear. These opinions, in large part formally embodied in the Kellogg Pact, are the basis for the law of Nuremberg. With the detailed reasoning by which the prosecution has supported the law set forth in the Charter of the International Military Tribunal, we cannot here concern ourselves. The proposition sustained by the Tribunal is simple: if a man plans aggression when aggression has been formally renounced by his nation, he is a criminal. Those who are concerned with the law of this proposition cannot do better than to read the pertinent passages in the opening address of Mr. Justice Jackson, the closing address of Sir Hartley Shawcross, and the opinion of the Tribunal itself.

What really troubles the critics of Nuremberg is that they see no evidence that before 1945 we considered the capture and conviction of such aggressors to be our legal duty. In this view they are in the main correct, but it is vitally important to remember that a legal right is not lost merely because temporarily it is not used. What happened before World War II was that we lacked the courage to enforce the authoritative decision of the international world. We agreed with the Kellogg Pact that aggressive war must end. We renounced it, and we condemned those who might use it. But it was a moral condemnation only. We thus did not reach the second half of the question: What will you do to an aggressor when you catch him? If we *had* reached it, we should easily have found the right answer. But that answer escaped us, for it implied a duty to catch the criminal, and such a chase meant war. It was the Nazi confidence that we would never chase and catch them, and not a misunderstanding of our opinion of them, that led them to commit their crimes. Our offense was thus that of the man who passed by on the other side. That we have finally recognized our negligence and named the criminals for what they are is a piece of righteousness too long delayed by fear.

We did not ask ourselves, in 1939 or 1940, or even in 1941, what punishment, if any, Hitler and his chief assistants deserved. We asked simply two questions: How do we avoid war, and how do we keep this wickedness from overwhelming us? These seemed larger questions to us than the guilt or innocence of individuals. In the end we found an answer to the second question, but none to the first. The crime of the Nazis, against *us,* lay in this very fact: that their making of aggressive war made peace here impossible. We have now seen again, in hard and deadly terms, what had been proved in 1917—that "peace is indivisible." The man who makes aggressive war at all makes war against mankind. That is an exact, not a rhetorical, description of the crime of aggressive war.

Thus the Second World War brought it home to us that our repugnance to aggressive war was incomplete without a judgment of its leaders. What we had called a crime demanded punishment; we must bring our law in balance with the universal moral judgment of mankind. The wickedness of aggression must be punished by a trial and judgment. This is what has been done at Nuremberg.

Now this is a new judicial process, but it is not *ex post*

facto law. It is the enforcement of a moral judgment which dates back a generation. It is a growth in the application of law that any student of our common law should recognize as natural and proper, for it is in just this manner that the common law grew up. There was, somewhere in our distant past, a first case of murder, a first case where the tribe replaced the victim's family as judge of the offender. The tribe had learned that the deliberate and malicious killing of any human being was, and must be treated as, an offense against the whole community. The analogy is exact. All case law grows by new decisions, and where those new decisions match the conscience of the community, they are law as truly as the law of murder. They do not become *ex post facto* law merely because until the first decision and punishment comes, a man's only warning that he offends is in the general sense and feeling of his fellow men.

The charge of aggressive war is unsound, therefore, only if the community of nations did not believe in 1939 that aggressive war was an offense. Merely to make such a suggestion, however, is to discard it. Aggression is an offense, and we all know it; we have known it for a generation. It is an offense so deep and heinous that we cannot endure its repetition.

The law made effective by the trial at Nuremberg is righteous law long overdue. It is in just such cases as this one that the law becomes more nearly what Mr. Justice Holmes called it: "the witness and external deposit of our moral life."

With the Judgment of Nuremberg we at last reach to the very core of international strife, and we set a penalty not merely for war crimes, but for the very act of war itself, except in self-defense. If a man will argue that this is bad law, untrue to our ideals, I will listen. But I feel only pity for the casuist who would dismiss the Nazi leaders because "they were not warned it was a crime." They were warned, and they sneered contempt. Our shame is that their contempt was so nearly justified, not that we have in the end made good our warning.

III. FAIR TRIAL

Next after its assertion of the criminality of aggressive war, the triumph of Nuremberg rests in the manner and degree to which it has discharged with honor the true functions of a legal instrument. The crimes charged were punishable as we have seen—so clearly punishable that the only important suggested alternative to a trial was summary execution of the accused. It is in its pursuit of a different course that the Nuremberg Tribunal has demonstrated at once the dignity and the value of the law, and students of law everywhere will find inspiration and enlightenment in close study of its work. In its skilful development of a procedure satisfying every tradition and material safeguard of the varying legal forms of the prosecuting nations, it represents a signal success in the field of international negotiation, and in its rigid fidelity to the fundamental principles of fair play it has insured the lasting value of its work.

In their insistence on fairness to the defendants, the Charter and the Tribunal leaned over backwards. Each defendant was allowed to testify for himself, a right denied by Continental law. At the conclusion of the trial, each defendant was allowed to address the Tribunal, at great length, a right denied by Anglo-American law. The difference between Continental and Anglo-American law was thus adjusted by allowing to the defendant his rights under both. Counsel for the defendants were leading German lawyers and professors from the German universities, some of them ardent and unrepentant Nazis. Counsel were paid, fed, sheltered and transported at the expense of the Allies, and were furnished offices and secretarial help. The defense had full access to all documents. Every attempt was made to produce desired witnesses when the Tribunal believed that they had any relevant evidence to offer. In the summation of the trial the defense had 20 days and the prosecution three, and the defense case as a whole occupied considerably more time than the prosecution.

The record of the Nuremberg trial thus becomes one of the foundation stones of the peace. Under the most rigid safeguards of jurisprudence, subject to challenge, denial and disproof by men on trial for their lives and assisted by counsel of their own choosing, the great conspiracy has been unmasked. In documents unchallenged by the defense and often in the words of the defendants themselves, there is recorded the whole black history of murder, enslavement and aggression. This record, so established, will stand as a demonstration, on a wholly new level of validity and strength, of the true character of the Nazi régime. And this is so not in spite of our insistence upon law, but because of it.

In this connection it is worth noting that the trial has totally exploded many of the strange notions that seem to lurk in the minds of some who have expressed their doubts about Nuremberg. Some of the doubters are not basically concerned with "*ex post facto* law" or with "vengeance." Their real trouble is that they did not think the Nazis could be proved guilty. To these gentlemen I earnestly commend a reading of the record. If after reading it they do not think there was in fact aggressive war, in its most naked form, then I shall be constrained to believe that they do not think any such thing exists or can exist.

IV. FAIR JUDGMENT

Not having made a study of the evidence presented in the case with special reference to each defendant, I am not qualified to pass judgment on the verdicts and sentences of the Tribunal against individuals and criminal groups. I have, however, heard no claim that these sentences were too severe. The Tribunal's findings as to the law are on the whole encouraging. The charge of aggressive war was accepted and ably explained. The charge of war crimes was sustained almost without comment. The charge of crimes against humanity was limited by the Tribunal to include only activities pursued in connection with the crime of war. The Tribunal eliminated from its jurisdiction the question of the criminal accountability of those responsible for wholesale persecution before the outbreak of the war in 1939. With this decision I do not here venture to quarrel, but its effect appears to me to involve a reduction of the meaning of crimes against humanity to a point where they become practically synonymous with war crimes.

If there is a weakness in the Tribunal's findings, I believe it lies in its very limited construction of the legal concept of conspiracy. That only eight of the 22 defendants should have been found guilty on the count of conspiracy to commit the various crimes involved in the indictment seems to me surprising. I believe that the Tribunal would have been justified in a broader construction of the law of conspiracy, and under such a construction it might well have found a different verdict in a case like that of Schacht.

In this first great international trial, however, it is perhaps as well that the Tribunal has very rigidly interpreted both the law and the evidence. In this connection we may observe that only in the case of Rudolf Hess, sentenced to life imprisonment, does the punishment of any of the defendants depend solely on the count of aggressive war. All of those who have been hanged were convicted of war crimes or crimes against humanity, and all but one were convicted of both. Certainly, then, the charge of aggressive war has not been established in international law at the expense of any innocent lives.

The judgment of the Tribunal is thus, in its findings of guilt, beyond challenge. We may regret that some of the charges were not regarded as proven and some of the defendants not found clearly guilty. But we may take pride in the restraint of a tribunal which has so clearly insisted upon certain proof of guilt. It is far better that a Schacht should go free than that a judge should compromise his conscience.

V. THE MEANING OF NUREMBERG

A single landmark of justice and honor does not make a world of peace. The Nazi leaders are not the only ones who have renounced and denied the principles of western civilization. They are unique only in the degree and violence of their offenses. In every nation which acquiesced even for a time in their offense, there were offenders. There have been still more culpable offenders in nations which joined before or after in the brutal business of aggression. If we claimed for Nuremberg that it was final justice, or that only these criminals were guilty, we might well be criticized as being swayed by vengeance and not justice. But this is not the claim. The American prosecutor has explicitly stated that he looks uneasily and with great regret upon certain brutalities that have occurred since the ending of the war. He speaks for us all when he says that there has been enough bloodletting in Europe. But the sins of others do not make the Nazi leaders less guilty, and the importance of Nuremberg lies not in any claim that by itself it clears the board, but rather in the pattern it has set. The four nations prosecuting, and the 19 others subscribing to the Charter of the International Military Tribunal, have firmly bound themselves to the principle that aggressive war is a personal and punishable crime.

It is this principle upon which we must henceforth rely for our legal protection against the horrors of war. We must never forget that under modern conditions of life, science and technology, all war has become greatly brutalized, and that no one who joins in it, even in self-defense, can escape becoming also in a measure brutalized. Modern war cannot be limited in its destructive methods and in the inevitable debasement of all participants. A fair scrutiny of the last two World Wars makes clear the steady intensification in the inhumanity of the weapons and methods employed by both the aggressors and the victors. In order to defeat Japanese aggression, we were forced, as Admiral Nimitz has stated, to employ a technique of unrestricted submarine warfare not unlike that which 25 years ago was the proximate cause of our entry into World War I. In the use of strategic air power, the Allies took the lives of hundreds of thousands of civilians in Germany, and in Japan the destruction of civilian life wreaked by our B-29s, even before the final blow of the atomic bombs, was at least proportionately great. It is true that our use of this destructive power, particularly of the atomic bomb, was for the purpose of winning a quick victory over aggressors, so as to minimize the loss of life, not only of our troops but of the civilian populations of our enemies as well, and that this purpose in the case of Japan was clearly effected. But even so, we as well as our enemies have contributed to the proof that the central moral problem is war and not its methods, and that a continuance of war will in all probability end with the destruction of our civilization.

International law is still limited by international politics, and we must not pretend that either can live and grow without the other. But in the judgment of Nuremberg there is affirmed the central principle of peace—that the man who makes or plans to make aggressive war is a criminal. A standard has been raised to which Americans, at least, must repair; for it is only as this standard is accepted, supported and enforced that we can move onward to a world of law and peace.

❖ ❖ ❖

The article entitled "The Sources of Soviet Conduct," which appeared in Foreign Affairs in July 1947, was at once widely recognized as being of quite exceptional interest, both as an analysis of Russian policy and as a statement of the attitude which the United States would be wise to adopt in consequence. In view of the apparently remorseless division of One World into a "western" half and a Communist half, and the awesome dangers which such a development brings in its train, the problems here considered are perforce the major concern of every foreign office. This concern is shared by the public, as indicated by the extent to which excerpts from the article in question were reprinted in newspapers and periodicals, both in the United States and abroad. Republication of the full text here may therefore be useful. The anonymity of the author is retained, in keeping with the custom of Foreign Affairs to print occasional unsigned contributions by writers in and out of government.

THE SOURCES OF SOVIET CONDUCT

By X

THE political personality of Soviet power as we know it today is the product of ideology and circumstances: ideology inherited by the present Soviet leaders from the movement in which they had their political origin, and circumstances of the power which they now have exercised for nearly three decades in Russia. There can be few tasks of psychological analysis more difficult than to try to trace the interaction of these two forces and the relative rôle of each in the determination of official Soviet conduct. Yet the attempt must be made if that conduct is to be understood and effectively countered.

It is difficult to summarize the set of ideological concepts with which the Soviet leaders came into power. Marxian ideology, in its Russian-Communist projection, has always been in process of subtle evolution. The materials on which it bases itself are extensive and complex. But the outstanding features of Communist thought as it existed in 1916 may perhaps be summarized as follows: (a) that the central factor in the life of man, the factor which determines the character of public life and the "physiognomy of society," is the system by which material goods are produced and exchanged; (b) that the capitalist system of production is a nefarious one which inevitably leads to the exploitation of the working class by the capital-owning class and is incapable of developing adequately the economic resources of society or of distributing fairly the material goods produced by human labor; (c) that capitalism contains the seeds of its own destruction and must, in view of the inability of the capital-owning class to adjust itself to economic change, result eventually and inescapably in a revolutionary transfer of power to the working class; (d) that imperialism, the final phase of capitalism, leads directly to war and revolution.

The rest may be outlined in Lenin's own words: "Unevenness of economic and political development is the inflexible law of capitalism. It follows from this that the victory of Socialism may come originally in a few capitalist countries or even in a single capitalist country. The victorious proletariat of that country, having expropriated the capitalists and having organized Socialist production at home, would rise against the remaining capitalist world, drawing to itself in the process the oppressed classes of other countries." It must be noted that there was no assumption that capitalism would perish without proletarian revolution. A final push was needed from a revolutionary proletariat movement in order to tip over the tottering structure. But it was regarded as inevitable that sooner or later that push be given.

For 50 years prior to the outbreak of the Revolution, this pattern of thought had exercised great fascination for the members of the Russian revolutionary movement. Frustrated, discontented, hopeless of finding self-expression—or too impatient to seek it—in the confining limits of the Tsarist political system, yet lacking wide popular support for their choice of bloody revolution as a means of social betterment, these revolutionists found in Marxist theory a highly convenient rationalization for their own instinctive desires. It afforded pseudo-scientific justification for their impatience, for their categoric denial of all value in the Tsarist system, for their yearning for power and revenge, and foı their inclination to cut corners in the pursuit of it. It is therefore no wonder that they had come to believe implicitly in the truth and soundness of the Marxian-Leninist teachings, so congenial to their own impulses and emotions. Their sincerity need not be impugned. This is a phenomenon as old as human nature itself. It has never been more aptly described than by Edward Gibbon, who wrote in "The Decline and Fall of the Roman Empire": "From enthusiasm to imposture the step is perilous and slippery; the demon of Socrates affords a memorable instance how a wise man may deceive himself, how a good man may deceive others, how the conscience may slumber in a mixed and middle state between self-illusion and voluntary fraud." And it was with this set of conceptions that the members of the Bolshevik Party entered into power.

Now it must be noted that through all the years of preparation for revolution, the attention of these men, as indeed of Marx himself, had been centered less on the future form which Socialism would take than on the necessary overthrow of rival power which, in their view, had to precede the introduction of Socialism. Their views, therefore, on the positive program to be put into effect, once power was attained, were for the most part nebulous, visionary and impractical. Beyond the nationalization of industry and the expropriation of large private capital holdings there was no agreed program. The treatment of the peasantry, which according to the Marxist formulation was not of the proletariat, had always been a vague spot in the pattern of Communist thought; and it remained an object of controversy and vacillation for the first ten years of Communist power.

The circumstances of the immediate post-revolution period —the existence in Russia of civil war and foreign intervention, together with the obvious fact that the Communists represented only a tiny minority of the Russian people— made the establishment of dictatorial power a necessity. The experiment with "war Communism" and the abrupt attempt to eliminate private production and trade had unfortunate economic consequences and caused further bitterness against the new revolutionary régime. While the temporary relaxation of the effort to communize Russia, represented by the New Economic Policy, alleviated some of this economic distress and thereby served its purpose, it also made it evident that the "capitalistic sector of society" was still prepared to profit at once from any relaxation of governmental pressure, and would, if permitted to continue to exist, always constitute a powerful opposing element to the Soviet régime and a serious rival for influence in the country. Somewhat the same situation prevailed with respect to the individual peasant who, in his own small way, was also a private producer.

Lenin, had he lived, might have proved a great enough

man to reconcile these conflicting forces to the ultimate benefit of Russian society, though this is questionable. But, be that as it may, Stalin, and those whom he led in the struggle for succession to Lenin's position of leadership, were not the men to tolerate rival political forces in the sphere of power which they coveted. Their sense of insecurity was too great. Their particular brand of fanaticism, unmodified by any of the Anglo-Saxon traditions of compromise, was too fierce and too jealous to envisage any permanent sharing of power. From the Russian-Asiatic world out of which they had emerged they carried with them a skepticism as to the possibilities of permanent and peaceful coexistence of rival forces. Easily persuaded of their own doctrinaire "rightness," they insisted on the submission or destruction of all competing power. Outside of the Communist Party, Russian society was to have no rigidity. There were to be no forms of collective human activity or association which would not be dominated by the Party. No other force in Russian society was to be permitted to achieve vitality or integrity. Only the Party was to have structure. All else was to be an amorphous mass.

And within the Party the same principle was to apply. The mass of Party members might go through the motions of election, deliberation, decision and action; but in these motions they were to be animated not by their own individual wills but by the awesome breath of the Party leadership and the overbrooding presence of "the word."

Let it be stressed again that subjectively these men probably did not seek absolutism for its own sake. They doubtless believed—and found it easy to believe—that they alone knew what was good for society and that they would accomplish that good once their power was secure and unchallengeable. But in seeking that security of their own rule they were prepared to recognize no restrictions, either of God or man, on the character of their methods. And until such time as that security might be achieved, they placed far down on their scale of values and of operational priorities the comforts and happiness of the peoples who were entrusted to their care.

Now the outstanding circumstance concerning the Soviet régime is that down to the present day this process of political consolidation has never been completed and the men in the Kremlin have continued to be predominantly absorbed with the struggle to secure and make absolute the power which they seized in November 1917. They have endeavored to secure it primarily against forces at home, within Soviet society itself. But they have also endeavored to secure it against the outside world. For ideology, as we have seen, taught them that the outside world was hostile and that it was their duty eventually to overthrow the political forces beyond their borders. The powerful hands of Russian history and tradition reached up to sustain them in this feeling. Finally, their own aggressive intransigence with respect to the outside world began to find its own reaction; and they were soon forced, to use another Gibbonesque phrase, "to chastise the contumacy" which they themselves had provoked. It is an undeniable privilege of every man to prove himself right in the thesis that the world is his enemy; for if he reiterates it frequently enough and makes it the background of his conduct he is bound eventually to make that enmity a reality.

Now it lies in the nature of the mental world of the Soviet leaders, as well as in the character of their ideology, that no opposition to them can be officially recognized as having any merit or justification whatsoever. Such opposition can flow, in theory, only from the hostile and incorrigible forces of dying capitalism. As long as remnants of capitalism were officially recognized as existing in Russia, it was possible to place on them, as an internal element, part of the blame for the maintenance of a dictatorial form of society. But as these remnants were liquidated, little by little, this justification fell away; and when it was indicated officially that they had been finally destroyed, it disappeared altogether. And this fact created one of the most basic of the compulsions which came to act upon the Soviet régime: since capitalism no longer existed in Russia and since it could not be admitted that there could be serious or widespread opposition to the Kremlin springing spontaneously from the liberated masses under its authority, it became necessary to justify the retention of the dictatorship by stressing the menace of capitalism abroad.

This began at an early date. In 1924 Stalin specifically defended the retention of the "organs of suppression," meaning, among others, the army and the secret police, on the ground that "as long as there is a capitalist encirclement there will be danger of intervention with all the consequences that flow from that danger." In accordance with that theory, and from that time on, all internal opposition forces in Russia have consistently been portrayed as the agents of foreign forces of reaction antagonistic to Soviet power.

By the same token, tremendous emphasis has been placed on the original Communist thesis of a basic antagonism between the capitalist and Socialist worlds. It is clear, from many indications, that this emphasis is not founded in reality. The real facts concerning it have been confused by the existence abroad of genuine resentment provoked by Soviet philosophy and tactics and occasionally by the existence of great centers of military power, notably the Nazi régime in Germany and the Japanese Government of the late 1930's, which did indeed have aggressive designs against the Soviet Union. But there is ample evidence that the stress laid in Moscow on the menace confronting Soviet society from the world outside its borders is founded not in the realities of foreign antagonism but in the necessity of explaining away the maintenance of dictatorial authority at home.

Now the maintenance of this pattern of Soviet power, namely, the pursuit of unlimited authority domestically, accompanied by the cultivation of the semi-myth of implacable foreign hostility, has gone far to shape the actual machinery of Soviet power as we know it today. Internal organs of administration which did not serve this purpose withered on the vine. Organs which did serve this purpose became vastly swollen. The security of Soviet power came to rest on the iron discipline of the Party, on the severity and ubiquity of the secret police, and on the uncompromising economic monopolism of the state. The "organs of suppression," in which the Soviet leaders had sought security from rival forces, became in large measure the masters of those whom they were designed to serve. Today the major part of the structure of Soviet power is committed to the perfection of the dictatorship and to the maintenance of the concept of Russia as in a state of siege, with the enemy lowering beyond the walls. And the millions of human beings who form that part of the structure of power must defend at all costs this concept of Russia's position, for without it they are themselves superfluous.

As things stand today, the rulers can no longer dream of parting with these organs of suppression. The quest for absolute power, pursued now for nearly three decades with a ruthlessness unparalleled (in scope at least) in modern times, has again produced internally, as it did externally, its own reaction. The excesses of the police apparatus have fanned the potential opposition to the régime into something far greater and more dangerous than it could have been before those excesses began.

But least of all can the rulers dispense with the fiction by which the maintenance of dictatorial power has been defended. For this fiction has been canonized in Soviet philosophy by the excesses already committed in its name; and it is now anchored in the Soviet structure of thought by bonds far greater than those of mere ideology.

II

So much for the historical background. What does it spell in terms of the political personality of Soviet power as we know it today?

Of the original ideology, nothing has been officially junked.
tariat to assist in that destruction and to take power into
Belief is maintained in the basic badness of capitalism, in the inevitability of its destruction, in the obligation of the prole-
its own hands. But stress has come to be laid primarily on those concepts which relate most specifically to the Soviet régime itself: to its position as the sole truly Socialist régime in a dark and misguided world, and to the relationships of power within it.

The first of these concepts is that of the innate antagonism between capitalism and Socialism. We have seen how deeply that concept has become imbedded in foundations of Soviet power. It has profound implications for Russia's conduct as a member of international society. It means that there can never be on Moscow's side any sincere assumption of a community of aims between the Soviet Union and powers which are regarded as capitalist. It must invariably be assumed in Moscow that the aims of the capitalist world are antagonistic to the Soviet régime, and therefore to the interests of the peoples it controls. If the Soviet Government occasionally sets its signature to documents which would indicate the contrary, this is to be regarded as a tactical manœuvre permissible in dealing with the enemy (who is without honor) and should be taken in the spirit of *caveat emptor*. Basically, the antagonism remains. It is postulated. And from it flow many of the phenomena which we find disturbing in the Kremlin's conduct of foreign policy: the secretiveness, the lack of frankness, the duplicity, the wary suspiciousness, and the basic unfriendliness of purpose. These phenomena are there to stay, for the foreseeable future. There can be variations of degree and of emphasis. When there is something the Russians want from us, one or the other of these features of their policy may be thrust temporarily into the background; and when that happens there will always be Americans who will leap forward with gleeful announcements that "the Russians have changed," and some who will even try to take credit for having brought about such "changes." But we should not be misled by tactical manœuvres. These characteristics of Soviet policy, like the postulate from which they flow, are basic to the internal nature of Soviet power, and will be with us, whether in the foreground or the background, until the internal nature of Soviet power is changed.

This means that we are going to continue for a long time to find the Russians difficult to deal with. It does not mean that they should be considered as embarked upon a do-or-die program to overthrow our society by a given date. The theory of the inevitability of the eventual fall of capitalism has the fortunate connotation that there is no hurry about it.

The forces of progress can take their time in preparing the final *coup de grâce*. Meanwhile, what is vital is that the "Socialist fatherland"—that oasis of power which has been already won for Socialism in the person of the Soviet Union—should be cherished and defended by all good Communists at home and abroad, its fortunes promoted, its enemies badgered and confounded. The promotion of premature, "adventuristic" revolutionary projects abroad which might embarrass Soviet power in any way would be an inexcusable, even a counter-revolutionary act. The cause of Socialism is the support and promotion of Soviet power, as defined in Moscow.

This brings us to the second of the concepts important to contemporary Soviet outlook. That is the infallibility of the Kremlin. The Soviet concept of power, which permits no focal points of organization outside the Party, requires that the Party leadership remain in theory the sole repository of truth. For if truth were to be found elsewhere, there would be justification for its expression in organized activity. But it is precisely that which the Kremlin cannot and will not permit.

The leadership of the Communist Party is therefore always right, and has been always right ever since in 1929 Stalin formalized his personal power by announcing that decisions of the Politburo were being taken unanimously.

On the principle of infallibility there rests the iron discipline of the Communist Party. In fact, the two concepts are mutually self-supporting. Perfect discipline requires recognition of infallibility. Infallibility requires the observance of discipline. And the two together go far to determine the behaviorism of the entire Soviet apparatus of power. But their effect cannot be understood unless a third factor be taken into account: namely, the fact that the leadership is at liberty to put forward for tactical purposes any particular thesis which it finds useful to the cause at any particular moment and to require the faithful and unquestioning acceptance of that thesis by the members of the movement as a whole. This means that truth is not a constant but is actually created, for all intents and purposes, by the Soviet leaders themselves. It may vary from week to week, from month to month. It is nothing absolute and immutable—nothing which flows from objective reality. It is only the most recent manifestation of the wisdom of those in whom the ultimate wisdom is supposed to reside, because they represent the logic of history. The accumulative effect of these factors is to give to the whole subordinate apparatus of Soviet power an unshakeable stubbornness and steadfastness in its orientation. This orientation can be changed at will by the Kremlin but by no other power. Once a given party line has been laid down on a given issue of current policy, the whole Soviet governmental machine, including the mechanism of diplomacy, moves inexorably along the prescribed path, like a persistent toy automobile wound up and headed in a given direction, stopping only when it meets with some unanswerable force. The individuals who are the components of this machine are unamenable to argument or reason which comes to them from outside sources. Their whole training has taught them to mistrust and discount the glib persuasiveness of the outside world. Like the white dog before the phonograph, they hear only the "master's voice." And if they are to be called off from the purposes last dictated to them, it is the master who must call them off. Thus the foreign representative cannot hope that his words will make any impression on them. The most that he can hope is that they will be transmitted to those at the top, who are capable of changing the party line. But even those are not likely to be swayed by any normal logic in the words of the bourgeois representative. Since there can be no appeal to common purposes, there can be no appeal to common mental approaches. For this reason, facts speak louder than words to the ears of the Kremlin; and words carry the greatest weight when they have the ring of reflecting, or being backed up by, facts of unchallengeable validity.

But we have seen that the Kremlin is under no ideological compulsion to accomplish its purposes in a hurry. Like the Church, it is dealing in ideological concepts which are of long-term validity, and it can afford to be patient. It has no right to risk the existing achievements of the revolution for the sake of vain baubles of the future. The very teachings of Lenin himself require great caution and flexibility in the pursuit of Communist purposes. Again, these precepts are fortified by the lessons of Russian history: of centuries of obscure battles between nomadic forces over the stretches of a vast unfortified plain. Here caution, circumspection, flexibility and deception are the valuable qualities; and their value finds natural appreciation in the Russian or the oriental mind. Thus the Kremlin has no compunction about retreating in the face of superior force. And being under the compulsion of no timetable, it does not get panicky under the necessity for such retreat. Its political action is a fluid stream which moves constantly, wherever it is permitted to move, toward a given goal. Its main concern is to make sure that it has filled every nook and cranny available to it in the basin of world power. But if it finds unassailable barriers in its path, it accepts these philosophically and accommodates itself to them. The main thing is that there should always be pressure, unceasing constant pressure, toward the desired goal. There is no trace of any feeling in Soviet psychology that that goal must be reached at any given time.

These considerations make Soviet diplomacy at once easier and more difficult to deal with than the diplomacy of individual aggressive leaders like Napoleon and Hitler. On the one hand it is more sensitive to contrary force, more ready to yield on individual sectors of the diplomatic front when that force is felt to be too strong, and thus more rational in the logic and rhetoric of power. On the other hand it cannot be easily defeated or discouraged by a single victory on the part of its opponents. And the patient persistence by which it is animated means that it can be effectively countered not by sporadic acts which represent the momentary whims of democratic opinion but only by intelligent long-range policies on the part of Russia's adversaries—policies no less steady in their purpose, and no less variegated and resourceful in their application, than those of the Soviet Union itself.

In these circumstances it is clear that the main element of any United States policy toward the Soviet Union must be that of a long-term, patient but firm and vigilant containment of Russian expansive tendencies. It is important to note, however, that such a policy has nothing to do with outward histrionics: with threats or blustering or superfluous gestures of outward "toughness." While the Kremlin is basically flexible in its reaction to political realities, it is by no means unamenable to considerations of prestige. Like almost any other government, it can be placed by tactless and threatening gestures in a position where it cannot afford to yield even though this might be dictated by its sense of realism. The Russian leaders are keen judges of human psychology, and as such they are highly conscious that loss of temper and of self-control is never a source of strength in political affairs. They are quick to exploit such evidences of weakness. For these reasons, it is a *sine qua non* of successful dealing with Russia that the foreign government in question should remain at all times cool and collected and that its demands on Russian policy should be put forward in such a manner as to leave the way open for a compliance not too detrimental to Russian prestige.

III

In the light of the above, it will be clearly seen that the Soviet pressure against the free institutions of the western world is something that can be contained by the adroit and vigilant application of counter-force at a series of constantly shifting geographical and political points, corresponding to the shifts and manœuvres of Soviet policy, but which cannot be charmed or talked out of existence. The Russians look forward to a duel of infinite duration, and they see that already they have scored great successes. It must be borne in mind that there was a time when the Communist Party represented far more of a minority in the sphere of Russian national life than Soviet power today represents in the world community.

But if ideology convinces the rulers of Russia that truth is on their side and that they can therefore afford to wait, those of us on whom that ideology has no claim are free to examine objectively the validity of that premise. The Soviet thesis not only implies complete lack of control by the west over its own economic destiny, it likewise assumes Russian unity, discipline and patience over an infinite period. Let us bring this apocalyptic vision down to earth, and suppose that the western world finds the strength and resourcefulness to contain Soviet power over a period of ten to fifteen years. What does that spell for Russia itself?

The Soviet leaders, taking advantage of the contributions of modern technique to the arts of despotism, have solved the question of obedience within the confines of their power. Few challenge their authority; and even those who do are unable to make that challenge valid as against the organs of suppression of the state.

The Kremlin has also proved able to accomplish its purpose of building up in Russia, regardless of the interests of the inhabitants, an industrial foundation of heavy metallurgy, which is, to be sure, not yet complete but which is nevertheless continuing to grow and is approaching those of the other major industrial countries. All of this, however, both the maintenance of internal political security and the building of heavy industry, has been carried out at a terrible cost in human life and in human hopes and energies. It has necessitated the use of forced labor on a scale unprecedented in modern times under conditions of peace. It has involved the neglect or abuse of other phases of Soviet economic life, particularly agriculture, consumers' goods production, housing and transportation.

To all that, the war has added its tremendous toll of destruction, death and human exhaustion. In consequence of this, we have in Russia today a population which is physically and spiritually tired. The mass of the people are disillusioned, skeptical and no longer as accessible as they once were to the magical attraction which Soviet power still radiates to its followers abroad. The avidity with which people seized upon the slight respite accorded to the Church for tactical reasons during the war was eloquent testimony to the fact that their capacity for faith and devotion found little expression in the purposes of the régime.

In these circumstances, there are limits to the physical and nervous strength of people themselves. These limits are absolute ones, and are binding even for the cruelest dictatorship, because beyond them people cannot be driven. The forced labor camps and the other agencies of constraint provide temporary means of compelling people to work longer hours than their own volition or mere economic pressure would dictate; but if people survive them at all they become old before their time and must be considered as human casualties to the demands of dictatorship. In either case their best powers are no longer available to society and can no longer be enlisted in the service of the state.

Here only the younger generation can help. The younger generation, despite all vicissitudes and sufferings, is numerous and vigorous; and the Russians are a talented people. But it still remains to be seen what will be the effects on mature performance of the abnormal emotional strains of childhood which Soviet dictatorship created and which were enormously increased by the war. Such things as normal security and placidity of home environment have practically ceased to exist in the Soviet Union outside of the most remote farms and villages. And observers are not yet sure whether that is not going to leave its mark on the over-all capacity of the generation now coming into maturity.

In addition to this, we have the fact that Soviet economic development, while it can list certain formidable achievements, has been precariously spotty and uneven. Russian Communists who speak of the "uneven development of capitalism" should blush at the contemplation of their own national economy. Here certain branches of economic life, such as the metallurgical and machine industries, have been pushed out of all proportion to other sectors of economy. Here is a nation striving to become in a short period one of the great industrial nations of the world while it still has no highway network worthy of the name and only a relatively primitive network of railways. Much has been done to increase efficiency of labor and to teach primitive peasants something about the operation of machines. But maintenance is still a crying deficiency of all Soviet economy. Construction is hasty and poor in quality. Depreciation must be enormous. And in vast sectors of economic life it has not yet been possible to instill into labor anything like that general culture of production and technical self-respect which characterizes the skilled worker of the west.

It is difficult to see how these deficiencies can be corrected at an early date by a tired and dispirited population working largely under the shadow of fear and compulsion. And as long as they are not overcome, Russia will remain economically a vulnerable, and in a certain sense an impotent, nation, capable of exporting its enthusiasms and of radiating the strange charm of its primitive political vitality but unable to back up those articles of export by the real evidences of material power and prosperity.

Meanwhile, a great uncertainty hangs over the political life of the Soviet Union. That is the uncertainty involved in the transfer of power from one individual or group of individuals to others.

This is, of course, outstandingly the problem of the personal position of Stalin. We must remember that his succession to Lenin's pinnacle of preëminence in the Communist movement was the only such transfer of individual authority which the Soviet Union has experienced. That transfer took 12 years to consolidate. It cost the lives of millions of people and shook the state to its foundations. The attendant tremors were felt all through the international revolutionary movement, to the disadvantage of the Kremlin itself.

It is always possible that another transfer of preëminent power may take place quietly and inconspicuously, with no repercussions anywhere. But again, it is possible that the questions involved may unleash, to use some of Lenin's words, one of those "incredibly swift transitions" from "delicate deceit" to "wild violence" which characterize Russian history, and may shake Soviet power to its foundations.

But this is not only a question of Stalin himself. There has been, since 1938, a dangerous congealment of political life in the higher circles of Soviet power. The All-Union Party Congress, in theory the supreme body of the Party, is supposed to meet not less often than once in three years. It will soon be eight full years since its last meeting. During this period membership in the Party has numerically doubled. Party mortality during the war was enormous; and today well over half of the Party members are persons who have entered since the last Party congress was held. Meanwhile, the same small group of men has carried on at the top through an amazing series of national vicissitudes. Surely there is some reason why the experiences of the war brought basic political changes to every one of the great governments of the west. Surely the causes of that phenomenon are basic enough to be present somewhere in the obscurity of Soviet political life, as well. And yet no recognition has been given to these causes in Russia.

It must be surmised from this that even within so highly disciplined an organization as the Communist Party there must be a growing divergence in age, outlook and interest between the great mass of Party members, only so recently recruited into the movement, and the little self-perpetuating clique of men at the top, whom most of these Party members have never met, with whom they have never conversed, and with whom they can have no political intimacy.

Who can say whether, in these circumstances, the eventual rejuvenation of the higher spheres of authority (which can only be a matter of time) can take place smoothly and peacefully, or whether rivals in the quest for higher power will not eventually reach down into these politically immature and inexperienced masses in order to find support for their respective claims? If this were ever to happen, strange consequences could flow for the Communist Party: for the membership at large has been exercised only in the practices of iron discipline and obedience and not in the arts of compromise and accommodation. And if disunity were ever to seize and paralyze the Party, the chaos and weakness of Russian society would be revealed in forms beyond description. For we have seen that Soviet power is only a crust concealing an amorphous mass of human beings among whom no independent organizational structure is tolerated. In Russia there is not even such a thing as local government. The present generation of Russians have never known spontaneity of collective action. If, consequently, anything were ever to occur to disrupt the unity and efficacy of the Party as a political instrument, Soviet Russia might be changed overnight from one of the strongest to one of the weakest and most pitiable of national societies.

Thus the future of Soviet power may not be by any means as secure as Russian capacity for self-delusion would make it appear to the men in the Kremlin. That they can keep power themselves, they have demonstrated. That they can quietly and easily turn it over to others remains to be proved. Meanwhile, the hardships of their rule and the vicissitudes of international life have taken a heavy toll of the strength and hopes of the great people on whom their power rests. It is curious to note that the ideological power of Soviet authority is strongest today in areas beyond the frontiers of Russia, beyond the reach of its police power. This phenomenon brings to mind a comparison used by Thomas Mann in his great novel "Buddenbrooks." Observing that human institutions often show the greatest outward brilliance at a moment when inner decay is in reality farthest advanced, he compared the Buddenbrook family, in the days of its greatest glamour, to one of those stars whose light shines most brightly on this world when in reality it has long since ceased to exist. And who can say with assurance that the strong light still cast by the Kremlin on the dissatisfied peoples of the western world is not the powerful afterglow of a constellation which is in actuality on the wane? This cannot be proved. And it cannot be disproved. But the possibility remains (and in the opinion of this writer it is a strong one) that Soviet power, like the capitalist world of its conception, bears within it the seeds of its own decay, and that the sprouting of these seeds is well advanced.

IV

It is clear that the United States cannot expect in the foreseeable future to enjoy political intimacy with the Soviet régime. It must continue to regard the Soviet Union as a rival, not a partner, in the political arena. It must continue to expect that Soviet policies will reflect no abstract love of peace and stability, no real faith in the possibility of a permanent happy coexistence of the Socialist and capitalist worlds, but a cautious, persistent pressure toward the disruption and weakening of all rival influence and rival power.

Balanced against this are the facts that Russia, as opposed to the western world in general, is still by far the weaker party, that Soviet policy is highly flexible, and that Soviet society may well contain deficiencies which will eventually weaken its own total potential. This would of itself warrant the United States entering with reasonable confidence upon a policy of firm containment, designed to confront the Russians with unalterable counter-force at every point where they show signs of encroaching upon the interests of a peaceful and stable world.

But in actuality the possibilities for American policy are by no means limited to holding the line and hoping for the best. It is entirely possible for the United States to influence by its actions the internal developments, both within Russia and throughout the international Communist movement, by which Russian policy is largely determined. This is not only a question of the modest measure of informational activity which this government can conduct in the Soviet Union and elsewhere, although that, too, is important. It is rather a question of the degree to which the United States can create among the peoples of the world generally the impression of a country which knows what it wants, which is coping successfully with the problems of its internal life and with the responsibilities of a World Power, and which has a spiritual vitality capable of holding its own among the major ideological currents of the time. To the extent that such an impression can be created and maintained, the aims of Russian Communism must appear sterile and quixotic, the hopes and enthusiasm of Moscow's supporters must wane, and added strain must be imposed on the Kremlin's foreign policies. For the palsied decrepitude of the capitalist world is the keystone of Communist philosophy. Even the failure of the United States to experience the early economic depression which the ravens of the Red Square have been predicting with such complacent confidence since hostilities ceased would have deep and important repercussions throughout the Communist world.

By the same token, exhibitions of indecision, disunity and internal disintegration within this country have an exhilarating effect on the whole Communist movement. At each evidence of these tendencies, a thrill of hope and excitement goes through the Communist world; a new jauntiness can be noted in the Moscow tread; new groups of foreign supporters climb on to what they can only view as the band wagon of international politics; and Russian pressure increases all along the line in international affairs.

It would be an exaggeration to say that American behavior unassisted and alone could exercise a power of life and death over the Communist movement and bring about the early fall of Soviet power in Russia. But the United States has it in its power to increase enormously the strains under which Soviet policy must operate, to force upon the Kremlin a far greater degree of moderation and circumspection than it has had to observe in recent years, and in this way to promote tendencies which must eventually find their outlet in either the break-up or the gradual mellowing of Soviet power. For no mystical, Messianic movement—and particularly not that of the Kremlin—can face frustration indefinitely without eventually adjusting itself in one way or another to the logic of that state of affairs.

Thus the decision will really fall in large measure in this country itself. The issue of Soviet-American relations is in essence a test of the over-all worth of the United States as a nation among nations. To avoid destruction the United States need only measure up to its own best traditions and prove itself worthy of preservation as a great nation.

Surely, there was never a fairer test of national quality than this. In the light of these circumstances, the thoughtful observer of Russian-American relations will find no cause for complaint in the Kremlin's challenge to American society. He will rather experience a certain gratitude to a Providence which, by providing the American people with this implacable challenge, has made their entire security as a nation dependent on their pulling themselves together and accepting the responsibilities of moral and political leadership that history plainly intended them to bear.

❖ ❖ ❖

HAVE the ideas of this quarter century of history, described here by men who often were protagonists of some of its major actions, resolved themselves into any discernible pattern? Surely no other short period offers its students less temptation to flatter themselves with the production of convenient conclusions. The era began with the end of one world war, it ends with the close of another. The commonly-accepted designation for the interval in which there was no open fighting is merely "the inter-war period." How can such a time be pictured now save as a cycle of destruction, in which men were the prey of forces which they did not understand and could not control?

But if the pattern of the era escapes present comprehension, there seems at least one fixed point of reference for future study in the analyses and descriptions given in this volume from such varying points of view. The constant is man's need of freedom. It was in relation to this fixed point that Benedetto Croce drew a balance sheet of postwar society in 1932. With but slight alterations, the article seems a summing up of the situation today. Of the three disastrous "ideals" of the early 1930's which Croce evaluates—the trend toward authoritarian truth through rule imposed from above, the philosophy of "action for action's sake," and the manifestation of Communism as autocracy—the second (the Fascist ideology) is under a cloud. That, at any rate, is a gain. How one estimates the present strength of the first and the third ideals depends upon how one evaluates the power of a fourth—the ideal of liberty.

During a quarter of a century of close combat, the standard which Benedetto Croce raised, as Senator, Minister of Public Instruction, historian and philosopher, was never lowered. Even during Mussolini's régime he did not fear to send out of Italy a great and confident statement like this article for FOREIGN AFFAIRS in 1932. "There are those who question the future of the ideal of freedom," he said. "To them we answer that it has more than a future; it has eternity." In his own life, Benedetto Croce has shown the meaning of his greatest philosophic truth. Freedom is a fighting faith.

❖ ❖ ❖

OF LIBERTY

By Benedetto Croce

BETWEEN the orderly Europe that we used to know and the distracted Europe of today is fixed the great gulf of the World War. We remember the old Europe with its riches, its flourishing trade, its abundance of goods, its ease of life, its bold sense of security; we see today the new Europe—impoverished, discouraged, crisscrossed with high tariff walls, each nation occupied solely with its own affairs, too distraught to pay heed to the things of the spirit and tormented by the fear of worse to come. Gone is the gay international society once the pride of Europe's capitals; extinct, or almost so, is the old community of thought, art, civilization. How many astounding changes there have been in frontiers and in political relationships! In the place of the Germany of the Hohenzollerns we see the German Republic; Austria-Hungary has been dismembered and cut up into new states; French sway has been reëstablished over the provinces lost in 1870, and the Italian frontiers now include the unredeemed territories and extend to the Brenner; Poland has been reconstituted; Russia is ruled, not by the Tsars but by the Soviets; and the United States has become a dominant factor in European policy.

Yet if we pass from externals to essentials and try to identify the controlling forces now at work, we soon discern that these two Europes, so dissimilar in appearance, have continuity and homogeneity. When we leave out superficial impressions and make a careful analysis we detect the same characteristics in both, though in the Europe of today they have been exaggerated by the war. The same proclivities and the same spiritual conflicts are there, though aggravated by the general intellectual decay which was to be expected after a war which counted its victims by the millions, accustomed its survivors to violence, and destroyed the habit of critical, constructive and concentrated mental labor.

Nationalistic and imperialistic impulses have seized the victorious nations because they are victors, and the vanquished because they are vanquished; while the new states add new nationalisms, new imperialisms to the list. Impatience with free institutions has led to open or masked dictatorships, and, where dictatorships do not exist, to the desire for them. Liberty, which before the war was a faith, or at least a routine acceptance, has now departed from the hearts of men even if it still survives in certain institutions. In its place is an atavistic libertarianism which more than ever ponders disorder and destruction, gives rein to extravagant impulses, and produces spectacular and sterile works. Indifferent and contemptuous, its followers scorn meditative and loving labor, labor with a reverent affection for the past and a courageous mastery of the future. They scorn actions which spring from the heart and speak to the heart, speculations which hold the germs of truth, history based on a realization of all that man has achieved by painful struggle, poetry which is beautiful.

Under the name of Socialism, Communism had already been introduced into the political life and institutions of Europe before the war. Now it has reappeared, crude and disruptive. Liberalism it ridicules as something naïvely moralistic. Like atavism, into which it often blends, this Communism is a sterile thing that kills thought, religion and art: seeking to subjugate them to its own purposes, it can only destroy them. All the distortions and decrepit sophistries of historical materialism have reappeared in the current opinions and theories of the day as if they were new and full of promise, although any man with a slight knowledge of criticism and the history of ideas passed judgment upon them long ago. They have taken on an air of novelty and modernness merely because, although originally introduced by Europe to Russia, they now come out of Russia; if anything they are more immature and shallow than ever; but in this age of unprecedented callowness and crudity they gain unprecedented credence. Catholicism, moreover, which before the war sought to draw new strength from the forces of irrationalism and mysticism, has been gathering into its fold many weak and bewildered souls. Thus once again is heard that chorus of pessimism and decadence which echoed through prewar literature, this time announcing the decline of western civilization and of the human race itself. According to these prophets it is about to sink back to the level of beasts after having failed to reach the estate of man.

All these are facts, and it is useless to deny them or to say that they are true only of certain people in certain countries. Like the situation from which they spring they are common to all Europe and all the world. And since they are facts, they must have a function to fill in the development of the human spirit and in social and human progress—if not as direct creators of new values, then at least as resources and stimuli for the deepening and broadening of old values. This function, whatever it may be, will be understood and described only by the future historian. He will have before him as a completed story the movement in which we are now involved and its subsequent developments. We cannot understand it or even attempt to describe it as a whole because we are part of it. Being in it, moving with it, we can, it is true, observe and understand many of its aspects, but that is all.

And what practical moral is there for each of us in the fact that we cannot know the future? This: that we must take part in what is going on about us, and not waste our forces in the contemplation of the unknowable, that we must act, to the degree that each of us can, as our conscience and duty command. Those who in disregard of the ancient admonition of Solon strive to understand and judge a life "before it is finished," and who lose themselves in conjecture and surmise, should be on their guard lest these digressions into the unknown prove a snare set by a bad demon to keep them from their goal.

Not "a history of the future" (as the old thinkers used to define prophecy), but a history of the past which is summed up in the present, is what we need for our work, for our action. And what we need most at the moment is to examine, or at least to review, those ideals which are generally accepted today. We must discover whether they contain the power to dissolve or surpass or correct the ideals which we ourselves hold; so that thereafter we may change or modify our ideals, and in any event reëstablish them upon a surer, sounder foundation.

The ideal of a transcendental system of truth, and, corollary to it, of a system of government from on high, exercised on earth by a vicar and represented by a church, has not yet acquired the intellectual proof which past ages found it to lack. Like all obvious statements this one runs the risk of seeming ungenerous. Nonetheless, it is a fact that the spiritual impulse which has prompted many persons to return to Catholicism or to take refuge in it (or in similar if less venerable and authoritative havens) is merely a craving, amid the turmoil of clashing and changing ideals, for a truth that is fixed and a rule of life that is imposed from above. In some cases it may have no nobler basis than fear and renunciation, a childish terror in the presence of the perception that all truth is absolute and at the same time relative. But a moral ideal cannot conform to the needs of the discouraged and the fearful.

Nor can a moral ideal conform to the purposes of those who are drunk with action for action's sake; for action thus conceived leaves only nausea, a profound indifference toward all that has stirred the human race, and an incapacity for objective work. Humanity has drunk deep of nationalism and imperialism and the taste of them is already bitter as gall: *inveni amariorem felle.* Those who love action for its own sake still rage on. But where is their serenity of soul, their joy in life? The best of them are enveloped in gloom; the great mass of them are merely raw and stupid.

Communism, it is the fashion to claim, has passed from theory to practice and is being applied in Russia. But it is being practised not as Communism but—in keeping with its inner contradiction—as a form of autocracy, as its critics had always predicted would be the case. Under it the people of Russia are denied even that faint breath of freedom which they managed to obtain under the autocracy of the Tsars. The abolition of the state, that "transition from the régime of necessity to the régime of liberty" about which Marx theorized, has not taken place. Communism has not abolished the state—it could not and never will be able to do so—but, as irony would have it, has forged for itself one of the most oppressive state systems which it is possible to imagine. In saying this we are not trying to deny that perhaps there were circumstances which forced the Russian revolutionists to choose the course they did and no other. Neither do we wish to detract from the immensity of their endeavors to develop, under these circumstances, the productive forces of the country. Neither do we minimize the importance of the lessons to be learned from their endeavors, or fail to admire the mystic enthusiasm, materialistic though it be, which inspires them and keeps them from sinking beneath the load which they have put on their own backs. It is this enthusiasm which gives them courage to trample on religion, thought, poetry, on everything in a word which we in the west revere as sacred or noble.

Nevertheless the Russian Communists have not solved, nor will their violent and repressive methods ever enable them to solve, the fundamental problem of human society, the problem of freedom. For in freedom only can human society flourish and bear fruit. Freedom alone gives meaning to life: without it life is unbearable. Here is an inescapable problem. It cannot be eliminated. It springs from the very vitals of things and stirs in the souls of all those countless human beings whom the Communists are trying to control and reshape in accordance with their arbitrary concepts. And on the day that this problem is faced, the materialistic foundations of the Soviet structure will crumble and new and very different supports will have to be found for it. Then, even as now, pure Communism will not be practised in Russia.

Outside of Russia this pseudo-Communism has not gained much ground in spite of the fascination that always attaches to things remote in time and space—as the old adage has it, *maior e longinquo reverentia*. Two conditions present in

Russia are indeed lacking in western and central Europe: the Tsarist tradition and mysticism. Miliukov was not far from the truth when he wrote of Lenin some twelve or more years ago that "in Russia he was building on the solid foundations of the good old autocratic tradition, but that as far as other countries were concerned he was merely building castles in the air." Even if such experiments should develop in other parts of Europe, the fact that other countries differ so from Russia in religion, civilization, education, customs, traditions—in historical background, in short—would produce something quite new, whatever its name and appearance; or else, after an indeterminate period of blind groping and struggle, there would sooner or later emerge that liberty which is only another name for humanity.

For liberty is the only ideal which unites the stability that Catholicism once possessed with the flexibility which it could never attain, the only ideal which faces the future without proposing to mould it to some particular form, the only ideal that can survive criticism and give human society a fixed point by which from time to time to reëstablish its balance. There are those who question the future of the ideal of freedom. To them we answer that it has more than a future: it has eternity. And today, despite the contempt and ridicule heaped upon it, liberty still endures in many of our institutions and customs and still exercises a beneficent influence upon them. More significant still, it abides in the hearts and minds of many noble men all over the world, men who though scattered and isolated, reduced to a small but aristocratic *res publica literaria,* still keep faith with it, reverently hallow its name, and love it more truly than ever they did in the days when no one denied or questioned its absolute sovereignty, when the mob proclaimed its glory and contaminated it with a vulgarity of which it is now purged.

And not only does freedom abide in such men, and not only does it exist and persist in the constitutions of many important countries and in institutions and customs. Its virtue is operative in things themselves and is gradually opening a way through many difficulties. We see it at work in the present wish for a truce in suspicions, a reduction in armaments and a peaceful settlement among the nations of Europe. That this is true is apparent in the general feeling that somehow these nations must contrive to harmonize their plans and efforts if they are to retain not their political and economic supremacy only, but even their leadership as creators of civilization and the aptitudes for this unending task which they have acquired through centuries of labor.

Disarmament and world peace are the only statesmanlike projects among the many put forward since the war which have not faded out or been dissipated; rather are they gaining ground from year to year and converting many who were once antagonistic or incredulous or faint-hearted. We are entitled to hope that they will not be allowed to fail but will be carried forward to fulfilment in the face of all opposition. It is true that the World War, which future historians may well regard as the *reductio ad absurdum* of nationalism, has embittered the relations of certain states as a result of an unjust and foolish peace treaty; but it also has made the peoples aware in their innermost consciousness that they have common virtues and defects, common strengths and weaknesses, that they share a common destiny, are inspired by the same affections, afflicted by the same sorrows, glory in the same patrimony of ideals. This explains why already in all parts of Europe we are witnessing the birth of a new consciousness, a new nationality—for nations are not, as has been imagined, data of nature but results of conscious acts, historical formations. Just as seventy years ago the Neapolitans and the Piedmontese decided to become Italians, not by abjuring their original nationality but by exalting and merging it in the new one, so Frenchmen and Germans and Italians and all the others will rise to becoming Europeans; they will think as Europeans, their hearts will beat for Europe as they now do for their smaller countries, not forgetting them but loving them the better.

This process of amalgamation is directly opposed to competitive nationalism and will in time destroy it entirely; meanwhile it tends to free Europe from the psychology of nationalism and its attendant habits of thought and action. If and when this happens, the liberal ideal will again prevail in the European mind and resume its sway over European hearts. But we must not see in this rebirth of liberalism merely a way to bring back the "old times" for which the Romantics idly yearn. Present events, those still to take place, will have their due effect; certain institutions of the old liberalism will have to be modified and replaced by ones better adapted to their tasks; new governing classes will arise; and experience will bring forth new concepts and give a new direction to the popular will.

In this new mental and moral atmosphere it will be imperative to take up again the so-called "social" problems. They are certainly not of recent making; thinkers and statesmen have struggled with them for centuries, dealing with them as they arose, case by case and in the spirit of the times. During the nineteenth century they were the object of deep attention and most heroic remedies, and were dealt with in such a way as to improve greatly the conditions of the working classes, to raise their standards of living and to better their legal and moral status. "Planned" economy, as it is now being called, although it holds a foremost position in talk today is not essentially new; and the question cannot be seriously raised of finding a collective substitute for individual economy or free individual initiative, both of themselves necessary to human life and economic progress. Discussion can turn only on the proportions, great or small, to be assigned to one form of economic organization rather than to another, differing with different means, places, times and other circumstances. This is primarily a question for technical experts and statesmen, who will have to devise solutions suitable to the times and favorable to an increase of wealth and its more equitable distribution. It is a question for experts and statesmen; but they will be unable to fulfil their function or attain their ends unless liberty be there to prepare and maintain the intellectual and moral atmosphere indispensable to labors so arduous, and to quicken the legal systems within which their duties must be performed.